The Compendium
of Catholic Philosophy

The Compendium of Catholic Philosophy

The texts contained in this work are in the public domain.

Copyright © 2017 by John Laney.

All rights reserved. No part of this publication may be reproduced, distributed, or transmitted in any form or by any means, including photocopying, recording, or other electronic or mechanical methods, without the prior written permission of the publisher.

De Wulf, Maurice. "Philosophy." The Catholic Encyclopedia. Vol. 12. New York: Robert Appleton Company, 1911.

Hagen, John. "Science and the Church." The Catholic Encyclopedia. Vol. 13. New York: Robert Appleton Company, 1912.

Aveling, Francis. "Man." The Catholic Encyclopedia. Vol. 9. New York: Robert Appleton Company, 1910.

Maher, Michael. "Psychology." The Catholic Encyclopedia. Vol. 12. New York: Robert Appleton Company, 1911.

Nys, Désiré. "Cosmology." The Catholic Encyclopedia. Vol. 4. New York: Robert Appleton Company, 1908.

Turner, William. "Metaphysics." The Catholic Encyclopedia. Vol. 10. New York: Robert Appleton Company, 1911.

Toner, Patrick. "The Existence of God." The Catholic Encyclopedia. Vol. 6. New York: Robert Appleton Company, 1909.

Toner, Patrick. "The Nature and Attributes of God." The Catholic Encyclopedia. Vol. 6. New York: Robert Appleton Company, 1909.

Toner, Patrick. "Relation of God to the Universe." The Catholic Encyclopedia. Vol. 6. New York: Robert Appleton Company, 1909.

Kempf, Constantine. "Theodicy." The Catholic Encyclopedia. Vol. 14. New York: Robert Appleton Company, 1912.

Joyce, George. "Morality." The Catholic Encyclopedia. Vol. 10. New York: Robert Appleton Company, 1911.

Cathrein, Victor. "Ethics." The Catholic Encyclopedia. Vol. 5. New York: Robert Appleton Company, 1909.

Fox, James. "Natural Law." The Catholic Encyclopedia. Vol. 9. New York: Robert Appleton Company, 1910.

Lehmkuhl, Augustinus. "Moral Theology." The Catholic Encyclopedia. Vol. 14. New York: Robert Appleton Company, 1912.

O'Hara, Frank. "Political Economy." The Catholic Encyclopedia. Vol. 12. New York: Robert Appleton Company, 1911.

Turner, William. "Logic." The Catholic Encyclopedia. Vol. 9. New York: Robert Appleton Company, 1910.

Dubray, Charles. "Knowledge." The Catholic Encyclopedia. Vol. 8. New York: Robert Appleton Company, 1910.

Walker, Leslie. "Truth." The Catholic Encyclopedia. Vol. 15. New York: Robert Appleton Company, 1912.

Dubray, Charles. "Epistemology." The Catholic Encyclopedia. Vol. 5. New York: Robert Appleton Company, 1909.

Pope, Hugh. "Faith." The Catholic Encyclopedia. Vol. 5. New York: Robert Appleton Company, 1909.

Walker, Leslie. "Scepticism." The Catholic Encyclopedia. Vol. 13. New York: Robert Appleton Company, 1912.

Kennedy, Daniel. "St. Thomas Aquinas." The Catholic Encyclopedia. Vol. 14. New York: Robert Appleton Company, 1912.

Kennedy, Daniel. "Thomism." The Catholic Encyclopedia. Vol. 14. New York: Robert Appleton Company, 1912.

Turner, William. "Scholasticism." The Catholic Encyclopedia. Vol. 13. New York: Robert Appleton Company, 1912.

Contents

Preface	7
I. Philosophy	9
II. Science and the Church	83
III. Man	140
IV. Psychology	153
V. Cosmology	175
VI. Metaphysics	194
VII. The Existence of God	235
VIII. Nature and Attributes of God	267
IX. Relation of God to the Universe	301
X. Theodicy	306
XI. Morality	314
XII. Ethics	324
XIII. Natural Law	374
XIV. Moral Theology	388
XV. Political Economy	441

XVI. Logic	456
XVII. Knowledge	482
XVIII. Truth	496
XIX. Epistemology	518
XX. Faith	531
XXI. Scepticism	568
XXII. St. Thomas Aquinas	579
XXIII. Thomism	629
XXIV. Scholasticism	656

Preface

My purpose in organizing this book was to provide Catholics who want to defend their faith with a useful collection of encyclopedia articles centered on the topic of philosophy. With the exception of the article on Logic, the selection of key articles follows the traditional ordering of philosophical instruction: natural philosophy, metaphysics, ethics, politics, and epistemology. Additional articles were included where I thought they would be of some supplementary benefit. Thus, this compendium can serve as both a general introduction to the broad topic of philosophy, as well as a guide to more specific topics. These articles have served me well over the years, and I hope they will do the same for you.

John Laney
September 2017

The Compendium
of Catholic Philosophy

than his master at compressing ideas, writes: tên onomazomenên sophian peri ta prôta aitia kai tas archas hupolambanousi pantes — "All men consider philosophy as concerned with first causes and principles" (Metaph., I, i). These notions were perpetuated in the post-Aristotelean schools (Stoicism, Epicureanism, neo-Platonism), with this difference, that the Stoics and Epicureans accentuated the moral bearing of philosophy ("Philosophia studium summae virtutis", says Seneca in "Epist.", lxxxix, 7), and the neo-Platonists its mystical bearing (see section V below). The Fathers of the Church and the first philosophers of the Middle Ages seem not to have had a very clear idea of philosophy for reasons which we will develop later on (section IX), but its conception emerges once more in all its purity among the Arabic philosophers at the end of the twelfth century and the masters of Scholasticism in the thirteenth. St. Thomas, adopting the Aristotelean idea, writes: "Sapientia est scientia quae considerat causas primas et universales causas; sapientia causas primas omnium causarum considerat" — Wisdom [i.e. philosophy] is the science which considers first and universal causes; wisdom considers the first causes of all causes" (In Metaph., I, lect. ii).

In general, modern philosophers may be said to have adopted this way of looking at it. Descartes regards philosophy as wisdom: "Philosophiae voce sapientiae studium denotamus" — "By the term philosophy we denote the pursuit of wisdom" (Princ. philos., preface); and he understands by it "cognitio veritatis per primas suas causas" — "knowledge of truth by its first causes" (ibid.). For Locke, philosophy is the true knowledge of things; for Berkeley, "the study of wisdom and truth" (Princ.). The many conceptions of philosophy given by Kant reduce it to that of a science of the general principles of knowledge and of the ultimate objects attainable by knowledge — "Wissenschaft von den letzten Zwecken der menschlichen Vernunft". For the numerous German philosophers who derive their inspiration from his criticism — Fichte, Hegel, Schelling, Schleiermacher, Schopenhauer, and the rest — it is the general teaching of science (Wissenschaftslehre). Many contemporary authors regard it as the synthetic theory of the particular sciences: "Philosophy", says Herbert Spencer, "is completely unified knowledge" (First Principles, #37). Ostwald has the same idea. For Wundt, the object of philosophy is "the acquisition of such a general conception of the world and of life as will satisfy the exigencies of the reason and the needs of the heart" — "Gewinnung einer allgemeinen Welt — und Lebensanschauung, welche die Forderungen unserer Vernunft und die Bedurfnisse unseres Gemüths befriedigen soll" (Einleit. in d. Philos., 1901, p. 5). This idea of philosophy as the ultimate science of values (Wert lehre) is emphasized by Windelband, Déring, and others.

    The list of conceptions and definitions might be indefinitely prolonged. All of them affirm the eminently synthetic character of philosophy. In the opinion of the present writer, the most exact and comprehensive definition is that of Aristotle. Face to face with nature and with himself, man reflects and endeavours to discover what the world is, and what he is himself. Having made the real the object of studies in detail, each of which constitutes science (see section VIII), he is led to a study of the whole, to inquire into the principles or reasons of the totality of things, a study which supplies the answers to the last Why's. The last Why of all rests upon all that is and all that becomes: it does not apply, as in any one particular science (e.g. chemistry), to this or that process of becoming, or to this or that being (e.g. the combination of two bodies), but to all being and all becoming. All being has within it its constituent principles, which account for its substance (constitutive material and formal causes); all becoming, or change, whether superficial or profound, is brought about by an efficient cause other than its subject; and lastly things and events have their bearings from a finality, or final cause. The harmony of principles, or causes, produces the universal order. And thus philosophy is the profound knowledge of the universal order, in the sense of having for its object the simplest and most general principles, by means of which all other objects of thought are, in the last resort, explained.

By these principles, says Aristotle, we know other things, but other things do not suffice to make us know these principles (dia gar tauta kai ek toutôn t'alla gnôrizetai, all' ou tauta dia tôn hupokeimenôn — Metaph., I). The expression universal order should be understood in the widest sense. Man is one part of it: hence the relations of man with the world of sense and with its Author belong to the domain of philosophy. Now man, on the one hand, is the responsible author of these relations, because he is free, but he is obliged by nature itself to reach an aim, which is his moral end. On the other hand, he has the power of reflecting upon the knowledge which he acquires of all things, and this leads him to study the logical structure of science. Thus philosophical knowledge leads to philosophical acquaintance with morality and logic. And hence we have this more comprehensive definition of philosophy: "The profound knowledge of the universal order, of the duties which that order imposes upon man, and of the knowledge which man acquires from reality" — "La connaissance approfondie de l'ordre universel, des devoirs qui en résultent pour l'homme et de la science que l'homme acquiert de la rémite" (Mercier, "Logique", 1904, p. 23). — The development of these same ideas under another aspect will be found in section VIII of this article.

Divisions of Philosophy

Since the universal order falls within the scope of philosophy (which studies only its first principles, not its reasons in detail), philosophy is led to the consideration of all that is: the world, God (or its cause), and man himself (his nature, origin, operations, moral end, and scientific activities).

logic, the vestibule of philosophy, which Aristotle studied at length, and of which he may be called the creator.

To metaphysics Aristotle rightly accords the place of honour in the grouping of philosophical studies. He calls it "first philosophy". His classification was taken up by the Peripatetic School and was famous throughout antiquity; it was eclipsed by the Platonic classification during the Alexandrine period, but it reappeared during the Middle Ages.

In the Middle Ages

Though the division of philosophy into its branches is not uniform in the first period of the Middle Ages in the West, i.e. down to the end of the twelfth century, the classifications of this period are mostly akin to the Platonic division into logic, ethics, and physics. Aristotle's classification of the theoretic sciences, though made known by Boethius, exerted no influence for the reason that in the early Middle Ages the West knew nothing of Aristotle except his works on logic and some fragments of his speculative philosophy (see section V below). It should be added here that philosophy, reduced at first to dialectic, or logic, and placed as such in the Trivium, was not long in setting itself above the liberal arts.

The Arab philosophers of the twelfth century (Avicenna, Averroes) accepted the Aristotelean classification, and when their works — particularly their translations of Aristotle's great original treatises —

penetrated into the West, the Aristotelean division definitively took its place there. Its coming is heralded by Gundissalinus (see section XII), one of the Toletan translators of Aristotle, and author of a treatise, "De divisione philosophiae", which was imitated by Michael Scott and Robert Kilwardby. St. Thomas did no more than adopt it and give it a precise scientific form. Later on we shall see that, conformably with the medieval notion of sapientia, to each part of philosophy corresponds the preliminary study of a group of special sciences. The general scheme of the division of philosophy in the thirteenth century, with St. Thomas's commentary on it, is as follows:

There are as many parts of philosophy as there are distinct domains in the order submitted to the philosopher's reflection. Now there is an order which the intelligence does not form but only considers; such is the order realized in nature. Another order, the practical, is formed either by the acts of our intelligence or by the acts of our will, or by the application of those acts to external things in the arts: e.g., the division of practical philosophy into logic, moral philosophy, and æsthetics, or the philosophy of the arts ("Ad philosophiam naturalem pertinet considerare ordinem rerum quem ratio humana considerat sed non facit; ita quod sub naturali philosophia comprehendamus et metaphysicam. Ordo autem quem ratio considerando facit in proprio actu, pertinet ad rationalem philosophiam, cujus est considerare ordinem partium orationis ad invicem et ordinem principiorum ad invicem et ad conclusiones. Ordo autem actionum voluntariarum pertinet ad considerationem moralis philosophiae. Ordo autem quem ratio considerando facit in rebus exterioribus per rationem humanam pertinet ad artes mechanicas.") To natural philosophy pertains the consideration of the order of things which human reason considers but does not create — just as we include metaphysics also under natural philosophy. But the order which reason creates of its own act by consideration pertains to rational philosophy, the office of which is to consider the order of the parts of speech with reference to one another and the order of the principles with reference to one another and to the conclusions. The order of voluntary actions pertains to the consideration of moral philosophy, while the order which the reason creates in external things through the human reason pertains to the mechanical arts. — In "X Ethic. ad Nic.", I, lect. i.

The philosophy of nature, or speculative philosophy, is divided into metaphysics, mathematics, and physics, according to the three stages traversed by the intelligence in its effort to attain a synthetic comprehension of the universal order, by abstracting from movement (physics), intelligible quantity (mathematics), being (metaphysics) (In lib. Boeth. de Trinitate, Q. v., a. 1). In this classification it is to be noted that, man being one element of the world of sense, psychology ranks as a part of physics.

In Modern Philosophy

The Scholastic classification may be said, generally speaking, to have lasted, with some exceptions, until the seventeenth century. Beginning with Descartes, we find a multitude of classifications arising, differing in the principles which inspire them. Kant, for instance, distinguishes metaphysics, moral philosophy, religion, and anthropology. The most widely accepted scheme, that which still governs the division of the branches of philosophy in teaching, is due to Wolff (1679-1755), a disciple of Leibniz, who has been called the educator of Germany in the eighteenth century. This scheme is as follows:

1. Logic.
2. Speculative Philosophy.
   * Ontology, or General Metaphysics.
   * Special Metaphysics.
     * Theodicy (the study of God).
     * Cosmology (the study of the World).
     * Psychology (the study of Man).
1. Practical Philosophy.
   * Ethics
   * Politics
   * Economics

Wolff broke the ties binding the particular sciences to philosophy, and placed them by themselves; in his view philosophy must remain purely rational. It is easy to see that the members of Wolff's scheme are found in the

Aristotelean classification, wherein theodicy is a chapter of metaphysics and psychology a chapter of physics. It may even be said that the Greek classification is better than Wolff's in regard to speculative philosophy, where the ancients were guided by the formal object of the study — i.e. by the degree of abstraction to which the whole universe is subjected, while the moderns always look at the material object — i.e., the three categories of being, which it is possible to study, God, the world of sense, and man.

In Contemporary Philosophy

The impulse received by philosophy during the last half-century gave rise to new philosophical sciences, in the sense that various branches have been detached from the main stems. In psychology this phenomenon has been remarkable: criteriology, or epistemology (the study of the certitude of knowledge) has developed into a special study. Other branches which have formed themselves into new psychological sciences are: physiological psychology or the study of the physiological concomitant of psychic activities; didactics, or the science of teaching; pedagogy, or the science of education; collective psychology and the psychology of people (Volkerpsychologie), studying the psychic phenomena observable in human groups as such, and in the different races. An important section of logic (called also noetic, or canonic) is tending to sever itself from the main body, viz., methodology, which studies the special logical formation of various sciences. On moral philosophy, in the wide sense, have been grafted the philosophy of law, the philosophy of society, or social philosophy (which is much the same as sociology), and the philosophies of religion and of history.

The Principal Systematic Solutions

From what has been said above it is evident that philosophy is beset by a great number of questions. It would not be possible here to enumerate all those questions, much less to detail the divers solutions which have been given to them. The solution of a philosophic question is called a philosophic doctrine or theory. A philosophic system (from sunistêmi, put together) is a complete and organized group of solutions. It is not an incoherent assemblage or an encyclopedic amalgamation of such solutions; it is dominated by an organic unity. Only those philosophic systems which are constructed conformably with the exigencies of organic unity are really powerful: such are the systems of the Upanishads, of Aristotle, of neo-Platonism, of Scholasticism, of Leibniz, Kant and Hume. So that one or several theories do not constitute a system; but some theories, i.e. answers to a philosophic question, are important enough to determine the solution of other important problems of a system. The scope of this section is to indicate some of these theories.

Monism, or Pantheism, and Pluralism, Individualism, or Theism

Are there many beings distinct in their reality, with one Supreme Being, God at the summit of the hierarchy; or is there but one reality (monas, hence monism), one All-God (pan-theos) of whom each individual is but a member or fragment (Substantialistic Pantheism), or else a force, or energy (Dynamic Pantheism)? Here we have an important question of metaphysics the solution of which reacts upon all other domains of philosophy. The system of Aristotle, of the Scholastics, and of Leibniz are Pluralistic and Theistic; the Indian, neo-Platonic, and Hegelian are Monistic. Monism is a fascinating explanation of the real, but it only postpones the difficulties which it imagines itself to be solving (e.g. the difficulty of the interaction of things), to say nothing of the objection, from the human point of view, that it runs counter to our most deep-rooted sentiments.

Objectivism and Subjectivism

Does being, whether one or many, possess its own life, independent of our mind, so that to be known by us is only accident to being, as in the objective system of metaphysics (e.g. Aristotle, the Scholastics, Spinoza)? Or is being no other reality than the mental and subjective presence which it acquires in our representation of it as in the Subjective system (e.g. Hume)? It is in this sense that the "Revue de métaphysique et de morale" (see bibliography) uses the term metaphysics in its title. Subjectivism cannot explain the passivity of our mental representations, which we do not draw out of ourselves, and which therefore oblige us to infer the reality of a non-ego.

Substantialism and Phenomenism

Is all reality a flux of phenomena (Heraclitus, Berkeley, Hume, Taine), or does the manifestation appear upon a basis, or substance, which manifests itself, and does the phenomenon demand a noumenon (the Scholastics)? Without an underlying substance, which we only know through the medium of the phenomenon, certain realities, as walking, talking, are inexplicable, and such facts as memory become absurd.

Mechanism and Dynamism (Pure and Modified)

Natural bodies are considered by some to be aggregations of homogeneous particles of matter (atoms) receiving a movement which is extrinsic to them, so that these bodies differ only in the number and arrangement of their atoms (the Atomism, or Mechanism, of Democritus, Descartes, and Hobbes). Others reduce them to specific, unextended, immaterial forces, of which extension is only the superficial manifestation (Leibniz). Between the two is Modified Dynamism (Aristotle), which distinguishes in bodies an immanent specific principle (form) and an indeterminate element (matter) which is the source of limitation and extension. This theory accounts for the specific characters of the entities in question as well as for the reality of their extension in space.

Materialism, Agnosticism, and Spiritualism

That everything real is material, that whatever

might be immaterial would be unreal, such is the cardinal doctrine of Materialism (the Stoics, Hobbes, De Lamettrie). Contemporary Materialism is less outspoken: it is inspired by a Positivist ideology (see section VI), and asserts that, if anything supra-material exists, it is unknowable (Agnosticism, from a and gnôsis, knowledge; Spencer, Huxley). Spiritualism teaches that incorporeal, or immaterial, beings exist or that they are possible (Plato, Aristotle, St. Augustine, the Scholastics, Descartes, Leibniz). Some have even asserted that only spirits exist: Berkeley, Fichte, and Hegel are exaggerated Spiritualists. The truth is that there are bodies and spirits; among the latter we are acquainted (though less well than with bodies) with the nature of our soul, which is revealed by the nature of our immaterial acts, and with the nature of God, the infinite intelligence, whose existence is demonstrated by the very existence of finite things. Side by side with these solutions relating to the problems of the real, there is another group of solutions, not less influential in the orientation of a system, and relating to psychical problems or those of the human ego.

Sensualism and Rationalism, or Spiritualism

These are the opposite poles of the ideogenetic question, the question of the origin of our knowledge. For Sensualism the only source of human knowledge is sensation: everything reduces to transformed sensations. This theory, long ago put forward in Greek philosophy

(Stoicism, Epicureanism), was developed to the full by the English Sensualists (Locke, Berkeley, Hume) and the English Associationists (Brown, Hartley, Priestley); its modern form is Positivism (John Stuart Mill, Huxley, Spencer, Comte, Taine, Littré etc.). Were this theory true, it would follow that we can know only what falls under our senses, and therefore cannot pronounce upon the existence or non-existence, the reality or unreality, of the super-sensible. Positivism is more logical than Materialism. In the New World, the term Agnosticism has been very happily employed to indicate this attitude of reserve towards the super-sensible. Rationalism (from ratio, reason), or Spiritualism, establishes the existence in us of concepts higher than sensations, i.e. of abstract and general concepts (Plato, Aristotle, St. Augustine, the Scholastics, Descartes, Leibniz, Kant, Cousin etc.). Ideologic Spiritualism has won the adherence of humanity's greatest thinkers. Upon the spirituality, or immateriality, of our higher mental operations is based the proof of the spirituality of the principle from which they proceed and, hence, of the immortality of the soul.

Scepticism, Dogmatism, and Criticism

So many answers have been given to the question whether man can attain truth, and what is the foundation of certitude, that we will not attempt to enumerate them all. Scepticism declares reason incapable of arriving at the truth, and holds certitude to be a purely subjective affair

(Sextus Empiricus, Ænesidemus). Dogmatism asserts that man can attain to truth, and that, in measure to be further determined, our cognitions are certain. The motive of certitude is, for the Traditionalists, a Divine revelation, for the Scotch School (Reid) it is an inclination of nature to affirm the principles of common sense; it is an irrational, but social, necessity of admitting certain principles for practical dogmatism (Balfour in his "Foundations of Belief" speaks of "non-rational impulse", while Mallock holds that "certitude is found to be the child, not of reason but of custom" and Brunetière writes about "the bankruptcy of science and the need of belief"); it is an affective sentiment, a necessity of wishing that certain things may be verities (Voluntarism; Kant's Moral Dogmatism), or the fact of living certain verities (contemporary Pragmatism and Humanism, William James, Schiller). But for others — and this is the theory which we accept — the motive of certitude is the very evidence of the connection which appears between the predicate and the subject of a proposition, an evidence which the mind perceives, but which it does not create (Moderate Dogmatism). Lastly for Criticism, which is the Kantian solution of the problem of knowledge, evidence is created by the mind by means of the structural functions with which every human intellect is furnished (the categories of the understanding). In conformity with these functions we connect the impressions of the senses and construct the world. Knowledge, therefore, is valid only for the world as represented to the mind. Kantian Criticism ends in excessive Idealism, which is also called Subjectivism or Phenomenalism, and according to which the mind draws all its representations out of itself, both the sensory impressions and the categories which connect them: the world becomes a mental poem, the object is created by the subject as representation (Fichte, Schelling, Hegel).

Nominalism, Realism, and Conceptualism

Nominalism, Realism, and Conceptualism are various answers to the question of the real objectivity of our predications, or of the relation of fidelity existing between our general representations and the external world.

Determinism and Indeterminism

Has every phenomenon or fact its adequate cause in an antecedent phenomenon or fact (Cosmic Determinism)? And, in respect to acts of the will, are they likewise determined in all their constituent elements (Moral Determinism, Stoicism, Spinoza)? If so, then liberty disappears, and with it human responsibility, merit and demerit. Or, on the contrary, is there a category of volitions which are not necessitated, and which depend upon the discretionary power of the will to act or not to act and in acting to follow freely chosen direction? Does liberty exist? Most Spiritualists of all schools have adopted a libertarian philosophy, holding that liberty alone gives the moral life an acceptable meaning; by various arguments they have confirmed the testimony of conscience and the data of common consent. In physical nature causation and determinism rule; in the moral life, liberty. Others, by no means numerous, have even pretended to discover cases of indeterminism in physical nature (the so-called Contingentist theories, e.g. Boutroux).

Utilitarianism and the Morality of Obligation

What constitutes the foundation of morality in our actions? Pleasure or utility say some, personal or egoistic pleasure (Egoism — Hobbes, Bentham, and "the arithmetic of pleasure"); or again, in the pleasure and utility of all (Altruism — John Stuart Mill). Others hold that morality consists in the performance of duty for duty's sake, the observance of law because it is law, independently of personal profit (the Formalism of the Stoics and of Kant). According to another doctrine, which in our opinion is more correct, utility, or personal advantage, is not incompatible with duty, but the source of the obligation to act is in the last analysis, as the very exigencies of our nature tell us, the ordinance of God.

Philosophical Methods

Method (meth' hodos) means a path taken to reach some objective point. By philosophical method is understood the path leading to philosophy, which, again, may mean either the process employed in the construction of a philosophy (constructive method, method of invention), or the way of teaching philosophy (method of teaching, didactic method). We will deal here with the former of these two senses; the latter will be treated in section XI. Three methods can be, and have been, applied to the construction of philosophy.

Experimental (Empiric, or Analytic) method

The method of all Empiric philosophers is to observe facts, accumulate them, and coordinate them. Pushed to its ultimate consequences, the empirical method refuses to rise beyond observed and observable fact; it abstains from investigating anything that is absolute. It is found among the Materialists, ancient and modern, and is most unreservedly applied in contemporary Positivism. Comte opposes the "positive mode of thinking", based solely upon observation, to the theological and metaphysical modes. For Mill, Huxley, Bain, Spencer, there is not one philosophical proposition but is the product, pure and simple, of experience: what we take for a general idea is an aggregate of sensations; a judgment is the union of two sensations; a syllogism, the passage from particular to particular (Mill, "A System of Logic, Rational and Inductive", ed. Lubbock, 1892; Bain, "Logic", New York, 1874). Mathematical propositions, fundamental axioms such as $a = a$, the principle of contradiction, the principle of causality are only "generalizations from facts of experience" (Mill, op. cit., vii, #5). According to this author, what we believe to be superior to experience in the enunciation of scientific laws is derived from our subjective incapacity to conceive its contradictory; according to Spencer, this inconceivability of the negation is developed by heredity.

Applied in an exaggerated and exclusive fashion, the experimental method mutilates facts, since it is powerless to ascend to the causes and the laws which govern facts. It suppresses the character of objective necessity which is inherent in scientific judgments, and reduces them to collective formulae of facts observed in the past. It forbids our asserting, e.g., that the men who will be born after us will be subject to death, seeing that all certitude rests on experience, and that by mere observation we cannot reach the unchangeable nature of things. The empirical method, left to its own resources, checks the upward movement of the mind towards the causes or object of the phenomena which confront it.

Deductive, or Synthetic a Priori, Method

At the opposite pole to the preceding, the deductive method starts from very general principles, from higher causes, to descend (Latin deducere, to lead down) to more and more complex relations and to facts. The dream of the Deductionist is to take as the point of departure an intuition of the Absolute, of the Supreme Reality — for the Theists, God; for the Monists, the Universal Being — and to draw from this intuition the synthetic knowledge of all that depends upon it in the universe, in conformity with the metaphysical scale of the real.

Plato is the father of deductive philosophy: he starts from the world of Ideas, and from the Idea of the Sovereign Good, and he would know the reality of the world of sense only in the Ideas of which it is the reflection. St. Augustine, too, finds his satisfaction in studying the universe, and the least of the beings which compose it, only in a synthetic contemplation of God, the exemplary, creative, and final cause of all things. So, too, the Middle Ages attached great importance to the deductive method. "I propose", writes Boethius, "to build science by means of concepts and maxims, as is done in mathematics." Anselm of Canterbury draws from the idea of God, not only the proof of the real existence of an infinite being, but also a group of theorems on His attributes and His relations with the world. Two centuries before Anselm, Scotus Eriugena, the father of anti-Scholasticism, is the completest type of the Deductionist: his metaphysics is one long description of the Divine Odyssey, inspired by the neo-Platonic, monistic conception of the descent of the One in its successive generations. And, on the very threshold of the thirteenth century, Alain de Lille would apply to philosophy a mathematical methodology. In the thirteenth century Raymond Lully believed that he had found the secret of "the Great Art" (ars magna), a sort of syllogism-machine, built of general tabulations of ideas, the combination of which would give the solution of any question whatsoever. Descartes, Spinoza, and Leibniz are Deductionists: they would construct philosophy after the manner of geometry (more geometrico), linking the most special and complicated theorems to some very simple axioms. The same tendency appears among the Ontologists and the post-Kantian Pantheists in Germany (Fichte, Schelling, Hegel), who base their philosophy upon an intuition of the Absolute Being.

The deductive philosophers generally profess to disdain the sciences of observation. Their great fault is the compromising of fact, bending it to a preconceived explanation or theory assumed a priori, whereas the observation of the fact ought to precede the assignment of its cause or of its adequate reason. This defect in the deductive method appears glaringly in a youthful work of Leibniz's, "Specimen demonstrationum politicarum pro rege Polonorum eligendo", published anonymously in 1669, where he demonstrates by geometrical methods (more geometrico), in sixty propositions, that the Count Palatine of Neuburg ought to be elected to the Polish Throne.

Analytico-Synthetic Method

This combination of analysis and synthesis, of observation and deduction, is the only method appropriate to philosophy. Indeed, since it undertakes to furnish a general explanation of the universal order (see section I), philosophy ought to begin with complex effects, facts known by observation, before attempting to include them in one comprehensive explanation of the universe. This is manifest in psychology, where we begin with a careful examination of activities, notably of the phenomena of sense, of intelligence, and of appetite; in cosmology, where we observe the series of changes, superficial and profound, of bodies; in moral philosophy, which sets out from the observation of moral facts; in theodicy, where we interrogate religious beliefs and feelings; even in metaphysics, the starting-point of which is really existing being.

But observation and analysis once completed, the work of synthesis begins. We must pass onward to a synthetic psychology that shall enable us to comprehend the destinies of man's vital principle; to a cosmology that shall explain the constitution of bodies, their changes, and the stability of the laws which govern them; to a synthetic moral philosophy establishing the end of man and the ultimate ground of duty; to a theodicy and deductive metaphysics that shall examine the attributes of God and the fundamental conceptions of all being.

As a whole and in each of its divisions, philosophy applies the analytic-synthetic method. Its ideal would be to give an account of the universe and of man by a synthetic knowledge of God, upon whom all reality depends. This panoramic view — the eagle's view of things — has allured all the great geniuses. St. Thomas expresses himself admirably on this synthetic knowledge of the universe and its first cause. The analytico-synthetic process is the method, not only of philosophy, but of every science, for it is the natural law of thought, the proper function of which is unified and orderly knowledge. "Sapientis est ordinare." Aristotle, St. Thomas, Pascal, Newton, Pasteur, thus understood the method of the sciences. Men like Helmholtz and Wundt adopted synthetic views after doing analytical work. Even the Positivists are metaphysicians, though they do not know it or wish it. Does not Herbert Spencer call his philosophy synthetic? and does he not, by reasoning, pass beyond that domain of the "observable" within which he professes to confine himself?

The Great Historical Currents

Among the many peoples who have covered the globe philosophic culture appears in two groups: the Semitic and the Indo-European, to which may be added the Egyptians and the Chinese. In the Semitic group (Arabs, Babylonians, Assyrians, Aramaeans, Chaldeans) the Arabs are the most important; nevertheless, their part becomes insignificant when compared with the intellectual life of the Indo-Europeans. Among the latter, philosophic life appears successively in various ethnic divisions, and the succession forms the great periods into which the history of philosophy is divided; first, among the people of India (since 1500 B.C.); then among the Greeks and the Romans (sixth century B.C. to sixth century of our era); again, much later, among the peoples of Central and Northern Europe.

Indian Philosophy

The philosophy of India is recorded principally in the sacred books of the Veda, for it has always been closely united with religion. Its numerous poetic and religious productions carry within themselves a chronology which enables us to assign them to three periods.

(1) The Period of the Hymns of the Rig Veda (1500-1000 B.C.)

This is the most ancient monument of Indo-Germanic civilization; in it may be seen the progressive appearance of the fundamental theory that a single Being exists under a thousand forms in the multiplied phenomena of the universe (Monism).

(2) The Period of the Brahmans (1000-500 B.C.)

This is the age of Brahminical civilization. The theory of the one Being remains, but little by little the concrete and anthropomorphic ideas of the one Being are replaced by the doctrine that the basis of all things is in oneself (âtman). Psychological Monism appears in its entirety in the Upanishads: the absolute and adequate identity of the Ego — which is the constitutive basis of our individuality (âtman) — and of all things, with Brahman, the eternal being exalted above time, space, number, and change, the generating principle of all things in which all things are finally reabsorbed — such the fundamental theme to be found in the Upanishad under a thousand variations of form. To arrive at the âtman, we must not stop at empirical reality which is multiple and cognizable; we must pierce this husk, penetrate to the unknowable and ineffable superessence, and identify ourselves with it in an unconscious unity.

(3) The Post-Vedic or Sanskrit, Period (since 500 B.C.)

From the germs of theories contained in the Upanishad a series of systems spring up, orthodox or heterodox. Of the orthodox systems, Vedanta is the most interesting; in it we find the principles of the Upanishads developed in an integral philosophy which comprise metaphysics, cosmology, psychology, and ethics (transmigration, metempsychosis). Among the systems not in harmony with the Vedic dogmas, the most celebrated is Buddhism, a kind of Pessimism which teaches liberation from pain in a state of unconscious repose, or an extinction of personality (Nirvâna). Buddhism spread in China, where it lives side by side with the doctrines of Lao Tse and that of Confucius. It is evident that even the systems which are not in harmony with the Veda are permeated with religious ideas.

Greek Philosophy

This philosophy, which occupied six centuries before, and six after, Christ, may be divided into four periods, corresponding with the succession of the principal lines of research (1) From Thales of Miletus to Socrates (seventh to fifth centuries B.C. — preoccupied with cosmology) (2) Socrates, Plato, and Aristotle (fifth to fourth centuries B.C. — psychology); (3) From the death of

Aristotle to the rise of neo-Platonism (end of the fourth century B.C. to third century after Christ — moral philosophy); (4) neo-Platonic School (from the third century after Christ, or, including the systems of the forerunners of neo-Platonism, from the first century after Christ, to the end of Greek philosophy in the seventh century — mysticism).

(1) The Pre-Socratic Period

The pre-Socratic philosophers either seek for the stable basis of things — which is water, for Thales of Miletus; air, for Anaximenes of Miletus; air endowed with intelligence, for Diogenes of Apollonia; number, for Pythagoras (sixth century B.C.); abstract and immovable being, for the Eleatics — or they study that which changes: while Parmenides and the Eleatics assert that everything is, and nothing changes or becomes. Heraclitus (about 535-475) holds that everything becomes, and nothing is unchangeable. Democritus (fifth century) reduces all beings to groups of atoms in motion, and this movement, according to Anaxagoras, has for its cause an intelligent being.

(2) The Period of Apogee: Socrates, Plato, Aristotle.

When the Sophists (Protagoras, Gorgias) had demonstrated the insufficiency of these cosmologies, Socrates (470-399) brought philosophical investigation to bear on man himself, studying man chiefly from the moral point of view. From the presence in us of abstract ideas Plato (427-347) deduced the existence of a world of supersensible realities or ideas, of which the visible world is but a pale reflection. These ideas, which the soul in an earlier life contemplated, are now, because of its union with the body, but faintly perceived. Aristotle (384-322), on the contrary, shows that the real dwells in the objects of sense. The theory of act and potentiality, of form and matter, is a new solution of the relations between the permanent and the changing. His psychology, founded upon the principle of the unity of man and the substantial union of soul and body, is a creation of genius. And as much may be said of his logic.

(3) The Moral Period

After Aristotle (end of the fourth Century B.C.) four schools are in evidence: Stoic, Epicurean, Platonic, and Aristotelean. The Stoics (Zeno of Citium, Cleanthes, Chrysippus), like the Epicureans, make speculation subordinate to the quest of happiness, and the two schools, in spite of their divergencies, both consider happiness to be ataraxia or absence of sorrow and preoccupation. The teachings of both on nature (Dynamistic Monism with the Stoics, and Pluralistic Mechanism with the Epicureans) are only a prologue to their moral philosophy. After the latter half of the second century B.C. we perceive reciprocal infiltrations between the various schools. This issues in Eclecticism. Seneca (first century B.C.) and Cicero (106-43 B.C.) are attached to Eclecticism with a Stoic basis; two great commentators of Aristotle, Andronicus of Rhodes (first century B.C.) and Alexander of Aphrodisia about

200), affect a Peripatetic Eclecticism. Parallel with Eclecticism runs a current of Scepticism (Ænesidemus, end of first century B.C., and Sextus Empiricus, second century A.D.).

(4) The Mystical Period

In the first century B.C. Alexandria had become the capital of Greek intellectual life. Mystical and theurgic tendencies, born of a longing for the ideal and the beyond, began to appear in a current of Greek philosophy which originated in a restoration of Pythagorism and its alliance with Platonism (Plutarch of Chieronea, first century B.C.; Apuleius of Madaura; Numenius, about 160 and others), and still more in the Graeco-Judaic philosophy of Philo the Jew (30 B.C. to A.D. 50). But the dominance of these tendencies is more apparent in neo-Platonism. The most brilliant thinker of the neo-Platonic series is Plotinus (A.D. 20-70). In his "Enneads" he traces the paths which lead the soul to the One, and establishes, in keeping with his mysticism, an emanationist metaphysical system. Porphyry of Tyre (232-304), a disciple of Plotinus, popularizes his teaching, emphasizes its religious bearing, and makes Aristotle's "Organon" the introduction to neo-Platonic philosophy. Later on, neo-Platonism, emphasizing its religious features, placed itself, with Jamblichus, at the service of the pagan pantheon which growing Christianity was ruining on all sides, or again, as with Themistius at Constantinople (fourth century), Proclus and Simplicius at Athens (fifth century), and Ammonius at Alexandria, it took an Encyclopedic turn. With Ammonius and John Philoponus (sixth century) the neo-Platonic School of Alexandria developed in the direction of Christianity.

Patristic Philosophy

In the closing years of the second century and, still more, in the third century, the philosophy of the Fathers of the Church was developed. It was born in a civilization dominated by Greek ideas, chiefly neo-Platonic, and on this side its mode of thought is still the ancient. Still, if some, like St. Augustine, attach the greatest value to the neo-Platonic teachings, it must not be forgotten that the Monist or Pantheistic and Emanationist ideas, which have been accentuated by the successors of Plotinus, are carefully replaced by the theory of creation and the substantial distinction of beings; in this respect a new spirit animates Patristic philosophy. It was developed, too, as an auxiliary of the dogmatic system which the Fathers were to establish. In the third century the great representatives of the Christian School of Alexandria are Clement of Alexandria and Origen. After them Gregory of Nyssa, Gregory of Nazianzus, St. Ambrose, and, above all, St. Augustine (354-430) appear. St. Augustine gathers up the intellectual treasures of the ancient world, and is one of the principal intermediaries for their transmission to the modern world. In its definitive form Augustinism is a fusion of intellectualism and mysticism, with a study of God as the centre of interest. In the fifth century, pseudo-Dionysius perpetuates many a neo-Platonic doctrine adapted to Christianity, and his writings exercise a powerful influence in the Middle Ages.

Medieval Philosophy

The philosophy of the Middle Ages developed simultaneously in the West, at Byzantium, and in divers Eastern centres; but the Western philosophy is the most important. It built itself up with great effort on the ruins of barbarism: until the twelfth century, nothing was known of Aristotle, except some treatises on logic, or of Plato, except a few dialogues. Gradually, problems arose, and, foremost, in importance, the question of universals in the ninth, tenth, and eleventh centuries. St. Anselm (1033-1109) made a first attempt at systematizing Scholastic philosophy, and developed a theodicy. But as early as the ninth century an anti-Scholastic philosophy had arisen with Eriugena who revived the neo-Platonic Monism.

In the twelfth century Scholasticism formulated new anti-Realist doctrines with Adelard of Bath, Gauthier de Mortagne, and, above all, Abelard and Gilbert de la Porrée, whilst extreme Realism took shape in the schools of Chartres. John of Salisbury and Alain de Lille, in the twelfth century, are the co-ordinating minds that indicate the maturity of Scholastic thought. The latter of these waged a campaign against the Pantheism of David of Dinant and the Epicureanism of the Albigenses — the two most important forms of anti-Scholastic philosophy. At

Byzantium, Greek philosophy held its ground throughout the Middle Ages, and kept apart from the movement of Western ideas. The same is true of the Syrians and Arabs.

But at the end of the twelfth century the Arabic and Byzantine movement entered into relation with Western thought, and effected, to the profit of the latter, the brilliant philosophical revival of the thirteenth century. This was due, in the first place, to the creation of the University of Paris; next, to the foundation of the Dominican and Franciscan orders; lastly, to the introduction of Arabic and Latin translations of Aristotle and the ancient authors. At the same period the works of Avicenna and Averroes became known at Paris. A pleiad of brilliant names fills the thirteenth century — Alexander of Hales, St. Bonaventure, Bl. Albertus Magnus, St. Thomas Aquinas, Godfrey of Fontaines, Henry of Ghent, Giles of Rome, and Duns Scotus — bring Scholastic synthesis to perfection. They all wage war on Latin Averroism and anti-Scholasticism, defended in the schools of Paris by Siger of Brabant. Roger Bacon, Lully, and a group of neo-Platonists occupy a place apart in this century, which is completely filled by remarkable figures.

In the fourteenth century Scholastic philosophy betrays the first symptoms of decadence. In place of individualities we have schools, the chief being the Thomist, the Scotist, and the Terminist School of William of Occam, which soon attracted numerous partisans. With John of Jandun, Averroism perpetuates its most audacious propositions; Eckhart and Nicholas of Cusa formulate philosophies which are symptomatic of the approaching revolution. The Renaissance was a troublous period for philosophy. Ancient systems were revived: the Dialectic of the Humanistic philologists (Laurentius Valla, Vivés), Platonism, Aristoteleanism, Stoicism. Telesius, Campanella, and Giordano Bruno follow a naturalistic philosophy. Natural and social law are renewed with Thomas More and Grotius. All these philosophies were leagued together against Scholasticism, and very often against Catholicism. On the other hand, the Scholastic philosophers grew weaker and weaker, and, excepting for the brilliant Spanish Scholasticism of the sixteenth century (Bañez, Francisco Suárez, Vasquez, and so on), it may be said that ignorance of the fundamental doctrine became general. In the seventeenth century there was no one to support Scholasticism: it fell, not for lack of ideas, but for lack of defenders.

Modern Philosophy

The philosophies of the Renaissance are mainly negative: modern philosophy is, first and foremost, constructive. The latter is emancipated from all dogma; many of its syntheses are powerful; the definitive formation of the various nationalities and the diversity of languages favour the tendency to individualism.

The two great initiators of modern philosophy are Descartes and Francis Bacon. The former inaugurates a spiritualistic philosophy based on the data of consciousness, and his influence may be traced in Malebranche, Spinoza, and Leibniz. Bacon heads a line of Empiricists, who regarded sensation as the only source of knowledge.

In the seventeenth and eighteenth centuries, a Sensualist philosophy grew up in England, based on Baconian Empiricism, and soon to develop in the direction of Subjectivism. Hobbes, Locke, Berkeley, and David Hume mark the stages of this logical evolution. Simultaneously an Associationist psychology appeared also inspired by Sensualism, and, before long, it formed a special field of research. Brown, David Hartley, and Priestley developed the theory of association of ideas in various directions. At the outset Sensualism encountered vigorous opposition, even in England, from the Mystics and Platonists of the Cambridge School (Samuel Parker and, especially, Ralph Cudworth). The reaction was still more lively in the Scotch School, founded and chiefly represented by Thomas Reid, to which Adam Ferguson, Oswald, and Dugald Stewart belonged in the seventeenth and eighteenth centuries, and which had great influence over Eclectic Spiritualism, chiefly in America and France. Hobbes's "selfish" system was developed into a morality by Bentham, a partisan of Egoistic Utilitarianism, and by Adam Smith, a defender of Altruism, but provoked a reaction among the advocates of the moral sentiment theory (Shaftesbury, Hutcheson, Samuel Clarke). In England, also, Theism or Deism was chiefly developed, instituting a criticism of all positive religion, which it sought to supplant with a philosophical religion. English Sensualism spread in France during the eighteenth century: its influence is traceable in de Condillac, de la Mettrie, and the Encyclopedists; Voltaire popularized it in France and with Jean-Jacques Rousseau it made its way among the masses, undermining their Christianity and preparing the Revolution of 1789. In Germany, the philosophy of the eighteenth century is, directly or indirectly, connected with Leibniz — the School of Wolff, the Æsthetic School (Baumgarten), the philosophy of sentiment. But all the German philosophers of the eighteenth century were eclipsed by the great figure of Kant.

With Kant (1724-1804) modern philosophy enters its second period and takes a critical orientation. Kant bases his theory of knowledge, his moral and æsthetic system, and his judgments of finality on the structure of the mind. In the first half of the eighteenth century, German philosophy is replete with great names connected with Kantianism — after it had been put through a Monistic evolution, however — Fichte, Schelling, and Hegel have been called the triumvirate of Pantheism; then again, Schopenhauer, while Herbart returned to individualism. French philosophy in the nineteenth century is at first dominated by an eclectic Spiritualistic movement with which the names of Maine de Biran and, especially, Victor Cousin are associated. Cousin had disciples in America (C. Henry), and in France he gained favour with those whom the excesses of the Revolution had alarmed. In the first half of the nineteenth century French Catholics approved the Traditionalism inaugurated by de Bonald and de Lamennais, while another group took refuge in Ontologism. In the same period Auguste Comte founded Positivism, to which Littré and Taine adhered, though it rose to its greatest height in the English-speaking countries. In fact, England may be said to have been the second fatherland of Positivism; John Stuart Mill, Huxley, Alexander Bain and Herbert Spencer expanded its doctrines, combined them with Associationism and emphasized it criteriological aspect, or attempted (Spencer) to construct a vast synthesis of human sciences. The Associationist philosophy at this time was confronted by the Scotch philosophy which, in Hamilton, combined the teachings of Reid and of Kant and found an American champion in Noah Porter. Mansel spread the doctrines of Hamilton. Associationism regained favour with Thomas Brown and James Mill, but was soon enveloped in the large conception of Positivism, the dominant philosophy in England. Lastly, in Italy, Hegel was for a long time the leader of nineteenth-century philosophical thought (Vera and d'Ercole), whilst Gioberti, the ontologist and Rosmini occupy a distinct position. More recently, Positivism has gained numerous adherents in Italy. In the middle of the century, a large Krausist School existed in Spain, represented chiefly by Sanz del Rio (d. 1869) and N. Salmeron. Balmes (1810-48), the author of "Fundamental Philosophy" is an original thinker whose doctrines have many points of contact with Scholasticism.

Contemporary Orientations
Favourite Problems

Leaving aside social questions, the study of which belongs to philosophy in only some of their aspects, it may be said that in the philosophic interest of the present day psychological questions hold the first place, and that chief among them is the problem of certitude. Kant, indeed, is so important a factor in the destinies of contemporary philosophy not only because he is the initiator of critical formalism, but still more because he obliges his successors to deal with the preliminary and fundamental question of the limits of knowledge. On the other hand the experimental investigation of mental processes has become the object of a new study, psycho-physiology, in which men of science co-operate with philosophers, and which meets with increasing success. This study figures in the programme of most modern universities. Originating at Leipzig (the School of Wundt) and Würzburg, it has quickly become naturalized in Europe and America. In America, "The Psychological Review" has devoted many articles to this branch of philosophy. Psychological studies are the chosen field of the American (Ladd, William James, Hall).

The great success of psychology has emphasized the subjective character of æsthetics, in which hardly anyone now recognizes the objective and metaphysical element. The solutions in vogue are the Kantian, which represents the æsthetic judgment as formed in accordance with the subjective, structural function of the mind, or other psychologic solutions which reduce the beautiful to a psychic impression (the "sympathy", or Einfühlung, of Lipps; the "concrete intuition" of Benedetto Croce). These explanations are insufficient, as they neglect the objective aspect of the beautiful — those elements which, on the part of the object, are the cause of the æsthetic impression and enjoyment. It may be said that the neo-Scholastic philosophy alone takes into account the objective æsthetic factor.

The absorbing influence of psychology also manifests itself to the detriment of other branches of philosophy; first of all, to the detriment of metaphysics, which our contemporaries have unjustly ostracized — unjustly, since, if the existence or possibility of a thing-in-itself is considered of importance, it behooves us to inquire under what aspects of reality it reveals itself. This ostracism of metaphysics, moreover, is largely due to misconception and to a wrong understanding of the theories of substance, of faculties, of causes etc., which belong to the traditional metaphysics. Then again, the invasion of psychology is manifest in logic: side by side with the ancient logic or dialectic, a mathematical or symbolic logic has developed (Peano, Russell, Peirce, Mitchell, and others) and, more recently, a genetic logic which would study, not the fixed laws of thought, but the changing process of mental life and its genesis (Baldwin).

We have seen above (section II, D) how the increasing cultivation of psychology has produced other scientific ramifications which find favour with the learned world. Moral philosophy, long neglected, enjoys a renewed vogue notably in America, where ethnography is devoted to its service (see, e.g., the publications of the Smithsonian Institution). "The International Journal of Ethics" is a review especially devoted to this line of work. In some quarters, where the atmosphere is Positivist, there is a desire to get rid of the old morality, with its notions of value and of duty, and to replace it with a collection of empiric rules subject to evolution (Sidgwick, Huxley, Leslie Stephen, Durkheim, Levy-Bruhl).

As to the history of philosophy, not only are very extended special studies devoted to it, but more and more room is given it in the study of every philosophic question. Among the causes of this exaggerated vogue are the impulse given by the Schools of Cousin and of Hegel, the progress of historical studies in general, the confusion arising from the clash of rival doctrines, and the distrust engendered by that confusion. Remarkable works have been produced by Deussen, on Indian and Oriental philosophy; by Zeller, on Greek antiquity; by Denifle, Hauréau, Bäumker, and Mandonnet, on the Middle Ages; by Windelband, Kuno Fischer, Boutroux and Höffding, on the modern period; and the list might easily be considerably prolonged.

The Opposing Systems

The rival systems of philosophy of the present time may be reduced to various groups: Positivism, neo-Kantianism, Monism, neo-Scholasticism. Contemporary philosophy lives in an atmosphere of Phenomenism, since Positivism and neo-Kantianism are at one on this important doctrine: that science and certitude are possible only within the limits of the world of phenomena, which is the immediate object of experience. Positivism, insisting on the exclusive rights of sensory experience, and Kantian criticism, reasoning from the structure of our cognitive faculties, hold that knowledge extends only as far as appearances; that beyond this is the absolute, the dark depths, the existence of which there is less and less disposition to deny, but which no human mind can fathom. On the contrary, this element of the absolute forms an integral constituent in neo-Scholasticism which has revived, with sobriety and moderation, the fundamental notions of Aristotelean and Medieval metaphysics, and has succeeded in vindicating them against attack and objection.

Positivism

Positivism, under various forms, is defended in England by the followers of Spencer, by Huxley, Lewes, Tyndall, F. Harrison, Congreve, Beesby, J. Bridges, Grant Allen (James Martineau is a reactionary against Positivism); by Balfour, who at the same time propounds a characteristic theory of belief, and falls back on Fideism. From England Positivism passed over to America, where it soon dethroned the Scottish doctrines (Carus). De Roberty, in Russia, and Ribot, in France, are among its most distinguished disciples. In Italy it is found in the writings of Ferrari, Ardigo, and Morselli; in Germany, in those of Laas, Riehl, Guyau, and Durkheim. Less brutal than Materialism, the radical vice of Positivism is its identification of the knowable with the sensible. It seeks in vain to reduce general ideas to collective images, and to deny the abstract and universal character of the mind's concepts. It vainly denies the super-experiential value of the first logical principles in which the scientific life of the mind is rooted; nor will it ever succeed in showing that the certitude of such a judgment as $2 + 2 = 4$ increases with our repeated addition of numbers of oxen or of coins. In morals, where it would reduce precepts and judgments to sociological data formed in the collective conscience and varying with the period and the environment, Positivism stumbles against the judgments of value, and the supersensible ideas of obligation, moral good, and law, recorded in every human conscience and unvarying in their essential data.

Kantianism

Kantianism had been forgotten in Germany for some thirty years (1830-60); Vogt, Büchner, and Molesehott had won for Materialism an ephemeral vogue; but Materialism was swept away by a strong Kantian reaction. This reversion towards Kant (Rückkehr zu Kant) begins to be traceable in 1860 (notably as a result of Lange's "History of Materialism"), and the influence of Kantian doctrines may be said to permeate the whole contemporary German philosophy (Otto Liebmann, von Hartmann, Paulsen, Rehmke, Dilthey, Natorp, Fueken, the Immanentists, and the Empirico-criticists). French neo-Criticism, represented by Renouvier, was connected chiefly with Kant's second "Critique" and introduced a specific Voluntarism. Vacherot, Secrétan, Lachelier, Boutroux, Fouillée, and Bergson are all more or less under tribute to Kantianism. Ravaisson proclaims himself a follower of Maine de Biran. Kantianism has taken its place in the state programme of education and Paul Janet, who, with F. Bouillier and Caro, was among the last legatees of Cousin's Spiritualism, appears, in his "Testament philosophique", affecting a Monism with a Kantian inspiration. All those who, with Kant and the Positivists, proclaim the "bankruptcy of science" look for the basis of our certitude in an imperative demand of the will. This Voluntarism, also called Pragmatism (William James), and, quite recently, Humanism (Schiller at Oxford), is inadequate to the establishment of the theoretic moral and social sciences upon an unshakable base: sooner or later, reflection will ask what this need of living and of willing is worth, and then the intelligence will return to its position as the supreme arbiter of certitude.

From Germany and France Kantianism has spread

everywhere. In England it has called into activity the Critical Idealism associated with T.H. Green and Bradley. Hodgson, on the contrary, returns to Realism. S. Laurie may be placed between Green and Martineau. Emerson, Harris, Everett, and Royce spread Idealistic Criticism in America; Shadworth Hodgson, on the other hand, and Adamson tend to return to Realism, whilst James Ward emphasizes the function of the will.

Monism

With a great many Kantians, a stratum of Monistic ideas is superimposed on Criticism, the thing in itself being considered numerically one. The same tendencies are observable among Positivist Evolutionists like Clifford and Romanes, or G.T. Ladd.

Neo-Scholasticism

Neo-Scholasticism, the revival of which dates from the last third of the nineteenth century (Liberatore, Taparelli, Cornoldi, and others), and which received a powerful impulse under Leo XIII, is tending more and more to become the philosophy of Catholics. It replaces Ontologism, Traditionalism, Gunther's Dualism, and Cartesian Spiritualism, which had manifestly become insufficient. Its syntheses, renewed and completed, can be set up in opposition to Positivism and Kantianism, and even its adversaries no longer dream of denying the worth of its doctrines. The bearings of neo-Scholasticism have been treated elsewhere.

Is Progress in Philosophy Indefinite, or is there a Philosophia Perennis?

Considering the historic succession of systems and the evolution of doctrines from the remotest ages of India down to our own times, and standing face to face with the progress achieved by contemporary scientific philosophy, must we not infer the indefinite progress of philosophic thought? Many have allowed themselves to be led away by this ideal dream. Historic Idealism (Karl Marx) regards philosophy as a product fatally engendered by pre-existing causes in our physical and social environment. Auguste Comte's "law of the three states", Herbert Spencer's evolutionism, Hegel's "indefinite becoming of the soul", sweep philosophy along in an ascending current toward an ideal perfection, the realization of which no one can foresee. For all these thinkers, philosophy is variable and relative: therein lies their serious error. Indefinite progress, condemned by history in many fields, is untenable in the history of philosophy. Such a notion is evidently refuted by the appearance of thinkers like Aristotle and Plato three centuries before Christ, for these men, who for ages have dominated, and still dominate, human thought, would be anachronisms, since they would be inferior to the thinkers of our own time. And no one would venture to assert this. History shows, indeed, that there are adaptations of a synthesis to its environment, and that every age has its own aspirations and its special way of looking at problems and their solutions; but it also presents unmistakable evidence of incessant new beginnings, of rhythmic oscillations from one pole of thought to the other. If Kant found an original formula of Subjectivism and the reine Innerlichkeit, it would be a mistake to think that Kant had no intellectual ancestors: he had them in the earliest historic ages of philosophy: M. Deussen has found in the Vedic hymn of the Upanishads the distinction between noumenon and phenomenon, and writes, on the theory of Mâyâ, "Kants Grunddogma, so alt wie die Philosophie" ("Die Philos. des Upanishad's", Leipzig, 1899, p. 204).

It is false to say that all truth is relative to a given time and latitude, and that philosophy is the product of economic conditions in a ceaseless course of evolution, as historical Materialism holds. Side by side with these things, which are subject to change and belong to one particular condition of the life of mankind, there is a soul of truth circulating in every system, a mere fragment of that complete and unchangeable truth which haunts the human mind in its most disinterested investigations. Amid the oscillations of historic systems there is room for a philosophia perennis — as it were a purest atmosphere of truth, enveloping the ages, its clearness somehow felt in spite of cloud and mist.

"The truth Pythagoras sought after, and Plato, and Aristotle, is the same that Augustine and Aquinas pursued. So far as it is developed in history, truth is the daughter of time; so far as it bears within itself a content independent of time, and therefore of history, it is the daughter of eternity" [Willmann, "Gesch. d Idealismus", II (Brunswick, 1896), 550; cf. Commer "Die immerwahrende Philosophie" (Vienna, 1899)].

This does not mean that essential and permanent verities do not adapt themselves to the intellectual life of each epoch. Absolute immobility in philosophy, no less than absolute relativity, is contrary to nature and to history. It leads to decadence and death. It is in this sense that we must interpret the adage: Vita in motu.

Philosophy and the sciences

Aristotle of old laid the foundation of a philosophy supported by observation and experience. We need only glance through the list of his works to see that astronomy, mineralogy, physics and chemistry, biology, zoology, furnished him with examples and bases for his theories on the constitution, of the heavenly and terrestrial bodies, the nature of the vital principle, etc. Besides, the whole Aristotelean classification of the branches of philosophy (see section II) is inspired by the same idea of making philosophy — general science — rest upon the particular sciences. The early Middle Ages, with a rudimentary scientific culture, regarded all its learning, built up on the Trivium (grammar, rhetoric, dialectic) and Quadrivium (arithmetic, geometry, astronomy, music), as preparation for philosophy. In the thirteenth century, when Scholasticism came under Aristotelean influences, it incorporated the sciences in the programme of philosophy itself. This may be seen in regulation issued by the Faculty of Arts of Paris 19 March, 1255, "De libris qui legendi essent" This order prescribes the study of commentaries or various scientific treatises of Aristotle, notably those on the first book of the "Meteorologica", on the treatises on Heaven and Earth, Generation, the Senses and Sensations, Sleeping and Waking, Memory, Plants, and Animals. Here are amply sufficient means for the magistri to familiarize the "artists" with astronomy, botany, physiology, and zoology to say nothing of Aristotle's "Physics", which was also prescribed as a classical text, and which afforded opportunities for numerous observations in chemistry and physics as then understood. Grammar and rhetoric served as preliminary studies to logic, Bible history, social science, and politics were introductory to moral philosophy. Such men as Albertus Magnus and Roger Bacon expressed their views on the necessity of linking the sciences with philosophy and preached it by example. So that both antiquity and the Middle Ages knew and appreciated scientific philosophy.

In the seventeenth century the question of the relation between the two enters upon a new phase: from this period modern science takes shape and begins that triumphal march which it is destined to continue through the twentieth century, and of which the human mind is justly proud. Modern scientific knowledge differs from that of antiquity and the Middle Ages in three important respects: the multiplication of sciences; their independent value; the divergence between common knowledge and scientific knowledge. In the Middle Ages astronomy was closely akin to astrology, chemistry to alchemy, physics to divination; modern science has severely excluded all these fantastic connections. Considered now from one side and again from another, the physical world has revealed continually new aspects, and each specific point of view has become the focus of a new study. On the other hand, by defining their respective limits, the sciences have acquired autonomy; useful in the Middle Ages only as a preparation for rational physics and for metaphysics, they are nowadays of value for themselves, and no longer play the part of handmaids to philosophy. Indeed, the progress achieved within itself by each particular science brings one more revolution in knowledge. So long as instruments of observation were imperfect, and inductive methods restricted, it was practically impossible to rise above an elementary knowledge. People knew, in the Middle Ages, that wine, when left exposed to the air, became vinegar; but what do facts like this amount to in comparison with the complex formulae of modern chemistry? Hence it was that an Albertus Magnus or a Roger Bacon could flatter himself, in those days, with having acquired all the science of his time, a claim which would now only provoke a smile. In every department progress has drawn the line sharply between popular and scientific knowledge; the former is ordinarily the starting-point of the latter, but the conclusions and teachings involved in the sciences are unintelligible to those who lack the requisite preparation.

Do not, then, these profound modifications in the condition of the sciences entail modifications in the relations which, until the seventeenth century, had been accepted as existing between the sciences and philosophy? Must not the separation of philosophy and science widen out to a complete divorce? Many have thought so, both scientists and philosophers, and it was for this that in the eighteenth and nineteenth centuries so many savants and philosophers turned their backs on one another. For the former, philosophy has become useless; the particular sciences, they say, multiplying and becoming perfect, must exhaust the whole field of the knowable, and a time will come when philosophy shall be no more. For the philosophers, philosophy has no need of the immeasurable mass of scientific notions which have been acquired, many of which possess only a precarious and provisional value. Wolff, who pronounced the divorce of science from philosophy, did most to accredit this view, and he has been followed by certain Catholic philosophers who held that scientific study may be excluded from philosophic culture.

What shall we say on this question? That the reasons which formerly existed for keeping touch with science are a thousand times more imperative in our day. If the profound synthetic view of things which justifies the existence of philosophy presupposes analytical researches, the multiplication and perfection of those researches is certainly reason for neglecting them. The horizon of detailed knowledge widens incessantly; research of every kind is busy exploring the departments of the universe which it has mapped out. And philosophy, whose mission is to explain the order of the universe by general and ultimate reasons applicable, not only to a group of facts, but to the whole body of known phenomena, cannot be indifferent to the matter which it has to explain. Philosophy is like a tower whence we obtain the panorama of a great city — its plan, its monuments, its great arteries, with the form and location of each — things which a visitor cannot discern while he goes through the streets and lanes, or visits libraries, churches, palaces, and museums, one after another. If the city grows and develops, there is all the more reason, if we would know it as a whole, why we should hesitate to ascend the tower and study from that height the plan upon which its new quarters have been laid out.

It is, happily, evident that contemporary philosophy is inclined to be first and foremost a scientific philosophy; it has found its way back from its wanderings of yore. This is noticeable in philosophers of the most opposite tendencies. There would be no end to the list if we had to enumerate every case where this orientation of ideas has been adopted. "This union", says Boutroux, speaking of the sciences and philosophy, "is in truth the classic tradition of philosophy. But there had been established a psychology and a metaphysics which aspired to set themselves up beyond the sciences, by mere reflection of the mind upon itself. Nowadays all philosophers are agreed to make scientific data their starting-point" (Address at the International Congress of Philosophy in 1900; Revue de Métaph. et de Morale, 1900, p. 697). Boutroux and many others spoke similarly at the International Congress of Bologna (April, 1911). Wundt introduces this union into the very definition of philosophy, which, he says, is "the general science whose function it is to unite in a system free of all contradictions the knowledge acquired through the particular sciences, and to reduce to their principles the general methods of science and the conditions of knowledge supposed by them" ("Einleitung in die Philosophie", Leipzig, 1901, p. 19). And R. Eucken says: "The farther back the limits of the observable world recede, the more conscious are we of the lack of an adequately comprehensive explanation" — "Gesammelte Aufsatze zur Philos. u. Lebensanschanung" (Leipzig, 1903), p. 157]. This same thought inspired Leo XIII when he placed the parallel and harmonious teaching of philosophy and of the sciences on the programme of the Institute of Philosophy created by him in the University of Louvain.

On their side, the scientists have been coming to the same conclusions ever since they rose to a synthetic view of that matter which is the object of their study. So it was with Pasteur, so with Newton. Ostwald, professor of chemistry at Leipzig, has undertaken to publish the "Annalen der Naturphilosophie", a review devoted to the cultivation of the territory which is common to philosophy and the sciences A great many men of science, too, are engaged in philosophy without knowing it: in their constant discussions of "Mechanism", "Evolutionism", "Transformism", they are using terms which imply a philosophical theory of matter.

If philosophy is the explanation as a whole of that world which the particular sciences investigate in detail, it follows that the latter find their culmination in the former, and that as the sciences are so will philosophy be. It is true that objections are put forward against this way of uniting philosophy and the sciences. Common observation, it is said, is enough support for philosophy. This is a mistake: philosophy cannot ignore whole departments of knowledge which are inaccessible to ordinary experience biology, for example, has shed a new light on the philosophic study of man. Others again adduce the extent and the growth of the sciences to show that scientific philosophy must ever remain an unattainable ideal; the practical solution of this difficulty concerns the teaching of philosophy (see section XI).

Philosophy and Religion

Religion presents to man, with authority, the solution of man's problems which also concern philosophy. Such are the questions of the nature of God, of His relation with the visible world, of man's origin and destiny. Now religion, which precedes philosophy in the social life, naturally obliges it to take into consideration the points of religious doctrine. Hence the close connection of philosophy with religion in the early stages of civilization, a fact strikingly apparent in Indian philosophy, which, not only at its beginning but throughout its development, was intimately bound up with the doctrine of the sacred books (see above). The Greeks, at least during the most important periods of their history, were much less subject to the influences of pagan religions; in fact, they combined with extreme scrupulosity in what concerned ceremonial usage a wide liberty in regard to dogma. Greek thought soon took its independent flight; Socrates ridicules the gods in whom the common people believed; Plato does not banish religious ideas from his philosophy; but Aristotle keeps them entirely apart, his God is the Actus purus, with a meaning exclusively philosophic, the prime mover of the universal mechanism. The Stoics point out that all things obey an irresistible fatality and that the wise man fears no gods. And if Epicurus teaches cosmic determinism and denies all finality, it is only to conclude that man can lay aside all fear of divine intervention in mundane affairs. The question takes a new aspect when the influences of the Oriental and Jewish religions are brought to bear on Greek philosophy by neo-Pythagorism, the Jewish theology (end of the first century), and, above all, neo-Platonism (third century B.C.). A yearning for religion was stirring in the world, and philosophy became enamoured of every religious doctrine Plotinus (third century after Christ), who must always remain the most perfect type of the neo-

Platonic mentality, makes philosophy identical with religion, assigning as its highest aim the union of the soul with God by mystical ways. This mystical need of the supernatural issues in the most bizarre lucubrations from Plotinus's successors, e.g. Jamblicus (d. about A.D. 330), who, on a foundation of neo-Platonism, erected an international pantheon for all the divinities whose names are known.

It has often been remarked that Christianity, with its monotheistic dogma and its serene, purifying morality, came in the fulness of time and appeased the inward unrest with which souls were afflicted at the end of the Roman world. Though Christ did not make Himself the head of a philosophical school, the religion which He founded supplies solutions for a group of problems which philosophy solves by other methods (e.g. the immortality of the soul). The first Christian philosophers, the Fathers of the Church, were imbued with Greek ideas and took over from the circumambient neo-Platonism the commingling of philosophy and religion. With them philosophy is incidental and secondary, employed only to meet polemic needs, and to support dogma; their philosophy is religious. In this Clement of Alexandria and Origen are one with St. Augustine and Pseudo-Dionysius the Areopagite. The early Middle Ages continued the same traditions, and the first philosophers may be said to have received neo-Platonic influences through the channel of the Fathers. John Scotus Eriugena (ninth century), the most remarkable mind of this first period, writes that "true religion is true philosophy and, conversely, true philosophy is true religion" (De div. praed., I, I). But as the era advances a process of dissociation sets in, to end in the complete separation between the two sciences of Scholastic theology or the study of dogma, based fundamentally on Holy Scripture, and Scholastic philosophy, based on purely rational investigation. To understand the successive stages of this differentiation, which was not completed until the middle of the thirteenth century, we must draw attention to certain historical facts of capital importance.

(1) The origin of several philosophical problems, in the early Middle Ages, must be sought within the domain of theology, in the sense that the philosophical discussions arose in reference to theological questions. The discussion, e.g. of transubstantiation (Berengarius of Tours), raised the problem of substance and of change, or becoming.

(2) Theology being regarded as a superior and sacred science, the whole pedagogic and didactic organization of the period tended to confirm this superiority (see section XI).

(3) The enthusiasm for dialectics, which reached its maximum in the eleventh century, brought into fashion certain purely verbal methods of reasoning bordering on the sophistical. Anselm of Besata (Anselmus Peripateticus) is the type of this kind of reasoner. Now the dialecticians, in discussing theological subjects, claimed absolute validity for their methods, and they ended in such heresies as

Gottschalk's on predestination, Berengarius's on transubstantiation, and Roscelin's Tritheism. Berengarius's motto was: "Per omnia ad dialecticam confugere". There followed an excessive reaction on the part of timorous theologians, practical men before all things, who charged dialectics with the sins of the dialecticians. This antagonistic movement coincided with an attempt to reform religious life. At the head of the group was Peter Damian (1007-72), the adversary of the liberal arts; he was the author of the saying that philosophy is the handmaid of theology. From this saying it has been concluded that the Middle Ages in general put philosophy under tutelage, whereas the maxim was current only among a narrow circle of reactionary theologians. Side by side with Peter Damian in Italy, were Manegold of Lautenbach and Othloh of St. Emmeram, in Germany.

(4) At the same time a new tendency becomes discernible in the eleventh century, in Lanfranc, William of Hirschau, Rodulfus Ardens, and particularly St. Anselm of Canterbury; the theologian calls in the aid of philosophy to demonstrate certain dogmas or to show their rational side. St. Anselm, in an Augustinian spirit, attempted this justification of dogma, without perhaps invariably applying to the demonstrative value of his arguments the requisite limitations. In the thirteenth century these efforts resulted in a new theological method, the dialectic.

(5) While these disputes as to the relations of philosophy and theology went on, many philosophical

questions were nevertheless treated on their own account, as we have seen above (universals, St. Anselm's theodicy, Abelard's philosophy, etc.).

(6) The dialectic method, developed fully in the twelfth century, just when Scholastic theology received a powerful impetus, is a theological, not a philosophical, method. The principal method in theology is the interpretation of Scripture and of authority; the dialectic method is secondary and consists in first establishing a dogma and then showing its reasonableness, confirming the argument from authority by the argument from reason. It is a process of apologetics. From the twelfth century onward, these two theological methods are fairly distinguished by the words auctoritates, rationes. Scholastic theology, condensed in the "summae" and "books of sentences", is henceforward regarded as distinct from philosophy. The attitude of theologians towards philosophy is threefold: one group, the least influential, still opposes its introduction into theology, and carries on the reactionary traditions of the preceding period (e.g. Gauthier de Saint-Victor); another accepts philosophy, but takes a utilitarian view of it, regarding it merely as a prop of dogma (Peter Lombard); a third group, the most influential, since it includes the three theological schools of St. Victor, Abelard, and Gilbert de la Porrée, grants to philosophy, in addition to this apologetic role, an independent value which entitles it to be cultivated and studied for its own sake. The members of this group are at once both theologians and philosophers.

(7) At the opening of the thirteenth century one section of Augustinian theologians continued to emphasize the utilitarian and apologetic office of philosophy. But St. Thomas Aquinas created new Scholastic traditions, and wrote a chapter on scientific methodology in which the distinctness and in dependence of the two sciences is thoroughly established. Duns Scotus, again, and the Terminists exaggerated this independence. Latin Averroism, which had a brilliant but ephemeral vogue in the thirteenth and fourteenth centuries, accepted whole and entire in philosophy Averroistic Peripateticism, and, to safeguard Catholic orthodoxy, took refuge behind the sophism that what is true in philosophy may be false in theology, and conversely — wherein they were more reserved than Averroes and the Arab philosophers, who regarded religion as something inferior, good enough for the masses, and who did not trouble themselves about Moslem orthodoxy. Lully, going to extremes, maintained that all dogma is susceptible of demonstration, and that philosophy and theology coalesce. Taken as a whole, the Middle Ages, profoundly religious, constantly sought to reconcile its philosophy with the Catholic Faith. This bond the Renaissance philosophy severed. In the Reformation period a group of publicists, in view of the prevailing strife, formed projects of reconciliation among the numerous religious bodies. They convinced themselves that all religions possess a common fund of essential truths relating to God, and that their content is identical, in spite of

divergent dogmas. Besides, Theism, being only a form of Naturism applied to religion, suited the independent ways of the Renaissance. As in building up natural law, human nature was taken into consideration, so reason was interrogated to discover religious ideas. And hence the wide acceptance of Theism, not among Protestants only, but generally among minds that had been carried away with the Renaissance movement (Erasmus, Coornheert).

For this tolerance or religious indifferentism modern philosophy in more than one instance substituted a disdain of positive religions. The English Theism or Deism of the seventeenth and eighteenth centuries criticizes all positive religion and, in the name of an innate religious sense, builds up a natural religion which is reducible to a collection of theses on the existence of God and the immortality of the soul. The initiator of this movement was Herbert of Cherbury (1581-1648); J. Toland (1670-1722), Tindal (1656-1733), and Lord Bolingbroke took part in it. This criticizing movement inaugurated in England was taken up in France, where it combined with an outright hatred of Catholicism. Pierre Bayle (1646-1706) propounded the thesis that all religion is anti-rational and absurd, and that a state composed of Atheists is possible. Voltaire wished to substitute for Catholicism an incoherent mass of doctrines about God. The religious philosophy of the eighteenth century in France led to Atheism and paved the way for the Revolution. In justice to contemporary philosophy it must be credited with teaching the amplest tolerance towards the various religions; and in its programme of research it has included religious psychology, or the study of the religious sentiment.

For Catholic philosophy the relations between philosophy and theology, between reason and faith, were fixed, in a chapter of scientific methodology, by the great Scholastic thinkers of the thirteenth century. Its principles, which still retain their vitality, are as follows:

(a) Distinctness of the two sciences.

The independence of philosophy in regard to theology, as in regard to any other science whatsoever, is only an interpretation of this undeniable principle of scientific progress, as applicable in the twentieth century as it was in the thirteenth, that a rightly constituted science derives its formal object, its principles, and its constructive method from its own resources, and that, this being so, it cannot borrow from any other science without compromising its own right to exist.

(b) Negative, not positive, material, not formal, subordination of philosophy in regard to theology.

This means that, while the two sciences keep their formal independence (the independence of the principles by which their investigations are guided), there are certain matters where philosophy cannot contradict the solutions afforded by theology. The Scholastics of the Middle Ages justified this subordination, being profoundly convinced that Catholic dogma contains the infallible word of God, the expression of truth. Once a proposition, e.g. that two and two make four, has been accepted as certain, logic forbids any other science to form any conclusion subversive of that proposition. The material mutual subordination of the sciences is one of those laws out of which logic makes the indispensable guarantee of the unity of knowledge. "The truth duly demonstrated by one science serves as a beacon in another science." The certainty of a theory in chemistry imposes its acceptance on physics, and the physicist who should go contrary to it would be out of his course. Similarly, the philosopher cannot contradict the certain data of theology, any more than he can contradict the certain conclusions of the individual sciences. To deny this would be to deny the conformity of truth with truth, to contest the principle of contradiction, to surrender to a relativism which is destructive of all certitude. "It being supposed that nothing but what is true is included in this science (sacred theology) . . . it being supposed that whatever is true by the decision and authority of this science can nowise be false by the decision of right reason: these things, I say, being supposed, as it is manifest from them that the authority of this science and reason alike rest upon truth, and one verity cannot be contrary to another, it must be said absolutely that reason can in no way be contrary to the authority of this Scripture, nay, all right reason is in accord with it" (Henry of Ghent, "Summa Theologica", X, iii, n.4).

But when is a theory certain? This is a question of fact, and error is easy. In proportion as the principle is simple and absolute, so are its applications complex and variable. It is not for philosophy to establish the certitude of theological data, any more than to fix the conclusions of chemistry or of physiology. The certainty of those data and those conclusions must proceed from another source. "The preconceived idea is entertained that a Catholic savant is a soldier in the service of his religious faith, and that, in his hands, science is but a weapon to defend his Credo. In the eyes of a great many people, the Catholic savant seems to be always under the menace of excommunication, or entangled in dogmas which hamper him, and compelled, for the sake of loyalty to his Faith, to renounce the disinterested love of science and its free cultivation" (Mercier, "Rapport sur les études supér. de philos.", 1891, p. 9). Nothing could be more untrue.

The Catholic Church and Philosophy

The principles which govern the doctrinal relations of philosophy and theology have moved the Catholic Church to intervene on various occasions in the history of philosophy. As to the Church's right and duty to intervene for the purpose of maintaining the integrity of theological dogma and the deposit of faith, there is no need of discussion in this place. It is interesting, however, to note the attitude taken by the Church towards philosophy throughout the ages, and particularly in the Middle Ages, when a civilization saturated with Christianity had established extremely intimate relations between theology and philosophy.

A. The censures of the Church have never fallen upon philosophy as such, but upon theological applications, judged false, which were based upon philosophical reasonings. John Scotus Eriugena, Roscelin, Berengarius, Abelard, Gilbert de la Porrée were condemned because their teachings tended to subvert theological dogmas. Eriugena denied the substantial distinction between God and created things; Roscelin held that there are three Gods; Berengarius, that there is no real transubstantiation in the Eucharist; Abelard and Gilbert de la Porrée essentially modified the dogma of the Trinity. The Church, through her councils, condemned their theological errors; with their philosophy as such she does not concern herself. "Nominalism", says Hauréau, "is the old enemy. It is, in fact, the doctrine which, because it best accords with reason, is most remote from axioms of faith. Denounced before council after council, Nominalism was condemned in the person of Abelard as it had been in the person of Roscelin" (Hist. philos. scol., I, 292).

No assertion could be more inaccurate. What the Church has condemned is neither the so-called Nominalism, nor Realism, nor philosophy in general, nor the method of arguing in theology, but certain applications of that method which are judged dangerous, i.e. matters which are not philosophical. In the thirteenth century a host of teachers adopted the philosophical theories of Roscelin and Abelard, and no councils were convoked to condemn them. The same may be said of the condemnation of David of Dinant (thirteenth century), who denied the distinction between God and matter, and of various doctrines condemned in the fourteenth century as tending to the negation of morality. It has been the same in modern times. To mention only the condemnation of Gunther, of Rosmini, and of Ontologism in the nineteenth century, what alarmed the Church was the fact that the theses in question had a theological bearing.

B. The Church has never imposed any philosophical system, though she has anathematized many doctrines, or branded them as suspect. This corresponds with the prohibitive, but not imperative attitude of theology in regard to philosophy. To take one example, faith teaches that the world was created in time; and yet St. Thomas maintains that the concept of eternal creation (ab aeterno) involves no contradiction. He did not think himself obliged to demonstrate creation in time: his teaching would have been heterodox only if, with the Averroists his day, he had maintained the necessary eternity of the world. It may, perhaps, be objected that many Thomistic doctrines were condemned in 1277 by Etienne Tempier, Bishop of Paris. But it is well to note, and recent works on the subject have abundantly proved this, that Tempier's condemnation, in so far as it applied to Thomas Aquinas, was the issue of intrigues and personal animosity, and that, in canon law, it had no force outside of the Diocese of Paris. Moreover, it was annulled by one of Tempier's successors, Etienne de

Borrète, in 1325.

C. The Church has encouraged philosophy. To say nothing of the fact that all those who applied themselves to science and philosophy in the Middle Ages were churchmen, and that the liberal arts found an asylum in capitular and monastic schools until the twelfth century, it is important to remark that the principal universities of the Middle Ages were pontifical foundations. This was the case with Paris. To be sure, in the first years of the university's aquaintance with the Aristotelean encyclopaedia (late twelfth century) there were prohibitions against reading the "Physics", the "Metaphysics", and the treatise "On the Soul". But these restrictions were of a temporary character and arose out of particular circumstances. In 1231, Gregory IX laid upon a commission of three consultors the charge to prepare an amended edition of Aristotle "ne utile per inutile vitietur" (lest what is useful suffer damage through what is useless). The work of expurgatio was done, in point of fact, by the Albertine-Thomist School, and, beginning from the year 1255, the Faculty of Arts, with the knowledge of the ecclesiastical authority, ordered the teaching of all the books previously prohibited (see Mandonnet, "Siger de Brabant et l'averroïsme latin au XIIIe s.", Louvain, 1910). It might also be shown how in modern times and in our own day the popes have encouraged philosophic studies. Leo XIII, as is well known, considered the restoration of philosophic Thomism on of the chief tasks of his pontificate.

The Teaching of Philosophy

The methods of teaching philosophy have varied in various ages. Socrates used to interview his auditors, and hold symposia in the market-place, on the porticoes and in the public gardens. His method was interrogation; he whetted the curiosity of the audience and practised what had become known as Socratic irony and the maieutic art (maieutikê techne), the art of delivering minds of their conceptions. His successor opened schools properly so called, and from the place occupied by these schools several systems took their names (the Stoic School, the Academy, the Lyceum). In the Middle Ages and down to the seventeenth century, the learned language was Latin. The German discourses of Eckhart are mentioned as merely sporadic examples. From the ninth to the twelfth century teaching was confined to the monastic and cathedral schools. It was the golden age of schools. Masters and students went from one school to another: Lanfranc travelled over Europe; John of Salisbury (twelfth century) heard at Paris all the then famous professors of philosophy; Abelard gathered crowds about his rostrum. Moreover, as the same subjects were taught everywhere, and from the same text-books, scholastic wanderings were attended with few disadvantages. The books took the form of commentaries or monographs. From the time of Abelard a method came into use which met with great success, that of setting forth the pros and cons of a question, which was later perfected by the addition of a solutio. The application of this method was extended in the thirteenth century (e.g. in the "Summa theologica" of St. Thomas). Lastly, philosophy being an educational preparation for theology, the "Queen of the Sciences", philosophical and theological topics were combined in one and the same book, or even in the same lecture.

At the end of the twelfth century and the beginning of the thirteenth, the University of Paris was organized, and philosophical teaching was concentrated in the Faculty of Arts. Teaching was dominated by two principles: internationalism and freedom. The student was an apprentice-professor: after receiving the various degrees, he obtained from the chancellor of the university a licence to teach (licentia docendi). Many of the courses of this period have been preserved, the abbreviated script of the Middle Ages being virtually a stenographic system. The programme of courses drawn up in 1255 is well known: it comprises the exegesis of all the books of Aristotle. The commentary, or lectio (from legere, to read), is the ordinary form of instruction (whence the German Vorlesungen and the English lecture). There were also disputations, in which questions were treated by means of objections and answers; the exercise took a lively character, each one being invited to contribute his thoughts on the subject. The University of Paris was the model for all the others, notably those of Oxford and Cambridge. These forms of instruction in the universities lasted as long as Aristoteleanism, i.e. until the seventeenth century. In the eighteenth century — the siècle des lumières (Erklärung) — philosophy took a popular and encyclopedic form, and was circulated in the literary productions of the period. In the nineteenth century it resumed its didactic attitude in the universities and in the seminaries, where, indeed its teaching had long continued. The advance of philological and historical studies had a great influence on the character of philosophical teaching: critical methods were welcomed, and little by little the professors adopted the practice of specializing in this or that branch of philosophy — a practice which is still in vogue. Without attempting to touch on all the questions involved in modern methods of teaching philosophy, we shall here indicate some of the principal features.

The Language of Philosophy

The earliest of the moderns — as Descartes or Leibniz — used both Latin and the vernacular, but in the nineteenth century (except in ecclesiastical seminaries and in certain academical exercises mainly ceremonial in character) the living languages supplanted Latin; the result has been a gain in clearness of thought and interest and vitality of teaching. Teaching in Latin too often contents itself with formulae: the living language effects a better comprehension of things which must in any case be difficult. Personal experience, writes Fr. Hogan, formerly superior of the Boston Seminary, in his "Clerical Studies" (Philadelphia, 1895-1901), has shown that among students who have learned philosophy, particularly Scholastic, only in Latin, very few have acquired anything more than a mass of formulae, which they hardly understand; though this does not always prevent their adhering to their formulae through thick and thin. Those who continue to write in Latin — as many Catholic philosophers, often of the highest worth, still do — have the sad experience of seeing their books confined to a very narrow circle of readers.

Didactic Processes

Aristotle's advice, followed by the Scholastics, still retains its value and its force: before giving the solution of a problem, expound the reasons for and against. This explains, in particular, the great part played by the history of philosophy or the critical examination of the solutions proposed by the great thinkers. Commentary on a treatise still figures in some special higher courses; but contemporary philosophical teaching is principally divided according to the numerous branches of philosophy (see section II). The introduction of laboratories and practical seminaries (séminaires practiques) in philosophical teaching has been of the greatest advantage. Side by side with libraries and shelves full of periodicals there is room for laboratories and museums, once the necessity of vivifying philosophy by contact with the sciences is admitted (see section VIII). As for the practical seminary, in which a group of students, with the aid of a teacher, investigate to some special problem, it may be applied to any branch of philosophy with remarkable results. The work in common, where each directs his individual efforts towards one general aim, makes each the beneficiary of the researches of all; it accustoms them to handling the instruments of research, facilitates the detection of facts, teaches the pupil how to discover for himself the reasons for what he observes, affords a real experience in the constructive methods of discovery proper to each subject, and very often decides the scientific vocation of those whose efforts have been crowned with a first success.

The Order of Philosophical Teaching

One of the most complex questions is: With what branch ought philosophical teaching to begin, and what order should it follow? In conformity with an immemorial tradition, the beginning is often made with logic. Now logic, the science of science, is difficult to understand and unattractive in the earliest stages of teaching. It is better to begin with the sciences which take the real for their object: psychology, cosmology, metaphysics, and theodicy. Scientific logic will be better understood later on; moral philosophy presupposes psychology; systematic history of philosophy requires a preliminary acquaintance with all the branches of philosophy (see Mercier, "Manuel de philosophie", Introduction, third edition, Louvain, 1911).

Connected with this question of the order of teaching is another: viz. What should be the scientific teaching preliminary to philosophy? Only a course in the sciences specially appropriate to philosophy can meet the manifold exigencies of the problem. The general scientific courses of our modern universities include too much or too little: "too much in the sense that professional teaching must go into numerous technical facts and details with which philosophy has nothing to do; too little, because professional teaching often makes the observation of facts its ultimate aim, whilst, from our standpoint, facts are, and can be, only a means, a starting-point, towards acquiring a knowledge of the most general causes and laws" (Mercier, "Rapport sur les études supérieures de philosophie", Louvain, 1891, p. 25). M. Boutroux, a professor at the Sorbonne, solves the problem of philosophical teaching at the university in the same sense, and, according to him, the flexible and very liberal organization of the faculty of philosophy should include "the whole assemblage of the sciences, whether theoretic, mathematico-physical, or philologico-historical" ("Revue internationale de l'enseignement", Paris, 1901, p. 510). The programme of courses of the Institute of Philosophy of Louvain is drawn up in conformity with this spirit.

II.
Science and the Church

Science and the Church

The words "science" and "Church" are here understood in the following sense: Science is not taken in the restricted meaning of natural sciences, but in the general one given to the word by Aristotle and St. Thomas Aquinas. Aristotle defines science as a sure and evident knowledge obtained from demonstrations. This is identical with St. Thomas's definition of science as the knowledge of things from their causes. In this sense science comprises the entire curriculum of university studies. Church, in connexion with science, theoretically means any Church that claims authority in matters of doctrine and teaching; practically, however, only the Catholic Church is in question, on account of her universality and her claim of power to exercise this authority. The relation between the two is here treated under the two heads SCIENCE and CHURCH.

Science

Science is considered from three points of view: contact with faith, legitimate freedom, unlimited freedom.
Points of contact between science and faith

These are mainly confined to philosophical and historical sciences. They do not occur in theology, as it is the very science of faith itself. The points of contact of the various sciences with faith may be grouped as follows:

Philosophy

In the philosophical sciences: — the existence of

God and His qualities: — unity, personality, eternity infinity; God, the final end of man and of all created things; freedom of the human will, the natural law.

History

In the historical and linguistic sciences: the historical unity of the human race and of the original language; the history of the Patriarchs, of the Israelites, and of their Messianic belief; the history of Christ and His Church; the authenticity of the Sacred Books; the history of dogmas, of schisms, of heresies; hagiography.

Law

In the science of ethics and law: — the origin of right and duty (the realistic Positivism of Comte and the subjective Positivism of John Stuart Mill); the authority of civil governments (Rousseau's "Contrat social" and Kant's "Critique of Pure Reason"); the matrimonial contract, its unity and permanency; the natural rights and duties of parents and children; personal property; freedom of religion (separation of religion and state, toleration).

Medicine

The medical and biological sciences have occasioned serious discussion concerning the existence of the human soul, its spirituality and immortality, its difference from the vital principle in animals; the physiological unity of mankind; the justification of prevention and extinction of human life. In reality, however, all these questions lie outside the domain of medicine.

Natural sciences

In natural sciences, especially natural philosophy, the points of contact are: — the creation of the world and of man (materialistic doctrines, eternity of matter, absolute necessity of natural laws impossibility of miracles, Darwinian origin of man); the Deluge, its existence and ethnographical universality. The mathematical and experimental sciences, also known as exact sciences, have no contact whatever with faith, although at one time, it was erroneously believed that the geocentric system was contained in the Bible. The celestial phenomena mentioned in the Scripture, like the star of the magi, the solar eclipse during the Paschal full moon, the stars falling from heaven as forerunners of the Last Judgment, are all of the miraculous kind and beyond the laws of nature.

Legitimate freedom

Legitimate freedom is needed for science as well as for any human development. The only questions are these: what is legitimate freedom, and what are its limitations?

Research and teaching

Science comprises two functions: research and teaching.

Research

The object of scientific research is practically indefinite in extent and can never be exhausted by the human mind. In this field there is more freedom than has ever been claimed. Compared to its field, the progress of science appears small, so much so, that the greatest progress seems to consist in the knowledge of how little we know. This was the conclusion arrived at by Socrates, Newton, Humboldt, and so many others. The very instruments teach this lesson: the deeper the microscope descends into the secrets of nature and the higher the telescopic power reaches into the heavens, the vaster appears the ocean of undiscovered truths. This ought to be kept in mind, when the progress of science is loudly proclaimed. There has never been a general progress of all sciences; it was always progress in some branches, often at the cost of others. In our own days natural, medical, and historical sciences advance rapidly in comparison with past ages; at the same time the philosophical sciences fall just as rapidly behind the early ages. The science of law owes its foundation to the ancient world. Some of the theological sciences reached their height in the early part of the Middle Ages, others towards the beginning of the seventeenth century.

Teaching

By teaching is here understood every diffusion of

knowledge, by word or print, in school or museum, in public or private. Progress and the freedom necessary for it are as much to be desired in teaching as in research. There is a doctrinal freedom, a pedagogical freedom, and a professional freedom. Doctrinal freedom regards the doctrine itself which is taught; pedagogical freedom, the manner in which science is diffused among scholars or the general public; professional freedom, the persons who do the teaching. Science claims freedom of teaching in all these respects.

Limitations

It has to be seen whether there are limitations to research and teaching and what these limitations are. All things in this world may be considered from a triple point of view: from the logical, the physical, and the ethical. Applied to science we discover limitations in all three.

Logical

Logically science is limited by truth, which belongs to its very essence. Knowledge of things cannot be had from their causes, unless the knowledge be true. False knowledge cannot be derived from the causes of things; it has its origin in some spurious source. Should science ever have to choose between truth and freedom (a choice not at all imaginary), it must under all circumstances decide for truth, under penalty of self-annihilation. As long as the case is thus put theoretically, there is no difference of opinion.

Yet in practice, it is almost hopeless to reconcile conflicting sentiments. When, in 1901, a vacant chair at the University of Strasburg was to be filled by a Catholic historian, Mommsen published a protest, in which he exclaimed: "A sense of degradation is pervading German university circles". On that occasion he coined the shibboleth "voraussetzungslos", and claimed that scientific research must be "without presuppositions". The same cry was raised by Harnack (1908) when he demanded "unbounded freedom for research and knowledge". The demand was formulated a little more precisely by the congress of academicians in Jena (1908). Their claim for science was "freedom from every view foreign to scientific methods".

In the latter formula the claim has a legitimate meaning, viz., that unscientific views should not influence the results of science. In the meaning of Mommsen and Harnack, however, the claim is illogical in a double sense. First, there can be no "science without presuppositions". Every scientist must accept certain truths dictated by sound reason, among others, the truth of his own existence and of a world outside of himself; next, that he can recognize the external world through the senses, that a reasoning power is given to him for understanding the impressions received, and a will power free from physical constraint. As a philosopher, he reflects upon these truths and explains them on scientific methods, but will never prove all of them without involving himself in vicious circles. Whatever science he chooses he has to build it upon the natural or philosophical presuppositions on which his life as man rests. The fact is that every positive science borrows from philosophy a number of established principles.

So much for the general premises. They alone would show how illogical is the claim for "science without presuppositions". But this is not all. Each science has its own particular presuppositions or axioms, distinct from its own conclusions, just as every building has its foundation, distinct from its walls and roof. Nay, the various branches of any special science have all their own proper presuppositions. Euclid's geometry is built upon three kinds of presuppositions. He calls them definitions, postulates, and common notions. The latter were called axioms by Proclus. To show the difference between hypothesis and result no better example could be chosen than Euclid's fifth postulate of the first book. The postulate says: "When two straight lines are intersected by a third so as to make the inner adjacent angles on one side less than two right angles, the two lines, indefinitely prolonged, will intersect on the side of those lesser angles." By a mistake of Proclus (fifth century) the postulate was changed into a proposition. Innumerable attempts at proving the supposed proposition were made, until the error was recognized, only a century ago. The fifth postulate, or axiom of parallels as it is often called, proved to be a real hypothesis, distinct from all the other presuppositions. Non-euclidian geometries have been constructed by a simple change of the fifth postulate. All this shows that there is no geometry without presuppositions. And similarly, there is no algebra without presuppositions. Law starts from the existence of families and from their natural tendency towards association for common welfare. Medicine takes the human body as a living organism, subject to derangement, and the existence of remedies, before it constructs its science. History supposes human testimony to be, under certain conditions, a reliable source of knowledge, before it begins its researches. Linguistic sciences, likewise, take it or granted that human languages are not constructed arbitrarily but evolved logically from a variety of circumstances. Theology takes from philosophy a number of truths, such as the existence of God, the possibility of miracles, and others. In fact, one science borrows its presuppositions from the results of other sciences, a division of labour which is necessitated by the limitations of everything human. Hence, the cry for "science without presuppositions" is doubly illogical, unless by presupposition is meant an hypothesis that can be proved to be false or foreign to the particular science in question. The freedom of science therefore has its limitations from the point of view of logic.

Physical

From the physical point of view science requires material means. Buildings, endowments, and libraries are necessary to all branches of science, in research as well as in teaching. Medical and natural sciences require extraordinary means, such as laboratories, museums, and instruments. Material requirements have always imposed limitations upon scientific research and teaching. On the other hand, the appeals of science for freedom from the burden have been generously answered. Between the twelfth and the fourteenth centuries about forty universities were founded in Europe, partly by private initiative, partly by princes or popes, in most cases by the combined efforts of both together with the members of the university. Among the self-originating universities may be mentioned Bologna, Paris, Oxford, and Cambridge. With the help of princes, universities were erected at Palencia, Naples, Salamanca, Seville, and Siena. Of the universities founded by popes we mention only Rome, Pisa, Ferrara, Toulouse, Valladolid, Heidelberg, Cologne, and Erfurt. Most of the old universities, like Coimbra, Florence, Prague, Vienna, Cracow, Alcalá, Upsala, Louvain, Leipzig, Rostock, Tübingen, and many others, owe their origin to the combined efforts of princes and popes. The foundations consisted mainly of charters giving civil rights and authorizing scientific degrees, in most cases also of material contributions and endowments. To many of the professors' chairs, ecclesiastical benefices were applied by the popes without other obligation than that of teaching science. Naturally the founders retained a certain authority and influence over the schools. On the whole, the old universities enjoyed everywhere the same freedom which they have in England up to this day. After the Reformation the governments of continental Europe made the universities of their own territories State institutions, paying the professors as Government employees, sometimes prescribing textbooks, methods of teaching, and even doctrines. Although in the nineteenth century, governments were obliged to relax their supervision, they still keep the monopoly of establishing universities and of appointing the professors. Their influence on the progress of science is unmistakable; how far this may benefit science, need not be decided in this place. With the growing influence of the State that of the Church has been diminished, in most universities to total extinction. In the few European universities in which the faculty of Catholic theology is still allowed to exist, the supervision of the Church over her own science is almost reduced to a mere veto. The necessity of exempting the professors from the oath against the Modernistic heresy is an illustration of the case. Owing to the freedom of teaching in the United States of America there are, besides the public universities of the different states, a number of institutions founded by private endowment. In the face of the strong aid which anti-Christian and atheistic tendencies receive through the influence of universities, private endowments of schools that maintain the truth of Revelation cannot be too much recommended.

Ethical

The limitations of science from the ethical point of view are twofold. The direct action of science on ethics is readily understood; the reaction of ethics upon science is just as certain. And both action and reaction create limitations for science. The activity of man is guided by two spiritual faculties, understanding and will. From the understanding it derives light, from the will firmness. Naturally the understanding precedes the will and hence the influence of science upon ethics. This influence becomes an important factor in the welfare of the human race for the reason that it is not confined to the scientist in his own researches, but reaches the masses through the various forms of teaching by word and writing. If one is to judge aright in this matter, two general principles must be kept in view. First, ethics is more important for mankind than science. Those who believe in revelation, know that the Commandments are the criteria by which men will be judged (Matthew 25:35-46); and those who see only as far as the light of natural reason enables them to see, know from history that the happiness of peoples and nations consists rather in moral rectitude than in scientific progress. The conclusion is that if there should ever be a conflict between science and ethics, ethics should prevail. Now, there can be no such conflict except in two cases: when scientific research leads into error, and when the teaching of science, even if true, is applied against sound educational maxims. To see that these exceptions are not imaginary, one need only glance at the points of contact between science and faith, under A. All of them indicate actual conflicts. Unpedagogical teaching is sadly illustrated by the recent movement in Germany towards premature and even public instruction on sexual relations, which provoked a reaction on the part of the civil authorities.

So much about the direct action of science on ethics. The case ought not to be reversible, in other words, ethics should not influence science, except in the way of stimulating research and teaching. However, not only individuals but whole schools of scientists have been subject to that human frailty expressed in the adage: Stat pro rations voluntas. As Cicero expresses it: "Man judges much more frequently influenced by hatred or love or cupidity . . or some mental agitation, than by the truth, or a command, or the law" (De oratore, II, xlii). If Cicero is correct, then the freedom of knowledge, so highly praised and so loudly demanded, is perverted by men in a double sense. First, they carry the freedom of the will into the judgment. Love, hatred, desires, are passions or acts of the will, while judgments are formed by the understanding, a faculty entirely devoid of free choice. Secondly, they deprive the understanding of the necessary indifference and equilibrium, and force it to one side, whether the side of truth or that of falsehood. If the men of science, who clamour for freedom, belong to the class described by Cicero, then their idea of freedom is entirely confused and perverted. It may be answered that Cicero's statement applied to daily affairs rather than to the pursuits of science. This is perfectly true as far as exact sciences are concerned, and it is probably true also in regard to the formal object of every science. Yet when we consider the very first postulates that the sciences take from philosophy, we come very near to daily life. Men of science hear of Christ and know of the magna carta of His kingdom, proclaimed on the mountain (Luke 6). It cuts very sharply into daily life. It could be discarded, if that same Christ had not claimed all power in heaven and on earth, and if He had not prophesied His second coming, to judge the living and the dead.

Here it is that Cicero's love and hatred come in. It is quite safe to say: there is no place in the civilized world where Christ is not loved and hated. Those who are willing to take the steep and narrow path towards His kingdom accept the testimonies to His Divine mission with impartiality; others who prefer an easier and broader way of life try to persuade themselves that the claims of Christ are unfounded. For, besides those who either reject His claims through inherited or acquired prejudices, or treat them with indifference, a large number of men try to strengthen their anti-Christian position by scientific forms. Knowing that Christ's Divinity can be proved from the miracles to which He appealed as testimonies of His Father, they formulate the axiom: "Miracles are impossible". Seeing, however, the inconsistency of the formula as long as there is a Maker of the world, they are driven to the next postulate: "There is no Creator". Seeing again, that the existence of the Creator can be proved from the existence of the world, and convincingly so by a number of arguments, they require new axioms. First they treat the origin of matter as too remote for its cause to be ascertained, and plead that: "Matter is eternal". For a similar reason the origin of life is explained by the arbitrary postulate of "spontaneous generation" . Then the wisdom and order displayed in the starry heavens and in the flora and fauna of the earth must be disposed of. To say in plain words "All order in the world is causal" would be offensive to common sense. The axiom is then vested in more scientific language, thus: "From eternity the world has passed through an infinite number of forms, and only the fittest was able to survive".

The substructure of anti-Christian science has still one weak point: the human soul is not from eternity and its spiritual faculties point to a spiritual maker. The fabrication of axioms, once begun, has to be concluded: "The human soul is not essentially different from the vital principle of the animal". This conclusion recommends itself as especially strong against what the will dreads: the animal is not immortal, and hence neither is the human soul; consequently whatever judgment may follow, it will have no effect. The end of the fabrication is bitter. Man is a highly developed orang-outang. There is still one stumbling-block in the Sacred Scriptures, old and new. The Old Testament narrates the creation of man, his fall, the promise of a Redeemer; it contains prophecies of a Messias which seem to be fulfilled in Christ and His Church. The New Testament proves the fulfilment of the promises, and presents a superhuman Being, who offered His life for the expiation of sin and attested His Divinity by His own

Resurrection; it gives the constitution and early history of His Church, and promises her existence to the consummation of the world. This could not be allowed to stand in the face of anti-Christian science. A few postulates more or less will do no harm to science as it stands. The Hebrew literature is put on a par with that of Persia or China, the history of Paradise is relegated to the realm of legends, the authenticity of the books is denied, contradictions in the contents are pointed out, and the obvious sense is distorted. The axioms used for the annihilation of the Sacred Scriptures have the advantage of plausibility over those used against the Creator. They are draped in a mass of erudition taken from the linguistic and the historical sciences.

But we have not seen all of them yet. The greatest obstacle to anti-Christian science is the Church, which claims Divine origin, authority to teach infallible truth, maintains the inspiration of Scripture, and is confident of her own existence to the end of the world. With her, science cannot play as With philosophy or literature. She is a living institution wielding her sceptre over all the peoples of the world. She has all the weapons of science at her disposal, and members devoted to her, heart and soul. To grant to her equal rights on scientific grounds would be disastrous to the "science without presuppositions". The mere creating of new axioms would not seem to be efficient against a living organization. The axioms have to be proclaimed loudly, and kept alive, and finally enforced by organized opposition, even in some cases by government power. Books and journals and lecture halls announce the one text, sung in every key, the great axiom: that the Church is essentially unscientific as resting on unwarranted presuppositions, and that her scientists can never be true men of science. Mommsen's cry of degradation on the appointment of a Catholic historian in Strasburg (1901) re-echoed loudly from most German universities. And yet, there was question of only a fifth Catholic among seventy-two professors; and this at a university in Alsace-Lorraine, a territory almost entirely Catholic. Similar proportions prevail in most universities. All the axioms of anti-Christian science mentioned above are entirely arbitrary and false. Not one of them can be supported by solid reasons; on the contrary, every one of them has been proved to be false. Thus anti-Christian science has surrounded itself by a number of boundary stakes driven into scientific ground, and has thus limited its own freedom of progress; the "science without presuppositions" is entangled in its own axioms, for no other reason than its aversion to Christ. On the other hand, the scientist who accepts the teaching of Christ need not fall back on a single arbitrary postulate. If he is a philosopher, he starts from the premises dictated by reason. In the world around him he recognizes the natural revelation of a Creator, and by logical deductions concludes from the contingency of things created to the Being Un-created. The same reasoning makes him understand the spirituality and immortality of the soul. From both results combined he concludes further to moral obligations and the existence of a natural law. Thus prepared he can start into any scientific research without the necessity of erecting boundary stakes for the purpose of justifying his prejudices. If he wants to go further and put his faith upon a scientific basis, he may take the books, called the Sacred Scriptures, as a starting-point, apply methodical criticism to their authenticity, and find them just as reliable as any other historical record. Their contents, prophecies, and miracles convince him of the Divinity of Christ, and from the testimony of Christ he accepts the entire supernatural Revelation. He has constructed the science of his faith without any other than scientific premises. Thus the science of the Christian is the only one that gives freedom of research and progress; its boundaries are none but the pale of truth. Anti-Christian science, on the contrary, is the slave of its own preconceived ethics.

Unlimited Freedom

The demand for unlimited freedom in science is unreasonable and unjust, because it leads to licence and rebellion.

Does Not Exist

There is no unlimited freedom in the world, and liberty over-stepping its boundaries always leads to evil. Man himself is neither absolutely free, nor would he desire unbounded freedom. Freedom is not the greatest boon nor the final end of man; it is given to him as a means to reach his end. Within his own mind, man feels bound to truth. Around himself, he sees all nature bound to laws and even dreads disturbances in their regular course. In all his activity he gets along best by remaining within the laws set for him. Those judgments are the best which are formed in accordance with the rules of logic. Those machines and instruments are the finest which are allowed the smallest amount of freedom. Social intercourse is easiest within the rules of propriety. Widening these boundaries does not lead to higher perfection. Opinions are free only where certainty cannot be reached; scientific theories are free as long as they rest on probabilities. The freest of all in their thinking are the ignorant. In short, the more freedom of opinion, the less science. Similarly, a railway train with freedom in more than one line is disastrous, a ship not under the control of the helm is doomed. A nation that depreciates its code of law, that relaxes the administration of justice, that sets aside the strict rules of propriety, that does not protect its own industry, that gives no guarantee for personal and public property and safety is on the decline. Unlimited freedom leads to barbarism, and its nearest approach is found in the wilds of Australia.

Licence

   The cry of anti-Christian science is for license. The boundaries enumerated in the preceding paragraph circumscribe the logical, the physical, and the ethical realm of man. Whenever he steps outside, he falls into error, into misfortune, into licence. Now, to which realm does science belong? Aristotle's definition fixes it in the logical realm. And what becomes of the freedom of science? Within man, the logical realm is the intellectual faculty, and without, it is the realm of truth. Yet neither is free. Man's freedom is in the will not in the understanding. Truth is eternal and absolute. It follows that the cry for unbounded freedom of science has no place in the logical realm; evidently, it is not meant for the physical; so it must belong to the ethical realm; it is not a cry for truth, it is a cry with a purpose. What the purpose is can be inferred from what has been said under II. It may be summed up in the statement that it is rebellion against both supernatural and natural revelation. The former position is the primary but could not consistently be held without the latter. Rebellion is not too strong a word. If God pleases to reveal Himself in any way whatever, man is obliged to accept the revelation, and no arbitrary axiom will dispense him from the duty. Against natural revelation Paulsen and Wundt appeal to the postulate of "closed natural causality", meaning by "closed" the exclusion of the Creator. Supernatural revelation was styled by Kant "a dogmatic constraint", which, he says, may have an educational value for minors by filling them with pious fears. Wundt follows him by calling Catholicism the religion of constraint, and Paulsen praises Kant as "the redeemer from unbearable stress". All these expressions rest on the supposition that in science there is no place for a Creator, no place for a Redeemer. Many attempts have been made to put the axiom on a scientific basis; but it remains an assumed premise, an "unwavering conviction", as Harnack calls it.

Consequences

That the expressions "license" and "rebellion" are just is clear from the consequences of anti-Christian science.

Atheism

Anti-Christian science leads to Atheism. When science repudiates the claim of Christ as Son of God, it necessarily repudiates the Father who sent Him, and the Holy Ghost who proceeds from both. The logical inference does not find favour with the partisans of that science. When in 1892 the school laws were being discussed in the German Reichstag, Chancellor Caprivi had the courage to say: "The point in question is Christianity or Atheism . . . the essential in man is his relation to God." The outcry on the "liberal" side of the House showed that the chancellor had touched a sore point. Since the repudiation of the Creator is clearly an abuse of freedom and an infringement of the natural law, science has, by all means, to save appearances by scientifically sounding words. First it calls the two great divisions of spirits Monism and Dualism. German scientists have even formed the "Monists' Union" claiming that there is no real distinction between the world and God. When their system emphasizes the world it is Materialism; when it accentuates the Divinity it is Pantheism. Monism is only a gentler name for both. The plain word "atheism" seems to be too offensive. English Naturalists replaced it long ago by better-sounding words, like Deism and Agnosticism. Toland, Tindal, Bolingbroke, Shaftesbury, of the eighteenth century, took satisfaction in removing the Deity so far away from the world that he could have no influence on it. Yet "Deity" still had too religious an odour and implied a gross inconsistency. To Huxley and other scientists of the nineteenth century the well-sounding name "agnosticism" appeared more dignified. In the face of natural law, however, which binds man to know and to serve his Creator, pleading ignorance of God is as much a rebellion against Him as shutting Him out of the world.

All these and other tactful terms and phases cover the same crude Atheism and stand, without exception, confessedly; on a collection of arbitrary postulates. Dualism, on the contrary, has no need of postulates, except those dictated by common sense. Sound reason beholds in creation, as in a mirror, its Maker, and is thus able to refer natural phenomena to their ultimate cause. While science requires the knowledge of intermediate causes only, the knowledge of things by their ultimate cause raises science to its highest degree, or wisdom, as St. Thomas Aquinas calls it. This is why logical coherence and consistency are always and exclusively found in the dualistic doctrine. It is vain to hope that the abyss between the logical philosophy of Dualists and the "unwavering convictions" of Monists may be bridged over by discussions. This was well illustrated when Father Wasmann lectured in Berlin (1907) on the theory of Evolution and was opposed by Plate and ten other speakers. The result of the discussion was that each, Plate and Wasmann, put his respective views in print, the one his axioms and the other his philosophy, and that, moreover, Plate denied that Wasmann was entitled to be considered a scientist on account of what he called Wasmann's Christian presuppositions.

Subjectivism

After the exclusion of God, there is need of an idol; the necessity lies in human nature. All the nations of old had their idols, even the Israelites, when at times they rebelled against the Prophets. The shape of the idols varies with progress. The savages made them of wood, the civilized pagans of silver and gold, and our own reading age makes them of philosophical systems. Kant did not draw the last consequences from his "autonomy of reason"; it was done by Fichte, Schelling, and Hegel. This Idealism developed into Subjectivism in the widest sense of the word, viz., into the complete emancipation of the human mind and will from God. The idol is the human Ego. The consequences are that truth and justice lose their eternal character and become relative concepts; man changes with the ages, and with him his own creations; what he calls true and right in one century, may become false and wrong in another. In regard to truth we have the explicit statement of Paulsen, that "there is no philosophy eternally valid". Relative to justice, Hartmann defines Kant's autonomy in the following words: "It means neither more nor less than this, that in moral matters I am the highest tribunal without appeal." Religion, which forms the principal part of justice, becomes likewise a matter of subjective inclination. Harnack calls submission to the doctrine of others treason against personal religion; and Nietzsche defends his idol by calling Christianity the immortal shame of mankind. The axiom is pronounced in more dignified form by Pfleiderer (1907). "In the science of history", he says, "the appearance on earth of a superhuman being cannot be considered". Perhaps in the most general way it is formulated by Paulsen (1908): "Switching off the supernatural from the natural and historical world". Yet, all these subjective axioms are only more or less scientific forms of the plain Straussian postulate (1835): "We are no longer Christians".

Anarchism

Here we are confronted by two facts that need earnest consideration. On the one hand, the Government universities of nearly all countries in Europe and many American universities exclude all relation to God and practically favour the atheistic postulate just mentioned; and on the other hand, these are the very postulates summed up by Pius X under the name of "modernism". Hence the general outcry of the State universities against the Encyclical "Pascendi" of 1907. To begin with the first, the licence of subjective truth is the very hotbed of anarchistic theories and the rebellion against the teaching of Christ will end with the moral conditions of Greek and Roman paganism. As we are not concerned here with the relation between science and the State, it must suffice to show how the alarm is beginning to sound. It seems to be a matter of course, and yet it sounds unusual, when Count Apponyi as minister of education and worship in Hungary, on the occasion of an academic promotion, recommends to teachers of science a moral and earnest conscientiousness. More remarkable is the warning of Virchow at the meeting of scientists at Munich (1877) against teaching personal views and speculations as established truths, and in particular, against replacing the dogmas of the Church by a religion of evolution.

The moral state of a youth growing up under such teaching could be anticipated in general from the history of paganism. It was reserved to our anti-Christian age, however, to justify immorality with an appearance of science. The assertion has been made and circulated in journals and meetings, that a pure and moral life is detrimental from the point of view of medicine. The medical faculty of the University of Christiania found it necessary to declare the assertion entirely false, and to state positively that "we know of no harm or weakness owing to chastity". The same protest was expressed by Dr. Raoult in the words: "There is no such thing as pathology of continency"; and by Dr. Vidal (see below) in the statement, that the commandments of God are legitimate from the standpoint of medicine, and that their observance is not only possible but advantageous. Warnings like these may be called forth by anticipated effects; but we hear others that prove the effects already existing. Such was the unanimous vote of the International Conference for the protection of Health and Morals held at Brussels (September, 1902): "Young men have to be taught that the virtues of chastity and continency are not only not hurtful but most commendable from a purely medical and hygienic point of view". The effects in educational institutions must have been appalling before scientific authorities dared to lift the veil by public warnings. They were given by Dr. Fleury (1899) in regard to French colleges, and were repeated by Dr. Fournier (1905) and Dr. Francotte (1907). Even louder are the warnings of Paulsen, Förster, and especially Obermedicinalrat Dr. Gruber regarding the German gymnasia and universities. Dr. Desplats (see bibliography) insists that in order to stay the current which is carrying the French along towards irremediable decadence, it is necessary to react against the doctrinal and practical neo-paganism. No wonder that the licentious doctrines have found their way from books into journals and passed from the educated to the illiterate. Sosnosky, a literary authority, compares the present moral epidemic to that of pagan Rome and of the French Revolution, and protests, from a merely natural point of view, against the hypocrisy of covering crude animalism with the cloak of art and science (see Allgemeine Zeitung, No. 3, 21 January, 1911).

What the State either will not or dare not do, the Church does always, by keeping men mindful of the object or end of their existence and this last end is not science. The catechism points it out under three heads: the knowledge of God; the observance of His commandments; and the use of His grace. Knowledge of nature is intended by God as a subordinate means to this end. And for that very reason there can never be a conflict between science and our final destiny. The Church does not teach natural sciences, but she helps to make their principles tributary to wisdom, first by warning against error and then by pointing to the ultimate cause of all things. When science raises the cry against the guiding office of the Church, it is comparable to a system of navigation without any directions outside the ship itself and the surrounding waves. The formal object of each particular science is certainly different from faith just as the steering of a vessel is different from the knowledge of the stars; but the exclusion of all guiding lights beyond the billows of scientific opinions and hypotheses is entirely arbitrary, unwise, and disastrous.

The Church

The Church in her relation to science may be better understood by a division of the subject into the following parts: Opposite views; distinction between the teaching body and the ecclesia discens; the holders of the teaching office; science of faith; pretended conflicts.

Opposite Views

Leo XIII

On the relation of the Church to science there are two irreconcilable views:

Leo XIII in his Apostolic Letter of 22 January, 1899, calls attention to the dangers imminent at the present time to the minds of Catholics, and specifies them as a confusion between licence and freedom, as a passion for saying and reviling whatever one pleases, as a habit of thinking or printing without restraint. The shadows cast by these dangers on men's minds, he says, are so deep as to make the exercise of the teaching office of the Apostolic See more necessary now than ever. The pope strengthens his words by the authority of the Vatican Council, which claims Divine faith for all things proposed by the Church, whether in solemn decision or by the ordinary universal magisterium.

Virchow

Not so those outside the Church. To them spiritual restriction of thinking, speaking, writing is a remnant of the times when science was in fetters, a relic of the Dark Ages. Virchow, in discussing the appointment of professors of Protestant theology at Bonn and Marburg by the Prussian Government, made the following declaration in the Chamber (6 March, 1896): "If it is considered incumbent upon the theological faculties to preserve and to interpret a certain deposit of so-called Divine and revealed truths, then they do not fit into the framework of universities, they are in opposition to the scientific machinery prevailing there. The Reformers of the sixteenth century", he continued," are today replaced by free scientific criticism; consistently, instead of halting before the theological faculties, they should have abolished them, and the troubles ever arising from a certain class of men who claim to be holders of Divine truth, would have vanished" (reported by Hertling, see below, p. 49 sqq.). Such is the general voice of those who stand outside of any creed. There are others who wish to adhere to certain articles of faith established either by a congress of Reformers, or by a sovereign, or by Parliament. Although widely differing among themselves as to the inspired Books, the Divinity of Christ, and even the existence of Revelation, they all agree in considering the papacy a usurpation, and Catholic obedience in matters of faith and morals spiritual darkness and slavery.

History

      These conflicting views have existed from the very cradle of Christianity, and will last to the end of the world.

St. Ambrose (397) speaking of the wise of the world (sapientes mundi) says: "Deviating from faith, they are implicated in the darkness of perpetual blindness, although they have the day of Christ and the light of the Church before them; while seeing nothing, they open their mouth as if they knew everything, keen for vain things and dull for things eternal (Hexaemeron, V, xxiv, 86, in P.L., XIV, 240). Those who accept the teaching of Christ have always formed the smaller portion of mankind, and the mass of the small flock is not composed of the rich or the mighty or the wise of the world. They maintain that the Church is a Divine institution, endowed with the triple power of priesthood, teaching, and government; hence their submission, firmness, and union in matters of faith all over the world. Those who stand aloof and see in the Church nothing but a human institution, like the old Roman Empire for instance, may be consistent in condemning the Catholic position; at the same time they cannot help seeing even greater consistency in the Catholic point of view. To submit one's understanding to a doctrine supposed to be Divine and guaranteed to be infallible is undoubtedly more consistent than to accept prevailing postulates of science, or national doctrines, or a passing public opinion. Catholics must be permitted to interpret in their own favour what the Scripture says about the light of faith, the darkness of error, and the liberty of truth.

The Teaching Body and the Ecclesia Discens

The teaching and hearing bodies of Christ's Church are technically called "ecclesia docens" and "ecclesia discens".

Distinction

The distinction between the teaching body of the Church and the body of hearers was made by its Founder in the command: "Going therefore, teach ye all nations" (Matthew 28:19); "he that heareth you, heareth me" (Luke 10:16). The same division is illustrated by St. Paul in the comparison between the human body and the mystical body of Christ: "If the whole body were the eye, where would be the hearing?" (1 Corinthians 12:17). The office of teaching was communicated to the Church together with the dignity of priesthood and the authority of government. The triple power rests in St. Peter and the Apostles and their legal successors. The Divine office of teaching is not to impart scientific conviction, it is to give authoritative declaration, and the response to it, on the part of the hearers, is not science but faith. The Church may even use her ruling power to support her teaching. All this is exemplified in the early Christian centuries. The Twelve Apostles were not conversant with the schools of Athens, of Alexandria, or of Rome. St. Paul, who was called later, was probably the only scholar among them; and even he professes that his preaching was not in the persuasive words of human wisdom (1 Corinthians 2:4). He used his power against Hymeneus and Alexander, who had made shipwreck concerning the faith (1 Timothy 1:20), and exhorted Timothy to use the same authority against those who would not endure sound doctrine (2 Timothy 4:3). The Apostle St. John blamed several bishops of Minor Asia for not removing false teachers (Revelation 2:14-20).

Premises of Faith

The partition of the Church in two bodies, one teaching and one hearing, does not exclude science from the latter, any more than it necessarily includes it in the former. The assent of faith is a rational act; before it can be made, it must be known for certain that there is a God, that God has spoken, and what He has spoken. The Apostles, the early Fathers, councils, and popes bear witness to it (Pesch, see below, pp. 18-22). St. Peter wants the faithful to be ready always to satisfy every one that asketh a reason of that hope which is in them (1 Peter 3:15). St. Augustine asks: "Who does not see that knowledge precedes faith? Nobody believes unless he knows what to believe". The following is the declaration of the Vatican Council (Sess. III, de fide, cap. 3): "To render the service of our faith reasonable, God has joined to the interior actions of the Holy Ghost exterior proofs of His revelation: Divine facts, miracles especially and prophecies, which are speaking witnesses of His infinite power and wisdom, unfailing testimonies of Divine revelation and adapted to the understanding of every one". Innocent XI explicitly condemned the opinion that mere probability in the knowledge of revelation is sufficient for the supernatural assent of faith. Pius IX demands that human reason should inquire conscientiously into the facts of Divine revelation, to make sure that God has spoken, in order to render Him, according to the Apostle, a reasonable service.

In the knowledge of the premises of faith, man has to progress with age and education. The child cannot give supernatural assent of faith to what parents or teachers say, until its mind is sufficiently developed to be sure of the existence and contents of Divine revelation. Again, the knowledge that may suffice for a child will not do for a man. He must apply his mental faculties and interest himself in the foundations of his faith. The prudence of his mind should equal the simplicity of his will. Prof. Heis used to have the catechism on his desk beside the scientific books. Progress of knowledge is especially commendable in parents, teachers, students, above all in professors of theological science and in ecclesiastical dignitaries. Under their scientific methods the premises of faith have become a special branch of theology, called apologetics.

Contents of Faith

The contents of faith should be penetrated as far as mental faculties and Divine grace allow. Revelation points out the eternal destiny, shows the way, and gives the means; it warns against eternal loss, helps in temptation, and shields from evil. Without knowledge there is no interest, and the consequence is forgetfulness of the main purpose of life. Hence the duty of all men to listen to God, to meditate on His words, and to understand them in a way. The highest acts of mercy and charity are teaching the ignorant and correcting the erring. The study of revealed truth and the propagation by word and writing of the knowledge thus acquired was practised in the Church at all times and by all classes. Owing to this study the Divine deposit of faith has grown into a scientific system which, in clearness and firmness of structure, is not equalled by other branches of knowledge. From the frame of that system stand out in bold relief the deep mysteries, beyond human comprehension, indeed, but well defined in meaning and safe against objections. It must be remembered. though, that divines and doctors, as such, do not constitute the teaching body of the Church; they all belong to the "Ecclesia discens". Theology as a scientific system, with propositions, arguments, and objections, is not the direct object of the "Ecclesia docens". She leaves it to specialists, with all manner of encouragement and direction.

Dangers Against Faith

The dangers against faith. — Since faith, as the foundation of eternal life, is a supernatural virtue, it is exposed to temptation like all other virtues. Some difficulties are inherent in the deposit of faith, others arise from outside. A revealed truth may appear contrary to the mind as unintelligible, like the mysteries, or repugnant to the will as entailing unwelcome precepts. Temptations from outside may be the constant hostility of the world towards the Church, discrimination against Catholics, falsification of history, anti-Christian and infidel literature, scandals within, and defections from, the Church.

From her positive and exclusive right to teach all nations whatsoever Christ has commanded the Apostles (Matthew 28:19-20), the Church necessarily derives also the right of defence. To protect her flock against dangers of faith she calls in the full authority of her ruling power with its subdivisions of legislation, judiciary, and administration. By this power she regulates the appointment and removal of religious teachers, the admission or prohibition of religious doctrines, and even methods of teaching, in word or writing.

The Holders of the Teaching Office
Infallible Magisterium

These are the pope and the bishops, as successors to St. Peter and the Apostles. The promise of Divine assistance was given together with the command of teaching; it rests, therefore, in the same subjects, but is restricted to official, to the exclusion of private, acts regarding the deposit of faith.

The official activity of teaching may be exercised either in the ordinary, or daily, magisterium, or by occasional solemn decisions. The former goes on uninterruptedly; the latter are called forth in times of great danger, especially of growing heresies. The promise of

Divine assistance provides for the integrity of doctrine "all days, even to the consummation of the world" (Matthew 28:20). From the nature of the case it follows that individual bishops may fall into error, because ample provision is made when the entire teaching body of the Church and the supreme pastor in particular are protected by Providence. The "Ecclesia docens", as a whole, can never fall into error in matters of faith or morals, whether her teaching be the ordinary or the solemn; nor can the pope proclaim false doctrines in his capacity of supreme pastor of the universal Church. Without this prerogative, which is known by the name of Infallibility, the Divine promise of assistance would be a fallacy. To the right of teaching on the part of the "Ecclesia docens" naturally corresponds the obligation of hearing on the part of the "Ecclesia discens". Hearing is meant in the sense of submitting the understanding, and it is of a double nature, according as the teaching is, or is not, done under the guarantee of infallibility. The former submission is called assent of faith, the latter assent of religious obedience.

Other Tribunals

Submission of the understanding to other than Divine authority may appear objectionable, but is practised, in science as well as in daily life, in hundreds of ways. With regard to the Church submission of the understanding is especially appropriate, no matter whether she speaks with infallible or with administrative authority, in other words whether the submission is one of faith or one of obedience. Even from a human point of view her authority is exceptionally high and impartial. To the teaching that rests directly on the ruling authority only, without the prerogative of infallibility, belong the pastoral letters of bishops, particular diocesan catechisms, decrees of provincial synods, the decisions of Roman Congregations, and many official acts of the pope, even such as are obligatory on the universal Church. In each diocese the official authority in matters of faith and morals is the bishop. Without his (or higher) consent no professor of theology, no catechist, no preacher can exercise his official function, and no publication that touches upon matters of faith and morals is permitted within the diocese. The approbation of teachers is known as canonical mission, while the approval or refusal of books is called censorship. Above the diocesan tribunals stand the Roman Congregations to which certain matters are reserved and to which appeal can be made. Science, in particular, may come in contact with the Congregation of Rites, which examines miracles proposed in support of beatifications and canonizations. More frequently it is the Congregation of the Index, which officially examines and decides upon the danger, to faith and morals, of books (not persons) denounced or under suspicion, and the Holy Office of the Inquisition, which decides questions of orthodoxy, with the pope himself as prefect. All the ecclesiastical authorities, mentioned in this paragraph, participate, either officially or by delegation, in the legislative, judicial, and executive powers of the Church, in support of their functions. It goes without saying that their decisions become endowed with the prerogative of infallibility, when the pope approves them, not in an ordinary manner as, for instance, when he acts as prefect of a Congregation, but solemnly, or ex cathedra, with the obligation of acceptance by the whole Church.

Galilei

To men of science the Roman tribunals of the Index and the Inquisition are best known in connexion with the name of Galilei. Here seems to be the place to speak about the attitude of non-Catholic scientists towards the case. It can be shown that it is not always in keeping with the principles of science, from a triple point of view.

(a) The error involved in the condemnation of Galilei is used as an argument against the right of the tribunals to exist. This is illogical and partial. The error was purely accidental, just as the miscarriages of justice in criminal courts is often the unfortunate result of similar accidental errors. If the argument does not hold in the latter case, it holds much less in the former. The error was a universal opinion tenaciously defended by the Reformers of the sixteenth century. Besides, it is about the only seriously erroneous decision of its kind among the hundreds that issued from the Roman tribunals in the course of centuries.

(b) What is objected to in the Galilei case is not so

much the historical fact of the blunder, as the permanent claim of the Church to be, by Divine right, the guardian of the Scripture; it is the principle by which she adheres to the literal sense of Holy Writ, as long as either the context or the nature of the case does not suggest a metaphorical interpretation. Granted that the evidences, which convinced Copernicus, Kepler, and Galilei, should also have convinced the theologians of the time, the latter committed a blunder. It cannot be this, however, that is continually held up against the Church. Official blunders of the highest tribunals are easily and constantly pardoned, when they are committed in the exercise of an acknowledged right. Nobody condemns the administration of justice when a disputed case, in its course of appeals, is reversed two or three times, although each reversal puts a juridical blunder on record. Hence, what is condemned in the case of Galilei, must be the right itself, viz., the claim and the principle before mentioned. Evidently, however, they are in no way peculiar to the case of Galilei; they are as old as the Church; they have been applied in our own days, e.g. in the Syllabus of Pius IX (1864), in the Vatican Council (1870) and recently in the Encyclical "Pascendi" of Pius X (1907); and they will be applied in all the future. To attack the claim of the Church as guardian of the Scripture, there is no apparent need for going back again and again to the old Galilei incident. Nor is the legal procedure against Galilei in any way peculiar to his case. The historian judges it by the established laws of the seventeenth century and finds it unusually mild. What is it then that prevents the Galilei controversy from resting? It is hard to see any other motive in the agitation but the reluctance to admit the Church's claim to be the interpreter of the Scriptures.

(c) The vast Galilei literature shows a remarkable difference in the opposite points of view. Among Catholics little importance is attached to the case, simply because Catholics knew before and after, that the Roman Congregations are liable to error, and only wonder that not more mistakes are recorded in history. Among the others the sympathy shown for Galilei is not easily intelligible from a scientific point of view. The whole process was an entirely internal affair of the Church: Galilei appeared before his own legal superiors; for a time he was disobedient, but in the end submitted to his condemnation. The character which he displayed in the affair does not seem to call for the admiration paid to him. What then makes outsiders so sympathetic towards Galilei, if not his disobedience to the command of 1616? It would seem so, judging from the praises given to his "immortal" dialogues.

The science of Faith

Although faith is not science, yet there is a science of faith. The knowledge acquired by faith, on the one hand, rests upon science, and on the other lends itself to scientific methods.

Parallel Case

Faith is in many ways a parallel case to history. Although historical knowledge is not directly scientific, yet there is a science of history. Scientific inquiries precede historical knowledge, and the results of historical research are treated on scientific methods. All we know from history we know upon the authority of testimony. It belongs to the science of history to search into the existence and trustworthiness of the sources and into the unfalsified transmission of their testimony to us. Nor is that all. The science of history will arrange the chain of discovered facts, not chronologically only, but with a view of causality. It will explain the why and the how in the rise and the downfall of men, of cities, of nations.

Theology

The science of faith is theology. — Human testimony is here replaced by Divine authority. The premises of faith have been elaborated into a scientific system called apologetics. The Divinely revealed truths have been studied on historical, philosophical, and linguistic lines; they have been analyzed, defined, and classified; theoretical consequences have been drawn and applications to church discipline made; boundary lines between faith and science have been drawn and points of contact established; methodical objections and solutions have been applied; and attacks from outside logically refuted. The results of all these studies are embodied in a number of scientific branches, like the Biblical sciences, with their subdivisions of historical criticism, theoretical hermeneutics, and practical exegesis; then dogmatic and moral theology, with their consequences in canon law and sub-branches of pastoral theology, homiletics, liturgies; again church history and its branches, — patrology, history of dogmas, archæology, art-history. The men who represent these sciences are the Greek and Latin Fathers and the Doctors of the Church, among them the founders of Scholastic theology, not to mention more recent celebrities among the regular and secular clergy. A vast literature may be found in Migne's edition of the Fathers and in Hurter's "Nomenclator". The widest field is here open for research eminently scientific. If science is knowledge of things from their causes, theology is the highest grade of science, since it traces its knowledge to the ultimate cause of all things. Science of this kind is what St. Thomas defines as wisdom.

Progress

Let it not be said that there is no progress in the science of faith. Dogmatic theology may appear as the most rigid of its branches, and even there we find, with time, deeper understanding, preciser definitions, stronger proofs, better classifications, profounder knowledge of dogmas in their mutual relation and history. Canon law has not only kept abreast with, but has gone ahead of, civil law, above all in its scientific foundations. Progress in the Biblical, historical, and pastoral disciplines is so apparent as to need only a passing mention. The answer to the question, whether there should be no progress of religion in the Church of Christ, goes as far back as the fifth century and was given by St. Vincent of Lérins in the following words: "Certainly let there be progress, and as much as may be . . . but so that it be really progress in the faith, not an alteration of it. "About alterations he gives the following explanation: "It is the peculiarity of progress for a thing to be developed in itself; and the peculiarity of change, for a thing to be altered from what it was into something else" (Commonitorium, 1,23; see P.L., L). The same difference between evolution and change was established by the Vatican Council: "If any one shall say that it is possible that, with the progress of science, a sense may ever be given to the doctrines proposed by the Church, other than that which the Church has understood and understands, let him be anathema" (Sess. III, can. iv, de fide et ratione, 1, can. 3). Science that is changed is not developed but abandoned, and so it is with faith. True development is shown in the parable of the mustard seed which grows into a tree, without destroying the organic connexion between the root and the smallest branches.

Objections

The scientific character of theology has been called in question on the following grounds:

Mysteries

Mysteries are said to be foreign to human science,

for a double reason: they rest exclusively on Divine revelation, a source foreign to science; and then, they cannot be subjected to scientific methods. The objection has some appearance in its favour. Mysteries, properly so called, are truths which are essentially beyond the natural powers of any created intellect, and could never be known except by supernatural revelation. Yet the objection is only apparent. As far as the source of knowledge is concerned, science should be so eager for truth as to welcome it, no matter where it comes from. It should esteem the source of knowledge the higher the more certainty it gives. Science is bound to accept Divine Creation as its source; why should Divine Revelation be excluded from its domain? Natural sciences may confine themselves to the former, but the latter is in no way foreign to the historical and philosophical sciences, least of all to theology. The assertion that mysteries are beyond scientifico research is too general. First, their existence can be proved scientifically; secondly, they can be analysed and compared with other scientific concepts; finally, they yield scientific consequences not otherwise accessible. If the objection had any real force, it would apply similarly to mysteries improperly so called, i.e., to natural truths that we shall never know in this life. Every science is full of them, and they are the very reason why the most learned scientists consider themselves the most ignorant. The sources of their knowledge seem to be closed forever, and scientific methods fail to open them. If this be an objection to the scientific character of a branch, then let history, law, medicine, physics, and chemistry be cancelled from the list of sciences.

Methodical Doubt

Scientific research is said to be impossible, when a proposition cannot be called in question, being bound up by the consensus of the Fathers and Doctors and the vigilant authority of the Church. A simple distinction between interior and methodical doubt will remove the difficulty. Methodical doubt is so much applied in theology that it may be said to be essential to Scholastic methods. And it is quite sufficient for impartial research. This is proved to evidence by the notorious fact that all the scientific proofs we now have for the Copernican system, without exception, have been furnished by men who could never entertain any interior doubt of its truth. The Catholic divine sees in the traditional doctrine of the Church a guiding light that leads him with great security through the fundamental questions of his science, where human reason alone is apt to lose itself in a labyrinth of inventions, surmises, hypotheses. Other difficulties touching upon science in general are mentioned in the next section.

Conflicts

The conflicts between science and the Church are not real. They all rest on assertions like these: Faith is an obstacle to research; faith is contrary to the dignity of science; faith is discredited by history. Basing the answers on the principles explained above, we can dispel the phantoms in the following manner.

Faith No Obstacle

A believer, it is stated, can never be a scientist; his mind is bound by authority, and in case of a conflict he has to contradict science.

(a) The assertion is consistent on the supposition, that faith is a human invention. The believer, however, bases faith on Divine Revelation, and science on Creation. Both have their common source in God, the Eternal Truth. The principal points of contact between the two are enumerated above in section A (I), and only there can there be question of conflicts. It is shown in the same place (II) that every one of the pretended conflicts, without exception, rests on arbitrary axioms. As far as scientific facts are concerned, the believer rests assured that, so far, none of them has ever been in contradiction with an infallible definition. In case of an apparent difference between faith and science, he takes the following logical position: When a religious view is contradicted by a well-established scientific fact, then the sources of revelation have to be re-examined, and they will be found to leave the question open. When a clearly-defined dogma contradicts a scientific assertion, the latter has to be revised, and it will be found premature. When both contradicting assertions, the religious and the scientific, are nothing more than prevailing theories, research will be stimulated in both directions, until one of the theories appears unfounded. The conflict about the heliocentric system belonged, theoretically speaking, to the first case, and Darwinism, in its gross form, to the second; practically, however, disputed questions generally turn up in the third case, and so it was actually with the heliocentric system at the time of Copernicus, Kepler, and Galilei.

(b) It is true, the believer is less free in his knowledge than the unbeliever, but only because he knows more. The unbeliever has one source of knowledge, the believer has two. Instead of barring his mind against the supernatural stream of knowledge by arbitrary postulates, man ought to be grateful to his Creator for every bit of knowledge, and, panting for truth, drink from both streams that pour down from heaven. Hence it is, that a well-instructed Christian child knows more of the important truths than did Kant, Herbert Spencer, or Huxley. Believing scientists do not wish to be free-thinkers just as respectable people do not want to be vagabonds.

Dignity of Science

Blind acceptance of dogmas and submission to non-scientific authority is said to be contrary to the dignity of science; hence the conflict between the Church and science. The answer is as follows:

(a) The dignity of science consists in searching for and finding truth. What injures the dignity of science is error, sham theories, arbitrary postulates. None of these qualifications is found in faith. Infallible truth is guaranteed, and the assent is based on premises which are not blindly accepted but proved by reason, on the most scientific methods if desired. Unworthy of science are premises like the following: "Error can be removed only by science and scientific truth" (Lipps, 1908); or "The only authority is science" (Masaryk). Unworthy of science, again, is the inconsistency in not yielding to premises once reasonably established. No scientist hesitates to accept results furnished by branches other than his own or even from scientists within his own special line. Yet, many shrink from accepting faith, though the existence of revelation is as reasonably established as any historical fact.

(b) When it comes to authority outside of science, the believing scientist knows that the authority to which he gives the assent of faith is Divine. The motive of his faith is not the Church, it is God. In God he sees the highest logical truth (infinite Wisdom), the highest ontological truth (the infinite Being), the highest moral truth (infinite Veracity). Bowing to such authority, infinitely beyond human science, is so much in harmony with sound reason, that science ought to be the first to say: "Ecce ancilla Domini". The dignity of science is indeed overshadowed by the dignity of faith, yet by no means degraded.

(c) More difficulty is perhaps found in the assent of religious obedience than in the assent of faith. Here it is not an infallible authority which science is asked to respect, but one that may err, like any human tribunal, even the highest. The phrase "dignity of science" means practically the dignity of man in his qualification as a scientist. Now, we put before him an alternative: If he is a member of the Catholic Church, submission to lawful authority, which he knows is established by Christ, is not only not undignified but honourable to him in all cases, because he considers obedience a higher boon than science. His case is parallel to that of the law-abiding citizen in regard to the supreme court of justice. The citizen may appeal from lower tribunals to the highest, but should not revolt against the latter. If convinced that injustice has been done him, he will prefer the common good of peaceful order to private interests, and feel the more dignified for it as a citizen. But if the scientist stands outside the Catholic Church, he most probably feels quite unconcerned about her authority in regard to himself. He might then as well let the Church take care of her own internal affairs.

In general, all scientists may consider the remark made by the bishops of the Province of Westminster in their joint pastoral letter of 1901 (see below): "It has been a fashion to decry the Roman Congregations by persons who have little or no knowledge of their careful and elaborate methods, of their system of sifting and testing evidence, and of the pains taken by the Holy See to summon experts, even from distant parts of the Church, to take part in their proceedings". As regards the Congregation of the Index in particular, its purpose is to shield the community from intellectual and moral poison. The prohibition of erroneous and dangerous publications is imposed by natural law upon the authorities of the family, of civil and religious communities; and science ought to be the first in the rank of co-operators. Only then would its real dignity shine forth. The Catholic scientist sees furthermore a positive law in the exercise of this power, as derived from the Divine office of teaching all nations. And he sees this right made use of from the very beginning of the Church, although the Congregation of the Index was not founded until 1570, and the first Roman Index had appeared only in 1559. Before the art of printing was invented, it sufficed to burn a few manuscript copies to prevent the spreading of a doctrine. So it was done at Ephesus in the presence of St. Paul (Acts 19:19). It is known that the other Apostles, the Fathers of the Church, and the Council of Nice (325) exercised the same authority. The enumeration of the various censures, prohibitions, and indexes issued by cities, universities, bishops, provincial councils, and popes, through the Christian centuries, may be seen in Hilgers, "Der Index der Verbotenen Bücher" (Freiburg, 1904), 3-15.

    The necessity of restricting the licence of all manner of publications may be illustrated by the following facts. As regards heretical books one might suppose men like St. Francis of Sales and Balmes proof against all danger. Yet, the former thanked God for having preserved him from reading infidel books and from losing his faith. The latter confessed that he could not read a forbidden book without feeling the necessity of regaining the proper tune of mind by recurring to the Scripture, the "Imitation of Christ", and Louis of Granada. As to immoral productions of literature, the flood has now become so enormous and the criminal results are so alarming, that leagues for public morality are being formed, composed of men and women, comprising all the conservative elements and all religious denominations. Political and social dangers are not less to be feared than moral infection. For that reason there is hardly any country in the world where some censorship has not been exercised. The measures taken in England, in the Netherlands, Scandinavia, France, Switzerland, and Germany may be found in Hilgers, op. cit., 206-389. To say that all these measures of self-defence on the part of parents, of the State, and of the Church are against the dignity of science would be a very bold assertion.

Historical Testimony

Those who maintain that faith is discredited by history are the very ones that discredit history by falsifications. It must suffice in this place to allude to some principal points.

(a) If a believer cannot be a scientist, as is maintained, then all the great scientists must be unbelievers. In spite of its boldness the assertion is made, in order to save the appearance of consistency. The fact is, however, that up to the French Revolution, when Voltaire and Rousseau drew the last consequences from Atheism, the great scientists, almost to a man, speak with great reverence of God and of His wonderful Creation. Is it necessary to mention Copernicus, Kepler, Galilei, Tycho Brahe, Newton, Huyghens, Boyle, Haller, Mariotte, the Bernoullis, Euler, Linné, and many others? Since it is often the advocates of the glorious principles of 1789 that never tire of recounting the tragedy of Galilei, we beg to remind them of the great chemist Lavoisier, who died faithful to his Church under the guillotine, while the free-thinkers raised the cry: "Nous n'avous plus besoin de chimistes" [see "Etudes", cxxiii (Paris, 1910), 834 sqq.]. For the time after the French Revolution we find in Kneller's volume (see below) the names of a glorious array of believing scientists, taken only from the branch of natural sciences. According to Donat ("Die Freiheit der Wissenschaft", Innsbruck, 1910, p. 251) among the 8847 scientists enumerated in Poggendorff's "Biographisch-Literarisches Handwörterbuch" (Leipzig, 1863) there are no less than 862 Catholic clergymen, or nearly ten per cent of the number.

(b) The lack of true arguments for the theses "that faith is discredited by history" is supplied by falsification. Among the fables invented for the purpose may be mentioned the condemnation of the doctrine about the Antipodes. Its (probable) representative, Virgilius, was accused in Rome (747) but not condemned (Hefele, "Konziliengeschichte", III, 557). He became Bishop of Salzburg, and was afterwards canonized by Gregory IX. Another story is the alleged prohibition by Boniface VIII of the anatomy of the human body. Columbus is reported as excommunicated by the "Council" of Salamanca. The recent re-appearance of Halley's comet has revived the story of a papal Bull issued against the comet by Calixtus III (1456). The fable was started by Laplace, who invented the "conjuration", though he tried to tone for his untruthfulness by omitting the phrase in the fourth edition of his "Essai philosophique" (see LAPLACE). The atheist Arago changed the conjuration into excommunication. Vice-Admiral Smyth added the exorcism, Robert Grant the anathema, Flammarion the "maléfice", and finally John Draper the malediction. Here the vocabulary came to an end. Poetry, gross and fine, sarcasm, and even astronomical errors were resorted to, to illustrate the conflict between science and the Church. Babinet describes the Friar Minors, during the Battle of Belgrade, crucifix in hand, exorcising a comet which was not there; Halley's comet had disappeared more than a week before. Chambers (1861) honoured Callistus III with the title "the silly pope" for commemorating annually the victory of Belgrade. Daru lets the pope stand at the foot of the altar, with tears in his eyes and his forehead covered with ashes, and bids him look up and see how the comet continues its course unconcerned about conjurations. John Draper lets the pope scare the comet away by noisy bells after the fashion of savages. Dr. Dickson White composes a papal litany: "From the Turk and the comet, good Lord, deliver us", which was supplemented by another writer: "Lord save us from the Devil, the Turk and the Comet". In "Popular Astronomy"

(1908) the comet is left more than a week too long on the visible sky and in the "Rivista di Astronomia" (1909) even a full month too long; in "The Scientific American" (1909) it appears fully three years too soon. Such fictions and falsifications are needed to prove conflicts between Science and the Church (see quotations and rectifications in Stein, "Calixte III et la comète de Halley", Rome, 1909; BARTOLOMEO PLATINA).

(c) As a specimen of the anti-Catholic literature on this subject we may take the "History of the Conflicts between Religion and Science" of John W. Draper (see below), which deserves special mention, not for the difficulty it presents, but for its wide circulation in various languages. The author placed himself exclusively on philosophical and historical grounds. Neither of them formed the field of his special studies, and the many blunders in his work might be pardoned, if it were not for the boldness of style and the shallowness of its contents. As the book is on the Index, a short specimen may be welcome to those who are not allowed to read it. In connexion with the subject of the preceding paragraph, Draper writes: "When Halley's comet came in 1456, so tremendous was its apparition that it was necessary for the pope himself to interfere. He exorcised and expelled it from the skies. It shrank away into the abysses of space, terror-stricken by the maledictions of Callixtus III, and did not venture back for seventy-five years! . . . By order of the pope, all the church bells in Europe were rung to scare it away, the faithful were commanded to add each day another prayer; and as their prayers had often in so marked a manner been answered in eclipses and droughts and rains, so on this occasion it was declared that a victory over the comet had been vouchsafed to the Pope". Except the first half sentence, that the "comet came in 1456", all his statements, without exception, are historical falsifications. The scurrility of language, however, makes one think that the author did not expect to be taken seriously. The same manner of treatment is given to other historical points, like Giordano Bruno, de Dominis, the Library of Alexandria. How the Spanish Inquisition comes into the book is easily understood from its purpose; but how it comes under the title, "Conflicts between Religion and Science", remains a logical problem. The domination of the Church in the Middle Ages and its influence upon the progress of science is a subject that required a different mind from that of a chemist or physicist. It was taken up by one of the Bollandists, Ch. de Smedt, in answer to Draper. It was an easy but, at the same time, disgusting task for him to correct Draper in this, as in all other historical points (de Smedt, see below). Draper's philosophical reasonings on the scientific freedom of believing scientists, on the right of the Church in proclaiming dogmas and demanding assent, on the possibility of miracles, betray complete ignorance or confusion of the principles explained in the preceding paragraphs.

Vatican Council

A fitting conclusion to the chapter of "Conflicts between Science and the Church" may be found in the declaration of the Vatican Council (Sess. III, de fide, c. 4): "Faith and reason are of mutual help to each other: by reason, well applied, the foundations of faith are established, and, in the light of faith, the science of Divinity is built up. Faith, on the other hand frees and preserves reason from error and enriches it with knowledge. The Church, therefore, far from hindering the pursuit of arts and sciences, fosters and promotes them in many ways. . . . Nor does she prevent sciences, each in its sphere, from making use of their own principles and methods. Yet, while acknowledging the freedom due to them, she tries to preserve them from falling into errors contrary to Divine doctrine, and from overstepping their own boundaries and throwing into confusion matters that belong to the domain of faith. The doctrine of faith which God has revealed is not placed before the human mind for further elaboration, like a philosophical system; it is a Divine deposit, handed over to the Spouse of Christ, to be faithfully guarded and infallibly declared. Hence, the meaning once given to a sacred dogma by holy mother Church is to be maintained forever and not to be departed from under pretext of more profound understanding. Let knowledge, science and wisdom grow with the course of times and centuries, in individuals as well as in the community, in each man as in the whole Church, but in the proper manner, i.e., in the same dogma, in the same meaning, in the same understanding".

What was pronounced in the Decree of the Vatican Council was represented by a master's hand on a wall of the Vatican, three centuries ago. In his fresco (wrongly) called "Disputa", Raphael has assigned to arts and sciences their proper place in the kingdom of God. They are grouped around the altar, accept the Gospel from angels' hands, raise their eyes to the Redeemer, and from Him to the Father and the Spirit, surrounded by the Church triumphant, their own ultimate end.

III.
Man

The Nature of Man

According to the common definition of the School, Man is a rational animal. This signifies no more than that, in the system of classification and definition shown in the Arbor Porphyriana, man is a substance, corporeal, living, sentient, and rational. It is a logical definition, having reference to a metaphysical entity. It has been said that man's animality is distinct in nature from his rationality, though they are inseparably joined, during life, in one common personality. "Animality" is an abstraction as is "rationality". As such, neither has any substantial existence of its own. To be exact we should have to write: "Man's animality is rational"; for his "rationality" is certainly not something superadded to his "animality". Man is one in essence. In the Scholastic synthesis, it is a manifest illogism to hypostasize the abstract conceptions that are necessary for the intelligent apprehension of complete phenomena. A similar confusion of expression may be noticed in the statement that man is a "compound of body and soul". This is misleading. Man is not a body plus a soul — which would make of him two individuals; but a body that is what it is (namely, a human body) by reason of its union with the soul. As a special application of the general doctrine of matter and form which is as well a theory of science as of intrinsic causality, the "soul" is envisaged as the substantial form of the matter which, so informed, is a human "body". The union between the two is a "substantial" one. It cannot be maintained, in the Thomistic system, that the "substantial union is a relation by which two substances are so disposed that they form one". In the general theory, neither "matter" nor "form", but only the composite, is a substance. In the case of man, though the "soul" be proved a reality capable of separate existence, the "body" can in no sense be called a substance in its own right. It exists only as determined by a form; and if that form is not a human soul, then the "body" is not a human body. It is in this sense that the Scholastic phrase "incomplete substance", applied to body and soul alike, is to be understood. Though strictly speaking self-contradictory, the phrase expresses in a convenient form the abiding reciprocity of relation between these two "principles of substantial being".

Man is an individual, a single substance resultant from the determination of matter by a human form. Being capable of reasoning, he verifies the philosophical definition of a person: "the individual substance of a rational nature". This doctrine of St. Thomas Aquinas (cf. I.75.4) and of Aristotle is not the only one that has been advanced. In Greek and in modern philosophy, as well as during the Patristic and Scholastic periods, another celebrated theory laid claim to pre-eminence. For Plato the soul is a spirit that uses the body. It is in a non-natural state of union, and longs to be freed from its bodily prison (cf. Republic, X, 611). Plato has recourse to a theory of a triple soul to explain the union—a theory that would seem to make personality altogether impossible (see MATTER). St. Augustine, following him (except as to the triple-soul theory) makes the "body" and "soul" two substances; and man "a rational soul using a mortal and earthly body" (De Moribus, I, xxvii). But he is careful to note that by union with the body it constitutes the human being. St. Augustine's psychological doctrine was current in the Middle Ages up to the time and during the perfecting of the Thomistic synthesis. It is expressed in the "Liber de Spiritu et Anima" of Alcher of Clairvaux (?) (twelfth century). In this work "the soul rules the body; its union with the body is a friendly union, though the latter impedes the full and free exercise of its activity; it is devoted to its prison" (cf. de Wulf, "History of Philosophy", tr. Coffey). As further instances of Augustinian influence may be cited Alanus ab Insulis (but the soul is united by a spiritus physicus to the body); Alexander of Hales (union ad modum formæ cum materia); St. Bonaventure (the body united to a soul consisting of "form" and "spiritual matter"—forma completiva). Many of the Franciscan doctors seem, by inference if not explicitly, to lean to the Platonic Augustinian view; Scotus, who, however, by the subtlety of his "formal distinction a parte rei", saves the unity of the individual while admitting the forma corporeitatis; his opponent John Peter Olivi's "mode of union" of soul and body was condemned at the Council of Vienne (1311-12).

The theories of the nature of man so far noticed are purely philosophical. No one of them has been explicitly condemned by the Church. The ecclesiastical definitions have reference merely to the "union" of "body" and "soul".

With the exception of the words of the Council of Toledo, 688 (Ex libro responionis Juliani Archiep. Tolet.), in which "soul" and "body" are referred to as two "substances" (explicable in the light of subsequent definitions only in the hypothesis of abstraction, and as "incomplete" substances), other pronouncements of the Church merely reiterate the doctrine maintained in the School. Thus Lateran in 649 (against the Monothelites), canon ii, "the Word of God with the flesh assumed by Him and animated with an intellectual principle shall come . . ."; Vienne, 1311-12, "whoever shall hereafter dare to assert, maintain, or pertinaciously hold that the rational or intellectual soul is not per se and essentially the form of the human body, is to be regarded as a heretic"; Decree of Leo X, in V Lateran, Bull "Apostolici Regiminis", 1513, ". . . with the approval of this sacred council we condemn all who assert that the intellectual soul is mortal or is the same in all men . . . for the soul is not only really and essentially the form of the human body, but is also immortal; and the number of souls has been and is to be multiplied according as the number of bodies is multiplied"; Brief "Eximiam tuam" of Pius IX to Cardinal de Geissel, 15 June, 1857, condemning the error of Günther, says: "the rational soul is per se the true and immediate form of the body".

In the sixteenth century Descartes advanced a doctrine that again separated soul and body, and compromised the unity of consciousness and personality. To account for the interaction of the two substances—the one "thought", the other "extension"— "Occasionalism" (Malebranche, Geulincx), "Pre-established Harmony" (Leibniz), and "Reciprocal Influx" (Locke) were imagined. The inevitable reaction from the Cartesian division is to be found in the Monism of Spinoza. Aquinas avoids the difficulties and contradictions of the "two substance" theory and, saving the personality, accounts for the observed facts of the unity of consciousness. His doctrine:

* disproves the possibility of metempsychosis;
* establishes an inferential, though not an apodictic argument, for the resurrection of the body;
* avoids all difficulties as to the "seat of the soul", by asserting formal actuation;
* proves the immortality of the soul from the spiritual and incomplex activity observed in the individual man; it is not my soul that thinks, or my body that eats, but "I" that do both.

The particular creation of the soul is a corollary of the foregoing. This doctrine — the contradiction of Traducianism and Transmigration—follows from the consideration that the formal principle cannot be produced by way of generation, either directly (since it is proved to be simple in substance), or accidentally (since it is a subsistent form). Hence there remains only creation as the mode of its production. The complete argument may be found in the "Contra Gentiles" of St. Thomas, II, lxxxvii. See also Summa Theologica, I, Q. cxviii, aa. 1 and 2 (against Traducianism) and a. 3 (in refutation of the opinion of Pythagoras, Plato and Origen — with whom Leibniz might be grouped as professing a modified form of the same opinion—the creation of souls at the beginning of time).

The Origin of Man

This problem may be treated from the standpoints of Holy Scripture, theology, or philosophy.

A. The Sacred Writings are entirely concerned with the relations of man to God, and of God's dealings with man, before and after the Fall. Two accounts of his origin are given in the Old Testament. On the sixth and last day of the creation "God created man to his own image: to the image of God he created him" (Genesis 1:27); and "the Lord God formed man of the slime of the earth: and breathed into his face the breath of life, and man became a living soul" (Genesis 2:7; so Sirach 17:1: "God created man of the earth, and made him after his own image"). By these texts the special creation of man is established, his high dignity and his spiritual nature. As to his material part, the Scripture declares that it is formed by God from the "slime of the earth". This becomes a "living soul" and fashioned to the "image of God" by the inspiration of the "breath of life", which makes man man and differentiates him from the brute.

B. This doctrine is obviously to be looked for in all Catholic theology. The origin of man by creation (as opposed to emanative and evolutionistic Pantheism) is asserted in the Church's dogmas and definitions. In the earliest symbols (see the Alexandrian: di ou ta panta egeneto, ta en ouranois kai epi ges, horata te kai aorata, and the Nicene), in the councils (see especially IV Lateran, 1215; "Creator of all things visible and invisible, spiritual and corporeal, who by this omnipotent power . . . brought forth out of nothing the spiritual and corporeal creation, that, is the angelic world and the universe, and afterwards man, forming as it were one composite out of spirit and body"), in the writings of the Fathers and theologians the same account is given. The early controversies and apologetics of St. Clement of Alexandria and Origen defend the theory of creation against Stoics and neo-Platonists. St. Augustine strenuously combats the pagan schools on this point as on that of the nature and immortality of man's soul. A masterly synthetic exposition of the theological and philosophical doctrine as to man is given in the "Summa Theologica" of St. Thomas Aquinas (I.75-I.111). So again the "Contra Gentiles", II (on creatures), especially from xlvi onwards, deals with the subject from a philosophical standpoint — the distinction between the theological and the philosophical treatment having been carefully drawn in chap. iv. Note especially chap. lxxxvii, which establishes Creationism.

  C. Scholastic philosophy reaches a conclusion as to the origin of man similar to the teaching of revelation and theology. Man is a creature of God in a created universe. All things that are, except Himself, exist in virtue of a unique creative act. As to the mode of creation, there would seem to be two possible alternatives. Either the individual composite was created ex nihilo, or a created soul became the informing principle of matter already pre-existing in another determination. Either mode would be philosophically tenable, but the Thomistic principle of the successive and graded evolution of forms in matter is in favour of the latter view. If, as is the case with the embryo (St. Thomas, I, Q. cxviii, a. 2, ad 2um), a succession of preparatory forms preceded information by the rational soul, it nevertheless follows necessarily from the established principles of Scholasticism that this, not only in the case of the first man, but of all men, must be produced in being by a special creative act. The matter that is destined to become what we call man's "body" is naturally prepared, by successive transformations, for the reception of the newly created soul as its determinant principle. The commonly held opinion is that this determination takes place when the organization of the brain of the foetus is sufficiently complete to allow of imaginative life; i.e. the possibility of the presence of phantasmata. But note also the opinion that the creation of, and information by, the soul takes place at the moment of conception.

The End of Man

In common with all created nature (substance, or essence, considered as the principle of activity or passivity), that of man tends towards its natural end. The proof of this lies in the inductively ascertained principle of finality. The natural end of man may be considered from two points of view. Primarily, it is the procuring of the glory of God, which is the end of all creation. God's intrinsic perfection is not increased by creation, but extrinsically He becomes known and praised, or glorified by the creatures He endows with intelligence. A secondary natural end of man is the attainment of his own beatitude, the complete and hierarchic perfection of his nature by the exercise of its faculties in the order which reason prescribes to the will, and this by the observance of the moral law. Since complete beatitude is not to be attained in this life (considered in its merely natural aspect, as neither yet elevated by grace, nor vitiated by sin) future existence, as proved in psychology, is postulated by ethics for its attainment. Thus the present life is to be considered as a means to a further end. Upon the relation of the rational nature of man to his last end—God—is founded the science of moral philosophy, which thus presupposes as its ground, metaphysics, cosmology, and psychology. The distinction of good and evil rests upon the consonance or discrepancy of human acts with the nature of man thus considered; and moral obligation has its root in the absolute necessity and immutability of the same relation.

With regard to the last end of man (as "man" and not as "soul"), it is not universally held by Scholastics that the resurrection of the body is proved apodictically in philosophy. Indeed some (e.g. Scotus, Occam) have even denied that the immortality of the soul is capable of such demonstration. The resurrection is an article of faith. Some recent authors, however (see Cardinal Mercier, "Psychologie", II, 370), advance the argument that the formation of a new body is naturally necessary on account of the perfect final happiness of the soul, for which it is a condition sine qua non. A more cogent form of the proof would seem to lie in the consideration that the separated soul is not complete in ratione naturæ. It is not the human being; and it would seem that the nature of man postulates a final and permanent reunion of its two intrinsic principles.

But there is de facto another end of man. The Catholic Faith teaches that man has been raised to a supernatural state and that his destiny, as a son of God and member of the Mystical Body of which Christ is the Head, is the eternal enjoyment of the beatific vision. In virtue of God's infallible promise, in the present dispensation the creature enters into the covenant by baptism; he becomes a subject elevated by grace to a new order, incorporated into a society by reason of which he tends and is brought to a perfection not due to his nature (see CHURCH). The means to this end are justification by the merits of Christ communicated to man, co-operation with grace, the sacraments, prayer, good works, etc. The Divine law which the Christian obeys rests on this supernatural relation and is enforced with a similar sanction. The whole pertains to a supernatural providence which belongs not to philosophical speculation but to revelation and theological dogma. In the light of the finalistic doctrine as to man, it is evident that the "purpose of life" can have a meaning only in reference to an ultimate state of perfection of the individual. The nature tending towards its end can be interpreted only in terms of that end; and the activities by which it manifests its tendency as a living being have no adequate explanation apart from it.

The theories that are sometimes put forward of the place of man in the universe, as destined to share in a development to which no limits can be assigned, rest upon the Spencerian theory that man is but "a highly-differentiated portion of the earth's crust and gaseous envelope", and ignore or deny the limitation imposed by the essential materiality and spirituality of human nature. If the intellectual faculties were indeed no more than the developed animal powers., there would seem to be no possibility of limiting their progress in the future. But since the soul of man is the result, not of evolution, but of creation, it is impossible to look forward to any such advance as would involve a change in man's specific nature, or any essential difference in its relation to its material environment, in the physiological conditions under which it at present exists, or in its "relation" to its Divine Creator. The "Herrenmoralität" of Nietzsche—the "transvaluation of values" which is to revolutionize the present moral law, the new morality which man's changing relation to the Absolute may some day bring into existence — must, therefore, be considered to be not less inconsistent with the nature of man than it is wanting in historical probability.

IV.
Psychology

In the most general sense, psychology is the science which treats of the soul and its operations. During the past century, however, the term has come to be frequently employed to denote the latter branch of knowledge — the science of the phenomena of the mind, of the processes or states of human consciousness. Moreover, the increasing differentiation, characteristic of the advance of all departments of knowledge in recent years, has manifested itself in so marked a manner in psychological investigation that there are already severe distinct fields of psychological work, each putting forward claims to be recognized as a separate science. The term psychologia seems to have first come into use about the end of the sixteenth century (Goclenius, 1590, Casmann's "Psychologia Anthropologica", 1594). But the popularization of the name dates from Ch. Wolff in the eighteenth century.

History

Aristotle may well be deemed the founder of this as of so many other sciences, though by him it is not distinguished from general biology, which is itself part of physics, or the study of nature. His treatise peri psyches ("De Anima") was during two thousand years virtually the universal textbook of psychology, and it still well repays study. In the investigation of vital phenomena Aristotle employed to some extent all the methods of modern science: observation, internal and external; comparison; experiment; hypothesis; and induction; as well as deduction and speculative reasoning. He defines the soul as the "Entelechy or form of a natural body potentially possessing life". He distinguishes three kinds of souls, or grades of life, the vegetative, the sensitive, and the intellectual or rational. In man the higher virtually includes the lower. He investigates the several functions of nutrition, appetency, locomotion, sensuous perception, and intellect or reason. The last is confined to man. The working of the senses is discussed by him in detail; and diligent anatomical and physiological study, as well as careful introspective observation of our conscious processes, is manifested. Knowledge starts from sensation, but sense only apprehends the concrete and singular thing. It is the function of the intellect to abstract the universal essence. There is a radical distinction between thought and sentiency. The intellect or reason (nous) is separate from sense and immortal, though how precisely we are to conceive this nous and its "scparateness" is one of the most puzzling problems in Aristotle's psychology. Indeed, the doctrines of free will and personal immortality are not easily reconciled with parts of Aristotle's teaching.

Scholastic Period

There is little effort at systematic treatment of psychology from Aristotle to the medieval philosophers. For Epicurus, psychology was a branch of physics in subordination to a theory of hedonistic ethics. With the introduction of Christianity certain psychological problems such as the immortality and the origin of the soul, free will and moral habits at once assumed a vastly increased importance and raised the treatise "De Anima", to one of the most important branches of philosophy. Moreover, the angels being assumed to be spirits in many ways resembling the human soul conceived as separate from the human body, a speculative theory of the nature, attributes, and operations of the angelic beings, partly based on Scriptural texts, partly deduced by analogical reasoning from human psychology, gradually grew up and received its final elaboration in the Middle Ages in the metaphysical theology of the Schoolmen. The Christian mystics were naturally led to consider the character of the soul's knowledge of God. But their treatment of psychological questions is generally vague and obscure, whilst their language indulges much in allegory and symbolism. Indeed, the greatest of the mystics were not sympathetic with the employment of Scholastic or scientific methods in the handling of mystic experience. The great controversy between Realism and Nominalism from the early Middle Ages directed much attention to the theory of knowledge and the problem of the origin of ideas. However, although psychological observation was appealed to, the epistemological discussions were largely metaphysical in character during this period. To Albertus Magnus and St. Thomas the popularization of the psychology of Aristotle throughout Europe during the thirteenth century was mainly due. In Questions lxxv to xc of part I of the "Summa

Theologica", St. Thomas gives a very fairly complete and systematic account of the leading topics connected with the soul. However, questions of biology, general metaphysics, and theology were constantly interwoven with psychology for many centuries afterwards. Indeed, the liberal use made of physiological evidence in psychological discussions is a marked feature in the treatment of this branch of philosophy throughout the entire history of scholastic philosophy. But although there is plenty of proof of acute observation of mental activities, the usual appeal in discussion is rather to metaphysical analysis and deductive argument than to systematic introspective observation and induction, so characteristic of modern psychology. The treatise "De Anima" of Francisco Suárez is a very good example of scholastic psychology at the close of the Middle Ages. The treatise, containing six books, starts in book I with an inquiry into the essence of the soul. Recalling Aristotle's definition of the soul as the form of the body, the author proceeds to examine the relations of the vegetative, sensitive, and rational soul. Next, in book II he treats of the faculties of the soul in general and their relation to the soul as an essence. In book III he investigates the nature and working of the cognitive faculties, and especially of the senses. In book IV he inquires into the character of the activity of the intellect. In book V he deals with faculties of appetency and free will. Book VI is devoted to a speculative consideration of the condition and mode of operation of the soul in a future life. In each question he begins with a summary of previous opinions and then puts forward his own solution. The order of treatment starting from the essence and passing thence to the faculties and their operations is characteristic of the scholastic treatises generally. The method is mainly deductive and the argument metaphysical, though in dealing with the senses there is constant appeal to recognized physiological authorities from Aristotle to Vesalius.

In psychology as well as in other branches of philosophy the influence of Descartes was considerable though indirect. His subjective starting-point, cogito, ergo sum, his insistence on methodic doubt, his advocacy of reflection on thought and close scrutiny of our fundamental ideas, all tended to encourage the method of internal observation, whilst the mechanical explanation of the "Traité des Passions" favoured the advent of physiological psychology. It was probably, however, John Locke's "Essay on the Human Understanding" (1690) which did most to foster the method of analytic introspection which constitutes the principal feature of modern psychological method. Notwithstanding the confused and inconsistent metaphysics and the many grave psychological blunders with which that work abounds, yet his frequent appeal to inner experience, his honest efforts to describe mental processes, and the quantity of acute observations scattered throughout the work, coming also at an age when the inductive method was rapidly rising in popularity, achieved a speedy and wide success for his book, and gave a marked empirical bent to all future English psychology.

      Psychological observation and analysis were still more skilfully used by Bishop Berkeley as a principle of explanation in his "Theory of Vision", and then employed by him to establish his psychological creed of Idealism. Finally, David Hume, the true founder of the Associationist school of psychology, still further increased the importance of the method of introspective analysis by the daring sceptical conclusions he claimed to establish by its means. The subsequent British adherents of the Associationist school Hartley, the two Mills, Bain, and Herbert Spencer, continued this method and tradition along the same lines. There is constant direct appeal to inner experience combined with systematic effort to trace the genesis of the highest, most spiritual, and most complex mental conceptions back to elementary atomic states of sensuous consciousness. Universal ideas, necessary truths, the ideas of self, time, space, causality as well as the conviction of an external material world were all explained as the outcome of sensations and association. The reality of any higher activities or faculties essentially different from the lower sensuous powers was denied, and all the chief data formerly employed in establishing the simplicity, spirituality, and substantiality of the soul were rejected. Rational or metaphysical psychology was thus virtually extinguished and erased from English philosophical literature during the nineteenth century. Even the more orthodox representatives of the Scotch school, Reid and Dugald Stewart, who avoided all metaphysical argument and endeavoured to controvert Hume with his own weapons of appeal exclusively to experience and observation, had only further confirmed the tendency in the direction of a purely empirical psychology. The great need in English psychological literature throughout most of the nineteenth century, on the side of those defending a spiritual doctrine of the human mind, was a systematic and thorough treatment of empirical psychology. Excellent pieces of work on particular questions were done by Martineau, W.G. Ward, and other writers, but nearly all the systematic treatises on psychology were produced by the disciples of the Sensationist or Materialistic schools. Yet, if philosophy is to be based on experience, then assuredly it is on the carefully-scrutinized and well-established results of empirical psychology that any satisfactory rational metaphysical doctrine respecting the nature of the soul, its origin, and its destiny must be built. It was in their faulty though often plausible analysis and interpretation of our states of consciousness that the greatest errors in philosophy and psychology of Bain, the two Mills, Spencer, and their disciples had their source; it is only by more careful introspective observation and a more searching analysis of the same mental facts that these errors can be exposed and solid foundations laid for a true metaphysical psychology of the soul.

In France, Condillac, La Mettrie, Holbach, and Bonnet developed the Sensationalism of Locke's psychology into an increasingly crude Materialism. To oppose this school later on, Royer-Collard, Cousin, Jouffroy, and Maine de Biran turned to the work of Reid and the "common sense" Scotch school, appropriating their method and results in empirical psychology. Some of these writers, moreover, sought to carry their reasoning beyond the mere inductions of empirical psychology, in order to construct on this enlarged experience a genuine philosophy of the soul, as "principle" and subject of the states and activities immediately revealed to introspective observation.

In Germany the purely empirical tendency which had reduced psychology in England to a mere positivistic science of mental facts did not meet with quite the same success. Metaphysics and philosophy proper never fell there into the degradation which they experienced in England in the beginning of the nineteenth century. And although the old conception of a philosophical science of the nature and attributes of the soul was rejected by Kant, and abandoned in the systems of Fichte, Schelling, and Hegel, yet mere Phenomenalism was never completely triumphant in Germany. Herbart, whilst denying the reality of faculties, postulates a simple soul as the underlying subject of the presentations or ideas which form our conscious life. Hermann Lotze, laying similar stress on the importance of scientific observation of our mental states, insists even more strongly that our introspective experience correctly interpreted affords abundant metaphysical justification for the doctrine of an immaterial soul. Meanwhile the earlier attempts of Herbart to express mental activities in mathematical formulæ led to a more successful line of experimental research in the hands of Weber, Fechner, Wundt, and others. The aim of this school is to attain the possible quantitative measurement of conscious states. As this is ordinarily not directly possible, much industry and ingenuity have been devoted to measuring quantitatively, by the aid of skilfully devised instruments, the immediate physical antecedents and effects of sundry mental activities, by which it is hoped to secure accurate quantitative descriptions of the mental states themselves. Psychological laboratories devoted to research of this kind have been set up in several countries, especially in Germany and America. One of the most successful so far is that at the Catholic University of Louvain, and another has lately been established at that of Washington. In Great Britain, however, the special home of empirical psychology since Locke, the new movement in favour of experimental psychology has not, at all events down to the present time, met with much success. The advance of physiological science, and especially of that of the brain and nervous system, has also reacted on psychology, stimulating closer inquiry into the relations between mental and bodily processes. It cannot, however, be maintained that the progress of physiological knowledge, considerable though it is, has brought us appreciably nearer to the solution of the great problem, how body and mind act on each other. The study of nervous pathology, of mental disease and of abnormal mental states, such as those of hypnotism and double-consciousness, has also opened up new fields of psychological research, constantly widening with the last thirty years.

Scope of Psychology

As we have already observed, recent writers commonly confine the term psychology to the science of the phenomena of the mind. Thus William James, probably the psychologist of widest influence during the past twenty years, defines psychology as "The Science of Mental Life, both of its phenomena and their conditions". ("Principles", I, 1). Wundt's definition is: "the science which investigates the whole content of Experience in its relations to the Subject". ("Outlines", 3rd ed., 3). Other writers describe it as, "the science of the facts apprehended by our internal sense", or again, "the science of our states of consciousness, their laws of succession and concomitancy". The common feature of all these definitions is the limitation of the scope of psychology to the phenomena of the mind directly observable by introspection. In this view it is a purely positivist science from which all philosophical problems are to be excluded, as rigorously as from chemistry or geology. It is, in fact; la psychologie sans âme. If such questions as the nature, origin, or destiny of the soul are to be discussed at all, it must be, according to these writers, not in psychology, but in some branch of speculation to be styled the metaphysics or ontology of the human mind, and to be completely isolated from science.

In direct contrast with this view is that ordinarily adopted by Catholic writers hitherto. By them, psychology has usually been conceived as one of the most important branches of philosophy. In their view it may be best described as the philosophical science, which investigates the nature, attributes, and activities of the soul or mind of man. By soul, or mind, is understood the ultimate principle within me by which I think, feel, will, and by which my body is animated. Whilst the soul and the mind are conceived as fundamentally one, the latter term is usually employed to designate the animating principle viewed as subject of my conscious or mental operations; the former denotes it as the root of all vital activities. By terming their branch of knowledge a philosophical science, it is implied that psychology ought to include not only a doctrine of the laws of succession and concomitance of our conscious states, but an inquiry into their ultimate cause. Any adequate study of the human mind, it is contended, naturally presents itself in two stages, empirical or phenomenal psychology, and rational or metaphysical psychology. Though conveniently separated for didactic treatment the two are organically connected. Our metaphysical conclusions as to the nature of the soul must rest on the evidence supplied by our experience of the character of its activities. On the other hand, any effort at thorough treatment of our mental operations, and especially any attempt at explanation of the higher forms or products of consciousness, it is urged, is quite impossible without the adoption of some metaphysical theory as to the nature of the underlying subject or agents of these states. Professor Dewey has justly observed: "The philosophic implications embedded in the very heart of psychology are not got rid of when they are kept out of sight. Some opinion regarding the nature of the mind and its relations to reality will show itself on almost every page, and the fact that this opinion is introduced without the conscious intention of the writer, may serve to confuse both the author and his reader" ("Psychology", IV). Ladd, and others also, recognize the evil of "clandestine" metaphysics when smuggled into what claims to be purely "scientific" non-philosophical treatments of psychology.

Psychology is not in the same position as the physical sciences here. Whilst investigating a question in geology, chemistry, or mechanics, we may, at least temporarily, prescind from our metaphysical creed, but not so — judging from the past history — when giving our psychological accounts and explanations of mental products, such as universal concepts, the notions of moral obligation, responsibility, personal identity, time, or the perception of an external material world, or the simple judgment, two and two must make four. The view, therefore, of those philosophers who maintain that the intrinsic connexions between many of the questions of empirical and rational psychology are so indissoluble that they cannot be divorced, seems to have solid justification. Of course we can call the study of the phenomena of the mind, "Psychology", and that of its inner nature, the "Philosophy of the Mind"; and we may treat each in a separate volume. That is merely a matter of terminology and convenience. But the important point is that in the explanatory treatment of the higher intellectual and rational processes, it will practically be impossible for the psychologist to preserve a philosophically neutral attitude. A truly scientific psychology, therefore, should comprise:

* (1) a thorough investigation by introspective observation and analysis of our various mental activities — cognitive and appetitive, sensuous and rational — seeking to resolve all products of the mind back to their original elements, determining as far as possible their organic conditions, and tracing the laws of their growth;

* (2) based on the results of this study, a rational theory or explanatory account of the nature of the agent or subject of these activities, with its chief properties.

Method of psychology

The primary method of investigation in empirical or phenomenal psychology is introspection or reflective observation of our own mental states. This is the ultimate source of all knowledge of mental facts; even the information gathered immediately from other quarters has finally to be interpreted in terms of our own subjective experience. Introspection is, however, liable to error; consequently, it has to be employed with care and helped and corrected by all the supplementary sources of psychological knowledge available. Among the chief of these are: the internal experience of other observers communicated through language; the study of the human mind as exhibited in different periods of life from infancy to old age, and in different races and grades of civilization; as embodied in various languages and literatures; and as revealed in the absence of particular senses, and in abnormal or pathological conditions such as dreams, hypnotism, and forms of insanity. Moreover, the anatomy, physiology, and pathology of the brain and nervous system supply valuable data as to the organic conditions of conscious states. Experimental psychology, psychophysics, and psychometry help towards accuracy and precision in the description of certain forms of mental activity. And the comparative study of the lower animals may also afford useful assistance in regard to some questions of human psychology. By the utilization of these several sources of information the data furnished to the psychologist by the introspective observation of his own individual mind may be enlarged, tested and corrected, and may thus acquire in a certain degree the objective and universal character of the observations on which the physical sciences are built. Introspection is frequently spoken of as the subjective method, these other sources of information as supplementary objective methods of psychological study.

Branches of Psychology

Indeed some of them have rapidly grown to be such large and important fields of research that they now claim to be recognized as special departments of psychology, or even sciences in their own right. Thus we have comparative psychology including animal psychology, child psychology, and race psychology. Again psychiatry or psychopathology, the science of mental disease, also physiological psychology, which, in a broad sense, includes all systematic study of the organic conditions of mental life, or, as Ladd defines it, "psychology approached and studied from the physiological side".

Experimental Psychology

A special department of physiological psychology which has recently risen rapidly into favour in some countries is experimental psychology, alluded to above in our historical sketch. It is at times styled the "New Psychology" by its more enthusiastic supporters. It seeks to secure precision and an objective standard in the description of mental states by controlling their conditions by skilful devices and ingenious apparatus. Its chief success so far has been in its efforts to measure the varying intensity of sensations, the delicacy of sense-organs and "reaction-time" or the rapidity of a faculty's response to stimulation. Certain properties of memory have also been made the subject of measuring experiments and more recently considerable industry has been devoted, especially by Külpe and the Würzburg school, to bring some aspects of the higher activities of intellect and will within the range of the laboratory apparatus. Opinions still differ much as to both the present value and future prospects of experimental psychology. Whilst Wundt, the leader of the new movement for the past fifty years, places the only hope of psychological progress in the experimental method, William James's judgment on the entire literature of the subject since Fechner (1840) was that "its proper psychological outcome is just nothing at all" ("Principles", I, 534). Apart, however from the very modest positive results, especially in the higher forms of mental life, which the experimental method has achieved or may achieve in the future, its exercise may nevertheless prove a valuable agency in the training of the psychological specialist, both in increasing his appreciation of the value of the most minute accuracy in descriptions of mental states, and also by fostering in him habits of precision and skill in systematic introspection.

Classification
The Faculties

In empirical psychology, with modern writers, the next step after determining the method of the science is to attempt a classification of the phenomena of mental life. In the scholastic philosophy the equivalent operation was the systematic division of the faculties of the soul. Apart from vegetative and locomotive powers the Schoolmen, following Aristotle, adopted a bipartite division of faculties into those of cognition and appetency. The former they subdivided into sensuous, and intellectual or rational. The sensuous faculties they again subdivided into the five external senses and the internal activities of imagination, sensuous memory, sensus communis, and vis cogitativa. But there was much disagreement as to the number, character, and boundary lines of these internal forms of sensuous cognition. There were also divergences of opinion as to the nature of the faculties in general in themselves and to what extent there was a distinctio realis between faculties and the essence of the soul. But, on the other hand, there was general agreement as to an essential difference between all sensuous and intellectual or spiritual powers of the mind. The possession of the latter constitutes the differentia which separates man from the irrational animals.

Content of Empirical Psychology

The psychologist naturally begins with the treatment of the phenomena of sentiency. The several senses, their organic structure and functions, the various forms of sentient activity with their cognitive, hedonic and appetitive properties and their special characteristics have to be carefully analyzed, compared, and described. Next, imagination and memory are similarly studied, and the laws of their operation, growth, and development diligently traced. The discussion of the organic appetites springing from sensations, and the investigation of the nature and conditions of the most elementary forms of pleasure and pain may also appropriately come here. Intellect follows. The consideration of this faculty includes the study of the processes of conception, judgment, reasoning, rational attention, and selfconscious reflection. These, however, are all merely different functions of the same spiritual cognitive power — the intellect. Psychology inquires into their modes of operation, their special features, and the general conditions of their growth and development. From the higher power of cognition it proceeds to the study of spiritual appetency, rational desire, and free volition. The relations of will to knowledge, the qualities of conative activity, and the effects of repeated volitions in the production of habit, constitute the chief subjects of investigation here. In connexion with these higher forms of cognition and desire, there will naturally be undertaken the study of conscience and the phenomena of the emotions.

Genetic treatment a marked characteristic of modern empirical psychology

The constant aim of modern psychology is to analyse all complex mental operations into their simplest elements and to trace back to their first beginning all acquired or composite habits and faculties, and to show how they have been generated or could have been generated from the fewest original aptitudes or fundamental activities of the mind. This is sound scientific procedure — recognized in the Scholastic aphorism, Entia non sunt multiplicanda prœter necessitatem. We may not postulate a special faculty for any mental state which can be accounted for by the co-operation of already recognized activities of the soul. But the labour and skill devoted during the past century and a half to this combined analytic and synthetic procedure has developed one feature of modern psychology by which it is differentiated in a most marked manner from that of the Middle Ages and of Aristotle. The present-day treatment is pronouncedly genetic. Thus, whilst the Schoolmen in their account of mental operations, such as perception, conception, or desire, considered these processes almost solely as elicited by the normal adult human being already in full possession and control of matured mental powers, the chief interest of the modern psychologist is to trace the growth of these powers from their first and simplest manifestations in infancy, and to discriminate what is the product of experience and acquired habits from that which is the immediate outcome of the innate capabilities of the soul. This is particularly noticeable if we compare the treatment of the mental operation of perception as given in most Scholastic textbooks with that to be found in any modern handbook of psychology. The point of view is usually quite different. Since much of the most plausible modern attacks on Scholastic psychological doctrine has been made in this manner, the genetic treatment from the Thomist standpoint of many psychological questions seems to us to be among the most urgent tasks imposed nowadays on the neo-Scholastic psychologist. The value of such work from a philosophical standpoint would seem to be distinctly greater than that of any results likely to be achieved in quantitative experimental psychology. Obviously there is nothing in the Thomistic conception of the soul and its operations incompatible with a diligent investigation into the unfolding of its various aptitudes and powers.

Rational Psychology

From the study of the character of the activities of the mind in experimental psychology, the student now passes on to inquire into the nature of the principle from which they proceed. This constitutes the more philosophical or metaphysical division of the science. For, as we have indicated, the analysis and explanatory accounts of the higher forms and products of mental activity, which the scientific psychologist is compelled to undertake even in phenomenal psychology, involve metaphysical assumption and conclusions which he cannot escape — certainly not by merely ignoring them. Still, it is in this second stage that he will formally evolve the logical consequences to which his previous study of the several forms of mental activity lead up. His method here will be both inductive and deductive; both analytic and synthetic. He argues from effect to cause. From the character of the mental activities already scrutinized with so much care, he now concludes as to the nature of the subject to which they belong. From what the mind does, he seeks to learn what it is. In particular, from the simple spiritual nature of the higher activities of intellect and will, he infers that the being, the ultimate principle from which they proceed, must be of a simple and spiritual nature. Consequently, it cannot be the brain or any corporeal substance. Having established the simplicity and spirituality of the soul, he then goes on to deduce further conclusions as to its origin, the nature of its union with the body, and its future destiny. In this way by rational arguments the Scholastic thinkers claim to prove that the human soul can only have arisen by creation, that it is naturally incorruptible, and that the boundless aspirations of the intellect, the insatiable yearnings of the will, and the deepest convictions of the moral reason all combine to establish a future life of the soul after death.

V.
Cosmology

From its Greek etymology (kósmos world; lógos, knowledge or science) the word cosmology means the science of the world. It ought, therefore, to include in its scope the study of the whole material universe: that is to say, of inorganic substances, of plants, of animals, and of man himself. But, as a matter of fact, the wide range indicated by the etymology of the word has been narrowed in the actual meaning. In our day cosmology is a branch of philosophical study, and therefore excludes from its investigation whatever forms the object of the natural sciences. While the sciences of physics and biology seek the proximate causes of corporal phenomena, the laws that govern them, and the wonderful harmony resulting therefrom, cosmology aims to discover the deeper and remoter causes which neither observation nor experiment immediately reveals. This special purpose restricts in many ways the field of cosmology. There is another limitation not less important. Man's unique position in the universe makes him the object of a special philosophical study, viz. psychology, or anthropology; and, in consequence, that portion of the corporeal world with which these sciences deal has been cut off from the domain of cosmology properly so called.

There is a tendency at present to restrict the field still further; and limit it to what is known as inorganic creation. Psychology being by its very definition the study of human fife considered in its first principle and in the totality of its phenomena, its investigations ought to comprise, it would seem, the threefold life of man, vegetative, animal, and rational. And, indeed, the interdependence of these three lives in the one living human being appears to justify the enlargement demanded nowadays by many authors of note for the psychological field. Hence for those who accept this view, cosmology has nothing to do with organic life but is reduced to "a philosophical study of the inorganic world". Such, in our opinion, is the best definition that can be given. At the same time it should be remarked that many philosophers still favour a broader definition, which would include not only the mineral kingdom but also living things considered in a general way. In German-speaking countries cosmology, as a rule, is known as Naturphilosophie, i.e. philosophy of nature.

Under this name, philosophers usually understand a study of the universe along the lines of one of the foregoing definitions. Scientists, on the other hand, give a more scientific turn to this philosophy of nature, transforming it into a sort of general physics with an occasional excursion into the realm of sensitive and intellectual life. A notable instance is the work of Prof. Ostwald, "Vorlesungen über Naturphilosophie" (Leipzig, 1902).

Origin of Cosmology

The word itself is of recent origin. It was first used by Wolff when, in 1730, he entitled one of his works "Cosmologia Generalis" (Frankfort and Leipzig). In this treatise the author studies especially the laws of motion, the relations that exist among things in nature, the contingency of the universe, the harmony of nature, the necessity of postulating a God to explain the origin of the cosmos and its manifestation of purpose. Because of the advance the natural sciences were then making, Wolff omitted from his philosophic study of nature the purely scientific portion which till then had been closely allied with it. The cosmology of the ancients and especially of Aristotle was simply a branch of physics. The "Physics" of Aristotle treats of corporeal beings in as far as they are subject to motion. The work is divided into two parts:

* General physics, which embraces the general principles governing corporeal being. It treats of local motion and its various kinds; the origin of substantial compounds; changes in quality; changes in quantity by increase and decrease; and changes arising from motion in place, on which Aristotle hinges our notions of the infinite, of time, and of space.

* Special physics which deals with the various classes of beings: terrestrial bodies, celestial bodies, and man.

It is the first part of this work that comes nearest to what we mean by cosmology. The Schoolmen of the Middle Ages, as a rule, follow the path marked out for them by Aristotle. Cosmological subjects, properly so called, have no reserved place in philosophical study, and are generally treated as a part of physics. In our own time, philosophers employ the words "cosmology" and "philosophy of nature" to designate the philosophic study of the corporeal world.

Method

Cosmology is the natural complement of the special sciences. It begins where they leave off, and its domain is quite distinct from theirs. The scientist determines the immediate cause of the phenomena observed in the mineral or the organic world: he formulates their laws and builds these into a synthesis with the help of certain general theories, such as those of light, of heat, and of electricity. The cosmologist, on the other hand, seeks the ultimate causes, not off this or that class of beings or of phenomena, but of the whole material universe. He inquires into the constituent nature of corporeal beings, their destiny, and their first cause. It is clear that these larger problems are quite beyond the range and purpose of the various sciences, each of which is by its method confined to its own particular subject. Nevertheless, cosmology must borrow, and borrow largely, from the data of science, since the causes which it studies are not directly perceptible; they can be known only through phenomena which are their more or less faithful manifestations. It is on these that cosmology must rest in order to pass upward from cause to cause till the ultimate cause is reached. Since, then, it is the role of the natural sciences to analyze and classify the properties and phenomena of nature, cosmology is obliged to draw very freely upon those sciences and to neglect none of their definitive results. In a word, the cosmological method is essentially a posteriori. Descartes and his school followed a different, even an opposite, course. Being a mathematician above all else, he applies to cosmology the principles of mathematics, and as mathematics sets out from the simplest propositions and travels along the road of deduction to the most complex truths, so Descartes, starting from extension as the primordial and universal property of matter, in fact its very essence, ends by ascribing to all bodies in nature whatever extension implies and by eliminating from them whatever it excludes. This a priori method, being essentially deductive is anti-scientific; and is based, moreover, on a false supposition, since extension is only one of the many properties of matter, not its essence. As Leibniz pointed out, extension presupposes something extended, just as a repetition presupposes something to be repeated. Philosophers, therefore, have almost entirely abandoned this method; with the exception perhaps of the Idealistic Pantheists of whom we shall speak presently.

Division of Cosmology

Cosmology, as most philosophers understand it, has a threefold problem to solve: Whence this corporeal world? What is it? Why is it? Hence its three parts, concerned respectively with
* the primordial efficient cause of the cosmos;
* its actual constituent causes;
* its final cause.

The First Cause of the Material Universe

Geology, go back as it may and as far as it may in the scientific history of the earth, must ever remain face to face with a fact that calls for explanation, viz. the existence of matter itself. Even if it could decisively prove Laplace's hypothesis, according to which all portions of this universe, earth, sun, and the whole stellar system, originally made up a single nebular class, there would still remain the very reasonable question, whence came this mass and what was its origin? Now this is precisely the question cosmology asks; and in seeking the answer it has riven rise to many systems which can always be brought under one of the following headings:

(a) Monism;
(b) the theory of Transitive Emanation;
(c) Creationism.

Monism

The Monist theory is that all beings in the world are but one and the same necessary and eternal substance having within itself the sufficient reason of its existence; while the seeming diversity of things and their attributes, are but the various manifestations and evolutions of this single substance. Pantheism identifies the world with the Divine Being. This Being is ceaselessly in process of evolution; which, however, in no wise disturbs the universal identity of things. The Pantheist is either an Idealist or a Realist according to the view he takes of the nature and character of the original substance. If that substance is real he is styled a Realist, and such were Erigena, Amalric, David of Dinant, Giordano Bruno, and Spinoza. But if the original substance is something ideal, e.g. the Ego, the Absolute, the Concept, he is styled an idealist, and such were Hegel, Schelling, and Fichte. Kraus and Tiberghien support the Pantheistic view: God is in the world and the world is in God, although they are not identical. Schopenhauer devised a form of Pantheism which is known as Panthelism. According to his view the motive force of the whole universe is a single blind will. Hartmann goes a step farther and says the world is but the constant evolution of the unconscious: hence the name Panhylism. Modern Materialists, such as Büchner, Häckel, Baruch, as well as the old Greek Atomists, Leucippus, Democritus, and Epicurus, consider all the activities of the universe as so many purely material phenomena arising from one necessary and eternal substance. Lastly, according to the supporters of the Immanent Emanation theory, the Divine Being develops within itself so that it is continually identifying itself with the beings it evolves, or that come forth from it, just as the grub maintains its substantial identity throughout its transformation into chrysalis and butterfly. It is clear that such a theory hardly differs from Pantheism.

Transitive Emanation

In the Transitive Emanation theory all beings issue from the Divine Substance much in the same way as new fruits appear on the parent tree without changing its substance and without diminishing its productive power.

Creationism

Creationism is the view held by the generality of spiritualistic philosophers. The universe through its endless transformations reveals its contingency: that is to say, its existence is not a necessity: therefore it must have received its existence from some other being. This first cause must be a necessary and independent one, unless we admit an infinite series of dependent causes and so leave unsolved the problem of the world's existence. God has, therefore, drawn all things from nothingness by the free act of His Almighty Will; in a word, He has made them out of nothing, since any other explanation, e.g. Emanationism, which implies a real intrinsic change in God, is incompatible with the immutability, necessity, and absolute perfection of the Divine Being.

The Constituent Causes of the World

The composition of corporeal beings is also the subject of much discussion. There are actually four systems of note, each promising to solve this delicate problem: Mechanism; Hylomorphism (the Scholastic system); Dynamic Atomism; and Dynamism proper.

Mechanism

The characteristic tendency of Mechanism, i.e. of

the mechanical theory, is to disregard all qualitative difference in natural phenomena and to emphasize their quantitative differences. That is to say, in this system the constituent matter of all corporeal beings is everywhere the same and is essentially homogeneous; all the forces animating it are of the same nature; they are simply modes of local motion. Furthermore, there is no internal principle of finality; in the world everything is determined by mechanical laws. To explain all cosmic phenomena, nothing is needed but mass and motion; so that all the differences observable between corporeal beings are merely differences in the amount of matter and motion. Mechanism appeals especially to the law of the correlation of forces in nature and of the mechanical equivalent of heat. Heat, we know, does work; but it consumes itself in proportion to its own activity. In like manner mechanical causes produce heat and grow weaker in proportion to the intensity of their effect. So it is with all corporeal energy; one form may be substituted for another, but the quantity of the new force will be always equivalent to the quantity of the force that has disappeared. Having in this way identified mechanical force with motion, the holders of this theory felt authorized to unify all forces and reduce them to local motion; and it was then an easy step to consider substance as homogeneous since its only use is to serve as a background for phenomena. Other arguments are drawn from chemistry, especially from the facts of isomerism, polymerism, and allotropism.

The mechanical theory is of ancient origin. Amongst its earliest partisans were Thales, Anaximander, and Heraclitus, whose chief concern was to prove the derivation of the world from one simple primitive substance. Empedocles, however, held out for four elements--air, earth, water, fire. But Democritus, and later Epicurus, suppressed this distinction between the elements, proclaimed the essential homogeneity of matter, and referred the variety of natural phenomena to differences of motion. After the time of Epicurus (270 B.C.), this system disappeared from philosophical thought for eighteen centuries. Restored by Descartes it soon won the favour of most scientists, and it is still dominant in scientific research. The Cartesian philosophy was a restatement of the two basic principles of the old theory, the homogeneity of nature and the reduction of all forces to terms of motion; but it got new vigour by contact with the natural sciences, espccially physics and chemistry; hence the name Atomism by which it is usually known. It should, however, be noted that there are two Atomisms, the one purely chemical, the other philosophical. According to the former all simple bodies are made up of atoms, i.e. of particles so small that no chemical force known to us can divide them, but which have all the properties of visible bodies. Atoms form groups of two or four or sometimes more; these small tenacious groups, known as chemical molecules coalesce in physical molecules, and from these in turn are built up the material bodies we see around us. The material body thus results from a progressive aggregation of molecules, and the very smallest portion of it that is endowed with the properties of the compound contains many atoms of various species, since by definition the compound results from the union of numerous elements. On this atomic theory, independent as such of all philosophical systems, was grafted during the last century that philosophical Atomism which, while ascribing to all atoms the same nature, differentiates them only by varying amounts of mass and motion.

Dynamism

Another explanation of the material world is offered by Dynamism. If Mechanism attributes extension to matter and complete passivity to corporeal substances, Dynamism sees in the world only simple forces, unextended, yet essentially active. There is nothing strange in the antithesis of these two systems. The Dynamism of Leibniz--it was he who propounded it--was but a reaction against the Mechanism of Descartes. To these two matrix-ideas of unextended, active forces the majority of Dynamists add the principle of actio in distans. They soon found out that points without extension can touch only by completely merging the one with the other, and on their own hypothesis the points in contact would amount to nothing more than a mathematical point which could never give us even the illusion of apparent extension. To avoid this pitfall, the Dynamists bethought them of considering all bodies as aggregates of force unextended indeed but separated by intervals from one another. Conceived by Leibniz, who held the monads to be dowered with all immanent activity, this system has been amended and modernized by Father Boscovich, Kant, Father Palmieri, Father Carbonelle, Hirn, and Father Leroy. On the whole it has found few supporters; scientists as a rule prefer the mechanical view. It would seem, however, that a reaction towards it has set in since the discovery of the radioactivity of matter. The property manifested by a considerable number of bodies of emitting at ordinary temperatures a seemingly inexhaustible quantity of electric rays suggests the idea that matter is a focus of energy which tends to diffuse itself in space. But in point of fact there are only two arguments in favour of Dynamism. One is drawn from the difficulties of grasping the concept of extension; the other from the fact that all we know of matter comes to us through its action on our organs of sense; hence the inference that force is the only thing existing apart from ourselves.

Hylomorphism

Between these two extremes stands the Scholastic theory, known as Hylomorphism, or theory of matter and form (húle, matter; morphé, form), also as the Aristotelean theory, and later as the Thomistic theory from the name of its principal defender in the Middle Ages. Aristotle (384-322 B.C.), who was its author, gave it a large place in his treatises on physics and on metaphysics. It was discussed during centuries in the Peripatetic and neo-Platonic schools and in the schools of Constantinople and Athens; but from the sixth century to the twelfth, though its essential principles survived, it was an insignificant factor in philosophic thought. An exception, however, must be made in favour of Avicenna in the East (980-1037) and of Averroes in Spain (1126-1198), both famous commentators on the Aristotelean encyclopedia. In the thirteenth century, the Golden Age of Scholasticism, the system was restored, thanks to a number of Latin translations, and its long-forgotten treasures were brought to light by daring prospectors, such as Alexander of Hales, St. Albertus Magnus, St. Thomas Aquinas, St. Bonaventure, and Henry of Ghent. During the fourteenth and fifteenth centuries the cosmological theory, and indeed the whole Scholastic system, suffered a decline which lasted till the nineteenth century, though during the interval it found ardent supporters in some of the religious orders. The restoration movement began about the middle of the nineteenth century with the works of Kleutgen (1811-1883); Sanseverino (1811-1865), and Liberatore (1810-1892); but it was especially owing to the impulse given it by the famous Encyclical of Leo XIII, "Æterni Patris" (1879), that Scholasticism regained its place of honour beside the great modern systems.

The Scholastic theory can be summed up in the following propositions:

* Bodies both elementary and compound have an essential

unity; they differ specifically, and are by their very nature extended;

* they possess powers or energies both passive and active which spring from their substantial nature and are inseparable from it;

* they have an immanent tendency toward certain special ends to be realized by the exercise of their native energies.

The basic principle of this cosmology is that of immanent finality. The corporeal world is a masterpiece of order and harmony. In spite of ceaseless transformations, every species of body, simple and composite alike, reappears again and again with its characteristic properties to further the well-being of the individual and of the universe as a whole. Now this constant and harmonious co-operation of innumerable causes acting under conditions the most diverse can only be explained, say the Scholastics, by admitting in the material agents themselves fixed and permanent principles of order. The universe must therefore be composed of specific natures, i.e. of beings which by their constitution and properties are really adapted to the ends they have to attain. Substance and its distinctive energies form a whole which is completely subordinated to its appointed destiny; so that if serious alterations, such as chemical combinations, succeed in affecting these properties and in marring the harmony that ought to exist between them and their substantial base, the being so affected must put on a new nature in harmony with its new state. There takes place, in other words, what the

Scholastics call a substantial transformation. But this implies that an essential portion of the original being must persist throughout the change, and be carried over into the final result, otherwise transformation would involve the annihilation of the first being and the production of the second out of nothing. On the other hand, if we hold that during the process the being in question does not lose its own specific difference in exchange for another, it would be illogical to speak of a transformation, since a change which preserves the substantial integrity of the being can never have as its result the production of a new being. All bodies, then, that are subject to such a change must contain, in spite of their unity, two constituent principles. The one is a specifying or determining principle whence spring the actuality and distinguishing marks of the body itself; and it is this principle which is born and dies at every step in the deeper transformations of matter. It is called substantial form. The other, the indeterminate complement of this, is the substratum which receives the various essential forms; and it is called first matter. These are the fundamental ideas in the Scholastic theory.

As a system it is not at every point the direct antithesis of the two other systems outlined above. It is true that, while Mechanism claims that the properties of bodies are nothing but local motion, the Scholastics admit the existence of qualities properly so called in all bodies, i.e. accidental determinations, fixed and destined for action. These properties are generated with the new substance; they cling to it indissolubly during its existence and they are its natural manifestation. But, on the other hand, the Scholastics concede to the mechanical theory that local motion plays a large part in the world, that it is the accompaniment and the measure of every exertion of material force. Hence they give Mechanism credit for assigning a quantitative value to the phenomena of nature by measuring the movement proportionate to each; while, on their side, they explain the activity at work in each case by taking into account the qualitative elements as well as the kinetic. Again, with the mechanical theory the Scholastic recognizes in every corporeal being an essential principle of passivity, of inertia, divisibility, and extension--in a word, of all the properties so highly prized by Mechanism; this principle is first matter. But the Scholastic theory adds a substantial form, i.e. a determining principle and a root-cause of the activities and peculiar tendencies displayed by cach individual body.

A similar partial agreement exists between Scholasticism and Dynamism. In the hylomorphic constitution of bodies the dynamic element has a preponderating role, represented by the substantial form; but since the corporeal being does not appear to be a source of energy pure and simple, the dynamic element is joined with first matter, of which passivity and extension are the natural outcome.

Dynamic Atomism

A fourth and last system is called Dynamic Atomism. The only real difference between it and Mechanism lies in the fact that it attributes to bodies forces distinct from local motion; but at the same time it maintains that they are purely mechanical forces. Matter, it asserts, is homogeneous and the atom incapable of transformation. This theory, proposed by Martin and Tongiorgi, and upheld nowadays by certain scientists, is a transition between the mechanical and the Scholastic system. Its partisans, in fact, are persuaded that a theory which denies the reality of qualitative energies inherent in matter and reduces them to local motion thereby makes the true explanation of natural phenomena impossible and hands over the universe to the whims of chance. Some Dynamists, therefore, to meet the obvious requirements of order in the world, seek in substance itself the reasons of its secondary principles of activity. But in this hypothesis it seems rather hard not to admit, as the Scholastics maintain, that diversity of substance is the only explanation of the constancy observed in the accidental differences of things.

The Final Cause of the Material Universe

The last problem that cosmology attempts to solve is that of the final cause. It is intimately bound up with that of the first cause. Materialists like Hackel and Büchner, who refuse to see in the universe a plan or a purpose, can assign no goal to cosmic evolution. In their opinion, just as the world, during its eternal past, has undergone countless variations in form, so during its eternal future it is destined to ceaseless change. The laws of mechanics, the chance encounter of atoms and molecules, the capricious play of natural forces following no preconceived aim, will determine the number, nature, and form of the states through which matter is to pass. Pantheists and all who identify God with matter share as a rule the same view. For them the condition of the world is but the fatal result of purposeless evolution; so that the world is its own end or rather is itself the term of its existence and activity.

Those who believe in the existence of a personal God can never admit that an all-wise being created without a purpose. And since a perfect and independent being can have no other than himself as the final aim of his action, it follows that the ultimate end of creation is to manifest the glory of the Creator, man being the intermediary, and, as it were, the high-priest of the material world. The welfare of man himself is the secondary purpose of creation. According to St. Thomas the world is a vast hierarchy of which inorganic matter is the base and man the summit. The mineral order ministers to the vegetable and this in turn to the animal, while man finds in all these the satisfaction of his needs and the adornment of his earthly life. Above all he finds in the material universe and in the service it renders him a means of rising to perfect happiness in the possession of God.

VI.
Metaphysics

Metaphysics is that portion of philosophy which treats of the most general and fundamental principles underlying all reality and all knowledge.

The Name

The word metaphysics is formed from the Greek meta ta phusika, a title which, about the year A.D. 70, was related by Andronicus of Rhodes to that collection of Aristotelean treatises which since then goes by the name of the "Metaphysics". Aristotle himself had referred to that portion of philosophy as "the theological science" (theologikê), because it culminated in the consideration of the nature of God, and as "first philosophy" (prôtê philosophia), both because it considered the first causes of things, and because, in his estimation, it is first in importance. The editor, however, overlooked both these titles, and, because he believed that that part of the Aristotelean corpus came naturally after the physical treatises, he entitled it "after the physics". This is the historical origin of the term. However, once the name was given, the commentators sought to find intrinsic reasons for its appropriateness. For instance, it was understood to mean "the science of the world beyond nature", that is, the science of the immaterial. Again, it was understood to refer to the chronological or pedagogical order among our philosophical studies, so that the "metaphysical sciences would mean, those which we study after having mastered the sciences which deal with the physical world" (St.

Thomas, "In Lib, Boeth. de Trin.", V, 1). In the widespread, though erroneous, use of the term in current popular literature, there is a remnant of the notion that metaphysical means ultraphysical: thus, "metaphysical healing" means healing by means of remedies which are not physical.

Definition

The term metaphysics, as used by one school of philosophers, is narrowed down to mean the science of mental phenomena and of the laws of mind, In this sense, it is employed, for instance, by Hamilton ("Lectures on Metaph.", Lect. VII) as synonymous with psychology. Hamilton holds that empirical psychology, or the phenomenology of mind, treats of the facts of consciousness, rational psychology, or the nomology of mind, treats of the laws of mental phenomena, and metaphysics, or inferential psychology, treats of the results derived from the study of the facts and laws of mind. This use of the term metaphysics is unfortunate because it rests on Descartes's false assumption that the method in metaphysics is subjective, in other words, that all the conclusions of metaphysics are based on the study of subjective, or mental, phenemona.

Taking a wider view of the scope and method of metaphysics, the followers of Aristotle and many who do not acknowledge Aristotle as a leader in philosophy define the science in terms of all reality, both objective and subjective. Here five forms of definition are offered which ultimately mean one and the same thing:

Metaphysics is the Science of Being as Being

This is Aristotle's definition (peri tou ontos ê on) — Met., VI, 1026 a, 31). In this definition metaphysics is placed in the genus "science". As a science, it has, in common with other sciences, this characteristic that it seeks a knowledge of things in their causes. What is peculiar to metaphysics is the difference "of being as being". In this phrase are combined at once the material object and the formal object of metaphysics. The material object is being, the whole world of reality, whether subjective or objective, possible or actual, abstract or concrete, immaterial or material, infinite or finite. Everything that exists comes within the scope of metaphysical inquiry. Other sciences are restricted to one or several departments of being: physics has its limited field of inquiry, mathematics is concerned only with those things which have quantity. Metaphysics knows no such restrictions. Its domain is all reality. For instance, the human soul and God, because they have neither colour nor weight, thermic nor electric properties, do not fall within the scope of the physicist's investigation; because they are devoid of quantity, they do not come within the field of inquiry of the mathematician. But, since they are beings, they do come within the domain of metaphysical investigation. The material object of metaphysics is, therefore, all being. As Aristotle says (Met., IV, 1004 a, 34): "It is the function of the philosopher to be able to investigate all things." Its formal object is also "being", or "beingness." The formal object of any science is that particular phase, quality, or aspect of things which interests that science in a specific way. Man, for instance, is the material object of psychology, ethics, sociology, anthropology, philology, and various other sciences. The formal object, however, of each of these is different. The formal object of psychology is mental phenomena and the subject of them; the formal object of ethics is man's relation to his ultimate destiny; that of sociology is man's relation to his fellow-men in institutions, laws customs, etc.; that of anthropology is the origin of man, distinction of races, etc.; that of philology is man's use of articulate speech. The formal object of the physical group generally is the so-called physical properties of bodies, such as light, sound, heat, molecular constitution, in general, etc. The formal object of the mathematical group is quantity; what interests the mathematician is not the colour, heat, etc., of an object, but its size or bulk. Similarly the metaphysician is interested in a specific way neither in the physical nor the mathematical qualities of things, but in their entity or beingness. If, then, physics is the science of being as affected by physical properties, and mathematics is the science of being as possessing quantity, metaphysics is the science of being as being. Since the material object of metaphysics is all being, the metaphysician is interested in everything that is or can be. Since the formal object of his study is, again, being, the point of view of metaphysics is different from that of the other sciences. The metaphysician studies all reality; still, the resulting science is not a summing up of the departmental sciences which deal with portions of reality, because his point of view is different from that of the student of the departmental sciences.

Metaphysics is the Science of Immaterial Being

The first science", says Aristotle (Met., VI, 1026 a, 16), "deals with things which are both separate (from matter) and unmovable". In this connection the scholastics (cf. St. Thomas, ibid.), distinguished two kinds of immaterial:
* immaterial quoad esse or immaterial beings, such as God and the human soul, which exist without matter;
* immaterial quoad conceptum, or concepts, such as substance, cause, quality, into the comprehension of which matter does not enter.

Metaphysics, in so far as it treats of immaterial beings, is called special metaphysics and is divided into rational psychology, which treats of the human soul, rational theology, which treats of the existence and attributes of God, and cosmology, which treats of the ultimate principles of the universe. Metaphysics in so far as it treats of immaterial concepts, of those general notions in which matter is not included, is called general metaphysics, or ontology, that is, the science of Being. Taking the term now in its widest sense, so as to include both general and special metaphysics, when we say that metaphysics is the science of the immaterial, we mean that whatever exists whether it is an immaterial being or a material being so long as it offers to our consideration immaterial concepts, such as substance or cause, is the object of metaphysical investigation. In this way, it becomes evident that this definition coincides with that given in the preceding paragraph.

Metaphysics is the Science of the Most Abstract Conceptions

All science, according to the scholastics deals with the abstract. The knowledge of the concrete individual objects of our experience, with their ever changing qualities and the particular individuating characteristics which make them to be individual (for instance, the knowledge of this tree, of that flower, of this particular animal or person) may be very useful knowledge, but it is not scientific. Scientific knowledge begins, when we abstract from what makes the thing to be individual, when we know it in the general principles that constitute it. The first degree of abstraction is found in the physical sciences which abstract merely from the particularizing, individuating characteristics, and consider the general laws or principles, of motion, light, heat, substantial change, etc. The mathematical sciences ascend higher in the scale of abstraction. They leave out of consideration not only the individuating qualities but also the physical qualities of things, and consider only quantity and its laws. The metaphysical sciences reach the highest point of abstraction. They prescind, or abstract, not only from those qualities physics and mathematics abstract from, but also leave out of consideration the determination of quantity. They consider only Being and its highest determinations, such as substance, cause, quality, action etc. "There is a science", says Aristotle (Met. IV 1003 a, 21) "which investigates being as being, and the attributes which belong to this in virtue of its own nature" (ta toutô huparchonta kath hauto). The objection therefore, that metaphysics is an abstract science would, in the estimation of the scholastics, militate not only against metaphysics but against all the other sciences as well. The peculiarity of metaphysics is not that it is abstract, but that it carries the process of abstraction farther than do the other sciences. This, however, does not make it to be unreal. On the contrary, what is left out of consideration in metaphysics namely individuating qualities, physical movement and specific quantity, derive whatever reality they have as conceptions from the concept, Being, which is the object of metaphysics. Metaphysics, in fact, is the most real of all the sciences precisely because by abstracting from everything else, it has centred, so to speak, its thought on Being, which is the source and root of reality everywhere else in the other sciences.

Metaphysics is the Science of the Most Universal Conceptions

This would follow from the consideration offered

in the preceding paragraph because, by a well known law of logic, the less the comprehension the greater the extension of a term or concept. The science which deals with the most abstract conceptions must, therefore, be the science of the most universal conceptions. Among our ideas the most universal are Being, and the determinations of it which are called transcendental, namely unity, truth, goodness, and beauty, each of which is coextensive with being itself, according to the formulas, "Every being is one", "Every being is true", etc. Next in universality come the highest determinations of Being in the supreme genera, substance and accident, or, if Being be analyzed in the order of metaphysical constitution, essence and existence, potency and actuality. Very high up in the scale of extension will be cause and effect. All these are included within the range of metaphysical inquiry, and are dealt with in every scholastic manual of metaphysics. "Being in its highest determinations" is, then, another way of describing the object of metaphysics. Where, however, shall we draw the line? What determinations are not highest? For instance, are space and time determinations of Being, which are general enough to be considered in metaphysics? The answer to these questions is to be decided according to the dictates of practical convenience. Many of the problems sometimes included in general metaphysics may conveniently be treated in special parts, such as cosmology and psychology.

Metaphysics is the Science of the First Principles

This definition also is given by Aristotle (Met. IV, 1003 a, 26). Every science is an inquiry into the causes and principles of things; this science inquires into the first principles and highest causes, not only in the order of existence, but also in the order of thought. It belongs, then, to metaphysics

* to inquire into the nature of cause and principle in general and to determine the meaning of the different kinds of causality, formal, material, efficient, and final:

* to investigate the first principles in the order of knowledge, and establish the validity, for instance, of the principles of identity and contradiction.

All these definitions are expressions of the Aristotelean doctrine that metaphysics, like physics and mathematics, is a science of reality, it being beyond the scope of metaphysics to inquire whether reality is, or is not, given in experience. This question, which is a fundamentally important one in modern philosophy was discussed by the scholastics in that portion of logic which they called critical, major logic, or applied logic, but which is now generally called epistemology (see LOGIC). Nowadays however, the epistemological problem, by a fatal mistake of method, is assigned to metaphysics, and the result is a confusion between the two branches of philosophy, viz. metaphysics and epistemology. In works like Fullerton's "System of Metaphysics" (New York, 1906) and Hodgson's "Metaphysics of Experience" (London, 1898) no attempt is made to separate the two.

The Rejection of Metaphysics

The Rejection of Metaphysics, by many schools of philosophy in modern times, is one of the most remarkable developments of post-Cartesian philosophy. A difference in the point of view leads to a very great divergence in the estimate based on metaphysical studies. On the one side we have the verdict that metaphysics is nothing but "transcendental moonshine", on the other, the opinion that it is "organized common sense", or "an unusually obstinate effort to think accurately". Materialism, naturally, objects to the claim of metaphysics to be a science of the immaterial. If nothing exists except matter, a science of the immaterial has no justification. Materialists, however, forget that the assertion, "Nothing exists except matter", is either a summing up of the individual experience of the materialist himself, meaning that he as never experienced anything except matter and manifestations of matter, and then the assertion is merely of biographical interest; or it is an affirmation regarding possible human experience, a declaration of the impossibility of immaterial existence, and in that sense it is a statement which in itself has a metaphysical import. Materialism is, in fact, a metaphysical theory of reality and is a contribution to the science which it professes to reject. Philosophical agnosticism, which is derived ultimately from Kant's doctrine of the unknowableness of noumenal reality (Ding an sich), rejects metaphysics on the ground that while the immaterial does, indeed, exist, it is unknown and must remain unknowable to the speculative reason. Kant maintained that all metaphysical reasoning, since it attempts by means of the speculative reason to go beyond experience, is doomed to failure, because the a priori forms which the understanding imposes on the empirical data of knowledge modify the quality of that knowledge by making it to be transcendental, but do not extend it beyond the realm of actual sense experience. The followers of Kant stigmatize as intellectual formalism the view that the speculative reason does actually attain ultra-empirical knowledge. This is the contention of the modernists and other Catholic writers who are more or less influenced by Kant. These decry rational metaphysics and offer as a substitute a metaphysics based on sentiment, vital activity, or some other non-rational foundation.

The answer to this line of thought is a denial of its fundamental tenet, the doctrine, namely, that the rational faculty cannot attain a knowledge of the essential or noumenal natures of things. Gratuitous assertion is often best refuted by categorical denial. The rejection of metaphysics by the materialist and the Kantian agnostic does not meet the full approval of the idealist. Instead of banishing metaphysics from the republic of the sciences, the idealist, having deprived it of its scientific character, elevates it to the rank of æsthetic preeminence side by side with poetry. He considers that it furnishes a point of view from which to contemplate the beauty, harmony, and value of those things which science merely explains. He holds that it is not the province of metaphysics to assign reasons or causes, but to furnish motives for action and enhance the value of reality. For him, its uplifting and regenerating function is entirely independent of its alleged ability to explain: he considers metaphysics to be, not an ontology, or science of reality, but a teleology, or application of the principle of purpose. That this is a function of metaphysics no one will deny. It is only one function, however, and unless the doctrine of final causes has its foundation in a doctrine of formal and efficient causes, teleological metaphysics is a castle in the air. Finally, the positivist, and the scientist whom the positivist has influenced, reject metaphysics because all our knowledge is confined to facts and the relations among facts. To attempt to go beyond facts and the succession or concomitance of facts is to essay the impossible. Causes, essences, and so forth, are terms which clothe in fictitious garb our ignorance of the real scientific explanation. The whole gist of positivism is contained in Hume's verdict that "it is impossible to go beyond experience". This psychological dictum is accepted by the philosophical positivist, as the death sentence of metaphysics. With the scientist, however, other considerations weigh more than the psychological argument. The scientist points to the present condition of metaphysics; he calls attention to the fact that, while the physical sciences have advanced by leaps and bounds, metaphysics is still grappling with the most fundamental problems and has not even settled the questions on which its very existence depends. The condition of metaphysics is, indeed, such as to invite the contempt and provoke the disdain of the scientist; the fault, however, may lie not so much in the claims of metaphysics as in the vagaries of the metaphysicians.

Relation of Metaphysics to Other Sciences

The consideration of the relation in which metaphysics stands, or ought to stand, to the other sciences should result in a refutation of the positivist contention that metaphysics is useless. In the first place, metaphysics is the natural co-ordinating science which crowns the unifying efforts of the other sciences. It accomplishes in the highest plane of knowledge that process of unification towards which the human mind tends irresistibly. Without it, the explanations and co-ordinations attained in the lower sciences would be, perhaps, satisfactory within the limits of those sciences, but would fail to meet the requirements of that unifying instinct which the mind tends to apply to knowledge in general. So long as the mind of the knower is one, it is impossible not to attempt to bring under the most general conceptions and principles the conclusions of the various sciences. That is the task of metaphysics. Whenever we look around among the contents of the mind and try to discover order and hierarchical arrangement among them, we are attempting a system of metaphysics. In the next place, the process of explanation which belongs to each of the lower sciences, if pursued far enough, brings us face to face with the demand for a metaphysical explanation. Thus, the chemical problem of atomic or proto-atomic constitution of bodies leads inevitably to the question, "What is matter?" The biological problem of the nature and origin of life brings us to the point where it is imperative to answer the query, "What is life?" The questions: "What is substance? What is a cause? What is quantity?" are additional examples of problems to which physics, mathematics, etc., finally lead. Indeed, the world of science is completely surrounded by the metaphysical world, and every path of investigation brings us to a highroad of inquiry which sooner or later crosses the border and leads us into metaphysics. When therefore, the scientist rejects metaphysics, he suppresses a natural and ineradicable tendency of the individual mind towards unification and, at the same time, he tries to put up in every highway and byway of his own science a barrier against further progress in the direction of rational explanation. Besides, the cultivation of the metaphysical habit of mind is productive of excellent results in the sphere of general culture. The faculty of appreciating principles as well as facts is a quality which cannot be absent from the mind without detriment to that symmetry of development wherein true culture consists. The scientist who objects to metaphysics, rightly condemns the metaphysician who disdains to consider facts. He himself, unless he cultivate the metaphysical powers of his mind, is in danger of reaching the point where he is incapable of appreciating principles. Both the empirical talent for ascertaining facts and the metaphysical grasp of principles and laws are necessary for the rounding out of man's mental powers, and there is no reason why they should not both be cultivated.

Relation of Metaphysics to Theology

The nature of metaphysics determines its essential and intimate relation to theology. Theology, it need hardly be said, derives its conclusions from premises which are revealed, and in so far as it does this it rises above all schools of philosophy or metaphysics. At the same time, it is a human science, and, as such, it must formulate its premises in exact terminology and must employ processes of human reasoning in attaining its conclusions. For this, it depends on metaphysics. Sometimes, indeed, as when it deals with the supernatural mysteries of faith, theology acknowledges that metaphysical conceptions are inadequate and metaphysical formulae incompetent to express the truths discussed. Nevertheless, if theology had no metaphysical formularies to rely upon, it could neither express its premises nor deduce its conclusion in a scientific manner. Again, theology relies on metaphysics to prove certain truths, called the preambula, which are not revealed but are nevertheless presupposed before revelation can be considered reasonable or possible. These truths are not the foundation on which we rest our supernatural faith. If they should fail, faith would not suffer, though theology should then be rebuilt on another foundation. Furthermore, metaphysics, as Aristotle pointed out, culminates in the discussion of the existence and nature of God. God is the object of theology. It is only natural, therefore, that metaphysics and theology should have many points of contact, and that the latter should rely on the former. Finally, since all truth is one, both in the source from which it is derived, and in the subject, the human mind, which it adorns, there must be a kinship between two sciences which, like theology and metaphysics, treat of the most important conceptions of the human mind. The difference in the manner of treatment, theology relying on revelation, and metaphysics on reason alone, does not affect the unity of purpose and the final harmony of the conclusions of the two sciences.

But, while theology thus derives assistance from metaphysics, there can be no doubt that metaphysics has derived advantages from its close association with theology. Pre-Christian philosophy failed to arrive at precise metaphysical determinations of the notions of substance and person. This defect was corrected in part by Origen, Clement, and Athanasius, and in part by their successors, the scholastics, the impulse in both cases being given to philosophical definition by the requirements of theological speculation concerning the Blessed Trinity. Pre-Christian philosophy failed to give a coherent, satisfactory account of the origin of the world: Plato's myths and Aristotle's doctrine of the eternity of matter could not long continue to satisfy the Christian mind. It was, once more, the Alexandrian School of Christian metaphysics that, by elaborating the Biblical conception of creation ex nihilo, gave an explanation of the origin of the universe which is satisfactory to the metaphysician as well as to the theologian. Finally, the Catholic doctrine of Transubstantiation, as discussed by the scholastics, gave occasion for a more definite and detailed determination of the metaphysical conception of accident in general and of quantity in particular.

The Method of Metaphysics

Among the objections most frequently urged against metaphysics, especially against scholastic metaphysics, is the unscientific character of its method. The metaphysician, we are told, pursues the a priori path of knowledge; he neglects or even condemns the use of the a posteriori empirical method which is employed with so much profit in the investigation of nature; he spins as Bacon says, the threads of his metaphysical fabric from the contents of his own mind, as the spider spins her web from the substance of her body, instead of gathering from every source in the world around him the materials for his study, and then working them up into metaphysical principles, as the bee gathers nectar from the flowers and elaborates it into honey. In order to clear up the misunderstanding which underlies this objection, it is necessary to remark that there are three kinds of method:

* the a priori, which, assuming certain self-evident postulates, maxims, and definitions to be true, proceeds deductively to draw conclusions implicated in those assumptions;
* The subjective a posteriori method, which, from an examination of the phenomena of consciousness builds up empirically, that is, inductively, conclusions based on those phenomena;
* the objective a posteriori method, which builds on the facts of experience in general in the same way as the subjective method builds on the facts of introspection.

The second method is pre-eminently the method of the Cartesians, who, like their leader, Descartes, strive to build the whole edifice of philosophy on the foundation furnished by reflection on our thought-processes: Cogito, ergo sum. It is also the method of the Kantians, who, rejecting the psychological basis of metaphysics as unsafe, build on the moral basis, the categorical imperative: their line of reasoning is "I ought, therefore I am free", etc. The third is the method of those who, rejecting the Aristotelean conceptions, essence, substance, cause etc., substitute so-called empirical conceptions of force mass, and so forth, under which they attempt to subsume in a system of empirico-critical metaphysics the conceptions peculiar to the various sciences. The first method is admittedly unscientific (in the popular sense of the word) and is adopted only by those philosophers who, like Plato, consider that the true source of philosophical knowledge is above us not in the world around and beneath us. If the formula universalia ante rem is taken in the exclusive sense, then we may not look to experience, but to intuition of a higher order of truth, for our metaphysical principles. It is a calumny which originated in ignorance perhaps, more than in prejudice, that the scholastics followed this a priori method in metaphysics. True, the scholastic philosopher often invokes such principles as "Agere sequitur esse" "Quidquid recipitur per modum recipientis recipitur" etc. and therefrom deduces metaphysical conclusions. If, however, we examine more closely, if we go back from the "Summa", or text-book, where the adage is quoted without proof, to the "Commentary on Aristotle" where the axiom is first introduced, we shall find that it is proved by inductive or empirical argument, and is therefore a legitimate premise from which to deduce other truths. In point of fact, the scholastics use a method which is at once a priori and a posteriori, and the latter both in the objective and the subjective sense. In their exposition of truth they naturally use the a priori, or deductive, method, In their investigation of truth they explore empirically both the world of mental phenomena within us, and the world of physical phenomena without us, for the purpose of building up inductively those metaphysical principles from which they proceed. It may be conceded that many of the later scholastics are too ready to invoke authority instead of investigating; it may be conceded, even, that the greatest of the scholastics were too dependent on books, especially on

Aristotle's works, for their knowledge of nature. But, in principle, at least, the best representatives of scholasticism recognized that in philosophy the argument from authority is the weakest argument, and if the circumstances in which they lived and wrote made it imperative on them to master the contents of Aristotle's writings on natural science, it must, nevertheless, be granted by every fair minded critic that in metaphysics at least they improved on the doctrines of the Stagyrite.

History of Metaphysics

The history of metaphysics naturally falls into the same divisions as the history of philosophy in general. In a brief outline of the course which metaphysical speculation has followed, it will be possible to consider only the principal stages, namely (1) Hindu philosophy, (2) Greek philosophy, (3) Early Christian philosophy, (4) Medieval philosophy, (5) Modern philosophy.

Hindu Philosophy

Of all the peoples of antiquity, the Hindus were the most successful in rising immediately from the mythological explanation of the universe to an explanation in terms of metaphysics. Apparently without passing through the intermediary stage of scientific explanation, they reached at once the heights of the metaphysical point of view. From polytheism or monotheism they proceeded very early to pantheism, and from that to a monistic metaphysical conception of reality. Their starting-point was the realization that man is born into a state of bondage and that his chief business in life is to deliver himself from that condition by means of knowledge. The knowledge, they taught, which avails most in the struggle for freedom is this: the world of sense phenomena is an illusion (mâya), all real things are identical in the one supreme substance, the soul is part of this real substance, and will ultimately return to the Whole. The real substance is, as Max Müller remarks, spoken of as a neuter, and in this doctrine "is contained in nuce a whole system of philosophy" ("Six Systems of Indian Philosophy", London, 1899, p. 60). The first, and most important of all truths, then, is that reality is one, and each of us is identical with the All: "That art thou" is the highest expression of self-knowledge, and the gate to all salutary truth. Thus, the Hindus, actuated by an ethical, or ascetic, motive, attained a metaphysical formula to which they reduced all reality.

Greek Philosophy

The first Greek philosophers were students of nature. They were actuated not by an ethical motive, but by a kind of scientific curiosity to know the origins of things. There was no metaphysician among the Ionians. Out of the problem of origins, however, the metaphysical problem was developed by the Eleatics and Heraclitus. These philosophers considered that the explanations of the Ionians — that the world originated from water or air — were too naïve, relied too much on the verdict of the senses. Consequently, they began to contrast the real truth which the mind (nous) sees, and the illusory truth (doxa) which appears to the senses. The Eleatics, on the one hand, asserted that the permanent element, which they called Being, alone exists, and that change, motion, and multiplicity are illusions. Heraclitus, on the other hand, reached the conclusion that what mind reveals is change, which alone is real, while permanency is only apparent, is, in fact, an illusion of the senses. Thus, these thinkers thrust into the foreground the problem of change and permanency. They themselves, were not, however, wholly free from the limitations which confined the earlier Ionians to a physical view of the problems of philosophy. They formulated metaphysical principles of reality, but both in the language which they used and in the mode of thought which they adopted, they seemed to be unable to rise above the consideration of matter and material principles. Nevertheless, they did immense service to metaphysics by bringing out clearly the problem of change.

Socrates was primarily an ethical teacher. Still, in laying the foundation of ethics he formulated a theory of knowledge which had immediate application to the problem of metaphysics. He taught that the contrast and apparently irreconcilable contradiction between the verdict of the mind and the deliverance of the senses disappear if we determine the scientific conditions of true knowledge. He held that these conditions are summed up in the processes of induction and definition. His conclusion, therefore, is, that out of the data of the senses, which are contingent and particular, we may form concepts, which are the elements of true scientific knowledge. He himself applied the doctrine to ethics.

Plato, the pupil of Socrates, carried the Socratic teaching into the region of metaphysics. If knowledge through concepts is the only true knowledge, it follows, says Plato, that the concept represents the only reality, and all the reality, in the object of our knowledge. The sum of the reality of a thing, is therefore the Idea. Corresponding to the internal, or psychological, world of our concepts is not only the world of our sense experience (the shadow-world of phenomena), but also the world of Ideas, of which our world of concepts is only a reflection, and the world of sense phenomena, a shadow merely. That which makes anything to be what it is, the essence, as we should call it, is the Idea of that thing existing in the world above us. In the "thing" itself, the phenomenon presented by the senses, there is a participation of the Idea, limited, disfigured and debased by union with a negative principle of limitation called matter. The metaphysical constituents of reality are, therefore, the Ideas as positive factors and this negative principle. From the Ideas comes all that is positive, permanent, intelligible, eternal in the world. From the negative principle come imperfection, negation, change, and liability to dissolution. Thus, profiting by the epistemological doctrines of Socrates, without losing sight of the antagonistic teachings of the Eleatics and of Heraclitus, Plato evolved his theory of Ideas as a metaphysical solution of the problem of change, which had a baffled his predecessors.

Aristotle also was a follower of Socrates. He was influenced, too, by the theory of Ideas advocated by his master, Plato. For, although he rejected that theory, he did so after a study of it which enabled him to view the problem of change in the light of metaphysical principles. Like Plato, he accepted the Socratic doctrine that the only true knowledge is knowledge of concepts. Like Plato, too, he inferred from this that the concept must represent the reality of a thing. But unlike Plato, he made at this point an important distinction. The reality, he taught, which the concept represents is in the thing which it constitutes, not as an Idea, but as an essence. He considers that the Platonic world of Ideas is a meaningless duplication of things: the world of essences is in, not above, nor beyond, the world of phenomena: there is, consequently, no contradiction between sense experience and intellectual knowledge: the metaphysical principles of things are known by abstraction from those individuating qualities, which are presented in sense knowledge; the knowledge of them is ultimately empirical, and not to be explained by an intuition which we are alleged to have enjoyed in a previous existence. In the essence of material things Aristotle further distinguished a twofold principle, namely the Form, which is the source of perfection, determinateness, activity and of all positive qualities, and the Matter, which is the source of imperfection, indetermination, passivity and of all the limitations and privations of a thing. Coming now to the borderland of metaphysics and physics, Aristotle defined the nature of causality, and distinguished four supreme kinds of cause, Material, Formal, Efficient and Final (see CAUSE). In addition to these contributions to the solution of the problem of change, which had, by historical evolution, become the central problem of metaphysics, Aristotle contributed to metaphysics a discussion of the nature of Being in general, and drew up a scheme of classification of things which is known as his system of Categories. He is least satisfactory in his treatment of the problem of the existence and nature of God, a question in which, as he himself admits, all metaphysical speculation culminates.

After the time of Aristotle, philosophy among the Greeks became centered in problems of human destiny and human conduct. The Stoics and the Epicureans, who were the chief representatives of this tendency, devoted attention to questions of metaphysics, only in so far as they considered that such questions may influence human happiness. As a result of this subordination of metaphysics to ethics, the pantheistic materialism of the Stoics and the materialistic monism of the Epicureans fall far short of the perfection which the doctrines of Plato and Aristotle attained. Contemporaneously with the Stoic and Epicurean schools, a new school of Platonism, generally called Neo-

Platonism, interested itself very much in problems of asceticism and mysticism, and, in connection with these problems, gave a new turn to the drift of metaphysical speculation. The Neo-Platonists, influenced by the monotheism of the Orientals, and, later by that of the Christians, took up the task of explaining how the manifold, diversified, imperfect world originated from the One, Unchangeable, and Perfect Being. They exaggerated the Platonic doctrine of matter to the point of maintaining that all evil, moral as well as physical, originates from a material source. At the same time, they ascribed to the spiritualized Ideas which they called daimones (spirits) all actuality, intelligence, and force in the whole universe. These intelligences were derived, they said, from the One by a process of emanation, which is akin to the "streaming forth" of light from the illuminating body. This system of metaphysics teaches, therefore, that the One, and intelligences derived from the One, are the only positive principles, while matter is the only negative principle of things. This is the system which was most widely accepted in pagan circles during the first centuries of the Christian era.

Early Christian Philosophy

The first heretics among the Christian thinkers were influenced in their philosophy by Neo-Platonism. For the most part, they adopted the Gnostic view that in the last appeal, the test of Christian truth is not the official teaching of the Church or the exoteric doctrine of the gospels, but a secret gnosis, a body of doctrine imparted by Christ to the chosen few. This body of doctrine was in reality a modified Neo-Platonism. Its most salient point was the theory that evil is not a creation of God but the work of the devil. The problem of evil thus came to occupy an important place in the philosophical systems of orthodox Christian thinkers down to the time of St. Augustine. Other problems, too, claimed special attention, notably the question of the origin of the universe. From the theological controversies concerning the mysteries of the Trinity and the Incarnation, arose the discussion of the meaning of nature, substance, and person. From all these sources sprang the Christian Neo-Platonism of the great Alexandrian School, which included Clement and Origen, and the later phase of Christian Platonism exemplified by St. Augustine. In the philosophy of St. Augustine we have the greatest constructive effort of the Christian mind during the Patristic Era. It is a philosophy which centres in the problems arising from the nature of God, and the nature and destiny of the human soul: The most crucial of these problems is that of the existence of evil. How can evil exist in a world created and governed by a God, Who is at once supremely good and all-powerful? Rejecting the Manichean theory that evil has an origin distinct from God, St. Augustine devotes all his efforts to showing, from the nature of evil, that it does not demand a direct efficient act on the part of God, but only a permissive act and that this toleration of evil is justified by the gradation of beings which results from the existence of imperfection, and which is essential to the harmony and variety of the universe in general. Another question which attains a good deal of prominence in St. Augustine's metaphysics is that of the origin of the world. All things, he teaches, were created at the beginning, material creatures as well as angels, and the subsequent appearance of plants, animals, and men in a chronological series is merely the development in time of those "seeds of things" which were implanted in the material world at the beginning. However, St. Augustine is careful to make an exception in the case of the individual human soul. He avoids the doctrine of preexistence which Origen had taught, and maintains that the individual soul originates at the same time as the body, although he is not prepared to decide definitively whether it originates by a distinct creative act or is derived from the souls of the child's parents.

Medieval Philosophy

The first scholastic philosophers devoted their attention to the discussion of logical problems arising out of the interpretation of the texts which were studied in the schools, such as Porphyry's "Isagoge", and Boethius's translation of portions of Aristotle's "Organon". From these discussions they passed to problems of psychology, but it was not until the end of the twelfth century, when Aristotle's metaphysical treatise and his works on psychology became accessible in Latin, that scholastic metaphysics rose to the dignity and proportions of a system. By way of exception, John the Scot (see ERIUGENA), as early as the first half of the ninth century, developed a highly wrought system of metaphysical speculation characterized by idealism, pantheism, and Neo-Platonic mysticism. In the eleventh century the school of Chartres, under the influence of Platonism, discussed in a metaphysical spirit the problems of the nature of reality and the origin of the universe.

The philosophy of the thirteenth century, represented by Alexander of Hales, St. Bonaventure, Roger Bacon, Albert the Great, St. Thomas, and Duns Scotus, accorded to metaphysics its place as the science which completes and crowns the efforts of the mind to attain a knowledge of things human and divine. It acknowledged the importance of the relation which metaphysics bears, on the one hand, to the other portions of philosophy, and, on the other hand, to the science of theology. Fundamentally Aristotelean in its conception of method and scope, the metaphysics of the golden age of scholasticism departed from Aristotle's teaching only to supply the defects and correct the faults which it detected in Aristotle's philosophy. Thus, it worked out on Aristotelean lines the problems of person and nature, substance and accident, cause and effect; it took up and carried to higher systematic development St. Augustine's reconciliation of evil with the goodness of God; it elaborated in detail the question of the nature of matter and the origin of the universe by God's creative act. At the same time, the metaphysics of the schools was obliged to face new problems which were thrust on the attention of the schoolmen by the exegetical and educational activity of the Arabians. Thus, it drew the line of distinction between Theism and Pantheism, discussed the question of fatalism and free will, and rejected the Arabian interpretation of Aristotle which jeopardized the doctrine of personal immortality. Towards the end of the scholastic period the appearance of the anti-metaphysicai nominalism of Occam, Durandus, and others had the effect of driving some of the later schoolmen to adopt an extreme a priorism in philosophy, which more than any other single cause contributed to bring about the antagonism between metaphysics and natural science, which marks the era of scientific discovery. This condition, though widespread, was not, however, universal. Men like Francisco Suárez and other great commentators continued down to the seventeenth century to present in their metaphysical treatises the best traditions of the scholasticism of the thirteenth century.

Modern Philosophy

At the beginning of the modern era we find a divergence of opinion concerning the scope and value of metaphysical speculation. On the one hand, Bacon, while himself retaining the name metaphysics to designate the science of the essential properties of bodies, is opposed to the metaphysical philosophy of the scholastics, and chiefly because that philosophy gave too much prominence to final causes and the study of the mind. On the other hand, Descartes, while declaring that "philosophy is a tree, which has metaphysics for its root", understands that the science of metaphysics is based exclusively on the data of the subjective consciousness. Spinoza accepts this restriction, implicitly at least, although his explicit main philosophy is ethical, namely to present that view of reality which will lead to the deliverance of the soul from bondage. Leibniz takes a more objective view. He tries to adopt a definition of reality which will reconcile the idealism of Plato with the results of scientific research, and he aims at harmonizing the materialism of the atomists with the spiritualism of the scholastics. Locke, by limiting all our knowledge to the two sources, sensation and reflection precludes the possibility of metaphysical speculation beyond the facts of experience and of consciousness. In fact, he maintains (Essay, IV, 8) that all metaphysical formulae, when they are not merely tautological and, therefore "trifling", have only a hypothetical formulae. This line of thought is taken up by Hume who emphatically declares that "it is impossible to go beyond experience", and by Mill, who maintains the hypothetical nature of all so-called necessary truth, mathematical as well as metaphysical. The same position is taken by the French sensists and materialists of the eighteenth century. Berkeley, although his professed aim was merely "to remove the mist and veil of words" which hindered the clear vision of the truth, passed from empirical immaterialism to a system of Platonic mysticism based on the metaphysical principle of causality.

Beginning with Kant, the question of the existence and scope of metaphysical science assumes a new phase. Metaphysics is now the science which claims to know things in themselves, and as Kant sees it, all post-Cartesian metaphysics is wrong in its starting-point. Kant holds that both the empiricist's rejection of metaphysics and the dogmatist's defence of it are wrong. The empiricist is wrong in asserting that we cannot go beyond experience: the dogmatist is wrong in affirming that we can go beyond experience by means of the theoretical reason. The practical reason, the faculty of moral consciousness, can alone take us beyond experience, and lead us to a knowledge of things in themselves. Practical reason, therefore, or the moral law, of which we are immediately conscious, is the only foundation of metaphysical science. The successors of Kant, namely, Fichte, Schelling, Hegel, Schopenhauer, and Von Hartmann, no matter how much they may differ in other respects, hold that the aim of metaphysics is to attain the ultra-empirical, or absolute, reality, whether this be called self (Fichte), the absolute of indifference (Schelling), the dynamic absolute, spirit or Idea (Hegel), the Will (Schopenhauer), or the Unconscious (Von Hartmann). Another group, the empiro-critics, who also acknowledge their dependence on Kant, assign to metaphysics the task of discussing the fundamental principles of knowledge by means of a critical examination of experience. Finally, there is among German philosophers of our own day an inclination to use the word metaphysics to designate any view of reality which, transcending the limits of the particular sciences, strives to combine and relate the results of those sciences in a synthetic formula (Weltanschauung).

English philosophers either define metaphysics in terms of mental phenomena, as Hamilton does, or restrict its field of inquiry to the problem of the value of knowledge, thus confounding it with epistemology, or go over to the Hegelian point of view that metaphysics is the science of the genesis and development of dynamic categories of reality. The evolutionist school, represented by Herbert Spencer, while they deny the cogency of "metaphysical reasonings", attempt a general synthesis of all truth under the evolutionist formula, which is in reality metaphysics in disguise. Their effort in this direction is, at least, an acknowledgement of the justice of the scholastic claim that there must be a hegemonic science which unifies and co-ordinates in an articulate system the conclusions of the various sciences, and which corrects the tendencies of those sciences towards a specialization which ends in fragmentation.

In so far as pragmatism, represented by James, Dewey, and Schiller, rejects absolute truth, it may be said to cut the ground from under metaphysics. Nevertheless, the latest phase of pragmatism, in which interest is shifted from the epistemological problem to the question, What is reality? is manifestly a step towards a rehabilitation of metaphysics. An analysis of reality is followed inevitably by an attempt to synthesize. The pragmatic synthesis, naturally, will have for its foundation neither the law of entity, as that being is being, nor the law of contradiction, that being is not not-being, but some principle of "value", akin to that of the Werth-Theorie of Lotze. Of quite special interest is the attempt on the part of Professor Royce to interpret reality in terms of loyalty. With the exception, then, of Trendelenburg's "Studies", and critical expositions of the text of Aristotle, the only philosophical literature in recent times which adopts the Aristotelean view of the nature and scope of metaphysics, is that which has come from the pens of the Neo-Scholastics. The Neo-Scholastic doctrine on at least one point in metaphysics is given in the following paragraph.

Doctrine of Being

The three ideas which are most important in any system of metaphysics are Being, Substance, and Cause. These have a decisive influence, and may be said to determine the character of a metaphysical system. Substance and Cause are treated elsewhere under separate titles. It will, therefore, be sufficient here to give the outlines of the scholastic doctrine of Being, which, indeed, is the most fundamental of the three, and decides, so to speak, beforehand, what the scholastics teach regarding Substance and Cause.

(1) Description of Being

Being cannot be defined (a) because a definition, according to the scholastic formula, must be "by proximate genus and ultimate difference", and Being, having the widest extension, cannot be included in any genus; (b) because a definition is the analysis of the comprehension of a Concept, and Being, having the least comprehension, is, as it were, indivisible in its comprehension, resisting all efforts to resolve it into simpler thought elements. Nevertheless, Being may be described. The word "Being", taken either as a participle or as a noun, has reference to the "act" of existence. Whatever exists, therefore, is a Being, whether it exists in the mind or outside the mind, whether it is actual or only potential, whether it requires a subject in which to inhere or is capable of subsisting without a subject of inherence. Thus, the broadest division of Being is into, notional, which exists only in the mind (ens rationis), and, real, which exists independently of the created world (ens reale). Real Being is further divided into the potential and the actual. This is an important point of scholastic teaching, which is sometimes overlooked in the exposition and still more in the criticism of scholasticism. For the scholastics, the real world extends far beyond the actual world of our experience or even of possible experience. Beyond the realm of actually existing things they see a world of tendencies, potencies, and possibilities which are truly real. The oak is really present, though only potentially, in the acorn; the painting is really, though only potentially, present, in the mind of the artist; and so, in every case, before the effect becomes actual it is really present in the cause in the measure in which its actual existence depends on the cause.

(2) Relation of Being to Other Concepts

Scholastic psychology, adopting Aristotle's doctrine that all our ideas are acquired through the senses, teaches that the first knowledge which we acquire is sense-knowledge. Out of the material furnished by the senses the mind elaborates ideas or concepts. The first of these ideas is the most general, the poorest in representative content, namely, the idea of "Being". In this sense, therefore, the idea of being, or, more correctly, perhaps, the idea of "something", is the first of all our ideas.

Turning, now, to the logical relation, how, ask the scholastics, is the idea of Being predicated of the lower or less general concepts, such as substance, accident, body, plant, tree, etc.? In the first place, the predicate being is never univocally affirmed of lower concepts, because it is not a genus. Neither is it predicated equivocally, because its meaning when predicated of substance, for example, is not entirely distinct from its meaning when predicated of accident. The predication is, therefore, analogical. What, then, is the relation, in comprehension, between Being and the lower concepts? It is obvious that the lower concept has greater comprehension than Being. But can it be said that the lower concept adds to the comprehension of Being? Manifestly, that is impossible, because if anything distinct from being is added to being, what is added is nothing, and there is no addition. The schoolmen, therefore, teach that the lower concept simply brings out in an explicit manner a mode or modes of being which are contained implicitly but not expressed in the higher concept, Being. The comprehension, for example, of substance is greater than that of being. Nevertheless it is not correct to say that, Substance = Being + a; for if a is distinct from the term Being, to which it is added, it must be Nothing. The truth, then, is that Substance brings out explicitly a mode (namely the power of existing without a subject in which to inhere) which is neither explicitly affirmed nor explicitly denied but only implicitly contained in the concept of Being.

(3) Being and Nothing

Being, therefore, has a comprehension, which, though it is the least of all comprehensions, is definite. It is not a bare, empty concept, and, therefore, equal to "nothing", as the Hegelians teach. This doctrine of the scholastics is the line of demarcation between Aristoteleanism on the one hand and Hegelianism on the other. Aristotle teaches that being has a definite comprehension, that, therefore, the fundamental law of thought as well as the basic principle of reality is the identity of Being with itself: Being = Being, A is A, or Everything is what it is. Hegel does not deny that this Aristotelean principle is true. He holds, however, that Being has an indeterminate comprehension, a comprehension which is dynamic or, as it were, fluent.

Therefore, he says, the principle Being = Being, A is A, or Everything is what it is, is only part of the truth, for Being is also equal to Nothing, A not-A, Everything is its opposite. The full truth is: Being is Becoming; no static or fixed formula is true; everything is constantly passing into its opposite. The consequences which follow from this fundamental divergence of doctrine regarding Being are enormous. Not the least serious of these is the Hegelian conclusion that all reality is dynamic and that God Himself is a process.

(4) Being, Existence, and Essence

As wisdom (sapientia) is that by which a person is wise (sapere), so essence (essentia) is that by which a thing is (esse). If one inquires what is the intrinsic cause of a person being wise, the answer is, wisdom; if one asks what is the intrinsic cause of existence, the answer is, essence. Essence, therefore, is that by which a thing is what it is. It is the source of all the necessary and universal properties of a thing, and is itself necessary, universal, eternal, and unchangeable. The act to which it refers is existence, in the same way as the act to which wisdom refers, is the exercise of wisdom (sapere). Both existence and essence are realities, the one in the entitative order, the other in the quiddative order. Of course, the existence of a notional being (ens rationis) is only notional; its essence, too, is notional. But in the case of a real, created Being, the existence is one kind of reality, a real actuality, and the essence is another kind of reality, a reality in the potential order. This doctrine of the real distinction between essence and existence in real created beings is not admitted by all scholastic philosophers. Francisco Suárez, for instance, and his school, hold that the distinction is only logical or notional; the Scotists, too, maintain that the distinction in question is less than real. The Thomists, on the contrary, hold that in God alone essence and existence are identical, that in all creatures there is a real distinction, because in creatures existence is participated, diversified, and multiplied, not by reason of itself but by reason of the essence which it actualizes. There is much controversy not only over the question itself, but also concerning the interpretation of the words of St. Thomas, although there seems very little ground for denying that in the work "De Ente et Essentia" the Angelic Doctor holds a real distinction between essence and existence.

(5) Transcendental Properties of Being

Equally extensive with the concept of Being are the concepts good, true, one, and beautiful. Every being is good, true, one, and beautiful, in the metaphysical sense, or as the scholastics expressed it, Being and Good are convertible, Being and True are convertible, etc. (Bonum et ens convertuntur, etc.). Goodness, in this sense, means the fullness of entity or perfection which belongs to each being in its own order of existence; truth means the correspondence of a thing to the idea of it, which exists in the Divine Mind; oneness means the lack of actual division, and beauty means that completeness, harmony or symmetry of essential nature which is only an aspect of truth and goodness. These properties, goodness, truth, oneness, and beauty, are called transcendental, because they transcend, or exceed in extension, all the lower classes into which reality is divided.

(6) The Categories

Real Being is divided (not by strict logical division, but by a process analogous to it) into Finite and Infinite. Finite Being is divided into the supreme genera, Substance and Accident. Accident is further divided into Quantity, Quality, Relation, Action, "Passion", Place, Time, Posture, and Habit (or possession). These nine Accidents, together with the supreme genus, substance, are the ten Aristotelean Categories into which, as supreme classes, all Being is divided.

VII.
The Existence of God

The Problem Stated
Formal Anti-theism

Had the Theist merely to face a blank Atheistic denial of God's existence, his task would he comparatively a light one. Formal dogmatic Atheism is self-refuting, and has never de facto won the reasoned assent of any considerable number of men. Nor can Polytheism, however easily it may take hold of the popular imagination, ever satisfy the mind of a philosopher. But there are several varieties of what may be described as virtual Atheism which cannot be dismissed so summarily.

There is the Agnosticism, for instance, of Herbert Spencer, which, while admitting the rational necessity of postulating the Absolute or Unconditioned behind the relative and conditioned objects of our knowledge declares that Absolute to be altogether unknowable, to be in fact the Unknowable, about which without being guilty of contradiction we can predicate nothing at all, except perhaps that It exists; and there are other types of Agnosticism.

Then again there is Pantheism in an almost endless variety of forms, all of which, however, may be logically reduced to the three following types:
* the purely materialistic, which, making matter the only reality, would explain life by mechanics and chemistry, reduce abstract thought to the level of an organic process deny any higher ultimate moral value to the Ten Commandments than to Newton's law of gravitation, and,

finally, identify God Himself with the universe thus interpreted;

* the purely idealistic, which, choosing the contrary alternative, would make mind the only reality, convert the material universe into an idea, and identify God with this all-embracing mind or idea, conceived as eternally evolving itself into passing phases or expressions of being and attaining self-consciousness in the souls of men; and

* the combined materialistic-idealistic, which tries to steer a middle course and without sacrificing mind to matter or matter to mind, would conceive the existing universe, with which God is identified, as some sort of "double-faced" single entity.

Thus to accomplish even the beginning of his task the Theist has to show, against Agnostics, that the knowledge of God attainable by rational inference — however inadequate and imperfect it may be — is as true and valid, as far as it goes, as any other piece of knowledge we possess; and against Pantheists that the God of reason is a supra-mundane personal God distinct both from matter and from the finite human mind — that neither we ourselves nor the earth we tread upon enter into the constitution of His being.

Types of Theism

But passing from views that are formally anti-theistic, it is found that among Theists themselves certain differences exist which tend to complicate the problem, and increase the difficulty of stating it briefly and clearly. Some of these differences are brief and clear.

Some of these differences are merely formal and accidental and do not affect the substance of the theistic thesis, but others are of substantial importance, as, for instance, whether we can validly establish the truth of God's existence by the same kind of rational inference (e.g. from effect to cause) as we employ in other departments of knowledge, or whether, in order to justify our belief in this truth, we must not rather rely on some transcendental principle or axiom, superior and antecedent to dialectical reasoning; or on immediate intuition; or on some moral, sentimental, emotional, or æsthetic instinct or perception, which is voluntary rather than intellectual.

Kant denied in the name of "pure reason" the inferential validity of the classical theistic proofs, while in the name of "practical reason" he postulated God's existence as an implicate of the moral law, and Kant's method has been followed or imitated by many Theists — by some who fully agree with him in rejecting the classical arguments; by others, who, without going so far, believe in the apologetical expediency of trying to persuade rather than convince men to be Theists. A moderate reaction against the too rigidly mathematical intellectualism of Descartes was to be welcomed, but the Kantian reaction by its excesses has injured the cause of Theism and helped forward the cause of anti-theistic philosophy. Herbert Spencer, as is well known, borrowed most of his arguments for Agnosticism from Hamilton and Mansel, who had popularized Kantian criticism in England, while in trying to improve on Kant's reconstructive transcendentalism, his German disciples (Fichte, Schelling, Hegel) drifted into Pantheism. Kant also helped to prepare the way for the total disparagement of human reason in relation to religious truth, which constitutes the negative side of Traditionalism, while the appeal of that system on the positive side to the common consent and tradition of mankind as the chief or sole criterion of truth and more especially of religious truth — its authority as a criterion being traced ultimately to a positive Divine revelation — is, like Kant's refuge in practical reason, merely an illogical attempt to escape from Agnosticism.

Again, though Ontologism — like that of Malebranche (d. 1715) — is older than Kant, its revival in the nineteenth century (by Gioberti, Rosmini, and others) has been inspired to some extent by Kantian influences. This system maintains that we have naturally some immediate consciousness, however dim at first, or some intuitive knowledge of God — not indeed that we see Him in His essence face to face but that we know Him in His relation to creatures by the same act of cognition — according to Rosmini, as we become conscious of being in general — and therefore that the truth of His existence is as much a datum of philosophy as is the abstract idea of being.

Finally, the philosophy of Modernism — about which there has recently been such a stir — is a somewhat complex medley of these various systems and tendencies; its main features as a system are:

* negatively, a thoroughgoing intellectual Agnosticism, and
* positively, the assertion of an immediate sense or experience of God as immanent in the life of the soul — an experience which is at first only subconscious, but which, when the requisite moral dispositions are present, becomes an object of conscious certainty.

Now all these varying types of Theism, in so far as they are opposed to the classical and traditional type, may be reduced to one or other of the two following propositions:

* that we have naturally an immediate consciousness or intuition of God's existence and may therefore dispense with any attempt to prove this truth inferentially;
* that, though we do not know this truth intuitively and cannot prove it inferentially in such a way as to satisfy the speculative reason, we can, nevertheless, and must conscientiously believe it on other than strictly intellectual grounds.

But an appeal to experience, not to mention other objections, is sufficient to negative the first proposition — and the second, which, as history has already made clear, is an illogical compromise with Agnosticism, is best refuted by a simple statement of the theistic Proofs. It is not the proofs that are found to be fallacious but the criticism which rejects them. It is true of course — and no Theist denies it — that for the proper intellectual appreciation of theistic proofs moral dispositions are required, and that moral consciousness, the æsthetic faculty, and whatever other powers or capacities belong to man's spiritual nature, constitute or supply so many data on which to base inferential proofs. But this is very different from holding that we possess any faculty or power which assures us of God's existence and which is independent of, and superior to, the intellectual laws that regulate our assent to truth in general — that in the religious sphere we can transcend those laws without confessing our belief in God to be irrational. It is also true that a mere barren intellectual assent to the truth of God's existence — and such an assent is conceivable — falls very far short of what religious assent ought to be; that what is taught in revealed religion about the worthlessness of faith uninformed by charity has its counterpart in natural religion; and that practical Theism, if it pretends to be adequate, must appeal not merely to the intellect but to the heart and conscience of mankind and be capable of winning the total allegiance of rational creatures. But here again we meet with exaggeration and confusion on the part of those Theists who would substitute for intellectual assent something that does not exclude but presupposes it and is only required to complement it. The truth and pertinency of these observations will be made clear by the following summary of the classical arguments for God's existence.

Theistic Proofs

The arguments for God's existence are variously

classified and entitled by different writers, but all agree in recognizing the distinction between a priori, or deductive, and a posteriori, or inductive reasoning in this connection. And while all admit the validity and sufficiency of the latter method, opinion is divided in regard to the former. Some maintain that a valid a priori proof (usually called the ontological) is available; others deny this completely; while some others maintain an attitude of compromise or neutrality. This difference, it should be observed, applies only to the question of proving God's actual existence; for, His self-existence being admitted, it is necessary to employ a priori or deductive inference in order to arrive at a knowledge of His nature and attributes, and as it is impossible to develop the arguments for His existence without some working notion of His nature, it is necessary to some extent to anticipate the deductive stage and combine the a priori with the a posteriori method. But no strictly a priori conclusion need be more than hypothetically assumed at this stage.

A Posteriori Argument

St. Thomas (Summa Theologica I:2:3; Cont. Gent., I, xiii) and after him many scholastic writers advance the five following arguments to prove the existence of God:

* Motion, i.e. the passing from power to act, as it takes place in the universe implies a first unmoved Mover (primum movens immobile), who is God; else we should postulate an infinite series of movers, which is

inconceivable.

* For the same reason efficient causes, as we see them operating in this world, imply the existence of a First Cause that is uncaused, i.e. that possesses in itself the sufficient reason for its existence; and this is God.

* The fact that contingent beings exist, i.e. beings whose non-existence is recognized as possible, implies the existence of a necessary being, who is God.

* The graduated perfections of being actually existing in the universe can be understood only by comparison with an absolute standard that is also actual, i.e., an infinitely perfect Being such as God.

* The wonderful order or evidence of intelligent design which the universe exhibits implies the existence of a supramundane Designer, who is no other than God Himself. To these many Theists add other arguments:

* the common consent of mankind (usually described by Catholic writers as the moral argument),

* from the internal witness of conscience to the supremacy of the moral law, and, therefore, to the existence of a supreme Lawgiver (this may be called the ethical argument, or

* from the existence and perception of beauty in the universe (the aesthetical argument).

One might go on, indeed, almost indefinitely multiplying and distinguishing arguments; but to do so would only lead to confusion.

The various arguments mentioned — and the same

is true of others that might be added — are not in reality distinct and independent arguments, but only so many partial statements of one and the same general argument, which is perhaps best described as the cosmological. This argument assumes the validity of the principle of causality or sufficient reason and, stated in its most comprehensive form, amounts to this: that it is impossible according to the laws of human thought to give any ultimate rational explanation of the phenomena of external experience and of internal consciousness — in other words to synthesize the data which the actual universe as a whole supplies (and this is the recognized aim of philosophy) — unless by admitting the existence of a self-sufficient and self-explanatory cause or ground of being and activity, to which all these phenomena may be ultimately referred.

It is, therefore, mainly a question of method and expediency what particular points one may select from the multitude available to illustrate and enforce the general a posteriori argument. For our purpose it will suffice to state as briefly as possible

* the general argument proving the self-existence of a First Cause,
* the special arguments proving the existence of an intelligent Designer and
* of a Supreme Moral Ruler, and
* the confirmatory argument from the general Consent of mankind.

(a) The general causality argument

We must start by assuming the objective certainty and validity of the principle of causality or sufficient reason — an assumption upon which the value of the physical sciences and of human knowledge generally is based. To question its objective certainty, as did Kant, and represent it as a mere mental a priori, or possessing only subjective validity, would open the door to subjectivism and universal scepticism. It is impossible to prove the principle of causality, just as it is impossible to prove the principle of contradiction; but it is not difficult to see that if the former is denied the latter may also be denied and the whole process of human reasoning declared fallacious. The principle states that whatever exists or happens must have a sufficient reason for its existence or occurrence either in itself or in something else; in other words that whatever does not exist of absolute necessity - whatever is not self-existent — cannot exist without a proportionate cause external to itself; and if this principle is valid when employed by the scientist to explain the phenomena of physics it must be equally valid when employed by the philosopher for the ultimate explanation of the universe as a whole. In the universe we observe that certain things are effects, i.e. they depend for their existence on other things, and these again on others; but, however far back we may extend this series of effects and dependent causes, we must, if human reason is to be satisfied, come ultimately to a cause that is not itself an effect, in other words to an uncaused cause or self-existent being which is the ground and cause of all being. And this conclusion, as thus stated, is virtually admitted by agnostics and Pantheists, all of whom are obliged to speak of an eternal something underlying the phenomenal universe, whether this something be the "Unknown", or the "Absolute", or the "Unconscious", or "Matter" itself, or the "Ego", or the "Idea" of being, or the "Will"; these are so many substitutes for the uncaused cause or self-existent being of Theism. What anti-Theists refuse to admit is not the existence of a First Cause in an indeterminate sense, but the existence of an intelligent and free First Cause, a personal God, distinct from the material universe and the human mind. But the very same reason that compels us to postulate a First Cause at all requires that this cause should be a free and intelligent being. The spiritual world of intellect and free will must be recognized by the sane philosopher to be as real as the world of matter; man knows that he has a spiritual nature and performs spiritual acts as clearly and as certainly as he knows that he has eyes to see with and ears to hear with; and the phenomena of man's spiritual nature can only be explained in one way — by attributing spirituality, i.e. intelligence and free will, to the First Cause, in other words by recognizing a personal God. For the cause in all cases must be proportionate to the effect, i.e. must contain somehow in itself every perfection of being that is realized in the effect.

The cogency of this argument becomes more apparent if account be taken of the fact that the human species had its origin at a comparatively late period in the history of the actual universe. There was a time when neither man nor any other living thing inhabited this globe of ours; and without pressing the point regarding the origin of life itself from inanimate matter or the evolution of man's body from lower organic types, it may be maintained with absolute confidence that no explanation of the origin of man's soul can be made out on evolutionary lines, and that recourse must be had to the creative power of a spiritual or personal First Cause. It might also be urged, as an inference from the physical theories commonly accepted by present-day scientists, that the actual organization of the material universe had a definite beginning in time. If it be true that the goal towards which physical evolution is tending is the uniform distribution of heat and other forms of energy, it would follow clearly that the existing process has not been going on from eternity; else the goal would have been reached long ago. And if the process had a beginning, how did it originate? If the primal mass was inert and uniform, it is impossible to conceive how motion and differentiation were introduced except from without, while if these are held to be coeval with matter, the cosmic process, which is ex hypothesi is temporal, would be eternal, unless it be granted that matter itself had a definite beginning in time.

But the argument, strictly speaking, is conclusive even if it be granted that the world may have existed from eternity, in the sense, that is, that, no matter how far back one may go, no point of time can be reached at which created being was not already in existence. In this sense Aristotle held matter to be eternal and St. Thomas, while denying the fact, admitted the possibility of its being so. But such relative eternity is nothing more in reality than infinite or indefinite temporal duration and is altogether different from the eternity we attribute to God. Hence to admit that the world might possibly be eternal in this sense implies no denial of the essentially finite and contingent character of its existence. On the contrary it helps to emphasize this truth, for the same relation of dependence upon a self-existing cause which is implied in the contingency of any single being is implied a fortiori in the existence of an infinite series of such beings, supposing such a series to be possible.

Nor can it be maintained with Pantheists that the world, whether of matter or of mind or of both, contains within itself the sufficient reason of its own existence. A self-existing world would exist of absolute necessity and would be infinite in every kind of perfection; but of nothing are we more certain than that the world as we know it, in its totality as well as in its parts, realizes only finite degrees of perfection. It is a mere contradiction in terms, however much one may try to cover up and conceal the contradiction by an ambiguous and confusing use of language, to predicate infinity of matter or of the human mind, and one or the other or both must be held by the Pantheist to be infinite. In other words the distinction between the finite and the infinite must be abolished and the principle of contradiction denied. This criticism applies to every variety of Pantheism strictly so called, while crude, materialistic Pantheism involves so many additional and more obvious absurdities that hardly any philosopher deserving of the name will be found to maintain it in our day. On the other hand, as regards idealistic Pantheism, which enjoys a considerable vogue in our day, it is to be observed in the first place that in many cases this is a tendency rather than a formal doctrine, that it is in fact nothing more than a confused and perverted form of Theism, based especially upon an exaggerated and one-sided view of Divine immanence (see below, iii). And this confusion works to the advantage of Pantheism by enabling it to make a specious appeal to the very arguments which justify Theism. Indeed the whole strength of the pantheistic position as against Atheism lies in what it holds in common with Theism; while, on the other hand, its weakness as a world theory becomes evident as soon as it diverges from or contradicts Theism. Whereas Theism, for example, safeguards such primary truths as the reality of human personality, freedom, and moral responsibility, Pantheism is obliged to sacrifice all these, to deny the existence of evil, whether physical or moral, to destroy the rational basis of religion, and, under pretence of making man his own God, to rob him of nearly all his plain, common sense convictions and of all his highest incentives to good conduct. The philosophy which leads to such results cannot but be radically unsound.

(b) The argument from design

The special argument based on the existence of order or design in the universe (also called the teleological argument) proves immediately the existence of a supramundane mind of vast intelligence, and ultimately the existence of God. This argument is capable of being developed at great length, but it must be stated here very briefly. It has always been a favourite argument both with philosophers and with popular apologists of Theism; and though, during the earlier excesses of enthusiasm for or against Darwinianism, it was often asserted or admitted that the evolutionary hypothesis had overthrown the teleological argument, it is now recognized that the very opposite is true, and that the evidences of design which the universe exhibits are not less but more impressive when viewed from the evolutionary standpoint. To begin with particular examples of adaptation which may be appealed to in countless number — the eye, for instance, as an organ of sight is a conspicuous embodiment of intelligent purpose — and not less but more so when viewed as the product of an evolutionary process rather than the immediate handiwork of the Creator. There is no option in such cases between the hypothesis of a directing intelligence and that of blind chance, and the absurdity of supposing that the eye originated suddenly by a single blind chance is augmented a thousand-fold by suggesting that it may be the product of a progressive series of such chances. "Natural selection", "survival of the fittest", and similar terms merely describe certain phases in the supposed process of evolution without helping the least to explain it; and as opposed to teleology they mean nothing more than blind chance. The eye is only one of the countless examples of adaptation to particular ends discernible in every part of the universe, inorganic as well as organic; for the atom as well as the cell contributes to the evidence available. Nor is the argument weakened by our inability in many cases to explain the particular purpose of certain structures or organisms. Our knowledge of nature is too limited to be made the measure of nature's entire design, while as against our ignorance of some particular purposes we are entitled to maintain the presumption that if intelligence is anywhere apparent it is dominant everywhere. Moreover, in our search for particular instances of design we must not overlook the evidence supplied by the harmonious unity of nature as a whole. The universe as we know it is a cosmos, a vastly complex system of correlated and interdependent parts, each subject to particular laws and all together subject to a common law or a combination of laws as the result of which the pursuit of particular ends is made to contribute in a marvellous way to the attainment of a common purpose; and it is simply inconceivable that this cosmic unity should be the product of chance or accident. If it be objected that there is another side to the picture, that the universe abounds in imperfections — maladjustments, failures, seemingly purposeless waste — the reply is not far to seek. For it is not maintained that the existing world is the best possible, and it is only on the supposition of its being so that the imperfections referred to would be excluded. Admitting without exaggerating their reality — admitting, that is, the existence of physical evil — there still remains a large balance on the side of order and harmony, and to account for this there is required not only an intelligent mind but one that is good and benevolent, though so far as this special argument goes this mind might conceivably be finite. To prove the infinity of the world's Designer it is necessary to fall back on the general argument already explained and on the deductive argument to be explained below by which infinity is inferred from self-existence. Finally, by way of direct reply to the problem suggested by the objection, it is to be observed that, to appreciate fully the evidence for design, we must, in addition to particular instances of adaptation and to the cosmic unity observable in the world of today, consider the historical continuity of nature throughout indefinite ages in the past and indefinite ages to come. We do not and cannot comprehend the full scope of nature's design, for it is not a static universe we have to study but a universe that is progressively unfolding itself and moving towards the fulfilment of an ultimate purpose under the guidance of a master mind. And towards that purpose the imperfect as well as the perfect — apparent evil and discord as well as obvious good order — may contribute in ways which we can but dimly discern. The well-balanced philosopher, who realizes his own limitations in the presence of nature's Designer, so far from claiming that every detail of that Designer's purpose should at present be plain to his inferior intelligence, will be content to await the final solution of enigmas which the hereafter promises to furnish.

(c) The argument from conscience

To Newman and others the argument from conscience, or the sense of moral responsibility, has seemed the most intimately persuasive of all the arguments for God's existence, while to it alone Kant allowed an absolute value. But this is not an independent argument, although, properly understood, it serves to emphasize a point in the general a posteriori proof which is calculated to appeal with particular force to many minds. It is not that conscience, as such, contains a direct revelation or intuition of God as the author of the moral law, but that, taking man's sense of moral responsibility as a phenomenon to be explained, no ultimate explanation can be given except by supposing the existence of a Superior and Lawgiver whom man is bound to obey. And just as the argument from design brings out prominently the attribute of intelligence, so the argument from conscience brings out the attribute of holiness in the First Cause and self-existent Personal Being with whom we must ultimately identify the Designer and the Lawgiver.

(d) The argument from universal consent

The confirmatory argument based on the consent of mankind may be stated briefly as follows: mankind as a whole has at all times and everywhere believed and continues to believe in the existence of some superior being or beings on whom the material world and man himself are dependent, and this fact cannot be accounted for except by admitting that this belief is true or at least contains a germ of truth. It is admitted of course that Polytheism, Dualism, Pantheism, and other forms of error and superstition have mingled with and disfigured this universal belief of mankind, but this does not destroy the force of the argument we are considering. For at least the germinal truth which consists in the recognition of some kind of deity is common to every form of religion and can therefore claim in its support the universal consent of mankind. And how can this consent be explained except as a result of the perception by the minds of men of the evidence for the existence of deity? It is too large a subject to be entered upon here — the discussion of the various theories that have been advanced to account in some other way for the origin and universality of religion; but it may safely be said that, abstracting from revelation, which need not be discussed at this stage, no other theory will stand the test of criticism. And, assuming that this is the best explanation philosophy has to offer, it may further be maintained that this consent of mankind tells ultimately in favour of Theism. For it is clear from history that religion is liable to degenerate, and has in many instances degenerated instead of progressing; and even if it be impossible to prove conclusively that Monotheism was the primitive historical religion, there is nevertheless a good deal of positive evidence adducible in support of this contention. And if this be the true reading of history, it is permissible to interpret the universality of religion as witnessing implicitly to the original truth which, however much obscured it may have become, in many cases could never be entirely obliterated. But even if the history of religion is to read as a record of progressive development one ought in all fairness, in accordance with a well-recognized principle, to seek its true meaning and significance not at the lowest but at the highest point of development; and it cannot be denied that Theism in the strict sense is the ultimate form which religion naturally tends to assume.

If there have been and are today atheistic philosophers who oppose the common belief of mankind, these are comparatively few and their dissent only serves to emphasize more strongly the consent of normal humanity. Their existence is an abnormality to be accounted for as such things usually are. Could it be claimed on their behalf, individually or collectively, that in ability, education, character, or life they excel the infinitely larger number of cultured men who adhere on conviction to what the race at large has believed, then indeed it might be admitted that their opposition would be somewhat formidable. But no such claim can be made; on the contrary, if a comparison were called for it would be easy to make out an overwhelming case for the other side. Or again, if it were true that the progress of knowledge had brought to light any new and serious difficulties against religion, there would, especially in view of the modern vogue of Agnosticism, be some reason for alarm as to the soundness of the traditional belief. But so far is this from being the case that in the words of Professor Huxley — an unsuspected witness — "not a solitary problem presents itself to the philosophical Theist at the present day which has not existed from the time that philosophers began to think out the logical grounds and the logical consequences of Theism" (Life and Letters of Ch. Darwin by F. Darwin, II, p. 203). Substantially the same arguments as are used today were employed by old-time sceptical Atheists in the effort to overthrow man's belief in the existence of the Divine, and the fact that this belief has withstood repeated assaults during so many ages in the past is the best guarantee of its permanency in the future. It is too firmly implanted in the depths of man's soul for little surface storms to uproot it.

A priori, or Ontological, Argument

This argument undertakes to deduce the existence of God from the idea of Him as the Infinite which is present to the human mind; but as already stated, theistic philosophers are not agreed as to the logical validity of this deduction.

As stated by St. Anselm, the argument runs thus: The idea of God as the Infinite means the greatest Being that can be thought of, but unless actual existence outside the mind is included in this idea, God would not be the greatest conceivable Being since a Being that exists both in the mind as an object of thought, and outside the mind or objectively, would be greater than a Being that exists in the mind only; therefore God exists not only in the mind but outside of it.

Descartes states the argument in a slightly different way as follows: Whatever is contained in a clear and distinct idea of a thing must be predicated of that thing; but a clear and distinct idea of an absolutely perfect Being contains the notion of actual existence; therefore since we have the idea of an absolutely perfect Being such a Being must really exist.

To mention a third form of statement, Leibniz would put the argument thus: God is at least possible since the concept of Him as the Infinite implies no contradiction; but if He is possible He must exist because the concept of Him involves existence. In St. Anselm's own day this argument was objected to by Gaunilo, who maintained as a reductio ad absurdum that were it valid one could prove by means of it the actual existence somewhere of an ideal island far surpassing in riches and delights the fabled Isles of the Blessed. But this criticism however smart it may seem is clearly unsound, for it overlooks the fact that the argument is not intended to apply to finite ideals but only to the strictly infinite; and if it is admitted that we possess a true idea of the infinite, and that this idea is not self-contradictory, it does not seem possible to find any flaw in the argument. Actual existence is certainly included in any true concept of the Infinite, and the person who admits that he has a concept of an Infinite Being cannot deny that he conceives it as actually existing. But the difficulty is with regard to this preliminary admission, which if challenged — as it is in fact challenged by Agnostics — requires to be justified by recurring to the a posteriori argument, i.e. to the inference by way of causality from contingency to self-existence and thence by way of deduction to infinity. Hence the great majority of scholastic philosophers have rejected the ontological argument as propounded by St. Anselm and Descartes nor as put forward by Leibniz does it escape the difficulty that has been stated.

As known Through Faith — ("the God of revelation")
Sacred Scriptures

Neither in the Old or New Testament do we find any elaborate argumentation devoted to proving that God exists. This truth is rather taken for granted, as being something, for example, that only the fool will deny in his heart [Psalm 13:1 and 52:1]; and argumentation, when resorted to, is directed chiefly against polytheism and idolatry. But in several passages we have a cursory appeal to some phase of the general cosmological argument: v.g. Psalm 18:1 and 93:5 sqq., Isaiah 41:26 sqq.; II Mach., vii, 28, etc.; and in some few others — Wis. xiii, 1-9; Rom., i, 18,20 — the argument is presented in a philosophical way, and men who reason rightly are held to be inexcusable for failing to recognize and worship the one true God, the Author and Ruler of the universe.

These two latter texts merit more than passing attention. Wis., xiii, 1-9 reads:

But all men are vain in whom there is not the knowledge of God: and who by these good things that are seen, could not understand him that is, neither by attending to the works have acknowledged who was the workman: but have imagined either the fire, or the wind, or the swift air or the circle of the stars, or the great water, or the sun and moon, to be the gods that rule the world. With whose beauty, if they, being delighted, took them to be gods: let them know how much the Lord of them is more beautiful than they: for the first author of beauty made all those things. Or if they admired their power and effects, let them understand by them that he that made them, is mightier than they: for by the greatness of the beauty, and of the creature, the creator of them may be seen, so as to be known thereby. But yet as to these they are less to be blamed. For they perhaps err, seeking God, and desirous to find him. For being conversant among his works, they search: and they are persuaded that the things are good which are seen. But then again they are not to be pardoned. For if they were able to know so much as to make a judgment of the world: how did they not more easily find out the Lord thereof?

Here it is clearly taught

* that the phenomenal or contingent world — the things that are seen — requires a cause distinct from and greater than itself or any of its elements;

* that this cause who is God is not unknowable, but is

known with certainty not only to exist but to possess in Himself, in a higher degree, whatever beauty, strength, or other perfections are realized in His works,

* that this conclusion is attainable by the right exercise of human reason, without reference to supernatural revelation, and that philosophers, therefore, who are able to interpret the world philosophically, are inexcusable for their ignorance of the true God, their failure, it is implied, being due rather to lack of good will than to the incapacity of the human mind.

Substantially the same doctrine is laid down more briefly by St. Paul in Romans 1:18-20:

For the wrath of God is revealed from heaven against all ungodliness and injustice of those men that detain the truth of God in injustice: because that which is known of God is manifest in them. For God hath manifested it unto them. For the invisible things of him, from the creation of the world, are clearly seen, being understood by the things that are made, his eternal power also and divinity: so that they are inexcusable.

It is to be observed that the pagans of whom St. Paul is speaking are not blamed for their ignorance of supernatural revelation and the Mosaic law, but for failing to preserve or for corrupting that knowledge of God and of man's duty towards Him which nature itself ought to have taught them. Indeed it is not pure ignorance as such they are blamed for, but that wilful shirking of truth which renders ignorance culpable. Even under the corruptions of paganism St. Paul recognized the indestructible permanency of germinal religious truth (cf. Romans 2:14-15).

It is clear from these passages that Agnosticism and Pantheism are condemned by revelation, while the validity of the general proof of God's existence given above is confirmed. It is also clear that the extreme form of Traditionalism, which would hold that no certain knowledge of God's existence or nature is attainable by human reason without the aid of supernatural revelation, is condemned.

Church Councils

What the author of Wisdom and St. Paul and after them the Fathers and theologians had constantly taught, has been solemnly defined by the Vatican Council. In the first place, as against Agnosticism and Traditionalism, the council teaches (cap. ii, De revelat.) that God, the first cause (principium) and last end of all things, can, from created things, be known with certainty by the natural light of human reason (Denz., 1785-old no. 1634) and in the corresponding canon (can. i, De revelat.) it anathematizes anyone who would say that the one true God our Creator and Lord, cannot, through the things that are made, be known with certainty by the natural light of human reason (Denz., 1806-old no. 1653).

As against Agnosticism this definition needs no explanation. As against Traditionalism, it is to be observed that the definition is directed only against the extreme form of that theory, as held by Lamennais and others according to which — taking human nature as it is — there would not, and could not, have been any true or certain knowledge of God, among men, had there not been at least a primitive supernatural revelation — in other words, natural religion as such is an impossibility. There is no reference to milder forms of Traditionalism which hold social tradition and education to be necessary for the development of man's rational powers, and consequently deny, for example, that an individual cut off from human society from his infancy, and left entirely to himself, could ever attain a certain knowledge of God, or any strictly rational knowledge at all. That is a psychological problem on which the council has nothing to say. Neither does it deny that even in case of the homo socialis a certain degree of education and culture may be required in order that he may, by independent reasoning, arrive at a knowledge of God; but it merely affirms the broad principle that by the proper use of their natural reasoning power, applied to the phenomena of the universe, men are able to know God with certainty.

In the next place, as against Pantheism, the council (cap. i, De Deo) teaches that God, "since He is one singular, altogether simple and incommutable spiritual substance, must be proclaimed to be really and essentially [re et essentia) distinct from the world most happy in and by Himself, and ineffably above and beyond all things, actual or possible, besides Himself" (Denzinger, 1782-old no.

1631); and in the corresponding canons (ii-iv, De Deo) anathema is pronounced against anyone who would say "that nothing exists but matter"; or "that the substance or essence of God and of all things is one and the same"; or "that finite things both corporeal and spiritual, or at least spiritual, have emanated from the Divine substance; or that the Divine essence by a manifestation or evolution of itself becomes all things; or that God is universal or indefinite being, which by determining itself constitutes the universe of things distinguished into genera, species and individuals" (Denzinger, 1802-4; old no. 1648).

These definitions are framed so as to cover and exclude every type of the pantheistic theory, and nobody will deny that they are in harmony with Scriptural teaching. The doctrine of creation, for example, than which none is more clearly taught or more frequently emphasized in Sacred Scripture, is radically opposed to Pantheism — creation as the sacred writers understand it being the voluntary act of a free agent bringing creatures into being out of nothingness.

The Knowability of God

It will be observed that neither the Scriptural texts we have quoted nor the conciliar decrees say that God's existence can be proved or demonstrated; they merely affirm that it can be known with certainty. Now one may, if one wishes, insist on the distinction between what is knowable and what is demonstrable, but in the present connection this distinction has little real import. It has never been claimed that God's existence can be proved mathematically, as a proposition in geometry is proved, and most Theists reject every form of the ontological or deductive proof. But if the term proof or demonstration may be, as it often is, applied to a posteriori or inductive inference, by means of which knowledge that is not innate or intuitive is acquired by the exercise of reason, then it cannot fairly be denied that Catholic teaching virtually asserts that God's existence can be proved. Certain knowledge of God is declared to be attainable "by the light of reason", i.e. of the reasoning faculty as such from or through "the things that are made"; and this clearly implies an inferential process such as in other connections men do not hesitate to call proof.

Hence it is fair to conclude that the Vatican Council, following Sacred Scripture, has virtually condemned the Scepticism which rejects the a posteriori proof. But it did not deal directly with Ontologism, although certain propositions of the Ontologists had already been condemned as unsafe (tuto tradi non posse) by a decree of the Holy Office (18 September, 1861), and among the propositions of Rosmini subsequently condemned (14 December, 1887) several reassert the ontologist principle. This condemnation by the Holy Office is quite sufficient to discredit Ontologism, regarding which it is enough to say here

* that, as already observed, experience contradicts the

assumption that the human mind has naturally or necessarily an immediate consciousness or intuition of the Divine,

* that such a theory obscures, and tends to do away with, the difference, on which St. Paul insists (1 Corinthians 13:12), between our earthly knowledge of God ("through a glass in a dark manner") and the vision of Him which the blessed in heaven enjoy ("face to face") and seems irreconcilable with the Catholic doctrine, defined by the Council of Vienne, that, to be capable of the face to face or intuitive vision of God, the human intellect needs to be endowed with a special supernatural light, the lumen gloriae and

* finally that, in so far as it is clearly intelligible, the theory goes dangerously near to Pantheism.

In the decree "Lamentabili" (3 July, 1907) and the Encyclical "Pascendi" (7 September, 1907), issued by Pope Pius X, the Catholic position is once more reaffirmed and theological Agnosticism condemned. In its bearing on our subject, this act of Church authority is merely a restatement of the teaching of St. Paul and of the Vatican Council, and a reassertion of the principle which has been always maintained, that God must be naturally knowable if faith in Him and His revelation is to be reasonable; and if a concrete example be needed to show how, of logical necessity, the substance of Christianity vanishes into thin air once the agnostic principle is adopted, one has only to point the finger at Modernism. Rational theism is a necessary logical basis for revealed religion; and that the natural knowledge of God and natural religion, which Catholic teaching holds to be possible, are not necessarily the result of grace, i.e. of a supernatural aid given directly by God Himself, follows from the condemnation by Clement XI of one of the propositions of Quesnel (prop. 41) in which the contrary is asserted (Denzinger, 1391; old no. 1256).

VIII.
The Nature and Attributes of God

Infinity of God

When we say that God is infinite, we mean that He is unlimited in every kind of perfection or that every conceivable perfection belongs to Him in the highest conceivable way. In a different sense we sometimes speak, for instance, of infinite time or space, meaning thereby time of such indefinite duration or space of such indefinite extension that we cannot assign any fixed limit to one or the other. Care should be taken not to confound these two essentially different meanings of the term. Time and space, being made up of parts in duration or extension, are essentially finite by comparison with God's infinity. Now we assert that God is infinitely perfect in the sense explained, and that His infinity is deducible from His self-existence. For a self-existent being, if limited at all, could be limited only by itself; to be limited by another would imply causal dependence on that other, which the very notion of self-existence excludes. But the self-existing cannot be conceived as limiting itself, in the sense of curtailing its perfection of being, without ceasing to be self-existing. Whatever it is, it is necessarily; its own essence is the sole reason or explanation of its existence, so that its manner of existence must be as unchangeable as its essence, and to suggest the possibility of an increase or diminution of perfection would be to suggest the absurdity of a changeable essence. It only remains, then, to say that whatever perfection is compatible with its essence is actually realized in a self-existing being; but as there is no conceivable perfection as such — that is, no expression of positive being as such — that is not compatible with the essence of the self-existent, it follows that the self-existent must be infinite in all perfection. For self-existence itself is absolute positive being and positive being cannot contradict, and cannot therefore limit, positive being.

This general, and admittedly very abstract, conclusion, as well as the reasoning which supports it, will be rendered more intelligible by a brief specific illustration of what it involves.

(i) When, in speaking of the Infinite, we attribute all conceivable perfections to Him, we must not forget that the predicates we employ to describe perfections derive their meaning and connotation in the first instance from their application to finite beings; and on reflection it is seen that we must distinguish between different kinds of perfections, and that we cannot without palpable contradiction attribute all the perfections of creatures in the same way to God. Some perfections are such that even in the abstract, they necessarily imply or connote finiteness of being or imperfection; while some others do not of themselves necessarily connote imperfection. To the first class belong all material perfections — extension, sensibility and the like — and certain spiritual perfections such as rationality (as distinct from simple intelligence); to the second class belong such perfections as being truth, goodness, intelligence, wisdom, justice, holiness, etc. Now while it cannot be said that God is infinitely extended, or that He feels or reasons in an infinite way, it can be said that He is infinitely good, intelligent, wise, just, holy, etc. — in other words, while perfections of the second class are attributed to God formally (i.e., without any change in the proper meaning of the predicates which express them), those of the first class can only be attributed to Him eminently and equivalently, (i.e. whatever positive being they express belongs to God as their cause in a much higher and more excellent way than to the creatures in which they formally exist). By means of this important distinction, which Agnostics reject or neglect, we are able to think and to speak of the Infinite without being guilty of contradiction, and the fact that men generally — even Agnostics themselves when off their guard — recognize and use the distinction, is the best proof that it is pertinent and well founded. Ultimately it is only another way of saying that, given an infinite cause and finite effects, whatever pure perfection is discovered in the effects must first exist in the cause (via affirmationis) and at the same time that whatever imperfection is discovered in the effects must be excluded from the cause (via negationis vel exclusionis). These two principles do not contradict, but only balance and correct one another.

(ii) Yet sometimes men are led by a natural tendency to think and speak of God as if He were a magnified creature — more especially a magnified man — and this is known as anthropomorphism. Thus God is said to see or hear, as if He had physical organs, or to be angry or sorry, as if subject to human passions: and this perfectly legitimate and more or less unavoidable use of metaphor is often quite unfairly alleged to prove that the strictly Infinite is unthinkable and unknowable, and that it is really a finite anthropomorphic God that men worship. But whatever truth there may be in this charge as applied to Polytheistic religions, or even to the Theistic beliefs of rude and uncultured minds, it is untrue and unjust when directed against philosophical Theism. The same reasons that justify and recommend the use of metaphorical language in other connections justify and recommended it here, but no Theist of average intelligence ever thinks of understanding literally the metaphors he applies, or hears applied by others, to God, any more than he means to speak literally when he calls a brave man a lion, or a cunning one a fox.

(iii) Finally it should be observed that, while predicating pure perfections literally both of God and of creatures, it is always understood that these predicates are true in an infinitely higher sense of God than of creatures, and that there is no thought of coordinating or classifying God with creatures. This is technically expressed by saying that all our knowledge of God is analogical, and that all predicates applied to God and to creatures are used analogically, not univocally. I may look at a portrait or at its living original, and say of either, with literal truth, that is a beautiful face. And this is an example of analogical predication. Beauty is literally and truly realized both in the portrait and its living original, and retains its proper meaning as applied to either;

there is sufficient likeness or analogy to justify literal predication but there is not that perfect likeness or identity between painted and living beauty which univocal predication would imply. And similarly in the case of God and creatures. What we contemplate directly is the portrait of Him painted, so to speak, by Himself on the canvas of the universe and exhibiting in a finite degree various perfections, which, without losing their proper meaning for us, are seen to be capable of being realized in an infinite degree; and our reason compels us to infer that they must be and are so realized in Him who is their ultimate cause.

Hence we admit, in conclusion, that our knowledge of the Infinite is inadequate, and necessarily so since our minds are only finite. But this is very different from the Agnostic contention that the Infinite is altogether unknowable, and that the statements of Theists regarding the nature and attributes of God are so many plain contradictions. It is only by ignoring the well-recognized rules of predication that have just been explained, and consequently by misunderstanding and misrepresenting the Theistic position, that Agnostics succeed in giving an air of superficial plausibility to their own philosophy of blank negation. Anyone who understands those rules, and has learned to think clearly, and trusts his own reason and common sense, will find it easy to meet and refute Agnostic arguments, most of which, in principle, have been anticipated in what precedes. Only one general observation need be made here — that the principles to which the

Agnostic philosopher must appeal in his attempt to invalidate religious knowledge would, if consistently applied, invalidate all human knowledge and lead to universal scepticism — and it is safe to say that, unless absolute scepticism becomes the philosophy of mankind, Agnosticism will never supplant religion.

Unity or Unicity of God

Obviously there can be only one infinite being, only one God. If several were to exist, none of them would really be infinite, for, to have plurality of natures at all, each should have some perfection not possessed by the others. This will be readily granted by every one who admits the infinity of God, and there is no need to delay in developing what is perfectly clear. It should be noted, however, that some Theistic philosophers prefer to deduce unicity from self-existence and infinity from both combined, and in a matter so very abstract it is not surprising that slight differences of opinion should arise. But we have followed what seems to us to be the simpler and clearer line of argument. The metaphysical argument by which unicity, as distinct from infinity, is deduced from self-existence seems to be very obscure, while on the other hand infinity, as distinct from unicity, seems to be clearly implied in self-existence as such. If the question, for example, be asked: Why may there not be several self-existing beings? The only satisfactory answer, as it seems to us, is this: Because a self-existent being as such is necessarily infinite, and there cannot be several infinities. The unity of God as the First Cause might also be inductively inferred from the unity of the universe as we know it; but as the suggestion might be made, and could not be disproved, that there may be another or even several universes of which we have no knowledge, this argument would not be absolutely conclusive.

Simplicity of God

God is a simple being or substance excluding every kind of composition, physical or metaphysical. Physical or real composition is either substantial or accidental — substantial, if the being in question consists of two or more substantial principles, forming parts of a composite whole, as man for example, consists of body and soul; accidental, if the being in question, although simple in its substance (as is the human soul), is capable of possessing accidental perfections (like the actual thoughts and volition of man's soul) not necessarily identical with its substance. Now it is clear that an infinite being cannot be substantially composite, for this would mean that infinity is made up of the union or addition of finite parts — a plain contradiction in terms. Nor can accidental composition be attributed to the infinite since even this would imply a capacity for increased perfection, which the very notion of the infinite excludes. There is not, therefore, and cannot be any physical or real composition in God.

Neither can there be that kind of composition which

is known as metaphysical, and which results from "the union of diverse concepts referring to the same real thing in such a way that none of them by itself signifies either explicitly or even implicitly the whole reality signified by their combination." Thus every actual contingent being is a metaphysical compound of essence and existence, and man in particular, according to the definition, is a compound of animal and rational. Essence as such in relation to a contingent being merely implies its conceivableness or possibility, and abstracts from actual existence; existence as such must be added before we can speak of the being as actual. But this distinction, with the composition it implies, cannot be applied to the self-existent or infinite being in whom essence and existence are completely identified. We say of a contingent being that it has a certain nature or essence, but of the self-existent we say that it is its own nature or essence. There is no composition therefore of essence and existence — or of potentiality and actuality in God, nor can the composition of genus and specific difference, implied for example in the definition of man as a rational animal, be attributed to Him. God cannot be classified or defined, as contingent beings are classified and defined; for there is no aspect of being in which He is perfectly similar to the finite, and consequently no genus in which He can be included. From this it follows that we cannot know God adequately in the way in which He knows Himself, but not, as the Agnostic contends, that our inadequate knowledge is not true as far as it goes. In speaking of a being who transcends the limitations of formal logical definition our propositions are an expression of real truth, provided that what we state is in itself intelligible and not self-contradictory; and there is nothing unintelligible or contradictory in what Theists predicate of God. It is true that no single predicate is adequate or exhaustive as a description of His infinite perfection, and that we need to employ a multitude of predicates, as if at first sight infinity could be reached by multiplication. But at the same time we recognize that this is not so — being repugnant to the Divine simplicity; and that while truth, goodness, wisdom, holiness and other attributes, as we conceive and define them express perfections that are formally distinct, yet as applied to God they are all ultimately identical in meaning and describe the same ultimate reality — the one infinitely perfect and simple being.

Divine Personality

When we say that God is a personal being we mean that He is intelligent and free and distinct from the created universe. Personality as such expresses perfection, and if human personality as such connotes imperfection, it must be remembered that, as in the case of similar predicates, this connotation is excluded when we attribute personality to God. It is principally by way of opposition to Pantheism that Divine personality is emphasized by the Theistic philosopher. Human personality, as we know it, is one of the primary data of consciousness, and it is one of those created perfections which must be realized formally (although only analogically) in the First Cause. But Pantheism would require us to deny the reality of any such perfection, whether in creatures or in the Creator, and this is one of the fundamental objections to any form of Pantheistic teaching. Regarding the mystery of the Trinity or three Divine Persons in God, which can be known only by revelation, it is enough to say here that properly understood the mystery contains no contradiction, but on the contrary adds much that is helpful to our inadequate knowledge of the infinite.

As Known Through Faith ("the God of revelation")

Reason, as we have seen, teaches that God is one simple and infinitely perfect spiritual substance or nature. Sacred Scripture and the Church teach the same. The creeds, for example, usually begin with a profession of faith in the one true God, Who is the Creator and Lord of heaven and earth, and is also, in the words of the Vatican Council, "omnipotent, eternal, immense, incomprehensible, infinite in intellect and will and in every perfection" (Sess. III, cap. i, De Deo). The best way in which we can describe the Divine nature is to say that it is infinitely perfect, or that God is the infinitely perfect Being; but we must always remember that even being itself, the most abstract and universal term we possess, is predicated of God and of creatures not univocally or identically, but only analogically. But other predicates, which, as applied to creatures, express certain specific determinations of being, are also used of God — analogically, if in themselves they express pure or unmixed perfection, but only metaphorically if they necessarily connote imperfection. Now of such predicates as applied to creatures we distinguish between those that are used in the concrete to denote being as such more or less determined (v.g., substance, spirit, etc.), and those that are used in the abstract or adjectively to denote determinations, or qualities, or attributes of being (v.g., good, goodness; intelligent, intelligence, etc.); and we find it useful to transfer this distinction to God, and to speak of the Divine nature or essence and Divine attributes being careful at the same time, by insisting on Divine simplicity, to avoid error or contradiction in its application. For, as applied to God, the distinction between nature and attributes, and between the attributes themselves, is merely logical and not real. The finite mind is not capable of comprehending the Infinite so as adequately to describe its essence by any single concept or term; but while using a multitude of terms, all of which are analogically true, we do not mean to imply that there is any kind of composition in God. Thus, as applied to creatures, goodness and justice, for example, are distinct from each other and from the nature or substance of the beings in whom they are found, and if finite limitations compel us to speak of such perfections in God as if they were similarly distinct, we know, nevertheless, and are ready, when needful, to explain, that this is not really so, but that all Divine attributes are really identical with one another and with the Divine essence.

The Divine attributes or perfections which may thus logically be distinguished are very numerous, and it would be a needless task to attempt to enumerate them fully. But among them some are recognized as being of fundamental importance, and to these in particular is the term attributes applied and special notice devoted by theologians — though there is no rigid agreement as to the number or classification of such attributes. As good a classification as any other is that based on the analogy of entitative and operative perfections in creatures — the former qualifying nature or essence as such and abstracting from activity, the latter referring especially to the activity of the nature in question. Another distinction is often made between physical, and moral or ethical, attributes — the former of themselves abstracting from, while the latter directly express, moral perfection. But without labouring with the question of classification, it will suffice to notice separately those attributes of leading importance that have not been already explained. Nothing need be added to what has been said above concerning self-existence, infinity, unity, and simplicity (which belong to the entitative class); but eternity, immensity, and immutability (also of the entitative class), together with the active attributes, whether physical or moral, connected with the Divine intellect and will, call for some explanation here.

Eternity

By saying that God is eternal we mean that in essence, life, and action He is altogether beyond temporal limits and relations. He has neither beginning, nor end, nor duration by way of sequence or succession of moments. There is no past or future for God — but only an eternal present. If we say that He was or that He acted, or that He will be or will act, we mean in strictness that He is or that He acts; and this truth is well expressed by Christ when He says (John 8:58 — A.V.): "Before Abraham was, I am." Eternity, therefore, as predicated of God, does not mean indefinite duration in time — a meaning in which the term is sometimes used in other connections — but it means the total exclusion of the finiteness which time implies. We are obliged to use negative language in describing it, but in itself eternity is a positive perfection, and as such may be best defined in the words of Boethius as being "interminabilis vitae tota simul et perfecta possessio," i.e. possession in full entirety and perfection of life without beginning, end, or succession.

The eternity of God is a corollary from His self-existence and infinity. Time being a measure of finite existence, the infinite must transcend it. God, it is true, coexists with time, as He coexists with creatures, but He does not exist in time, so as to be subject to temporal relations: His self-existence is timeless. Yet the positive perfection expressed by duration as such, i.e. persistence and permanence of being, belongs to God and is truly predicated of Him, as when He is spoken of, for example, as "Him that is, and that was and that is to come" (Revelation 1:4); but the strictly temporal connotation of such predicates must always be corrected by recalling the true notion of eternity.

Immensity and Ubiquity, or Omnipresence

Space, like time, is one of the measures of the finite, and as by the attribute of eternity, we describe God's transcendence of all temporal limitations, so by the attribute of immensity we express His transcendent relation to space. There is this difference, however, to be noted between eternity and immensity, that the positive aspect of the latter is more easily realized by us, and is sometimes spoken of, under the name of omnipresence, or ubiquity, as if it were a distinct attribute. Divine immensity means on the one hand that God is necessarily present everywhere in space as the immanent cause and sustainer of creatures, and on the other hand that He transcends the limitations of actual and possible space, and cannot be circumscribed or measured or divided by any spatial relations. To say that God is immense is only another way of saying that He is both immanent and transcendent in the sense already explained. As some one has metaphorically and paradoxically expressed it, "God's centre is everywhere, His circumference nowhere."

That God is not subject to spatial limitations

follows from His infinite simplicity; and that He is truly present in every place or thing — that He is omnipresent or ubiquitous — follows from the fact that He is the cause and ground of all reality. According to our finite manner of thinking we conceive this presence of God in things spatial as being primarily a presence of power and operation — immediate Divine efficiency being required to sustain created beings in existence and to enable them to act; but, as every kind of Divine action ad extra is really identical with the Divine nature or essence, it follows that God is really present everywhere in creation not merely per virtuten et operationem, but per essentiam. In other words God Himself, or the Divine nature, is in immediate contact with, or immanent in, every creature — conserving it in being and enabling it to act. But while insisting on this truth we must, if we would avoid contradiction, reject every form of the pantheistic hypothesis. While emphasizing Divine immanence we must not overlook Divine transcendence.

There is no lack of Scriptural or ecclesiastical testimonies asserting God's immensity and ubiquity. It is enough to refer for example to:

* Hebrews 1:3 and 4:12-13
* Acts 17:24-28
* Ephesians 1:23;
* Colossians 1:16-17,
* Psalm 139:7-12
* Job 12:10, etc.

Immutability

In God "there is no change, nor shadow of alteration" (James 1:17); "They [i.e. "the works of thy hands"] shall perish, but thou shalt continue: and they shall all grow old as a garment. And as a vesture shalt thou change them, and they shall be changed: but thou art the selfsame and thy years shall not fail" (Hebrews 1:10-12, Psalm 101:26-28. Cf. Malachi 3:6; Hebrews 13:8). These are some of the Scriptural texts which clearly teach Divine immutability or unchangeableness, and this attribute is likewise emphasized in church teaching, as by the Council of Nicaea against the Arians, who attributed mutability to the Logos (Denzinger, 54-old No. 18), and by the Vatican Council in its famous definition.

That the Divine nature is essentially immutable, or incapable of any internal change, is an obvious corollary from Divine infinity. Changeableness implies the capacity for increase or diminution of perfection, that is, it implies finiteness and imperfection. But God is infinitely perfect and is necessarily what He is. It is true that some attributes by which certain aspects of Divine perfection are described are hypothetical or relative, in the sense that they presuppose the contingent fact of creation: omnipresence, for example, presupposes the actual existence of spatial beings. But it is obvious that the mutability implied in this belongs to creatures, and not to the Creator; and it is a strange confusion of thought that has led some modern Theists — even professing Christians — to maintain that such attributes can be laid aside by God, and that the Logos in becoming incarnate actually did lay them aside, or at least ceased from their active exercise. But as creation itself did not affect the immutability of God, so neither did the incarnation of a Divine Person; whatever change was involved in either case took place solely in the created nature.

The Divine Attributes

The so-called active Divine attributes are best treated in connection with the Divine Intellect and Will — principles of Divine operation ad extra — to which they are all ultimately reducible.

Divine Knowledge
Description of the Divine Knowledge

That God is omniscient or possesses the most perfect knowledge of all things, follows from His infinite perfection. In the first place He knows and comprehends Himself fully and adequately, and in the next place He knows all created objects and comprehends their finite and contingent mode of being. Hence He knows them individually or singularly in their finite multiplicity, knows everything possible as well as actual; knows what is bad as well as what is good. Everything, in a word, which to our finite minds signifies perfection and completeness of knowledge may be predicated of Divine omniscience, and it is further to be observed that it is on Himself alone that God depends for His knowledge. To make Him in any way dependent on creatures for knowledge of created objects would destroy His infinite perfection and supremacy. Hence it is in His eternal, unchangeable, comprehensive knowledge of Himself or of His own infinite being that God knows creatures and their acts, whether there is question of what is actual or merely possible. Indeed, Divine knowledge itself is really identical with Divine essence, as are all the attributes and acts of God; but according to our finite modes of thought we feel the need of conceiving them distinctly and of representing the Divine essence as the medium or mirror in which the Divine intellect sees all truth. Moreover, although the act of Divine knowledge is infinitely simple in itself, we feel the need of further distinctions — not as regards the knowledge in itself, but as regards the multiplicity of finite objects which it embraces. Hence the universally recognized distinction between the knowledge of vision (scientia visionis) and that of simple intelligence (simplicis intelligentiae), and the famous controversy regarding the scientia media. We shall briefly explain this distinction and the chief difficulties involved in this controversy.

Distinctions in the Divine Knowledge

In classifying the objects of Divine omniscience the most obvious and fundamental distinction is between things that actually exist at any time, and those that are merely possible. And it is in reference to these two classes of objects that the distinction is made between knowledge "of vision" and "of simple intelligence"; the former referring to things actual, and the latter to the merely possible. This distinction might appear at first sight to be absolutely comprehensive and adequate to the purpose for which we introduce distinctions at all, but some difficulty is felt once the question is raised of God's knowledge of the acts of creatures endowed with free will. That God knows infallibly and from eternity what, for example, a certain man, in the exercise of free will, will do or actually does in any given circumstances, and what he might or would actually have done in different circumstances is beyond doubt — being a corollary from the eternal actuality of Divine knowledge. So to speak, God has not to wait on the contingent and temporal event of the man's free choice to know what the latter's action will be; He knows it from eternity. But the difficulty is: how, from our finite point of view, to interpret and explain the mysterious manner of God's knowledge of such events without at the same time sacrificing the free will of the creature.

The Dominican school has defended the view that the distinction between knowledge of "vision" and of "simple intelligence" is the only one we need or ought to employ in our effort to conceive and describe Divine omniscience, even in relation to the free acts of intelligent creatures. These acts, if they ever take place, are known or foreknown by God as if they were eternally actual — and this is admitted by all; otherwise they remain in the category of the merely possible — and this is what the Jesuit school denies, pointing for example to statements such as that of Christ regarding the people of Tyre and Sidon, who would have done penance had they received the same graces as the Jews (Matthew 11:21). This school therefore maintains that to the actual as such and the purely possible we must add another category of objects: hypothetical facts that may never become actual, but would become actual were certain conditions realized. The hypothetical truth of such facts, it is rightly contended, is more than mere possibility, yet less than actuality; and since God knows such facts in their hypothetical character there is good reason for introducing a distinction to cover them — and this is the scientia media. And it is clear that even acts that take place and as such fall finally under the knowledge of vision may be conceived as falling first under the knowledge of simple intelligence and then under the scientia media, the progressive formula would be:

* first, it is possible Peter would do so and so;
* second, Peter would do so and so, given certain conditions;
* third, Peter will do or does so and so.

Now, were it not for the differences that lie behind there would probably be no objection raised to scientia media, but the distinction itself is only the prelude to the real problem. Admitting that God knows from eternity the future free acts of creatures the question is how or in what way He knows them or rather how we are to conceive and explain by analogy the manner of the divine foreknowledge, which in itself is beyond our powers of comprehension? It is admitted that God knows them first as objects of the knowledge of simple intelligence; but does he know them also as objects of the scientia media, i.e. hypothetically and independently of any decree of His will, determining their actuality, or does He know them only in and through such decrees? The Dominican contention is that God's knowledge of future free acts depends on the decrees of His free will which predetermine their actuality by means of the praemotio physica. God knows, for example, that Peter will do so and so, because He has decreed from eternity so to move Peter's free will that the latter will infallibly, although freely, cooperate with, or consent to, the Divine premotion. In the case of good acts there is a physical and intrinsic connection between the motion given by God and the consent of Peter's will, while as regards morally bad acts, the immorality as such — which is a privation and not a positive entity — comes entirely from the created will.

The principal difficulties against this view are that in the first place it seems to do away with human free will, and in the next place to make God responsible for sin. Both consequences of course are denied by those who uphold it, but, making all due allowance for the mystery which shrouds the subject, it is difficult to see how the denial of free will is not logically involved in the theory of the praemotio physica, how the will can be said to consent freely to a motion which is conceived as predetermining consent; such explanations as are offered merely amount to the assertion that, after all, the human will is free. The other difficulty consists in the twofold fact that God is represented as giving the praemotio physica in the natural order for the act of will by which the sinner embraces evil, and that He withholds the supernatural praemotio or efficacious grace which is essentially required for the performance of a salutary act. The Jesuit school, on the other hand — with whom probably a majority of independent theologians agree — using the scientia media maintains that we ought to conceive God's knowledge of future free acts not as being dependent and consequent upon decrees of His will, but in its character as hypothetical knowledge or being antecedent to them. God knows in the scientia media what Peter would do if in given circumstances he were to receive a certain aid, and this before any absolute decree to give that aid is supposed. Thus there is no predetermination by the Divine of what the human will freely chooses; it is not because God foreknows (having foredecreed) a certain free act that that act takes place, but God foreknows it in the first instance because as a matter of fact it is going to take place; He knows it as a hypothetical objective fact before it becomes an object of the scientia visionis — or rather this is how, in order to safeguard human liberty, we must conceive Him as knowing it. It was thus, for example, that Christ knew what would have been the results of His ministry among the people of Tyre and Sidon. But one must be careful to avoid implying that God's knowledge is in any way dependent on creatures, as if He had, so to speak, to await the actual event in time before knowing infallibly what a free creature may choose to do. From eternity He knows, but does not predetermine the creature's choice. And if it be asked how we can conceive this knowledge to exist antecedently to and independently of some act of the Divine will, on which all things contingent depend, we can only say that the objective truth expressed by the hypothetical facts in question is somehow reflected in the Divine Essence, which is the mirror of all truth, and that in knowing Himself God knows these things also. Whichever way we turn we are bound ultimately to encounter a mystery, and, when there is a question of choosing between a theory which refers the mystery to God Himself and one which only saves the truth of human freedom by making free-will itself a mystery, most theologians naturally prefer the former alternative.

The Divine Will
Description of the Divine Will

(a) The highest perfections of creatures are reducible to functions of intellect and will, and, as these perfections are realized analogically in God, we naturally pass from considering Divine knowledge or intelligence to the study of Divine volition. The object of intellect as such is the true; the object of will as such, the good. In the case of God it is evident that His own infinite goodness is the primary and necessary object of His will, created goodness being but a secondary and contingent object. This is what the inspired writer means when he says: "The Lord hath made all things for himself" (Proverbs 16:4). The Divine will of course, like the Divine intellect, is really identical with the Divine Essence but according to our finite modes of thought we are obliged to speak of them as if they were distinct and, just as the Divine intellect cannot be dependent on created objects for its knowledge of them, neither can the Divine will be so dependent for its volition. Had no creature ever been created, God would have been the same self-sufficient being that He is, the Divine will as an appetitive faculty being satisfied with the infinite goodness of the Divine Essence itself. This is what the Vatican Council means by speaking of God as "most happy in and by Himself" — not that He does not truly wish and love the goodness of creatures, which is a participation of His own, but that He has no need of creatures and is in no way dependent on them for His bliss.

(b) Hence it follows that God possesses the perfection of free will in an infinitely eminent degree. That is to say, without any change in Himself or in His eternal act of volition, He freely chooses whether or not creatures shall exist and what manner of existence shall be theirs, and this choice or determination is an exercise of that dominion which free will (liberty of indifference) essentially expresses. In itself free will is an absolute and positive perfection, and as such is most fully realized in God. Yet we are obliged to describe Divine liberty as we have done relatively to its effects in creation, and, by way of negation, we must exclude the imperfections associated with free will in creatures. These imperfections may be reduced to two:

* potentiality and mutability as opposed to immutable pure act, and
* the power of choosing what is evil.

Only the second need be noticed here.

(c) When a free creature chooses what is evil, he does not choose it formally as such, but only sub specie boni, i.e., what his will really embraces is some aspect of goodness which he truly or falsely believes to be discoverable in the evil act. Moral evil ultimately consists in choosing some such fancied good which is known more or less clearly to be opposed to the Supreme Good, and it is obvious that only a finite being can be capable of such a choice. God necessarily loves Himself, who is the Supreme Good, and cannot wish anything that would be opposed to Himself. Yet He permits the sins of creatures, and it has always been considered one of the gravest problems of theism to explain why this is so. We cannot enter on the Problem here, but must content ourselves with a few brief observations.

* First, however difficult or even mysterious, may be the problem of moral evil for the theist, it is many times more difficult for every kind of anti-theist.
* Secondly, so far as we can judge the possibility of moral defection seems to be a natural limitation of created free

will, and can only be excluded supernaturally, and, even viewing the question from a purely rational standpoint, we are conscious on the whole that, whatever the final solution may be, it is better that God should have created free beings capable of sinning than that He should not have created free beings at all. Few men would resign the faculty of free will just to escape the danger of abusing it.

* Thirdly, some final solution, not at present apparent to our limited intelligence, may be expected on merely rational grounds from the infinite wisdom and justice of God, and supernatural revelation, which gives us glimpses of the Divine plan, goes a long way towards supplying a complete answer to the questions that most intimately concern us. The clearly perceived truth to be emphasized here is that sin is hateful to God and essentially opposed to His infinite holiness, and that the wilful discord which sin introduces into the harmony of the universe will somehow be set right in the end.

There is no need to delay in discussing mere physical as distinct from moral evil, and it is enough to remark that such evil is not merely permitted, but willed by God, not indeed in its character as evil, but as being, in such a universe as the present, a means towards good and in itself relatively good.

Distinctions in the Divine Will

As distinctions are made in the Divine knowledge, so also in the Divine will, and one of these latter is of sufficient importance to deserve a passing notice here. This is the distinction between the antecedent and consequent will, and its principal application is to the question of man's salvation. God, according to St. Paul (1 Timothy 2:4),"wills that all men be saved", and this is explained to be an antecedent will; that is to say, abstracting from circumstances and conditions which may interfere with the fulfilment of God's will (e.g., sin on man's part, natural order in the universe, etc.), He has a sincere wish that all men should attain supernatural salvation, and this will is so far efficacious that He provides and intends the necessary means of salvation for all — sufficient actual graces for those who are capable of cooperating with them and the Sacrament of Baptism for infants. On the other hand, the consequent will takes account of those circumstances and conditions and has reference to what God wills and executes in consequence of them. It is thus, for example, that He condemns the wicked to punishment after death and excludes unbaptized infants from the beatific vision.

Intellect and Will Providence, Predestination, and Reprobation)

Several attributes and several aspects of Divine activity partake both of an intellectual and a volitional character and must be treated from the combined point of view. Such are omnipotence, holiness, justice, blessedness, and so forth, but it is unnecessary to delay on such attributes which are self-explanatory. Some notice, on the other hand, must be devoted to providence and to the particular aspects of providence which we call predestination and reprobation; and with a brief treatment of these which are elsewhere fully treated this article will be concluded.

Providence

Providence may be defined as the scheme in the Divine mind by which all things treated are ordered and guided efficiently to a common end or purpose (ratio perductionis rerum in finem in mente divina existens). It includes an act of intellect and an act of will, in other words knowledge and power. And that there is such a thing as Divine Providence by which the entire universe is ruled clearly follows from the fact that God is the author of all things and that order and purpose must characterize the action of an intelligent creator. Nor is any truth more insistently proclaimed in revelation. What the author of Wisdom (xiv, 3) says of a particular thing is applicable to the universe as a whole: "But your providence, O Father, governs it", and no more beautiful illustration of the same truth has ever been given than that given by Christ Himself when He instances God's care for the birds of the air and the lilies of the field (Matthew 6:25 sq.). But to rational creatures God's providential care is extended in a very special way, yet not so as to do away with the utility and efficacy of prayer, whether for temporal or spiritual favours (Matthew 7:8), nor to disturb or override the efficiency of secondary causes. It is in and through secondary causes that providence ordinarily works, and no miracle, as a rule, is to be expected in answer to prayer

Predestination and Reprobation

Predestination and reprobation are those special parts of Divine Providence which deal specially with man's salvation or damnation in the present supernatural order. Predestination is the foreknowledge on the part of God of those who will de facto be saved and the preparation and bestowal of the means by which salvation is obtained, while reprobation is the foreknowledge of those who will de facto be damned and the permission of this eventuality by God. In both cases an act of the intellect (infallible foreknowledge), and an act of the will are supposed; but whereas in predestination the antecedent and consequent will is the same, in reprobation God wills consequently what He does not antecedently will at all but only permits, namely, the eternal punishment of the sinner.

Many controversies have arisen on the subject of predestination and reprobation, into which we cannot enter here. But we shall briefly summarize the leading points on which Catholic theologians have agreed and the points on which they differ.

First, that predestination exists, i.e. that God knows from eternity with infallible certainty who will be saved and that He wills from eternity to give them the graces by which salvation will be secured, is obvious from reason and is taught by Christ Himself (John 10:27), and by St. Paul (Romans 8:29, 30).

Second, while God has this infallible foreknowledge, we on our part cannot have an absolutely certain assurance that we are among the number of the predestined — unless indeed by means of a special Divine revelation such as we know from experience is rarely, if ever, given. This follows from the Tridentine condemnation of the teaching of the Reformers that we could and ought to believe with the certainty of faith in our own justification and election (Sess. VI, cap. ix, can. xiii-xv).

Third, the principal controverted point regarding predestination between Catholic theologians is concerned with its gratuity, and in order to understand the controversy it is necessary to distinguish between predestination in intention, i.e. as it is a mere act of knowledge and of purpose in the Divine mind, and in execution, i.e. as it means the actual bestowal of grace and of glory; and also between predestination in the adequate sense, as referring both to grace and to glory, and in the inadequate sense, as referring particularly to one's destination to glory, and abstracting from the grace by which glory is obtained.

Now,
* speaking of predestination in execution, all Catholic theologians maintain in opposition to Calvinists that it is not entirely gratuitous, but in the case of adults depends partly on the free mercy of God and partly on human cooperation; the actual bestowal of glory is at least partly a

reward of true merit.

* Speaking of predestination in intention and in the adequate sense, Catholic theologians agree that it is gratuitous; so understood it includes the first grace which cannot be merited by man.

* But if we speak of predestination in intention and in the inadequate sense, i.e. to glory in abstraction from grace, there is no longer unanimity of opinion. Most Thomists and several other theologians maintain that predestination in this sense is gratuitous, i.e. God first destines a man to glory antecedently to any foreseen merits, and consequently upon this decrees to give the efficacious grace by which it is obtained. Predestination to grace is the result of an entirely gratuitous predestination to glory, and with this is combined for those not included in the decree of election what is known as a negative reprobation. Other theologians maintain on the contrary that there is no such thing as negative reprobation, and that predestination to glory is not gratuitous but dependent on foreseen merits. The order of dependence, according to these theologians, is the same in predestination in intention as it is in predestination in execution, and as already stated, the bestowal of glory only follows upon actual merit in the case of adults. These have been the two prevailing opinions followed for the most part in the schools, but a third opinion, which is a somewhat subtle via media, has been put forward by certain other theologians and defended with great skill by such an authority as Billot. The gist of this view is that while negative reprobation must be rejected, gratuitous election to glory ante praevisa merita must be retained, and an effort is made to prove that these two may be logically separated, a possibility overlooked by the advocates of the first two opinions. Without entering into details here, it is enough to observe that the success of this subtle expedient is very questionable.

Fourth, as regards reprobation,

* all Catholic theologians are agreed that God foresees from eternity and permits the final defection of some, but that the decree of His will destining them to eternal damnation is not antecedent to but consequent upon foreknowledge of their sin and their death in the state of sin. The first part of this proposition is a simple corollary from Divine omniscience and supremacy, and the second part is directed against Calvinistic and Jansenistic teaching, according to which God expressly created some for the purpose of punishing them, or at least that subsequently to the fall of Adam, He leaves them in the state of damnation for the sake of exhibiting His wrath. Catholic teaching on this point reechoes 2 Peter 3:9, according to which God does not wish that any should perish but that all should return to penance, and it is the teaching implied in Christ's own description of the sentence that is to be pronounced on the damned, condemnation being grounded not on the antecedent will of God, but on the actual demerits of men themselves (e.g. Matthew 25:41).

* So-called negative reprobation, which is commonly

defended by those who maintain election to glory antecedently to foreseen merits, means that simultaneously with the predestination of the elect God either positively excludes the damned from the decree of election to glory or at least fails to include them in it, without, however, destining them to positive punishment except consequently on their foreseen demerits. It is this last qualification that distinguishes the doctrine of negative reprobation from Calvinistic and Jansenistic teaching, leaving room, for instance, for a condition of perfect natural happiness for those dying with only original sin on their souls. But, notwithstanding this difference, the doctrine ought to be rejected, for it is opposed very plainly to the teaching of St. Paul regarding the universality of God's will to save all (1 Timothy 2:4), and from a rational point of view it is difficult to reconcile with a worthy concept of Divine justice.

IX.
Relation of God to the Universe

Essential Dependence of the Universe on God (Creation and Conservation)

In developing the argument of the First Cause we have seen that the world is essentially dependent on God, and this dependence implies in the first place that God is the Creator of the world — the producer of its whole being or substance — and in the next place, supposing its production, that its continuance in being at every moment is due to His sustaining power. Creation means the total production of a being out of nothing, i.e. the bringing of a being into existence to replace absolute nonexistence, and the relation of Creator is the only conceivable relation in which the Infinite can stand to the finite. Pantheistic theories, which would represent the varieties of being in the universe as so many determinations or emanations or phases of one and the selfsame eternal reality — Substance according to Spinoza, Pure Ego according to Fichte, the Absolute according to Schelling, the Pure Idea or Logical Concept according to Hegel — simply bristle with contradictions, and involve, as has been stated already, a denial of the distinction between the finite and the infinite. And the relation of Creator to created remains the same even though the possibility of eternal creation be admitted; the Infinite must be the producer of the finite even though it be impossible to fix a time at which production may not already have taken place. For certain knowledge of the fact that created being, and time itself, had a definite beginning in the past we can afford to rely on revelation, although, as already stated, science suggests the same fact.

It is also clear that if the universe depends on God for its production, it must also depend on Him for its conservation or continuance in being; and this truth will perhaps be best presented by explaining the much talked-of principle of Divine immanence as corrected and counterbalanced by the equally important principle of Divine transcendence.

Divine Immanence and Transcendence

To Deists is attributed the view — or at least a tendency towards the view — that God, having created the universe, leaves it to pursue its own course according to fixed laws and ceases, so to speak, to take any further interest in, or responsibility for what may happen; and Divine immanence is urged, sometimes too strongly, in opposition to this view. God is immanent, or intimately present, in the universe because His power is required at every moment to sustain creatures in being and to concur with them in their activities. Conservation and concursus are so to speak, continuations of creative activity, and imply an equally intimate relation of God towards creatures, or rather an equally intimate and unceasing dependence of creatures on God. Whatever creatures are, they are by virtue of God's conserving power; whatever they do, they do by virtue of God's concursus. It is not, of course, denied that creatures are true causes and produce real effects; but they are only secondary causes, their efficiency is always dependent and derived; God as the First Cause is an ever active cooperator in their actions. This is true even of the free acts of an intelligent creature like man; only it should be added in this case that Divine responsibility ceases at the point where sin or moral evil enters in. Since sin as such, however, is an imperfection, no limitation is thus imposed on God's supremacy.

But lest insistence on Divine immanence should degenerate into Pantheism — and there is a tendency in this direction on the part of many modern writers — it is important at the same time to emphasize the truth of God's transcendence, to recall, in other words, what has been stated several times already, that God is one simple and infinitely perfect personal Being whose nature and action in their proper character as Divine infinitely transcend all possible modes of the finite, and cannot, without contradiction, be formally identified with these.

Possibility of the Supernatural

From a study of nature we have inferred the existence of God and deduced certain fundamental truths regarding His nature and attributes, and His relation to the created universe. And from these it is easy to deduce a further important truth, with a brief mention of which we may fittingly conclude this section. However wonderful we may consider the universe to be, we recognize that neither in its substance nor in the laws by which its order is maintained, in so far as unaided reason can come to know them, does it exhaust God's infinite power or perfectly reveal His nature. If then it be suggested that, to supplement what philosophy teaches of Himself and His purposes, God may be willing to favour rational creatures with an immediate personal revelation, in which He aids the natural powers of reason by confirming what they already know, and by imparting to them much that they could not otherwise know, it will be seen at once that this suggestion contains no impossibility. All that is required to realize it is that God should be able to communicate directly with the created mind, and that men should be able to recognize with sufficient certainty that the communication is really Divine — and that both of these conditions are capable of being fulfilled no Theist can logically deny. This being so it will follow further that knowledge so obtained, being guaranteed by the authority of Him who is infinite Truth, is the most certain and reliable knowledge we can possess.

X.
Theodicy

Etymologically considered theodicy (theos dike) signifies the justification of God. The term was introduced into philosophy by Leibniz, who, in 1710, published a work entitled: "Essais de Théodicée sur la bonté de Dieu, la liberté de l'homme et l'origine du mal". The purpose of the essay was to show that the evil in the world does not conflict with the goodness of God, that, indeed, notwithstanding its many evils, the world is the best of all possible worlds. The problem of evil has from earliest times engrossed the attention of philosophers. The well-known sceptic Pierre Bayle had denied in his "Dictionnaire historique et critique" the goodness and omnipotence of God on account of the sufferings experienced in this earthly life. The "Théodicée" of Leibniz was directed mainly against Bayle. Imitating the example of Leibniz other philosophers now called their treatises on the problem of evil "theodicies". As in a thorough treatment of the question the proofs both of the existence and of the attributes of God cannot be disregarded, our entire knowledge of God was gradually brought within the domain of theodicy. Thus theodicy came to be synonymous with natural theology (theologia naturalis) that is, the department of metaphysics which presents the positive proofs for the existence and attributes of God and solves the opposing difficulties. Theodicy, therefore, may be defined as the science which treats of God through the exercise of reason alone. It is a science because it systematically arranges the content of our knowledge about God and demonstrates, in the strict sense of the word, each of its propositions. But it appeals to nature as its only source of proof, whereas theology sets forth our knowledge of God as drawn from the sources of supernatural revelation.

The first and most important task of theodicy is to prove the existence of God. It is of course presupposed that the suprasensible can be known and that the limits of experience pure and immediate can be transcended. The justification of this assumption must be furnished by other branches of philosophy, e.g. criteriology and general metaphysics. The natural demonstrability of God's existence was always accepted by the majority of theists. Hume and Kant were the first to awaken in the minds of would-be theists serious doubt on this point. Not that these philosophers presented any solid reason against the long-tested arguments for the existence of God, but because in their systems a scientific proof of the existence of a supernatural being is impossible. New ways of establishing theism were now sought. The Scotch School led by Thomas Reid taught that the fact of the existence of God is accepted by us without knowledge of reasons but simply by a natural impulse. That God exists, this school said, is one of the chief metaphysical principles that we accept not because they are evident in themselves or because they can be proved, but because common sense obliges us to accept them. In Germany the School of Jacobi taught that our reason is able to perceive the suprasensible. Jacobi distinguished three faculties: sense, reason, and understanding. Just as sense has immediate perception of the material so has reason immediate perception of the immaterial, while the understanding brings these perceptions to our consciousness and unites them to one another (Stöckl, "Geschichte der neueren Philosophie", II, 82 sqq.). God's existence, then, cannot be proved--Jacobi, like Kant, rejected the absolute value of the principle of causality--it must be felt by the mind. In his "Emile", Jean-Jacques Rousseau asserted that when our understanding ponders over the existence of God it encounters nothing but contradictions; the impulses of our hearts, however, are of more value than the understanding, and these proclaim clearly to us the truths of natural religion, e.g., the existence of God, the immortality of the soul, etc. The same theory was advocated in Germany by Friedrich Schleiermacher (d. 1834), who assumed an inner religious sense by means of which we feel religious truths. According to Schleiermacher, religion consists solely in this inner perception, dogmatic doctrines are unessential (Stöckl, loc. cit., 199 sqq.). Nearly all Protestant theologians who have not yet sunken into atheism follow in Schleiermacher's footsteps. They generally teach that the existence of God cannot be demonstrated; certainty as to this truth is only furnished us by inner experience, feeling, and perception.

As is well known the Modernists also deny the demonstrability of the existence of God. According to them we can only know something of God by means of the vital immanence, that is, under favourable circumstances the need of the Divine dormant in our subconsciousness becomes conscious and arouses that religious feeling or experience in which God reveals himself to us. In condemnation of this view the oath against Modernism formulated by Pius X says: "Deum ... naturali rationis lumine per ea quae facta sunt, hoc est per visibilia creationis opera, tanquam causam per effectus certo cognosci adeoque demostrari etiam posse, profiteor", i.e., I declare that by the natural light of reason, God can be certainly known and therefore His existence demonstrated through the things that are made, i.e., through the visible works of creation, as the cause is known through its effects.

There is, however, still another class of philosophers who assert that the proofs for the existence of God present indeed a fairly large probability but no absolute certainty. A number of obscure points, they say, always remain. In order to overcome these difficulties there is necessary either an act of the will, a religious experience, or the discernment of the misery of the world without God, so that finally the heart makes the decision. This view is maintained, among others, by the noted English statesman Arthur Balfour in his widely read book "The Foundations of Belief" (1895). The opinions set forth in this work were adopted in France by Brunetiére, the editor of the "Revue des deux Mondes". Many orthodox Protestants express themselves in the same manner, as, for instance, Dr. E. Dennert, President of the Kepler Society, in his work "Ist Gott tot?" (Stuttgart, 1908). It must undoubtedly be conceded that for the perception of religious truths the mental attitude and temper are of great importance. As the questions here under consideration are those that penetrate deeply into practical life and their solution is not directly evident, the will is thus able to hold fast to the opposing difficulties and to prevent the understanding from attaining to quiet, objective reflection. But it is false to say that the understanding cannot eliminate every reasonable doubt as to the existence of God, or that a subjective inclination of the heart is a guarantee of the truth, even though there is no evidence that it is based on objective facts. This latter view would open the door wide to religious extravagance. It is not, therefore, an excess of intellectualism to demand that the truths which serve as the rational basis of faith shall be strictly proved.

Even in earlier times there were those who denied that the existence of God could be proved absolutely by the understanding alone, and took refuge in Revelation. In his "Summa contra Gentiles" (I, c. xii) St. Thomas refers to such reasoners. At a later date this opinion was championed by the Nominalists, William of Occam and Gabriel Biel, as well as by the Reformers; the Jansenists demanded the special aid of grace. In the nineteenth century the Traditionalists asserted that only when some vestiges of the original revelation reached man could he deduce with certainty the existence of God. Dr. J. Kuhn, formerly professor at Tüubingen declares that the clear recognition of the existence of God requires a pure soul unstained by sin. Ontologism went to the other extreme and asserted the immediate cognition of God. St. Anselm offered an a priori proof of the existence of God. This, however, has been always and rightly rejected by the majority of Catholic philosophers, notwithstanding the modifications by which Duns Scotus, Leibniz, and Descartes sought to save it (cf. Dr. Otto Paschen, "Der ontologische Gottesbeweis in der Scholastik", Aachen, 1903; M. Esser, "Der ontologische Gottesbeweis und seine Geschichte", Bonn, 1905). In regard to the various a posteriori proofs for the existence of God, see the separate article. A dispute has arisen of late as to whether there are a number of proofs of the existence of God or whether all are not merely parts of one and the same proof (cf. Dr. C. Braig, "Gottesbeweis oder Gottesbeweise?", Stuttgart, 1889). It is certain that we always reach God as the cause, the last ground of all existence, and thus constantly follow as a guide the principle of sufficient reason. But the starting point of the individual proofs varies. St. Thomas calls them aptly (Summ. theol., I, Q. ii, a.3) Viæ i.e., roads to the apprehension of God which all open on the same highway.

After demonstrating the existence of God, theodicy investigates the question as to His nature and attributes. The latter are in part absolute (quiescentia) in part relative (operativa). In the first class belong the infinity, unity, immutability, omnipresence, and eternity; to the second class the knowledge, volition, and action of God. The action of God includes the creation, maintenance, and government of the world, the co-operation of God with the activity of the creature, and the working of miracles. The understanding affords us abundant knowledge concerning God, although it allows us faint glimpses of His essential greatness and beauty. For one thing should not be forgotten, namely, that all our cognition of God is incomplete and analogous, that is, is formed from notions that we have deduced from created things. Hence it is that much remains obscure to us, as for instance, how God's immutability harmonizes with His freedom, and how He knows the future. But the inadequacy of our knowledge does not justify the assertion of the Agnostic that God is unknowable and that consequently any attempt such as theodicy makes to reason about His attributes and our relations to Him is foredoomed to failure.

XI.
Morality

It is necessary at the outset of this article to distinguish between morality and ethics, terms not seldom employed synonymously. Morality is antecedent to ethics: it denotes those concrete activities of which ethics is the science. It may be defined as human conduct in so far as it is freely subordinated to the ideal of what is right and fitting.

This ideal governing our free actions is common to the race. Though there is wide divergence as to theories of ethics, there is a fundamental agreement among men regarding the general lines of conduct desirable in public and private life. Thus Mr. Hobhouse has well said:

"The comparative study of ethics, which is apt in its earlier stages to impress the student with a bewildering sense of the diversity of moral judgments, ends rather by impressing them with a more fundamental and far-reaching uniformity. Through the greatest extent of time and space over which we have records, we find a recurrence of the common features of ordinary morality, which to my mind at least is not less impressive than the variations which also appear" (Morals in Evolution, I, i, n. 11).

Plainly this uniformity regards principles rather than their application. The actual rules of conduct differ widely. While reverence to parents may be universally acknowledged as obligatory, certain savage tribes believe that filial piety requires them to despatch their parents when the infirmities of old age appear. Yet making allowance for all such diversities, it may be said that the common voice of the race proclaims it to be right for a man to reverence his parents; to care and provide for his children; to be master of his lower appetites; to be honest and just in his dealings, even to his own damage; to show benevolence to his fellows in time of distress; to bear pain and misfortune with fortitude. And only within comparatively recent years has anyone been found to deny that beyond this a man is bound to honour God and to prefer his country's interests to his own. Thus, indeed, the advance of morality lies not so much in the discovery of new principles as in the better application of those already accepted, in the recognition of their true basis and their ultimate sanction, in the widening of the area within which they are held to bind, and in the removal of corruptions inconsistent with their observance.

The relation of morality to religion has been a subject of keen debate during the past century. In much recent ethical philosophy it is strenuously maintained that right moral action is altogether independent of religion. Such is the teaching alike of the Evolutionary, Positivist, and Idealist schools. And an active propaganda is being carried on with a view to the general substitution of this independent morality for morality based on the beliefs of Theism. On the other hand, the Church has ever affirmed that the two are essentially connected, and that apart from religion the observance of the moral law is impossible. This, indeed, follows as a necessary consequence from the Church's teaching as to the nature of morality. She admits that the moral law is knowable to reason: for the due regulation of our free actions, in which morality consists, is simply their right ordering with a view to the perfecting of our rational nature. But she insists that the law has its ultimate obligation in the will of the Creator by whom our nature was fashioned, and who imposes on us its right ordering as a duty; and that its ultimate sanction is the loss of God which its violation must entail. Further, among the duties which the moral law prescribes are some which are directly concerned with God Himself, and as such are of supreme importance. Where morality is divorced from religion, reason will, it is true, enable a man to recognize to a large extent the ideal to which his nature points. But much will be wanting. He will disregard some of his most essential duties. He will, further, be destitute of the strong motives for obedience to the law afforded by the sense of obligation to God and the knowledge of the tremendous sanction attached to its neglect — motives which experience has proved to be necessary as a safeguard against the influence of the passions. And, finally, his actions even if in accordance with the moral law, will be based not on the obligation imposed by the Divine will, but on considerations of human dignity and on the good of human society. Such motives, however, cannot present themselves as, strictly speaking, obligatory. But where the motive of obligation is wanting, acting lacks an element essential to true morality. Moreover, in this connection the Church insists upon the doctrine of original sin. She teaches that in our present state there is a certain obscurity in reason's vision of the moral law, together with a morbid craving for independence impelling us to transgress it, and a lack of complete control over the passions; and that by reason of this inherited taint, man, unless supported by Divine aid, is unable to observe the moral law for any length of time. Newman has admirably described from the psychological point of view this weakness in our grasp of the moral law:

"The sense of right and wrong . . . is so delicate, so fitful, so easily puzzled, obscured, perverted, so subtle in its argumentative methods, so impressionable by education, so biassed by pride and passion, so unsteady in its course, that in the struggle for existence amid the various exercises and triumphs of the human intellect, the sense is at once the highest of all teachers yet the least luminous" (Newman, "Letter to the Duke of Norfolk", in section on conscience).

In dealing with this subject, however, it is further necessary to take account of the historical argument. Various facts are adduced, which, it is alleged, show that morality is, in point of fact, capable of dissociation from religion. It is urged (1) that the most primitive peoples do not connect their religious beliefs with such moral code as they possess; and (2) that even where the moral consciousness and the religious system have reached a high degree of development, the spheres of religion and morality are sometimes regarded as separate. Thus the Greeks of classical times were in moral questions influenced rather by non-religious conceptions such as that of aidos (natural shame) than by fear of the gods; while one great religious system, namely Buddhism, explicitly taught the entire independence of the moral code from any belief in God. To these arguments we reply, first: that the savages of today are not primitives, but degenerates. It is the merest superstition to suppose that these degraded races can enlighten us as to what were the beliefs of man in his primitive state. It is among civilized races, where man has developed normally, that we must seek for knowledge as to what is natural to man. The evidence gathered from them is overwhelmingly in favour of the contention that human reason proclaims the essential dependence of morality on religious belief. In regard to the contrary instances alleged, it must be denied that the morality of the Greeks was unconnected with religion. Though they may not have realized that the laws prescribed by natural shame were derived from a divine command, they most certainly believed that their violation would be punished by the gods. As to Buddhist belief, a distinction must be drawn between the metaphysical teaching of the Buddha or of some of his disciples, and the practical interpretation of that teaching as expressed in the lives of the great mass of the adherents of the creed. It is only the Buddhist monks who have really followed the speculative teaching of their master on this point and have dissociated the moral law from belief in God. The mass of adherents never did so. Yet even the monks, while denying the existence of a personal God, regarded as a heretic any who disputed the existence of heaven and hell. Thus they too help to bear witness to the universal consensus that the moral law is based on supernatural sanctions. We may, however, readily admit that where the religious conceptions and the moral code were alike immature and inadequate, the relation between them was less clearly grasped in thought, and less intimate in practice, than it became when man found himself in possession of a fuller truth regarding them. A Greek or a Buddhist community may have preserved a certain healthiness of moral tone even though the religious obligation of the moral law was but obscurely felt, while ancestral precept and civic obligation were viewed as the preponderating motives. A broad distinction must be made between such cases and that of those nations which having once accepted the Christian faith with its clear profession of the connection between moral obligation and a Divine law, have subsequently repudiated this belief in favour of a purely natural morality. There is no parity between "Fore-Christians" and "After-Christians". The evidence at our command seems to establish as certain that it is impossible for these latter to return to the inadequate grounds of obligation which may sometimes suffice for nations still in the immaturity of their knowledge; and that for them the rejection of the religious sanction is invariably followed by a moral decay, leading rapidly to the corruptions of the most degraded periods of our history. We may see this wherever the great revolt from Christianity, which began in the eighteenth century, and which is so potent a factor today, has spread. It is naturally in France, where the revolt began, that the movement has attained its fullest development. There its effects are not disputed. The birth-rate has shrunk until the population, were it not for the immigration of Flemings and Italians, would be a diminishing quantity; Christian family life is disappearing; the number of divorces and of suicides multiplies annually; while one of the most ominous of all symptoms is the alarming increase of juvenile crime. But these effects are not peculiar to France. The movement away from Christianity has spread to certain sections of the population in the United States in England, in Germany, in Australia, countries providing in other respects a wide variety of circumstances. Wherever it is found, there in varying degrees he same results have followed, so that the unprejudiced observer can draw but one conclusion, namely: that for a nation which has attained maturity, morality is essentially dependent on the religious sanction, and that when this is rejected, morality will soon decay.

Granting religion to be the essential basis of moral action, we may further inquire what are the chief conditions requisite for the growth and development of morality in the individual and in the community. Three such may be singled out as of primary moment, namely: (1) a right education of the young, (2) a healthy public opinion, (3) sound legislation. It will be unnecessary for us to do more than touch in the briefest manner on these points.

    (1) Under education we include the early training of the home as well as the subsequent years of school life. The

family is the true school of morality, a school which nothing can replace. There the child is taught obedience, truthfulness, self-restraint, and the other primary virtues. The obligation to practise them is impressed upon him by those whose claim on him he at once recognizes, and whose word he does not dream of doubting; while the observance of the precept is made easy by the affection which unites him with those who impose it. It is, therefore, with reason that the Church has ever declared divorce to be fatal to the truest interests of a nation. Where divorce is frequent, family life in its higher form disappears and with it perishes the foundation of a nation's morality. Similarly the Church maintains, that during the years of school life, the moral and religious atmosphere is of vital importance, and that apart from this the possession of intellectual culture is a danger rather than a safeguard.

(2) It is hardly necessary to do more than call attention to the necessity of a sound public opinion. The great mass of men have neither opportunity nor leisure to determine a standard of morals for themselves. They accept that which prevails around them. If it is high, they will not question it. If it is low, they will aim no higher. When the nations were Catholic, public opinion was predominantly swayed by the teaching of the Church. In these days it is largely formed by the press; and since the press as a whole views morality apart from religion, the standard proposed is inevitably very different from what the Church would desiderate. Hence the immense importance of a Catholic

press, which even in a non-Catholic environment will keep a true view before the minds of those who recognize the Church's authority. But public opinion is also largely influenced by voluntary associations of one form or another; and of recent years immense work has been done by Catholics in organizing associations with this purpose, the most notable instance being the German Volksverein.

(3) It may be said with truth that the greater part of a nation's legislation affects its morality in some way or other. This is of course manifestly the case with all laws connected with the family or with education; and with those, which like the laws regarding the drink traffic and the restriction of bad literature, have the public morals for their immediate object. But it is also true of all legislation which deals with the circumstances of the lives of the people. Laws, for instance, determining the conditions of labour and protecting the poor from the hands of the usurer, promote morality, for they save men from that degradation and despair in which moral life is practically impossible. It is thus evident how necessary it is, that in all such questions the Church should in every country have a definitely formed opinion and should make her voice heard.

XII.
Ethics

Many writers regard ethics (Gr. ethike) as any scientific treatment of the moral order and divide it into theological, or Christian, ethics (moral theology) and philosophical ethics (moral philosophy). What is usually understood by ethics, however, is philosophical ethics, or moral philosophy, and in this sense the present article will treat the subject. Moral philosophy is a division of practical philosophy. Theoretical, or speculative, philosophy has to do with being, or with the order of things not dependent on reason, and its object is to obtain by the natural light of reason a knowledge of this order in its ultimate causes. Practical philosophy, on the other hand, concerns itself with what ought to be, or with the order of acts which are human and which therefore depend upon our reason. It is also divided into logic and ethics. The former rightly orders the intellectual activities and teaches the proper method in the acquirement of truth, while the latter directs the activities of the will; the object of the former is the true; that of the latter is the good. Hence ethics may be defined as the science of the moral rectitude of human acts in accordance with the first principles of natural reason. Logic and ethics are normative and practical sciences, because they prescribe norms or rules for human activities and show how, according to these norms, a man ought to direct his actions. Ethics is pre-eminently practical and directive; for it orders the activity of the will, and the latter it is which sets all the other faculties of man in motion. Hence, to order the will is the same as to order the whole man. Moreover, ethics not only directs a man how to act if he wishes to be morally good, but sets before him the absolute obligation he is under of doing good and avoiding evil.

A distinction must be made between ethics and morals, or morality. Every people, even the most uncivilized and uncultured, has its own morality or sum of prescriptions which govern its moral conduct. Nature had so provided that each man establishes for himself a code of moral concepts and principles which are applicable to the details of practical life, without the necessity of awaiting the conclusions of science. Ethics is the scientific or philosophical treatment of morality. The subject-matter proper of ethics is the deliberate, free actions of man; for these alone are in our power, and concerning these alone can rules be prescribed, not concerning those actions which are performed without deliberation, or through ignorance or coercion. Besides this, the scope of ethics includes whatever has reference to free human acts, whether as principle or cause of action (law, conscience, virtue), or as effect or circumstance of action (merit, punishment, etc.). The particular aspect (formal object) under which ethics considers free acts is that of their moral goodness or the rectitude of order involved in them as human acts. A man may be a good artist or orator and at the same time a morally bad man, or, conversely, a morally good man and a poor artist or technician. Ethics has merely to do with the order which relates to man as man, and which makes of him a good man.

Like ethics, moral theology also deals with the moral actions of man; but unlike ethics it has its origin in supernaturally revealed truth. It presupposes man's elevation to the supernatural order, and, though it avails itself of the scientific conclusions of ethics, it draws its knowledge for the most part from Christian Revelation. Ethics is distinguished from the other natural sciences which deal with moral conduct of man, as jurisprudence and pedagogy, in this, that the latter do not ascend to first principles, but borrow their fundamental notions from ethics, and are therefore subordinate to it. To investigate what constitutes good or bad, just or unjust, what is virtue, law, conscience, duty, etc., what obligations are common to all men, does not lie within the scope of jurisprudence or pedagogy, but of ethics; and yet these principles must be presupposed by the former, must serve them as a groundwork and guide; hence they are subordinated to ethics. The same is tre of political economy. The latter is indeed immediately concerned with man's social activity inasmuch as it treats of the production, distribution and consumption of material commodities, but this activity is not independent of ethics; industrial life must develop in accordance with the moral law and must be dominated by justice, equity, and love. Political economy was wholly wrong in trying to emancipate itself from the requirements of ethics. Sociology is at the present day considered by many as a science distinct from ethics. If, however, by sociology is meant a philosophical treatment of society, it is a division of ethics; for the enquiry into the nature of society in general, into the origin, nature, object and purpose of natural societies (the family, the state) and their relations to one another forms an essential part of Ethics. If, on the other hand, sociology be regarded as the aggregate of the sciences which have reference to the social life of man, it is not a single science but a complexus of sciences; and among these, so far as the natural order is concerned, ethics has the first claim.

Sources and Methods of Ethics

The sources of ethics are partly man's own experience and partly the principles and truths proposed by other philosophical disciplines (logic and mataphysics). Ethics takes its origin from the empirical fact that certain general principles and concepts of the moral order are common to all people at all times. This fact has indeed been frequently disputed, but recent ethnological research has placed it beyond the possibility of doubt. All nations distinguish between what is good and what is bad, between good men and bad men, between virtue and vice; they are all agreed in this: that the good is worth striving for, and that evil must be shunned, that the one deserves praise, the other, blame. Though in individual cases they may not be one in denominating the same thing good or evil, they are nevertheless agreed as to the general principle, that good is to be done and evil avoided. Vice everywhere seeks to hide itself or to put on the mask of virtue; it is a universally recognized principle, that we should not do to others what we would not wish them to do to us. With the aid of the truths laid down in logic and mataphysics, ethics proceeds to give a thorough explanation of this undeniable fact, to trace it back to its ultimate causes, then to gather from fundamental moral principles certain conclusions which will direct man, in the various circumstances and relations of life, how to shape his own conduct towards the attainment of the end for which he was created. Thus the proper method of ethics is at once speculative and empirical; it draws upon experience and metaphysics. Supernatural Christian Revelation is not a proper source of ethics. Only those conclusions properly belong to ethics which can be reached with the help of experience and philosophical principles. The Christian philosopher, however, may not ignore supernatural revelation, but must at least recognise it as a negative norm, inasmuch as he is not to advance any assertion in evident contradiction to the revealed truth of Christianity. God is the fountain-head of all truth — whether natural as made known by Creation, or supernatural as revealed through Christ and the Prophets. As our intellect is an image of the Divine Intellect, so is all certain scientific knowledge the reflex and interpretation of the Creator's thoughts embodied in His creatures, a participation in His eternal wisdom. God cannot reveal supernaturally and command us to believe on His authority anything that contradicts the thoughts expressed by Him in his creatures, and which, with the aid of the faculty of reason which he has given us, we can discern in His works. To assert the contrary would be to deny God's omniscience and veracity, or to suppose that God was not the source of all truth. A conflict, therefore, between faith and science is impossible, and hence the Christian philosopher has to refrain from advancing any assertion which would be evidently antagonistic to certain revealed truth. Should his researches lead to conclusions out of harmony with faith, he is to take it for granted that some error has crept into his deductions, just as the mathematician whose calculations openly contradict the facts of experience must be satisfied that his demonstration is at fault.

After what has been said the following methods of ethics must be rejected as unsound.

1. Pure Rationalism. — This system makes reason the sole source of truth, and therefore at the very outset excludes every reference to Christian Revelation, branding any such reference as degrading and hampering free scientific investigation. The supreme law of science is not freedom, but truth. It is not derogatory to the true dignity and freedom of science to abstain from asserting what, according to Christian Revelation, is manifestly erroneous.

2. Pure Empiricism, which would erect the entire structure of ethics exclusively on the foundation of experience, must also be rejected. Experience can tell us merely of present or past phenomena; but as to what, of necessity, and universal, must, or ought to, happen in the future, experience can give us no clue without bringing in

the aid of necessary and universal principles. Closely allied to Empiricism is Historicism, which considers history as the exclusive source of ethics. What has been said of Empiricism may also be applied to Historicism. History is concerned with what has happened in the past and only too often has to rehearse the moral aberrations of mankind.

3. Positivism is a variety of Empiricism; it seeks to emancipate ethics from metaphysics and base it on facts alone. No science can be constructed on the mere foundation of facts, and independently of metaphysics. Every science must set out from evident principles, which form the basis of all certain cognition. Ethics especially is impossible without metaphysics, since it is according to the metaphysical view we take of the world that ethics shapes itself. Whoever considers man as nothing else than a more highly developed brute will hold different ethical views from one who discerns in man a creature fashioned to the image and likeness of God, possessing a spiritual, immortal soul and destined to eternal life; whoever refuses to recognize the freedom of the will destroys the very foundation of ethics. Whether man was created by God or possesses a spiritual, immortal soul which is endowed with free will, or is essentially different from brute creation, all these are questions pertaining to metaphysics. Anthropology, moreover, is necessarily presupposed by ethics. No rules can be prescribed for man's actions, unless his nature is clearly understood.

4. Another untenable system is Traditionalism,

which in France, during the last half of the nineteenth century, counted many adherents (among others, de Bonald, Bautain), and which advanced the doctrine that complete certainty in religious and moral questions was not to be attained by the aid of reason alone, but only by the light of revelation as made known to us through tradition. They failed to see that for all reasonable belief certain knowledge of the existence of God and of the fact of revelation is necessarily presupposed, and this knowledge cannot be gathered from revelation. Fideism, or, as Paulsen designated it, the Irrationalism of many Protestants, also denies the ability of reason to furnish certainty in matters relating to God and religion. With Kant, it teaches that reason does not rise above the phenomena of the visible world; faith alone can lead us into the realm of the supersensible and instruct us in matters moral and religious. This faith, however, is not the acceptance of truth on the strength of external authority, but rather consists in certain appreciative judgments, i.e. assumptions or convictions which are the result of each one's own inner experiences, and which have, therefore, for him a precise worth, and correspond to his own peculiar temperament. Since these persuasions are not supposed to come within the range of reason, exception to them cannot be taken on scientific grounds. According to this opinion, religion and morals are relegated to pure subjectivism and lose all their objectivity and universality of value.

Historical View of Ethics

As ethics is the philosophical treatment of the moral order, its history does not consist in narrating the views of morality entertained by different nations at different times; this is properly the scope of the history of civilisation, and of ethnology. The history of ethics is concerned solely with the various philosophical systems which in the course of time have been elaborated with reference to the moral order. Hence the opinions advanced by the wise men of antiquity, such as Pythagoras (582-500 B.C.), Heraclitus (535-475 B.C.), Confucius (558-479 B.C.), scarcely belong to the history of ethics; for, though they proposed various moral truths and principles, they did so in a dogmatic and didactic, and not in a philosophically systematic manner. Ethics properly so-called is first met with among the Greeks, i.e.in the teaching of Socrates (470-399 B.C.). According to him the ultimate object of human activity is happiness, and the necessary means to reach it, virtue. Since everybody necessarily seeks happiness, no one is deliberately corrupt. All evil arises from ignorance, and the virtues are one and all but so many kinds of prudence. Virtue can, therefore, be imparted by instruction. The disciple of Socrates, Plato (427-347 B.C.) declares that the summum bonum consists in the perfect imitation of God, the Absolute Good, an imitation which cannot be fully realised in this life. Virtue enables man to order his conduct, as he properly should, according to the dictates of reason, and acting thus he becomes like unto God. But

Plato differed from Socrates in that he did not consider virtue to consist in wisdom alone, but in justice, temperance, and fortitude as well, these constituting the proper harmony of man's activities. In a sense, the State is man writ large, and its function is to train its citizens in virtue. For his ideal State he proposed the community of goods and of wives and the public education of children. Though Socrates and Plato had been to the fore in this mighty work and had contributed much valuable material to the upbuilding of ethics; nevertheless, Plato's illustrious disciple, Aristotle (384-322 B.C.), must be considered the real founder of systematic ethics. With characteristic keenness he solved, in his ethical and political writings, most of the problems with which ethics concerns itself. Unlike Plato, who began with ideas as the basis of his observation, Aristotle chose rathe to take the facts of experience as his starting-point; these he analysed accurately, and sought to trace to their highest and ultimate causes. He set out from the point that all men tend to happiness as the ultimate object of all their endeavours, as the highest good, which is sought for its own sake, and to which all other goods merely serve as means. This happiness cannot consist in external goods, but only in the activity proper to human nature - not indeed in such a lower activity of the vegetative and sensitive life as man possesses in common with plants and brutes, but in the highest and most perfect activity of his reason, which springs in turn from virtue. This activity, however, has to be exercised in a perfect and enduring life. The highest pleasure is naturally bound up with this activity, yet, to constitute perfect happiness, external goods must also supply their share. True happiness, though prepared for him by the gods as the object and reward of virtue, can be attained only through a man's own individual exertion. With keen penetration Aristotle thereupon proceeds to investigate in turn each of the intellectual and moral virtues, and his treatment of them must, even at the present time, be regarded as in great part correct. The nature of the State and of the family were, in the main, rightly explained by him. The only pity is that his vision did not penetrate beyond this earthly life, and that he never saw clearly the relations of man to God.

A more hedonistic (edone, "pleasure") turn in ethics begins with Democritus (about 460-370 B.C.), who considers a perpetually joyous and cheerful disposition as the highest good and happiness of man. The means thereto is virtue, which makes us independent of external goods — so far as that is possible — and which wisely discriminates between the pleasures to be sought after and those that are to be shunned. Pure Sensualism or Hedonism was first taught by Aristippus of Cyrene (435-354 B.C.), according to whom the greatest possible pleasure, is the end and supreme good of human endeavour. Epicurus (341-270 B.C.) differs from Aristippus in holding that the largest sum total possible of spiritual and sensual enjoyments, with the greatest possible freedom from displeasure and pain, is man's highest good. Virtue is the proper directive norm in the attainment of this end.

The Cynics, Antisthenes (444-369 B.C.) and Diogenes of Sinope (414-324 B.C.), taught the direct contrary of Hedonism, namely that virtue alone suffices for happiness, that pleasure is an evil, and that the truly wise man is above human laws. This teaching soon degenerated into haughty arrogance and open contempt for law and for the remainder of men (Cynicism). The Stoics, Zeno (336-264 B.C.) and his disciples, Cleanthes, Chrysippus, and others, strove to refine and perfect the views of Antisthenes. Virtue, in their opinion, consist in man's living according to the dictates of his rational, and, as each one's individual nature is but a part of the entire natural order, virtue is, therefore, the harmonious agreement with the Divine Reason, which shapes the whole course of nature. Whether they conceived this relation of God to the world in a pantheistic or a theistic sense, is not altogether clear. Virtue is to be sought for its own sake, and it suffices for man's happiness. All other things are indifferent and are, as circumstances require, to be striven after or shunned. The passions and affections are bad, and the wise man is independent of them. Among the Roman Stoics were Seneca (4 B.C. — A.D. 65), Epictetus (born about A.D. 50), and the Emperor Marcus Aurelius (A.D. 121-180), upon whom however, at least upon the latter two, Christian influences had already begun to make themselves felt. Cicero (106-43 B.C.) elaborated no new philosophical system of his own, but chose those particular views from the various systems of Grecian philosophy which appeared best to him. He maintained that moral goodness, which is the general object of all virtues, consists in what is becoming to man as a rational being as distinct from the brute. Actions are often good or bad, just or unjust, not because of human institutions or customs, but of their own intrinsic nature. Above and beyond human laws there is a natural law embracing all nations and all times, the expression of the rational will of the Most High God, from obedience to which no human authority can exempt us. Cicero gives an exhaustive exposition of the cardinal virtues and the obligations connected with them; he insists especially on devotion to the gods, without which human society could not exist.

Parallel with the above-mentioned Greek and Roman ethical systems runs a sceptical tendency, which rejects every natural moral law, bases the whole moral order on custom or human arbitrariness, and frees the wise man from subjection to the ordinary precepts of the moral order. This tendency was furthered by the Sophists, against whom Socrates and Plato arrayed themselves, and later on by Carnea, Theodore of Cyrene, and others.

A new epoch in ethics begins with the dawn of Christianity. Ancient paganism never had a clear and definite concept of the relation between God and the world, of the unity of the human race, of the destiny of man, of the nature and meaning of the moral law. Christianity first shed full light on these and similar questions. As St. Paul teaches (Romans 2:24 sq.), God has written his moral law in the hearts of all men, even of those outside the influence of Christian Revelation; this law manifests itself in the conscience of every man and is the norm according to which the whole human race will be judged on the day of reckoning. In consequence of their perverse inclinations, this law had to a great extent become obscured and distorted among the pagans; Christianity, however, restored it to its prestine integrity. Thus, too, ethics received its richest and most fruitful stimulus. Proper ethical methods were now unfolded, and philosophy was in a position to follow up and develop these methods by means supplied from its own store-house. This course was soon adopted in the early ages of the Church by the Fathers and ecclesiastical writers, as Justin Martyr, Irenaeus, Tertullian, Clement of Alexandria, Origen, but especially the illustrius Doctors of the Church, Ambrose, Jerome, and Augustine, who, in the exposition and defence of Christian truth, made use of the principles laid down by the pagan philosophers. True, the Fathers had no occasion to treat moral questions from a purely philosophical standpoint, and independently of Christin Revelation; but in the explanation of Catholic doctrine their discussions naturally led to philosophical investigations. This is particularly true of St. Augustine, who proceeded to thoroughly develop along philosophical lines and to establish firmly most of the truths of Christian morality. The eternal law (lex aeterna), the original type and source of all temporal laws the natural law, conscience, the ultimate end of man, the cardinal virtues, sin, marriage, etc. were treated by him in the clearest and most penetrating manner. Hardly a single portion of ethics does he present to us but is enriched with his keen philosophical commentaries. Late ecclesiastical writers followed in his footsteps.

A sharper line of separation between philosophy and theology, and in particular between ethics and moral theology, is first met with in the works of the great Schoolmen of the Middle Ages, especially of Albert the Great (1193-1280), Thomas Aquinas (1225-1274), Bonaventure (1221-1274), and Duns Scotus (1274-1308). Philosophy and, by means of it, theology reaped abundant fruit from the works of Aristotle, which had until then been a sealed treasure to Western civilization, and had first been elucidated by the detailed and profound commentaries of St. Albert the Great and St. Thomas Aquinas and pressed into the service of Christian philosophy. The same is particularly true as regards ethics. St. Thomas, in his commentaries on the political and ethical writings of the Stagirite, in his "Summa contra Gentiles" and his "Quaestiones disputatae, treated with his wonted clearness and penetration nearly the whole range of ethics in a purely philosophical manner, so that even to the present day his words are an inexhaustible source whence ethics draws its supply. On the foundations laid by him the Catholic philosophers and theoologians of succeeding ages have continued to build. It is true that in the fourteenth and fifteenth centuries, thanks especially to the influence of theco-called Nominalists, a period of stagnation and decline set in, but the sixteenth century is marked by a revival. Ethical questions, also, though largely treated in connexion with theology, are again made the subject of careful investigation. We mention as examples the great theologians Victoria, Dominicus Soto, L. Molina, Francisco Suárez, Lessius, and De Lugo. Since the sixteenth century special chairs of ethics (moral philosophy) have been erected in many Catholic universities. The larger, purely philosophical works on ethics, however do not appear until the seventeenth and eighteenth centuries, as an example of which we may instance the production of Ign. Schwarz, "Instituitiones juris universalis naturae et gentium" (1743).

Far different from Catholic ethical methods were those adopted for the most part by Protestants. With the rejection of the Church's teaching authority, each individual became on principle his own supreme teacher and arbiter in matters appertaining to faith and morals. True it is that the Reformers held fast to Holy Writ as the infallible source of revelation, but as to what belongs or does not belong to it, whether, and how far, it is inspired, and what is its meaning — all this was left to the final decision of the individual. The inevitable result was that philosophy arrogantly threw to the winds all regard for revealed truth, and in many cases became involved in the most pernicious errors. Melanchthon, in his "Elementa philosophiae moralis", still clung to the Aristotelean philosophy; so, too, did Hugo Grotius, in his work, "De jure belli et pacis". But Cumberland and his follower, Samuel Pufendorf, moreover, assumed, with Descartes, that the ultimate ground for every distinction between good and evil lay in the free determination of God's will, a view which renders the philosophical treatment of ethics fundamentally impossible. Quite an influential factor in the development of ethics was Thomas Hobbes (1588-1679). He supposes that the human race originally existed in existed in a rude condition (status naturae) in which every man was free to act as he pleased, and possessed a right to all things, whence arose a war of all against all. Lest destruction should be the result, it was decided to abandon this condition of nature and to found a state in which, by agreement, all were to be subject to one common will (one ruler). This authority ordains, by the law of the State, what is to be considered by all as good and as evil, and only then does there arise a distinction between good and evil of universal binding force on all. The Pantheist Baruch Spinoza (1632-1677) considers the instinct to self-preservation as the foundation of virtue. Every being is endowed with the necessary impulse to assert itself, and, as reason demands nothing contrary to nature, it requires each one to follow this impulse and to strive after whatever is useful to him. And each individual possesses power and virtue just in so far as he obeys this impulse. Freedom of the will consists merely in the ability to follow unrestrainedly this natural impulse. Shaftesbury

(1671-1713) bases ethics on the affections or inclinations of man. There are sympathetic, idiopathic, and unnatural inclinations. The first of these regard the common good, the second the private good of the agent, the third are opposed to the other two. To lead a morally good life, war must be waged upon the unnatural impulses, while the idiopathic and sympathetic inclinations must be made to harmonize. This harmony constitutes virtue. In the attainment of virtue the subjective guiding principle of knowledge is the "moral sense", a sort of moral instinct. This "moral sense" theory was further developed by Hutcheson (1694-1747); meanwhile "common sense" was suggested by Thoms Reid (1710-1796) as the highest norm of moral conduct. In France the materialistic philosophers of the eighteenth century — as Helvetius, de la Mettrie, Holbach, Condillac, and others — disseminated the teachings of Sensualism and Hedonism as understood by Epicurus.

A complete revolution in ethics was introduced by Immanuel Kant (1724-1804). From the wreck of pure theoretical reason he turned for rescue to practical reason, in which he found an absolute, universal, and categorical moral law. This law is not to be conceived as an enactment of external authority, for this would be heteronomy, which is foreign to true morality; it is rather the law of our own reason, which is, therefore, autonomous, that is, it must be observed for its own sake, without regard to any pleasure or utility arising therefrom. Only that will is morally good which obeys the moral law under the influence of such a subjective principle or motive as can be willed by the individual to become the universal law for all men. The followers of Kant have selected now one now another doctrine from his ethics and combined therewith various pantheistical systems. Fichte places man's supreme good and destiny in absolute spontaneity and liberty; Schleiermacher, in co-operating with the progressive civilization of mankind. A similar view recurs substantially in the writings of Wilhelm Wundt and, to a certain extent, in those of the pessimist, Edward von Hartmann, though the latter regards culture and progress merely as means to the ultimate end, which, according to him, consists in delivering the Absolute from the torment of existence.

The system of Cumberland, who maintained the common good of mankind to be the end and criterion of moral conduct, was renewed on a positive basis in the nineteenth century by Auguste Comte and has counted many adherents, e.g., in England, John Stuart Mill, Henry Sidgwick, Alexander Bain; in Germany, G.T. Fechner, F.E. Beneke, F. Paulsen, and others. Herbert Spencer (1820-1903) sought to effect a compromise between social Utilitarianism (Altruism) and private Utilitarianism (Egoism) in accordance with the theory of evolution. In his opinion, that conduct is good which serves to augment life and pleasure without any admixture of displeasure. In consequence, however, of man's lack of adaptation to the conditions of life, such absolute goodness of conduct is not as yet possible, and hence various compromises must be made between Altruism and Egoism. With the progress of evolution, however, this adaptability to existing conditions will become more and more perfect, and consequently the benefits accruing to the individual from his own conduct will be most useful to society at large. In particular, sympathy (in joy) will enable us to take pleasure in altruistic actions.

The great majority of non-Christian moral philosophers have followed the path trodden by Spencer. Starting with the assumption that man, by a series of transformations, was gradually evolved from the brute, and therefore differs from it in degree only, they seek the first traces and beginnings of moral ideas in the brute itself. Charles Darwin had done some preparatory work along these lines, and Spencer did not hesitate to descant on brute-ethics, on the pre-human justice, conscience, and self-control of brutes. Present-day Evolutionists follow his view and attempt to show how animal morality has in man continually become more perfect. With the aid of analogies taken from ethnology, they relate how mankind originally wandered over the face of the earth in semi-savage hordes, knew nothing of marriage or the family, and only by degrees reached a higher level of morality. These are the merest creations of fancy. If man is nothing more than a highly developed brute, he cannot possess a spiritual and immortal soul, and there can no longer be question of the freedom of the will, of the future retribution of good and evil, nor can man in consequence be hindered from ordering his life as he pleases and regarding the weel-being of others only in so far as it redounds to his own profit.

As the Evolutionists, so too the Socialists favour the theory of evolution from their ethical viewpoint; yet the latter do not base their observations on scientific principles, but on social and economic considerations. According to K. Marx, F. Engels, and other exponents of the so-called "materialistic interpretation of history", all moral, religious, juridical and philosophical concepts are but the reflex of the economical conditions of society in the minds of men. Now these social relations are subject to constant change; hence the ideas of morality, religion, etc. are also continually changing. Every age, every people, and even each class in a given people forms its moral and religious ideas in accordance with its own peculiar economical situation. Hence, no universal code of morality exists binding on all men at all times; the morality of the present day is not of Divine origin, but the product of history, and will soon have to make room for another system of morality. Allied to this materialistic historical interpretation, though derived from other sources, is the system of Relativism, which recognizes no absolute and unchangeable truths in regard to ethics or anything else. Those who follow this opinion aver that nothing objectively true can be known by us. Men differ from one another and are subject to change, and with them the manner and means of viewing the world about them also change. Moreover the judgments passed on matters religious and moral depend essentially on the inclinations, interests, and character of the person judging, while these latter are constantly varying. Pragmatism differs from Relativism inasmuch as that not only is to be considered true which is proven by experience to be useful; and, since the same thing is not always useful, unchangeable truth is impossible.

In view of the chaos of opinions and systems just described, it need not surprise us that, as regards ethical problems, scepticism is extending its sway to the utmost limits, in fact many exhibit a formal contempt for the traditional morality. According to Max Nordau, moral precepts are nothing but "conventional lies"; according to Max Stirner, that alone is good which serves my interests, whereas the common good, the love for all men, etc. are but empty phantoms. Men of genius and superiority in particular are coming more and more to be regarded as exempt from the moral law. Nietzsche is the originator of a school whose doctrines are founded on these principles. According to him, goodness was originally identified with nobility and gentility of rank. Whatever the man of rank and power did, whatever inclinations he possessed were good. The down-trodden proletariat, on the other hand were bad, i.e. lowly and ignoble, without any other derogatory meaning being given to the word bad. It was only by a gradual process that the oppressed multitude through hatred and envy evolved the distinction between good and bad, in the moral sense, by denominating the characteristics and conduct of those in power and rank as bad, and their own behaviour as good. And thus arose the opposition between the morality of the master and that of the slave. Those in power still continued to look upon their own egoistic inclinations as noble and good, while the oppressed populace lauded the "instincts of the common herd", i.e. all those qualities necessary and useful to its existence — as patience, meekness, obedience and love of one's neighbour. Weakness became goodness, cringing obsequiousness became humility, subjection to hated oppressors was obedience, cowardice meant patience. "All morality is one long and audacious deception." Hence, the value attached to the prevailing concepts of morality must be entirely rearranged. Intellectual superiority is above and beyond good and evil as understood in the traditional sense. There is no higher moral order to which men of such calibre are amenable. The end of society is not the common good of its members; the intellectual aristocracy (the over-man) is its own end; in its behalf the common herd, the "too many", must be reduced to slavery and decimated. As it rests with each individual to decide who belongs to this intellectual aristocracy, so each man is at liberty to emancipate himself from the existing moral order.

In conclusion, one other tendency in ethics may be noted, which has manifested itself far and wide; namely, the effort to make all morality independent of all religion. It is clear that many of the above-mentioned ethical systems essentially exclude all regard for God and religion, and this is true especially of materialistic, agnostic, and in the last analysis, of all pantheistic systems. Apart, also, from these systems, "independent morality", called also "lay morality", has gained many followers and defenders. Kant's ideas formed the basis of this tendency, for he himself founded a code of morality on the categorical imperative and expressly declared that morality is sufficient for itself, and therefore has no need of religion. Many modern philosophers — Herbart, Eduard von Hartmann, Zeller, Wundt, Paulsen, Ziegler, and a number of others — have followed Kant in this respect. For several decades practical attempts have been made to emancipate morality from religion. In France religious instruction was banished from the schools in 1882 and moral instruction substituted. This tendency manifests a lively activity in what is known as the "ethical movement", whose home, properly speaking, is in the United States. In 1876, Felix Adler, professor at Cornell University, founded the "Society for Ethical Culture", in New York City. Similar societies were formed in other cities. These were consolidated in 1887 into the "Union of the Societies for Ethical Culture." Besides Adler, the chief propagators of the movement by word of mouth and writing were W.M. Salter and Stanton Coit. The purpose of these societies is declared to be "the improvement of the moral life of the members of the societies and of the community to which they belong, without any regard to theological or philosophical opinions". In most of the European countries ethical societies were founded on the model of the American organization. All these were combined in 1894 into the "International Ethical Asociation". Their purpose, i.e. the amelioration of man's moral condition, is indeed praiseworthy, but it is erroneous to suppose that any such moral improvement can be brought about without taking religion into consideration. In fact many members of the ethical societies are openly antagonistic to all religions, and would therefore do away with denominational schools and supplant religious teaching by mere moral instruction. Even upon purely ethical considerations such attempts must be unhesitatingly rejected. If it be true that even in the case of adults moral instruction without religion, without any higher obligation or sanction, is a nonentity, a meaningless sham, how much more so is it in the case of the young? It is evident that, judged from the standpoint of Christianity, these efforts must meet with a still more decided condemnation. Christians are bound to observe not only the prescriptions of the natural law, but also all the precepts given by Christ concerning faith, hope, love, Divine worship, and the imitation of Himself. The Christian, moreover, knows that without Divine grace and, hence, without prayer and the frequent reception of the sacraments, a morally good life for any considerable length of time is impossible. From their earliest years, therefore, the young must not only receive thorough instruction in all the Commandments, but must be exercised and trained in the practical use of the means of grace. Religion must be the soil and atmosphere in which education develops and flourishes.

While, among non-Catholics ever since the Reformation, and especially since Kant, there has been an increasing tendency to divorce ethics from religion, and to dissolve it into countless venturesome and frequently contradictory systems, Catholics for the most part have remained free from these errors, because, in the Church's infallible teaching authority, the Guardian of Christian Revelation, they have always found secure orientation. It is true that towards the end of the eighteenth, and at the beginning of the nineteenth century, Illuminism and Rationalism penetrated here and there into Catholic circles and attempted to replace moral theology by purely philosophical ethics, and in turn to transform the latter according to the Kantian autonomy. This movement, however, was but a passing phase. With a reawakening of the Church's activity, fresh impetus was given to Catholic science, which was of benefit to ethics also and produced in its domain some excellent fruits. Recourse was again had to the illustrius past of Catholicism, while, at the same time, modern ethical systems gave occasion to a thorough investigation and verification of principles of the moral order. Taparelli d'Azeglio led the way with his great work "Saggio teoretico di diritto naturale appogiato sul fatto" (1840-43). Then followed, in Italy, Audisio, Rosmini, Liberatore, Sanseverino, Rosselli, Zigliara, Signoriello, Schiffini, Ferretti, Talamo, and others. In Spain this revival of ethics was due to, among others, J. Balmes, Donoso Cortés, Zefirio Gonzalez, Mendive, R. de Cepeda; in

France and Belgium, to de Lehen (Institutes de droit naturel), de Margerie, Onclair, Ath, Vallet, Charles Périn, Piat, de Pascal, Moulart, Castelein; in England and America, to Joseph Rickaby, Jouin, Russo, Hollaind, J.J. Ming. In German-speaking countries the reawakening of Scolasticism in general begins with Kleutgen (Theologie der Vorzeit, 1853); Philosophie der Vorzeit, 1860), and of ethics in particular with Th. Meyer* (Die Grundsätze der Sittlichkeit und des Rechts, 1868; Institutiones juris naturalis seu philosophiae moralis universae, 1885-1900). After them came A. Stöckl, Ferd, Walter, Moy de Sons, C. Gutberlet, Fr. J. Stein, Brandis, Costa-Rossetti, A.M. Weiss, Renninger, Lehmen, Willems, V. Frins, Heinrich Pesch, and others. We pass over numerous Catholic writers, who have made a specialty of sociology and political economy.

Outlines of Ethics

It is clear that the following statement cannot pretend to treat thoroughly all ethical questions; it is intended rather to afford the reader an insight into the most important problems dealt with by ethics, as well as into the methods adopted in their treatment. Ethics is usually divided into two parts: general, or theoretical ethics, and special, or applied ethics. General ethics expounds and verifies the general principles and concepts of the moral order; special ethics applies these general principles to the various relations of man, and determines his duties in particular.

Reason itself can rise from the knowledge of the visible creation to the certain knowledge of the existence of God, the origin and end of all things. On this fundamental truth the structure of ethics must be based. God created man, as he created all things else, for His own honour and glory. The ultimate end is the proper motive of the will's activity. If God were not the ultimate object and end of His own activity, he would depend upon His creatures, and would not be infinitely perfect. He is, then, the ultimate end of all things, they are created for His sake, not, indeed, that he can derive any benefit from them, which would be repugnant to an infinitely perfect being, but for His glory. They are to manifest His goodness and perfection. Irrational creatures cannot of themselves directly glorify God, for they are incapable of knowing Him. The are intended as means to the end for which rational man was created. The end of man, however, is to know God, to love Him and serve Him, and thereby attain to perfect and unending happiness. Every man has within him an irresistible, indestructible desire for perfect happiness; he seeks to be free from every evil and to possess every attainable good. This impulse to happiness is founded on man's nature; it is implanted there by his Maker; and hence will be duly realised, if nothing is wanting on the part of man's own individual endeavour. But perfect happiness is unattainable in the present life, if for no other reason, at least for this, that inexorable death puts an early end to all earthly happiness. There is reserved for man a better life, if he freely chooses to glorify God here on earth. It will be the crown of victory to be conferred upon him hereafter, if at present he remains subject to God and keeps His Commandments. Only from the viewpoint of eternity do this earthly life and the moral order acquire their proper significance and value. But how does man, considered in the natural order, or apart from every influence of supernatural revelations, come to know what God requires of him here below, or how he is to serve and glorify Him, in order to arrive at eternal happiness? — By means of the natural law.

From eternity there existed in the mind of God the idea of the world, which he determined to create, as well as the plan of government according to which He wished to rule the world and direct it to its end. This ordination existing in the mind of God from all eternity, and depending on the nature and essential relations of rational beings, is the eternal law of God (lex aeterna Dei), the source from which all temporal laws take their rise. God does not move and govern His creatures by a mere external directive impetus, as the archer does the arrow, but by means of internal impulses and inclinations, which He has bound up with their natures. Irrational creatures are urged, by means of physical forces or natural impulses and instincts to exercise the activity peculiar to them and keep the order designed for them. Man, on the other hand, is a being endowed with reason and free will; as such, he cannot be led by blind impulses and instincts in a manner conformable to his nature, but must needs depend on practical principles and judgments, which point out to him how he is to order his conduct. These principles must somehow or other be manifested to him by nature. All created things have implanted in their natures certain guiding principles, necessary to their corresponding activities. Man must be no exception to this rule. He must be led by a natural inborn light, manifesting to him what he is to do, or not to do. This natural light is the natural law. When we speak of man as possessing a natural, inborn light, it is not to be understood in the sense that man has innate ideas. Innate ideas do not exist. It is true, nevertheless, that the Creator has endowed man with the ability and the inclination to form many concepts and develop principles. As soon as he comes to the use of reason, he forms, by a natural necessity, on the basis of experience, certain general concepts of theoretical reason — e.g. those of being and not being, of cause and effect, of space and time — and so he arrives at universal principles, e.g. that "nothing can exist and not exist at the same time", that "every effect has its cause", etc. As it is in the theoretical, so also in the practical order. As soon as reason has been sufficiently developed, and the individual can somehow or other practically judge that he is something more than a mere animal, by an intrinsic necessity of his nature he forms the concept of good and evil, i.e. of something that is proper to the rational nature which distinguishes him from the brute, and which is therefore worth striving for, and something which is unbecoming and therefore to be avoided. Adn, as by nature he feels himself attracted by what is good, and repelled by what is evil, he naturally forms the judgments, that "good is to be done and evil avoided", that "man ought to live according to the dictates of reason", etc. From hid own reflections, especially when assisted by instruction from others, he easily comes to the conclusion that in these judgments the will of a superior being, of the Creator and Designer of nature, has its expression. Around about him he perceives that all things are well ordered, so that it is very easy for him to discern in them the handiwork of a superior and all-wise power. He himself has been appointed to occupy in the domain of nature the position of lord and master; he, too, must lead a well regulated life, as befits a rational being, not merely because he himself chooses to do so, but also in obedience to his Creator. Man did not give himself his nature with all its faculties and inclinations; he received it from a superior being, whose wisdom and power are everywhere manifest to him in Creation.

The general practical judgments and principles: "Do good and avoid evil", "Lead a life regulated according to reason", etc., from which all the Commandments of the Decalogue are derived, are the basis of the natural law, of which St. Paul (Romans 2:14) says, that it is written in the hearts of all men. This law is an emanation of the Divine law, made known to all men by nature herself; it is the expression of the will of nature's Author, a participation of the created rational being in the eternal law of God. Hence the obligation it imposes does not arise from na's own autonomy, as Kant held, nor from any other human authority, but from the will of the Creator; and man cannot violate it without rebelling against God, his master, offending Him, and becoming amenable to his justice. How deeply rooted among all nations this conviction of the higher origin of the natural law was, is shown by the fact that for various violations of it (as murder, adultery, perjury, etc.) they did their utmost to propitiate the angered deity by means of prayers and sacrifices. Hence they looked upon the deity as the guardian and protector of the moral order, who would not let the contempt of it to go unpunished. The same conviction is manifested by the value all nations have attached to the moral order, a value far surpassing that all other earthly goods. The noblest among the nations maintained that it was better to undergo any hardship, even death itself, rather than prove recreant to one's duty. They understood, therefore, that, over and above earthly treasures, there were higher and more lasting goods whose attainment was dependent upon the observance of the moral order, and this not by reason of any ordinance of man, but because of the law of God. This being premised, it is clearly impossible to divorce morality from religion without robbing it of its true obligation and sanction, of its sanctity and inviolability and of its importance as transcending every other earthly consideration.

The natural law consists of general practical principles (commands and prohibitions) and the conclusion necessarily flowing therefrom. It is the peculiar function of man to formulate these conclusions himself, though instruction and training are to assist him in doing so. Besides this, each individual has to take these principles as a guide of his conduct and apply them to his particular actions. This, to a certain extent, everybody does spontaneously, by virtue of an innate tendency. As in the case of all practical things, so in regard to what concerns the moral order, reason uses syllogistic processes. When a person, e.g., is on the point of telling a lie, or saying what is contrary to his convictions, there rises before his mental vision the general precept of the natural law: "Lying is wrong and forbidden." Hence he avails himself, at least virtually, of the following syllogism: "Lying is forbidden; what you are about to say is a lie; therefore, what you are about to say is forbidden." The conclusion thus arrived at is our conscience, the proximate norm of our conduct. Conscience, therefore, is not an obscure feeling or a sort of moral instinct, but a practical judgment of our reason on the moral character of individual acts. If we follow the voice of conscience, our reward is peace and calm of soul, if we resist this voice, we experience disquiet and remorse.

The natural law is the foundation of all human laws and precepts. It is only because we recognize the necessity of authority for human society, and because the natural law enjoins obedience to regularly constituted authority, that it is possible for a human superior to impose laws and commands binding in conscience. Indeed all human laws and precepts are fundamentally the conclusions, or more minute determinations, of the general principles of the natural law, and for this very reason every deliberate infraction of a law or precept binding in conscience is a sin, i.e. the violation of a Divine commandment, a rebellion against God, an offence against Him, which will not escape punishment in this life or in the next, unless duly repented of before death.

The problems hitherto mentioned belong to general, or theoretical, ethics, and their investigation in nearly all cases bear upon the natural law, whose origin, nature, subject- matter, obligation, and properties it is the scope of ethics to explain thoroughly and verify. The general philosophical doctrine of right is usually treated in general ethics. Under no circumstances may the example of Kant and others be imitated in severing the doctrine of right from ethics, or moral philosophy, and developing it as a seperate and independent science. The juridical order is but a part of the moral order, even as justice is but one of the moral virtues. The first principle of right: "Give every man his due"; "Commit no injustice"; and the necessary conclusions from these: "Thou shalt not kill"; "Thou shalt not commit adultery", and the like, belong to the natural law, and cannot be deviated from without violating one's duty and one's neighbour's rights, and staining one's conscience with guilt in the sight of God.

Special ethics applies the principles of general, or theoretical, ethics to the various relations of man, and thus deduces his duties in particular. General ethics teaches that man must do good and avoid evil, and must inflict injury upon no one. Special ethics descends to particulars and demonstrates what is good or bad, right or wrong, and therefore to be done or avoided in the various relations of human life. First of all, it treats of man as an individual in his relations to God, to himself, and to his fellow-men. God is the Creator, Master, and ultimate end of man; from these relations arise man's duties toward God. Presupposing his own individual efforts, he is, with God's assistance, to hope for eternal happiness from Him; he must love God above all things as the highest, infinite good, in such a manner that no creature shall be preferred to Him; he must acknowledge Him as his absolute lord and master, adore and reverence Him, and resign himself entirely to His holy Will. The first, highest, and most essential business of man is to serve God. In case it is God's good pleasure to reveal a supernatural religion and to determine in detail the manner and means of our worship of Him, man is bound by the natural law to accept this revelation in a spirit of faith, and to order his life accordingly. Here, too, it is plain that to divorce morality from religion is impossible. Religious duties, those, namely, which have direct reference to God, are man's principal and most essential moral duties. Linked to these duties to God are man's duties regarding himself. Man loves himself by an intrinsic necessity of his nature. From this fact Schopenhauer drew the conclusion that the commandment concerning sel-love was superfluous. This would be true, if it were a matter of indifference how man loved himself. But such is not the case; he must love himself with a well-ordered love. He is to be solicitous for the welfare of his soul and to do what is necessary to attain to eternal happiness. He is not his own master, but was created for the service of God; hence the deliberate arbitrary destruction of one's own life (suicide), as well as the freely intended mutilation of self, is a criminal attack on the proprietary right God has to man's person. Furthermore, every man is supposed to take a reasonable care to preserve his health. He has certain duties also as regards temperance; for the body must not be his master, but an instrument in the service of the soul, and hence must be cared for in so far only as is conducive to this purpose. A further duty concerns the acquisition of external material goods, as far as they are necessary for man's support and the fulfillment of his other obligations. This again involves the obligation to work; furthermore, God has endowed man with the capacity for work in order that he might prove himself a beneficial member of society; for idleness is the root of all evil. Besides these self-regarding duties, there are similar ones regarding our fellow-men: duties of love, justice, fidelity, truthfullness, gratitude, etc. The commandment of the love of our neighbour first received its true appreciation in the Christian Dispensation. Though doubtlessly contained to a certain extent in the natural law, the pagans had so lost sight of the unity of the human race, and of the fact that all men are members of one vast family dependent upon God, that they looked on every stranger as an enemy. Christianity restored to mankind the consciousness of its unity and solidarity, and supernaturally transfigured the natural precept to love our neighbour, by demonstrating that all men are children of the same Father in heaven, were redeemed by the same blood of the same Saviour, and are destined to the same supernatural salvation. And, better still, Christianity provided man with the grace necessary to the fulfillment of this precept and thus renewed the face of the earth. In man's intercourse with his fellow-men the precepts of justice and of the other allied virtues go hand in hand with the precept of love. There exists in man the natural tendency to assert himself when there is question of his goods or property. He expects his fellow-men to respect what belongs to him, and instinctively resists any unjust attempt to violate this proprietorship. He will brook an injury from no one in all that regards his life or health, his wife or child, his honour or good name; he resents faithlessness and ingratitude on the part of others, and the lie by which they would lead him into error. Yet he clearly understands that only then can he reasonably expect others to respect his rights when he in turn respects theirs. Hence the general maxim: "Do not do to others, what you would not wish them to do to you"; from which are naturally deduced the general commandments known to all men: "Thou shalt not kill, nor commit adultery, nor steal, nor bear false witness against thy neighbour", etc. In this part of ethics it is customary to investigate the principles of right as regards private ownership. Has every man the right to acquire property? Or, at least, may not society (the State) abolish private ownership and assume possession and control of all material goods either wholly or in part, in order to thus distribute among the members of the community the products of their joint industry? This latter question is answered in the affirmative by the Socialists; and yet, it is the experience of all ages that the community of goods and of ownership is altogether impracticable in larger commonwealths, and would, if realized in any case, involve widespread slavery.

The second part of special, or applied, ethics, called by many sociology, considers man as a member of society, as far as this can be made the subject of philosophical investigation. Man is by nature a social being; out of his innate needs, inclinations, and tendencies the family and State necessarily arise. And first of all the Creator had to provide for the preservation and propagation of the human race. Man's life is brief, were no provision made for the perpetuation of the human species, the world would soon become an uninhabited solitude, a well-appointed abode without occupants. Hence God has given man the power and propensity to propagate his kind. The generative function was not primarily intended for man's individual well-being, but for the general good of his species, and in its exercise, therefore, he must be guided accordingly. This general good cannot be perfectly realized except in a lasting indissoluble monogamy. The unity and indissolubility of the marriage bond are requirements of the natural law, at least in the sense that man may not on his own authority set them aside. Marriage is a Divine institution, for which God Himself has provided by means of definite laws and in regard to which, therefore, man has not the power to make any change. The Creator might, of course, dispense for a time from the unity and indissolubility of the marriage tie; for, though the perfection of the married state demands these qualities, they are not of absolute necessity; the principal end of marriage may be attained to a certain degree without them. God could, therefore, for wise reasons grant a dispensation in regard to them for a certain length of time. Christ, however, restored marriage to the original perfection consonant with its nature. Moreover He raised marriage to the dignity of a sacrament and made it symbolic of His own union with the Church; and had he done nothing more in this respect than restore the natural law to its prestine integrity, mankind would be bound to Him by an eternal debt of gratitude. For it was chiefly be means of the unity and indissolubility of the married life that the sanctuary of the Christian family was established, from which mankind has reaped the choicest blessings, and compared with which paganism has no equivalent to offer. This exposition of the nature of marriage from a theistic standpoint is diametrically opposed to the views of modern Darwinists. According to them, men did not primitively recognize any such institution as the married state, but lived together in complete promiscuity. Marriage was the result of gradual development, woman was originally the centre about which the family crystallized, and from this latter circumstance there arises an explanation of the fact that many savage tribes reckon heredity and kinship between families according to the lineal descent of the female. We cannot dwell long upon these fantastic speculations, because they do not consider man as essentially different from the brute, but as gradually developed from a purely animal origin. Although marriage is of Divine institution, not every individual is obliged, as a human being, to embrace the married state. God intends marriage for the propagation of the human race. To achieve this purpose it is by no means necessary for each and every member of the human family to enter upon marriage, and this particularly at the present time, when the question of over-population presents so many grave difficulties to social economists. In this connexion certain other considerations from a Christian point of view arise, which do not, however, belong to philosophical ethics. Since the principal end of marriage is the procreation and education of children, it is incumbent upon both parents to co-operate according to the requirements of sex in the attainment of this end. From this it may readily be gathered what duties exist between husband and wife, and between parents and their children.

The second natural society, the State, is a logical and necessary outcome of the family. A completely isolated family could scarcely support itself, at all events it could never rise above the lowest grade of civilization. Hence we see that at all times and in all places, owing to natural needs and tendencies, larger groups of families are formed. A division of labour takes place. Each family devotes itself to some industry in which it may improve and develop its resources, and then exchanges its products for those of other families. And now the way is opened to civilization and progress. This grouping of families, in order to be permanent, has need of authority, which makes for security, order, and peace, and in general provides for what is necessary to the common good. Since God intends men to live together in harmony and order, He likewise desires such authority in the community as will have the right to procure what is needful for the common good. This authority, considered in itself and apart from the human vehicle in which it is placed, comes immediately from God, and hence, within its proper sphere, it imposes upon the consciences of the subjects the duty of obedience. In the light of this interpretation, the exercise of public power is vested with its proper dignity and inviolability, and at the same time is circumscribed by necessary limitations. A group of families under a common authoritative head, and not subject to any similar aggregation, forms the primitive State, however small this may be. By further development, or by coalition with other States, larger States gradually come into existence. It is not the purpose of the State to supplant the families, but to safeguard their rights, to protect them, and to supplement their efforts. It is not to forfeit their rights or to abandon their proper functions that individuals and families combine to form the State, but to be secured in these rights, and to find support and encouragement in the discharge of the various duties assigned them. Hence the State may not deprive the family of its right to educate and instruct the children, but must simply lend its assistance by supplying, whenever needful, opportunities for the better accomplishment of this duty. Only so far as the order and prosperity of the body politic requires it, may the State circumscribe individual effort and activity. In other words, the State is to posit the conditions under which, provided private endeavour be not lacking, each individual and each family may attain to true earthly happiness. By true earthly happiness is meant such as not only does not interfere with the free performance of the individual's moral duties, but even upholds and encourages him therin.

Having defined the end and aim of the State, we are now in a position to examine in detail its various functions and extent. Private morality is not subject to State interference; but it is the proper function of the State to concern itself with the interests of public morality. It must not only prevent vice from parading in public and becoming a snare to many (e.g. through immoral literature, theatres, plays, or other means of seduction), but also see to it that the public ordinances and laws facilitate and advance morally good behaviour. The State may not affect indifference as regards religion; the obligation to honour God publicly is binding upon the State as such. It is true that the direct supervision of religious matters in the present supernatural order was entrusted by Christ to His Church; nevertheless, it is the duty of the Christian State to protect and uphold the Church, the one true Church founded by Christ. Of course, owing to the unfortunate division of Christians into numerous religious systems, such an intimate relation betwen Church and State is at the present day but rarely maintained. The separation of Church and State, with complete liberty of conscience and worship, is often the only practical modus vivendi. In circumstances such as these the State must be satisfied to leave the affairs of religion to various bodies, and to protect the latter in those rights which have reference to the general public order. The education and instruction of children belongs per se to the family, and should not be monopolized by the State. The later has, however, the right and the duty to suppress schools which disseminate immoral doctrine or foster the practice of vice; beyond such control it may not set limits to free individual endeavour. It may, however, assist the individual in his efforts to secure an education, and, in case these do not suffice, it may establish schools and institutions for his benefit. Finally, the State has to exercise important economical functions. It must protect private property and see to it that in man's industrial life the laws affecting justice be carried out in all their force and vigour. But its duties do not stop here. It should pass such laws as will enable its subjects to procure what is needed for their respectable sustenance and even to attain a moderate competency. Both excessive wealth and extreme poverty involve many dangers to the individual and to society. Hence the State should pass such laws as will favour the sturdy middle class of citizens and add to their numbers. Much can be done to bring about this desirable condition by the enactment of proper tax and inheritance laws of laws which protect the labouring, manufacturing, and agricultural interests, and which supervise and control trusts, syndicates, etc.

Although the authority of the State comes immediately from God, the person who exercises it is not immediately designated by Him. This determination is left to the circumstances of men's progress and development or of their modes of social aggregation. According as the supreme power resides in one individual, or in a privileged class, or in the people collectively, governments are divided into three forms: the monarchy; the aristocracy; the democracy. The monarchy is hereditary or elective, according as succession to supreme power follows the right of primogeniture of a family (dynasty) or is subject to suffrage. At the present day the only existing kind of monarchy is the hereditary, the elective monarchies, such as Poland and the old German Sovereignty, having long since disappeared. Those States in which the sovereign power resides in the body of the people are called polycracies, or more commonly, republics, and are divided into aristocracies and democracies. In republics sovereignty is vested in the people. The latter elect from their number representatives who frame their laws and administer the affairs of government in their name. The almost universally prevailing form of government in Europe, fashioned upon the model created in England, is the constitutional monarchy, a mixture of the monarchical, aristocratic, and democratic forms. The law- making power is vested in the king and two chambers. The members of one chamber represent the aristocratic and conservative element, while the other chamber, elected from the body of citizens, represents the democratic element. The monarch himself is responsible to no one, yet his governmental acts require the counter-signature of the ministers, who in turn are responsible to the chamber.

With regard to its appointed functions the government of the State is divided into the legislative, judiciary, and executive powers. It is of primary importance that the State enact general and stable laws governing the activities of its subjects, as far as this is required for the good order and well-being of the whole body. For this purpose it must possess the right to legislate; it must, moreover, carry out these laws and provide, by means of the administrative, or rather executive, power for what is needful to the general good of the community; finally, it has to punish infractions of the laws and authoritatively settle legal disputes, and for this purpose it has need of the judiciary power (in civil and criminal courts). This right of the State to impose penalties is founded on the necessity to preserve good order and of providing for the security of the whole body politic. In a community there are always found those who can in no other way be effectually forced to observe the laws and respect the rights of others than by the infliction of punishment. Hence the State must have the right to enact penal statutes, calculated to deter its subjects from violating the laws and the right, moreover, to actually inflict punishment after the violation has occurred. Among the legitimate modes of punishment is capital punishment. It is considered, and rightly so, a step forward in civilization, that nowadays a milder practice has been adopted in this regard, and that capital punishment is more rarely inflicted, and then only for such heinous crimes as murder and high treason. Nevertheless humanitarian sentimentalism has no doubt been carried to an exaggerated degree, so much so that many would on principle do away with capital punishment altogether. And yet, this is the only sanction sufficiently effective to deter some men from committing the gravest crimes.

When it is asserted, with Aristotle, that the State is a society sufficient for itself, this is to be considered true in the sense that the State needs no further development to complete its organization, but not in the sense that it is independent in every respect. The greater the advance of mankind in progress and civilization, the more necessary and frequent the communication between nations becomes. Hence the question arises as to what rights and duties mutually exist between nation and nation. That portion of ethics which treats this question from a philosophical standpoint is called the theory of international law, or of the law of nations. Of course, many writers of the present day deny the propriety of a philosophical treatment of international law. According to them the only international rights and duties are those which have been established by some positive measure either implicitly or explicitly agreed upon. This, indeed, is the position that must be taken by all who reject the natural law. On the other hand, this position precludes the possibility of any positive international law whatever, for lasting and binding compacts between various States are possible only when the primary principle of right is recognized — that it is just and obligatory to stand by lawful agreements. Now this is a principle of natural law; hence, those who deny the existence of natural law (e.g. E. von Hartmann) must consequently reject any international law properly so called. In their opinion any international agreements are mere conventions, which each one observes as long as he finds it necessary or advantageous. And so we are eventually led back to the principle of ancient paganism, which, in the intercourse between nations, too often identified right with might. But Christianity brought the nations into a closer union and broke down the barriers of narrow-minded policy. It proclaimed, moreover, the duties of love and justice as binding on all nations, thus restoring and perfecting the natural law. The fundamental principles: "Give each one his due", "Do injury to no man",

"Do not to others what you would not have them do to you", etc., have an absolute and universal value, and hence must obtain also in the intercourse between nations. Purely natural duties and rights are comon to all nations; the acquired or positive ones may vary considerably. Various, too, are the rights and duties of nations in peace and in war. Since, however, there are, under this head, many details of a doubtful and changeable character, the codification of international law is a most urgent desideratum. Besides this an international court should be established to attend to the execution of the various measures promulgated by the law and to arbitrate in case of dispute. The foundations of such an international court of arbitration have been laid at The Hague; unfortunately, its competence has been hitherto very much restricted, and besides, it exercises its functions only when the Powers at variance appeal to it of their own accord. In the codification of international law no one would be more competent to lend effective cooperation and to maintain the principles of justice and love which should exist between nations in their intercourse with one another, than the pope. No one can offer sounder guarantees for the righteousness of the principles to be laid down, and no one can exert greater moral influence towards carrying them into effect. This is even recognized by unprejudiced Protestants. At the Vatican Council not only the many Catholic bishops present, but the Protestant David Urquhart appealed to the pope to draw up a schedule of the more important principles of international law, which were to be binding on all Christian nations. Religious prejudice, however, places many difficulties in the way of realizing this plan.

XIII.
Natural Law

In English this term is frequently employed as equivalent to the laws of nature, meaning the order which governs the activities of the material universe. Among the Roman jurists natural law designated those instincts and emotions common to man and the lower animals, such as the instinct of self-preservation and love of offspring. In its strictly ethical application—the sense in which this article treats it—the natural law is the rule of conduct which is prescribed to us by the Creator in the constitution of the nature with which He has endowed us.

According to St. Thomas, the natural law is "nothing else than the rational creature's participation in the eternal law" (I-II.94). The eternal law is God's wisdom, inasmuch as it is the directive norm of all movement and action. When God willed to give existence to creatures, He willed to ordain and direct them to an end. In the case of inanimate things, this Divine direction is provided for in the nature which God has given to each; in them determinism reigns. Like all the rest of creation, man is destined by God to an end, and receives from Him a direction towards this end. This ordination is of a character in harmony with his free intelligent nature. In virtue of his intelligence and free will, man is master of his conduct. Unlike the things of the mere material world he can vary his action, act, or abstain from action, as he pleases. Yet he is not a lawless being in an ordered universe. In the very constitution of his nature, he too has a law laid down for him, reflecting that ordination and direction of all things, which is the eternal law. The rule, then, which God has prescribed for our conduct, is found in our nature itself. Those actions which conform with its tendencies, lead to our destined end, and are thereby constituted right and morally good; those at variance with our nature are wrong and immoral.

The norm, however, of conduct is not some particular element or aspect of our nature. The standard is our whole human nature with its manifold relationships, considered as a creature destined to a special end. Actions are wrong if, though subserving the satisfaction of some particular need or tendency, they are at the same time incompatible with that rational harmonious subordination of the lower to the higher which reason should maintain among our conflicting tendencies and desires (see GOOD). For example, to nourish our bodies is right; but to indulge our appetite for food to the detriment of our corporal or spiritual life is wrong. Self-preservation is right, but to refuse to expose our life when the well-being of society requires it, is wrong. It is wrong to drink to intoxication, for, besides being injurious to health, such indulgence deprives one of the use of reason, which is intended by God to be the guide and dictator of conduct. Theft is wrong, because it subverts the basis of social life; and man's nature requires for its proper development that he live in a state of society. There is, then, a double reason for calling this law of conduct natural: first, because it is set up concretely in our very nature itself, and second, because it is manifested to us by the purely natural medium of reason. In both respects it is distinguished from the Divine positive law, which contains precepts not arising from the nature of things as God has constituted them by the creative act, but from the arbitrary will of God. This law we learn not through the unaided operation of reason, but through the light of supernatural revelation.

We may now analyse the natural law into three constituents: the discriminating norm, the binding norm (norma obligans), and the manifesting norm. The discriminating norm is, as we have just seen, human nature itself, objectively considered. It is, so to speak, the book in which is written the text of the law, and the classification of human actions into good and bad. Strictly speaking, our nature is the proximate discriminating norm or standard. The remote and ultimate norm, of which it is the partial reflection and application, is the Divine nature itself, the ultimate groundwork of the created order. The binding or obligatory norm is the Divine authority, imposing upon the rational creature the obligation of living in conformity with his nature, and thus with the universal order established by the Creator. Contrary to the Kantian theory that we must not acknowledge any other lawgiver than conscience, the truth is that reason as conscience is only immediate moral authority which we are called upon to obey, and conscience itself owes its authority to the fact that it is the mouthpiece of the Divine will and imperium. The manifesting norm (norma denuntians), which determines the moral quality of actions tried by the discriminating norm, is reason. Through this faculty we perceive what is the moral constitution of our nature, what kind of action it calls for, and whether a particular action possesses this requisite character.

The Contents of the Natural Law

Radically, the natural law consists of one supreme and universal principle, from which are derived all our natural moral obligations or duties. We cannot discuss here the many erroneous opinions regarding the fundamental rule of life. Some of them are utterly false—for instance, that of Bentham, who made the pursuit of utility or temporal pleasure the foundation of the moral code, and that of Fichte, who taught that the supreme obligation is to love self above everything and all others on account of self. Others present the true idea in an imperfect or one-sided fashion. Epicurus, for example, held the supreme principle to be, "Follow nature"; the Stoics inculcated living according to reason. But these philosophers interpreted their principles in a manner less in conformity with our doctrine than the tenor of their words suggests. Catholic moralists, though agreeing upon the underlying conception of the Natural Law, have differed more or less in their expression of its fundamental formula. Among many others we find the following: "Love God as the end and everything on account of Him"; "Live conformably to human nature considered in all its essential respects"; "Observe the rational order established and sanctioned by God"; "Manifest in your life the image of God impressed on your rational nature." The exposition of St. Thomas is at once the most simple and philosophic. Starting from the premise that good is what primarily falls under the apprehension of the practical reason—that is of reason acting as the dictator of conduct—and that, consequently, the supreme principle of moral action must have the good as its central idea, he holds that the supreme principle, from which all the other principles and precepts are derived, is that good is to be done, and evil avoided (I-II, Q, xciv, a. 2).

Passing from the primary principle to the subordinate principles and conclusions, moralists divide these into two classes: (1) those dictates of reason which flow so directly from the primary principle that they hold in practical reason the same place as evident propositions in the speculative sphere, or are at least easily deducible from the primary principle. Such, for instance, are "Adore God"; "Honour your parents"; "Do not steal"; (2) those other conclusions and precepts which are reached only through a more or less complex course of inference. It is this difficulty and uncertainty that requires the natural law to be supplemented by positive law, human and Divine. As regards the vigour and binding force of these precepts and conclusions, theologians divide them into two classes, primary and secondary. To the first class belong those which must, under all circumstances, be observed if the essential moral order is to be maintained. The secondary precepts are those whose observance contributes to the public and private good and is required for the perfection of moral development, but is not so absolutely necessary to the rationality of conduct that it may not be lawfully omitted under some special conditions. For example, under no circumstances is polyandry compatible with the moral order, while polygamy, though inconsistent with human relations in their proper moral and social development, is not absolutely incompatible with them under less civilized conditions.

The Qualities of the Natural Law

(a) The natural law is universal, that is to say, it applies to the entire human race, and is in itself the same for all. Every man, because he is a man, is bound, if he will conform to the universal order willed by the Creator, to live conformably to his own rational nature, and to be guided by reason. However, infants and insane persons, who have not the actual use of their reason and cannot therefore know the law, are not responsible for that failure to comply with its demands.

(b) The natural law is immutable in itself and also extrinsically. Since it is founded in the very nature of man and his destination to his end—two bases which rest upon the immutable ground of the eternal law—it follows that, assuming the continued existence of human nature, it cannot cease to exist. The natural law commands and forbids in the same tenor everywhere and always. We must, however, remember that this immutability pertains not to those abstract imperfect formulæ in which the law is commonly expressed, but to the moral standard as it applies to action in the concrete, surrounded with all its determinate conditions. We enunciate, for instance, one of the leading precepts in the words: "Thou shalt not kill"; yet the taking of human life is sometimes a lawful, and even an obligatory act. Herein exists no variation in the law; what the law forbids is not all taking of life, but all unjust taking of life.

With regard to the possibility of any change by abrogation or dispensation, there can be no question of such being introduced by any authority except that of God Himself. But reason forbids us to think that even He could exercise such power, because, given the hypothesis that He wills man to exist, He wills him necessarily to live conformably to the eternal law, by observing in his conduct the law of reason. The Almighty, then, cannot be conceived as willing this and simultaneously willing the contradictory, that man should be set free from the law entirely through its abrogation, or partially through dispensation from it. It is true that some of the older theologians, followed or copied by some later ones, hold that God can dispense, and, in fact in some instances, has dispensed from the secondary precepts of the natural law, while others maintain that the bearing of the natural law is changed by the operation of positive law. However, an examination of the arguments offered in support of these opinions shows that the alleged examples of dispensation are: (a) cases where a change of conditions modifies the application of the law, or (b) cases concerning obligations not imposed as absolutely essential to the moral order, though their fulfillment is necessary for the full perfection of conduct, or (c) instances of addition made to the law.

As examples of the first category are cited God's permission to the Hebrews to despoil the Egyptians, and His command to Abraham to sacrifice Isaac. But it is not necessary to see in these cases a dispensation from the precepts forbidding theft and murder. As the Sovereign Lord of all things, He could withdraw from Isaac his right to life, and from the Egyptians their right of ownership, with the result that neither would the killing of Isaac be an unjust destruction of life, nor the appropriation of the Egyptians' goods the unjust taking of another's property. The classic instance alleged as an example of (b) is the legalization of polygamy among the Hebrews. Polygamy, however, is not under all circumstances incompatible with the essential principles of a rationally ordered life, since the chief ends prescribed by nature for the marital union—the propagation of the race and the due care and education of offspring—may, in certain states of society, be attained in a polygamous union. The theory that God can dispense from any part of the law, even from the secondary precepts, is scarcely compatible with the doctrine, which is the common teaching of the School, that the natural law is founded on the eternal law, and, therefore, has for its ultimate ground the immutable essence of God himself. As regards (c), when positive law, human or Divine, imposes obligations which only modify the bearing of the natural law, it cannot correctly be said to change it. Positive law may not ordain anything contrary to the natural law, from which it draws its authority; but it may—and this is one of its functions—determine with more precision the bearing of the natural law, and for good reasons, supplement its conclusions. For example, in the eyes of the natural law mutual verbal agreement to a contract is sufficient; yet, in many kinds of contract, the civil law declares that no agreement shall be valid, unless it be expressed in writing and signed by the parties before witnesses. In establishing this rule the civil authority merely exercises the power which it derives from the natural law to add to the operation of the natural law such conditions as the common good may call for. Contrary to the almost universally received doctrine, a few theologians held erroneously that the natural law depends not on the essential necessary will of God, but upon His arbitrary positive will, and taught consistently with this view, that the natural law may be dispensed from or even abrogated by God. The conception, however, that the moral law is but an arbitrary enactment of the Creator, involves the denial of any absolute distinction between right and wrong—a denial which, of course, sweeps away the very foundation of the entire moral order.

Our Knowledge of the Law

Founded in our nature and revealed to us by our reason, the moral law is known to us in the measure that reason brings a knowledge of it home to our understanding. The question arises: How far can man be ignorant of the natural law, which, as St. Paul says, is written in the human heart (Romans 2:14)? The general teaching of theologians is that the supreme and primary principles are necessarily known to every one having the actual use of reason. These principles are really reducible to the primary principle which is expressed by St. Thomas in the form: "Do good and avoid evil". Wherever we find man we find him with a moral code, which is founded on the first principle that good is to be done and evil avoided. When we pass from the universal to more particular conclusions, the case is different. Some follow immediately from the primary, and are so self-evident that they are reached without any complex course of reasoning. Such are, for example: "Do not commit adultery"; "Honour your parents". No person whose reason and moral nature is ever so little developed can remain in ignorance of such precepts except through his own fault. Another class of conclusions comprises those which are reached only by a more or less complex course of reasoning. These may remain unknown to, or be misinterpreted even by persons whose intellectual development is considerable. To reach these more remote precepts, many facts and minor conclusions must be correctly appreciated, and, in estimating their value, a person may easily err, and consequently, without moral fault, come to a false conclusion.

A few theologians of the seventeenth and

eighteenth centuries, following some older ones, maintained that there cannot exist in anyone practical ignorance of the natural law. This opinion however has no weight (for the controversy see Bouquillon, "Theologia Fundamentalis", n. 74). Theoretically speaking, man is capable of acquiring a full kowledge of the moral law, which is, as we have seen, nothing but the dictates of reason properly exercised. Actually, taking into consideration the power of passion, prejudice, and other influences which cloud the understanding or pervert the will, one can safely say that man, unaided by supernatural revelation, would not acquire a full and correct knowledge of the contents of the natural law (cf. Vatican Council, Sess. III, cap. ii). In proof we need but recall that the noblest ethical teaching of pagans, such as the systems of Plato, Aristotle, and the Stoics, was disfigured by its approbation of shockingly immoral actions and practices.

As the fundamental and all-embracing obligation imposed upon man by the Creator, the natural law is the one to which all his other obligations are attached. The duties imposed on us in the supernatural law come home to us, because the natural law and its exponent, conscience, tell us that, if God has vouchsafed to us a supernatural revelation with a series of precepts, we are bound to accept and obey it. The natural law is the foundation of all human law inasmuch as it ordains that man shall live in society, and society for its constitution requires the existence of an authority, which shall possess the moral power necessary to control the members and direct them to the common good. Human laws are valid and equitable only in so far as they correspond with, and enforce or supplement the natural law; they are null and void when they conflict with it. The United States system of equity courts, as distinguished from those engaged in the administration of the common law, are founded on the principle that, when the law of the legislator is not in harmony with the dictates of the natural law, equity (æquitas, epikeia) demands that it be set aside or corrected. St. Thomas explains the lawfulness of this procedure. Because human actions, which are the subject of laws are individual and innumerable, it is not possible to establish any law that may not sometimes work out unjustly. Legislators, however, in passing laws attend to what commonly happens, though to apply the common rule will sometimes work injustice and defeat the intention of the law itself. In such cases it is bad to follow the law; it is good to set aside its letter and follow the dictates of justice and the common good (II-II.120.1). Logically, chronologically, and ontologically antecedent to all human society for which it provides the indispensable basis, the natural or moral law is neither—as Hobbes, in anticipation of the modern positivistic school, taught—a product of social agreement or convention, nor a mere congeries of the actions, customs, and ways of man, as claimed by the ethicists who, refusing to acknowledge the First Cause as a Personality with whom one entertains personal relations, deprive the law of its obligatory basis. It is a true law, for through it the Divine Mind imposes on the subject minds of His rational creatures their obligations and prescribes their duties.

XIV.
Moral Theology

Moral theology is a branch of theology, the science of God and Divine things. The distinction between natural and supernatural theology rests on a solid foundation. Natural theology is the science of God Himself, in as far as the human mind can by its own efforts reach a definite conclusion about God and His nature: it is always designated by the adjective natural. Theology, without any further modification, is invariably understood to mean supernatural theology, that is, the science of God and Divine things, in as far as it is based on supernatural Revelation. Its subject-matter embraces not only God and His essence, but also His actions and His works of salvation and the guidance by which we are led to God, our supernatural end. Consequently, it extends much farther than natural theology; for, though the latter informs us of God's essence and attributes, yet it can tell us nothing about His free works of salvation. The knowledge of all these truths is necessary for every man, at least in its broad outlines, and is acquired by Christian faith. But this is not yet a science. The science of theology demands that the knowledge won through faith, be deepened, expanded, and strengthened, so that the articles of faith be understood and defended by their reasons and be, together with their conclusions, arranged systematically.

The entire field of theology proper is divided into dogmatic and moral theology, which differ in subject-matter and in method. Dogmatic theology has as its end the scientific discussion and establishment of the doctrines of faith, moral theology of the moral precepts. The precepts of Christian morals are also part of the doctrines of faith, for they were announced or confirmed by Divine Revelation. The subject-matter of dogmatic theology is those doctrines which serve to enrich the knowledge necessary or convenient for man, whose destination is supernatural. Moral theology, on the other hand, is limited to those doctrines which discuss the relations of man and his free actions to God and his supernatural end, and propose the means instituted by God for the attainment of that end. Consequently, dogmatic and moral theology are two closely related parts of universal theology. Inasmuch as a considerable number of individual doctrines may be claimed by either discipline, no sharp line of demarcation can be drawn between the subject-matter of dogma and morals. In actual practice, however, a division and limitation must be made in accordance with practical needs. Of a similar nature is the relation between moral theology and ethics. The subject-matter of natural morals or ethics, as contained in the Decalogue, has been included in positive, Divine Revelation, and hence has passed into moral theology. Nevertheless, the argumentative processes differ in the two sciences, and for this reason a large portion of the matter is disregarded in moral theology and referred to ethics. For instance, the refutation of the false systems of the modern ethicists is generally treated under ethics, especially because these systems are refuted by arguments drawn not so much from faith, as from reason. Only in as far as moral theology requires a defence of revealed doctrines, does it concern itself with false systems. However, it must discuss the various requirements of the natural law, not only because this law has been confirmed and defined by positive revelation, but also because every violation of it entails a disturbance of the supernatural moral order, the treatment of which is an essential part of moral theology.

The field of moral theology, its contents, and the boundaries which separate it from kindred subjects, may be briefly indicated as follows: moral theology includes everything relating to man's free actions and the last, or supreme, end to be attained through them, as far as we know the same by Divine Revelation; in other words, it includes the supernatural end, the rule, or norm, of the moral order, human actions as such, their harmony or disharmony with the laws of the moral order, their consequences, the Divine aids for their right performance. A detailed treatment of these subjects may be found in the second part of St. Thomas's "Summa theologica", a work still unrivalled as a treatise of moral theology.

The position of moral theology in universal theology is briefly sketched by St. Thomas in the "Summa theol.", I, Q. i, a. 7 and Q. ii in the proemium and in the prologus of I-II; likewise by Fr. Suárez in the proemium of his commentaries on the I-II of St. Thomas. The subject-matter of the entire second part of the "Summa theol." is, man as a free agent. "Man was made after the image of

God, by his intellect, his free will, and a certain power to act of his own accord. Hence, after we have spoken of the pattern, viz. of God, and of those things which proceeded from His Divine power according to His will, we must now turn our attention to His image, that is, man, inasmuch as he also is the principle or his actions in virtue of his free will and his power over his own actions." He includes all this in theology, not only because it is viewed as the object of positive Divine Revelation (I, Q. i, a. 3), but also because God always is the principal object, for "theology treats all things in their relation to God, either in as far as they are God Himself or are directed towards God as their origin or last end" (I, Q. i, a. 7). "Since it is the chief aim of theology to communicate the knowledge of God, not only as He is in Himself but also as the beginning and end of all things and particularly of rational creatures . . ., we shall speak first of God, secondly of the tendency of the rational creature towards God", etc. (I, Q. ii, proem.). These words point out the scope and the subject-matter of the moral part of theology. Francisco Suárez, who pregnantly calls this tendency of the creatures towards God "the return of the creatures to God", shows that there is no contradiction in designating man created after the image of God, endowed with reason and free will and exercising these faculties, as the object of moral theology, and God as the object of entire theology. "If we are asked to name the proximate object of moral theology, we shall undoubtedly say that it is man as a free agent, who seeks his happiness by his free actions; but if we are asked in what respect this object must be treated chiefly, we shall answer that this must be done with respect to God as his last end."

A detailed account of the wide range of moral theology may be found in the analytical index of Pars Secunda of St. Thomas's "Summa theologica". We must confine ourselves to a brief summary. The first question treats of man's last end, eternal happiness, Its nature and possession. Then follows an examination of human acts in themselves and their various subdivisions, of voluntary and involuntary acts, of the moral uprightness or malice of both interior and exterior acts and their consequences; the passions in general and in particular; the habits or permanent qualities of the human soul, and the general questions about virtues, vices, and sins. Under this last title, while enquiring into the causes of sin, the author embodies the doctrine on original sin and its consequences. This portion might, however, be with equal right assigned to dogmatic theology in the stricter meaning of the word. Although St. Thomas regards sin chiefly as a transgression of the law, and in particular of the "lex æterna" (Q. ii, a. 6), still he places the chapters on the laws after the section on sin; because sin, a free human act like any other human act, is first discussed from the standpoint of its subjective principles, viz. knowledge, will, and the tendency of the will; only after this are the human actions viewed with regard to their objective or exterior principles, and the exterior principle, by which human actions are judged not merely as human, but as moral actions, either morally good or morally bad, is the law. Since morality is conceived by him as supernatural morality, which exceeds the nature and the faculties of man, Divine grace, the other exterior principle of man's morally good actions, is discussed after the law. In the exordium to Q. xc, St. Thomas states his division briefly as follows: "The exterior principle which moves us to good actions is God; He instructs us by His law and aids us with His grace. Hence we shall speak first of the law, secondly of grace. "

The following volume is wholly devoted to the special questions, in the order given by St. Thomas in the prologue: "After a cursory glance at the virtues, vices, and the moral principles in general, it is incumbent on us to consider the various points in detail. Moral discussions, if satisfied with generalities, are of little value, because actions touch particular, individual things. When there is question of morals, we may consider individual actions in two ways: one, by examining the matter, i.e., by discussing the different virtues and vices; another, by inquiring into the various avocations of individuals and their states of life." St. Thomas then goes on to discuss the whole range of moral theology from both these standpoints. First, he closely scrutinizes the various virtues, keeping in view the Divine aids, and the sins and vices opposed to the respective virtues. He examines first the three Divine virtues which are wholly supernatural and embrace the vast field of charity and its actual practice; then he passes to the cardinal virtues with their auxiliary and allied virtues. The volume concludes with a discussion of the particular states of life in the Church of God, including those which suppose an extraordinary, Divine guidance. This last part, therefore, discusses subjects which specifically belong to mystical or ascetical theology, such as prophecy and extraordinary modes of prayer, but above all the active and the contemplative life, Christian perfection, and the religious state in the Church. The contents of a modern work on moral theology, as, for instance, that of Slater (London, 1909), are: Human acts, conscience, law, sin, the virtues of faith, hope, charity; the precepts of the Decalogue, including a special treatise on justice; the commandments of the Church; duties attached to particular states or offices; the sacraments, in so far as their administration and reception are a means of moral reform and rectitude; ecclesiastical laws and penalties, only in so far as they affect conscience; these laws forming properly the subject-matter of canon law, in so far as they govern and regulate the Church as an organization, Its membership, ministry, the relations between hierarchy, clergy, religious orders, laity, or of spiritual and temporal authority.

One circumstance must not be overlooked. Moral theology considers free human actions only in their relation to the supreme order, and to the last and highest end, not in their relation to the proximate ends which man may and must pursue, as for instance political, social, economical. Economics, politics, social science are separate fields of science, not subdivisions of moral science. Nevertheless, these special sciences must also be guided by morals, and must subordinate their specific principles to those of moral theology, at least so far as not to clash with the latter. Man is one being, and all his actions must finally lead him to his last and highest end. Therefore, various proximate ends must not turn him from this end, but must be made subservient to it and its attainment. Hence moral theology surveys all the individual relations of man and passes judgment on political, economical, social questions, not with regard to their bearings on politics and economy, but with regard to their influence upon a moral life. This is also the reason why there is hardly another science that touches other spheres so closely as does moral theology, and why its sphere is more extensive than that of any other. This is true inasmuch as moral theology has the eminently practical scope of instructing and forming spiritual directors and confessors, who must be familiar with human conditions in their relation to the moral law, and advise persons in every state and situation.

The manner in which moral theology treats its subject-matter, must be, as in theology generally, chiefly positive, that is, drawing from Revelation and theological sources. Starting from this positive foundation, reason also comes into play quite extensively, especially since the whole subject-matter of natural ethics has been raised to the level of supernatural morals. It is true reason must be illumined by supernatural faith, but when illumined its duty is to explain, prove, and defend most of the principles of moral theology.

From what has been said it is manifest that the chief source of moral theology is Sacred Scripture and Tradition together with the teachings of the Church. however, the following points must be observed regarding the Old Testament. Not all precepts contained in it are universally valid, as many belong to the ritual and special law of the Jews. These statutes never obliged the non-Jewish world and have simply been abrogated by the New Covenant, so that now the ritual observances proper are illicit. The Decalogue, however, with the sole change in the law enjoining the celebration of the Sabbath, has passed Into the New Covenant a positive Divine confirmation of the natural law, and now constitutes the principal subject matter of Christian morality. Moreover, we must remember that the Old Covenant did not stand on the high moral level to which Christ elevated the New Covenant. Jesus Himself mentions things which were permitted to the Jews "on account of the hardness of their hearts", but against which He applied again the law at first imposed by God. Hence, not everything that was tolerated in the Old Testament and its writings, is tolerated now; on the contrary, many of the usages approved and established there would be counter to Christian perfection as counselled by Christ. With these limitations the writings of the Old Testament are sources of moral theology, containing examples of and exhortations to heroic virtues, from which the Christian moralist, following in the footsteps of Christ and His Apostles, may well draw superb models of sanctity.

Apart from Sacred Scripture, the Church recognizes also Tradition as a source of revealed truths, and hence of Christian morals. It has assumed a concrete shape chiefly in the writings of the Fathers. Furthermore, the decisions of the Church must be regarded as a source, since they are based on the Bible and Tradition, they are the proximate source of moral theology, because they contain the final judgment about the meaning of Sacred Scripture as well as the teachings of the Fathers. These include the long list of condemned propositions, which must be considered as danger signals along the boundary between lawful and illicit, not only when the condemnation has been pronounced by virtue of the highest Apostolic authority, but also when the congregation instituted by the pope has issued a general, doctrinal decision in questions bearing on morals. What Pius IX wrote concerning the meetings of scholars in Munich in the year 1863 may also be applied here: "Since there is question of that subjection which binds all Catholics in conscience who desire to advance the interests of the Church by devoting themselves to the speculative sciences; let the members of this assembly recall that it is not sufficient for Catholic scholars to accept and esteem the above-mentioned dogmas, but that they are also obliged to submit to the decisions of the papal congregations as well as to those teachings which are, by the constant and universal consent of Catholics, so held as theological truths and certain conclusions that the opposite opinion even when not heretical, still deserves some theological censure." If this is true of the dogmatic doctrines in the strict sense of the word, we might say that it is still more true of moral questions, because for them not only absolute and infallibility certain, but also morally certain decisions must be accounted as obligatory norms.

The words of Pius IX just quoted, point to another source of theological doctrines, and hence of morals, viz., the universal teachings of the Catholic schools. For these are the channels by which the Catholic doctrines on faith and morals must be transmitted without error, and which have consequently the nature of a source. From the unanimous doctrine of the Catholic schools follows naturally the conviction of the universal Church. But since it is a dogmatic principle that the whole Church cannot err in matters of faith and morals, the consent of the various Catholic schools must offer the guarantee of infallibility in these questions.

Moral theology, to be complete in every respect, must accomplish in moral questions what dogmatic theology does in questions pertaining to dogma. The latter has to explain clearly the truths of faith and prove them to be such; it must also, as far as possible, show their accordance with reason, defend them against objections, trace their connection with other truths, and, by means of theological argumentation, deduce further truths. Moral theology must follow the same processive questions of morals. — It is evident that this cannot be done in all branches of moral theology in such a way as to exhaust the subject, except by a series of monographs. It would take volumes to sketch but the beauty and the harmony of God's dispositions, which transcend the natural law, but which God enacted in order to elevate man to a higher plane and to lead him to his supernatural end in a future life — and yet all this is embraced in the subject of supernatural morals. Nor is moral theology confined to the exposition of those duties and virtues which cannot be shirked if man wishes to attain his last end; it includes all virtues, even those which mark the height of Christian perfection, and their practice, not only in the ordinary degree, but also in the ascetical and mystical life. Hence, it is entirely correct to designate asceticism and mysticism as parts of Christian moral theology, though ordinarily they are treated as distinct sciences.

The task of the moral theologian is by no means completed when he has explained the questions indicated. Moral theology, in more than one respect, is essentially a practical science. Its instructions must extend to moral character, moral behaviour, the completion and issue of moral aspirations, so that it can offer a definite norm for the complex situations of human life. For this purpose, it must examine the individual cases which arise and determine the limits and the gravity of the obligation in each. Particularly those whose office and position in the Church demand the cultivation of theological science, and who are called to be the teachers and counsellors, must find in it a practical guide. As jurisprudence must enable the future judge and lawyer to administer justice in individual cases, so must moral theology enable the spiritual director or confessor to decide matters of conscience in varied cases of everyday life; to weigh the violations of the natural law in the balance of Divine justice; it must enable the spiritual guide to distinguish correctly and to advise others as to what is sin and what is not, what is counselled and what not, what is good and what is better; it must provide a scientific training for the shepherd of the flock, so that he can direct all to a life of duty and virtue, warn them against sin and danger, lead from good to better those who are endowed with necessary light and moral power, raise up and strengthen those who have fallen from the moral level. Many of these tasks are assigned to the collateral science of pastoral theology; but this also treats a special part of the duties of moral theology, and falls, therefore, within the scope of moral theology in its widest sense. The purely theoretical and speculative treatment of the moral questions must be supplemented by casuistry. Whether this should be done separately, that is, whether the subject matter should be taken casuistically before or after its theoretical treatment, or whether the method should be at the same time both theoretical and casuistical, is unimportant for the matter itself; the practical feasibility will decide this point, while for written works on moral theology the special aim of the author will determine it. However, he who teaches or writes moral theology for the training of Catholic priests, would not do full justice to the end at which he must aim, if he did not unite the casuistical with the theoretical and speculative element.

What has been said so far, sufficiently outlines the concept of moral theology in its widest sense. Our next task is to follow up its actual formation and development.

Moral theology, correctly understood, means the science of supernaturally revealed morals. Hence, they cannot speak of moral theology who reject supernatural Revelation; the most they can do is to discourse on natural ethics. But to distinguish between moral theology and ethics is sooner or later to admit a science of ethics without God and religion. That this contains an essential contradiction, is plain to everyone who analyzes the ideas of moral rectitude and moral perversion, or the concept of an absolute duty which forces itself with unrelenting persistency on all who have attained the use of reason. Without God, an absolute duty is inconceivable, because there is nobody to impose obligation. I cannot oblige myself, because I cannot be my own superior; still less can I oblige the whole human race, and yet I feel myself obliged to many things, and cannot but feel myself absolutely obliged as man, and hence cannot but regard all those who share human nature with me as obliged likewise. It is plain then that this obligation must proceed from a higher being who is superior to all men, not only to those who live at present, but to all who have been and will be, nay, in a certain sense even to those who are merely possible, This superior being is the Lord of all, God. It is also plain that although this Supreme lawgiver can be known by natural reason, neither He nor His law can be sufficiently known without a revelation on His part. Hence if is that moral theology, the study of this Divine law is actually cultivated only by those who faithfully cling to a Divine Revelation, and by the sects which sever their connection with the Church, only as long as they retain the belief in a supernatural Revelation through Jesus Christ.

Wherever Protestantism has thrown this belief overboard, there the study of moral theology as a science has suffered shipwreck. Today it would be merely lost labour to look for an advancement of it on the part of a non-Catholic denomination. In the seventeenth and eighteenth centuries there were still men to be found who made an attempt at it. J. A. Dorner states in Herzog, "Real-Encyklopädie", IV, 364 sqq. (s.v. "Ethik"), that prominent Protestant writers upholding "theological morals" have grown very scarce since the eighteenth century. However, this is not quite correct. Of those who still cling to a positive Protestantism, we may name Martensen, who recently entered the lists with deep conviction for "Christian Ethics"; the same, though in his own peculiar manner, is done by Lemme in his "Christliche Ethik" (1905); both attribute to it a scope wider and objectively other than that of natural ethics. A few names from the seventeenth and eighteenth centuries may here suffice:

Hugo Grotius (d. 1645), Pufendorf (d. 1694) and Christian Thomasius (d. 1728), all see the difference between theological and natural morals in that the former is also positive, i.e. Divinely revealed, but with the same subject matter as the latter. This last assertion could spring only from the Protestant view which has staked its all on the "fides fiducialis"; but it can hardly acknowledge a range of duties widened by Christ and Christianity. Other writers of a "theologia moralis" based on this "fides fiducialis", are Buddeus, Chr. A. Crusius, and Jerem. Fr. Reuss. A logical result of Kantianism was the denial of the very possibility of moral theology, since Kant had made autonomous reason the only source of obligation. On this point Dorner says (loc. cit.): "It is true that the autonomy and the autocracy of the moral being separates morals and religion"; he would have been nearer the mark, had he said: "they destroy all morals". Generally speaking the modern Liberal Protestants hardly know any other than autonomous morals; even when they do speak of "religious" morals, they find its last explanation in man, religion, and God or Divine Revelation being taken in their Modernistic sense, that is subjective notions of whose objective value we have no knowledge and no certainty.

This being the case, there remains only one question to be discussed: What has been the actual development and method of moral theology in the Church? and here we must first of all remember that the Church is not an educational institution or a school for the advancement of the sciences. True, she esteems and promotes the sciences, especially theology, and scientific schools are founded by her; but this is not her only, or even her chief task. She is the authoritative institution, founded by Christ for the salvation of mankind; she speaks with power and authority to the whole human race, to all nations, to all classes of society, to every age, communicates to them the doctrine of salvation unadulterated and. offers them her aids. It is her mission to urge upon educated and uneducated persons alike the acceptance of truth, without regard to its scientific study and establishment. After this has been accepted on faith, she also promotes and urges, according to times and circumstances, the scientific investigation of the truth, but she retains supervision over it and stands above all scientific aspirations and labours. As a result, we see the subject matter of moral theology, though laid down and positively communicated by the Church, treated differently by ecclesiastical writers according to the requirements of times and circumstances.

In the first years of the early Church, when the Divine seed, nourished by the blood of the martyrs, was seen to sprout in spite of the chilling frosts of persecution, when, to the amazement of the hostile world, it grew into a mighty tree of heavenly plantation, there was hardly leisure for the scientific study of Christian doctrine. Hence morals were at first treated in a popular, parenetic form. Throughout the Patristic period, hardly any other method for moral questions was in vogue, though this method might consist now in a concise exposition, now in a more detailed discussion of individual virtues and duties. One of the earliest works of Christian tradition, if not the earliest after the Sacred Scripture, the "Didache" or "Teaching of the Apostles", is chiefly of a moral-theological nature. It Is hardly more than a code of laws an enlarged decalogue, to which are added the principal duties arising from the Divine institution of the means of salvation and from the Apostolic institutions of a common worship — in this respect valuable for dogmatic theology in its narrow sense. The "Pastor" of Hermas, composed a little later, is of a moral character, that is, it contains an ascetical exhortation to Christian morality and to serious penance if one should have relapsed into sin.

There exists a long series of occasional writings bearing on moral theology, from the first period of the Christian era; their purpose was either to recommend a certain virtue, or to exhort the faithful in general for certain times and circumstances. Thus, from Tertullian (d. about 240) we have: "De spectaculis", "De idololatria", "De corona militis", "De patientia", "De oratione", "De poenitentia", "Ad uxorem", not to take into consideration the works which he wrote after his defection to Montanism and which are indeed of interest for the history of Christian morals, but cannot serve as guides in it. Of Origen (d. 254) we still possess two minor works which bear on our question, viz., "Demartyrio", parenetic in character, and "De oratione", moral and dogmatic in content; the latter meets the objections which are advanced or rather reiterated even today against the efficacy of prayer. Occasional writings and monographs are offered to us in the precious works of St. Cyprian (d. 258); among the former must be numbered: "De mortalitate" and "De martyrio", in a certain sense also "De lapsis", though it bears rather a disciplinary and judicial character; to the latter class belong: "De habitu virginum", "De oratione", "De opere et eleemosynis", "De bono patientiæ", and "De zelo et livore". A clearer title to be classed among moral-theological books seems to belong to an earlier work, the "Pædagogus" of Clement of Alexandria (d. about 217). It is a detailed account of a genuine Christian's daily life, in which ordinary and everyday actions are measured by the standard of supernatural morality. The same author touches upon Christian morals also in his other works, particularly in the "Stromata"; but this work is principally written from the apologetic standpoint, since it was intended to vindicate the entire Christian doctrine, both faith and morals, against pagan and Jewish philosophies.

In subsequent years, when the persecutions ceased, and patristic literature began to flourish, we find not only exegetical writings and apologies written to defend Christian doctrine against various heresies, but also numerous moral-theological works, principally sermons, homilies, and monographs. First of these are the orations of St. Gregory of Nazianzus (d. 391), of St. Gregory of Nyssa (d. 395), of St. John Chrysostom (d. 406), of St. Augustine

(d. 430), and above all the "Catecheses" of St. Cyril of Jerusalem (d. 386). Of St. John Chrysostom we have "De sacerdotio"; of St. Augustine, "Confessiones", "Soliloquia", "De cathechizandis rudibus", "De patientia", "De continentia", "De bono coniugali", "De adulterinis coniugiis", "De sancta virginitate", "De bono viduitatis", "De mendacio", "De cura pro mortuis gerenda", so that the titles alone suffice to give an intimation of the wealth of subjects discussed with no less unction than originality and depth of thought. A separate treatment of the supernatural morality of Christians was attempted by St. Ambrose (d. 397) in his books "De officiis", a work which, imitating Cicero's "De officiis", forms a Christian counterpart of the pagan's purely natural discussions. A work of an entirely different stamp and of larger proportions is the "Expositio in Job, seu moralium lib. XXV", of Gregory the Great (d. 604). It is not a systematic arrangement of the various Christian duties, but a collection of moral instructions and exhortations based on the Book of Job; Alzog (Handbuch der Patrologie, 92) calls it a "fairly complete repertory of morals". More systematic is his work "De cura pastorali" which was intended primarily for the pastor and which is considered even today a classical work in pastoral theology.

Having broadly outlined the general progress of moral theology during the Patristic era proper, we must supplement it by detailing the development of a very special branch of moral theology and its practical application. For moral theology must necessarily assume a peculiar form when its purpose is restricted to the administration of the Sacrament of Penance. The chief result to be attained was a clear notion of the various sins and their species, of their relative grievousness and importance, and of the penance to be imposed for them. In order to ensure uniform procedure, it was necessary for ecclesiastical superiors to lay down more detailed directions; this they did either of their own accord or in answer to inquiries. Writings of this kind are the pastoral or canonical letters of St. Cyprian, St. Peter of Alexandria, St. Basil of Cappadocia, and St. Gregory of Nyssa; the decretals and synodal letters of a number of popes, as Siricius, Innocent, Celestine, Leo I, etc.; canons of several oecumenical councils. These decrees were collected at an early date and used by the bishops and priests as a norm in distinguishing sins and in imposing ecclesiastical penance for them.

The ascendancy of the so-called "penitential books" dated from the seventh century, when a change took place in the practice of ecclesiastical penance. Till then it had been a time-honoured law in the Church that the three capital crimes: apostasy, murder, and adultery, were to be atoned for by an accurately determined penance, which was public at least for public sins. This atonement, which consisted chiefly in severe fasts and public, humiliating practices, was accompanied by various religious ceremonies under the strict supervision of the Church; it included four distinct stations or classes of penitents and at times lasted from fifteen to twenty years. At an early period, however, the capital sins mentioned above were divided into sections, according as the circumstances were either aggravating or attenuating;, and a correspondingly longer or shorter period of penance was set down for them. When in the course of centuries, entire nations, uncivilized and dominated by fierce passions, were received into the bosom of the Church, and when, as a result, heinous crimes began to multiply, many offences, akin to those mentioned above, were included among sins which were subject to canonical penances, while for others, especially for secret sins, the priest determined the penance, its duration and mode, by the canons. The seventh century brought with It a relaxation, not indeed in canonical penance, but in the ecclesiastical control; on the other hand, there was an increase in the number of crimes which demanded a fixed penance if discipline was to be maintained; besides, many hereditary rights of a particular nature, which had led to a certain mitigation of the universal norm of penance, had to be taken into consideration; substitutes and so-called redemptiones, which consisted in pecuniary donations to the poor or to public utilities, gradually gained entrance and vogue; all this necessitated the drawing up of comprehensive lists of the various crimes and of the penances to be imposed for them, so that a certain uniformity among confessors might be reached as to the treatment of penitents and the administration of the sacraments.

There appeared a number of "penitential books" Some of them, bearing the sanction of the Church, closely followed the ancient canonical decrees of the popes and the councils, and the approved statutes of St. Basil, St. Gregory of Nyssa, and others; others were merely private works, which, recommended by the renown of their authors, found a wide circulation, others again went too far in their decisions and hence constrained ecclesiastical superiors either to reprehend or condemn them. A more detailed account of these works will be found in another article.

These books were not written for a scientific, but for a practical juridical purpose. Nor do they mark an advance in the science of moral theology, but rather a standing-still, nay, even a decadence. Those centuries of migrations, of social and political upheavals, offered a soil little adapted for a successful cultivation of the sciences, and though in the ninth century a fresh attempt was made to raise scientific studies to a higher level, still the work of the subsequent centuries consisted rather in collecting and renewing treasures of former centuries than in adding to them. This is true of moral-theological questions, no less than of other scientific branches. From this stagnation theology in general and moral theology in particular rose again to new life towards the end of the twelfth and the beginning of the thirteenth century. A new current of healthy development was noticeable in moral theology and that in two directions: one in the new strength infused into the practice of the confessors, the other in renewed vigour given to the speculative portion.

With the gradual dying out of the public penances, the "penitential books" lost their importance more and more. The confessors grew less concerned about the exact measure of penances than about the essential object of the sacrament, which is the reconciliation of the sinner with God. Besides, the "penitential books" were by far too defective for teaching confessors how to judge about the various sins, their consequences and remedies. In order to meet this need, St. Raymond of Peñafort wrote towards the year 1235 the "Summa de poenitentia et matrimonio". Like his famous collection of decretals, it is a repertory of canons on various matters, i.e. important passages from the Fathers, councils, and papal decisions. More immediately adapted for actual use was the "Summa de casibus conscientiæ", which was written about 1317 by an unknown member of the Order of St. Francis at Asti in Upper Italy, and which is, therefore, known as "Summa Astensana" or "Summa Astensis". Its eight books cover the whole subject matter of moral theology and the canonical decrees, both indispensable for the pastor and confessor: Book I, the Divine commandments; II, virtues and vices; III, contracts and wills; IV-VI, sacraments, except matrimony; VII, ecclesiastical censures; VIII, matrimony. The fourteenth and fifteenth centuries produced a number of similar summoe for confessors; all of them, however, discarded the arrangement in books and chapters, and adopted the alphabetical order. Their value is, of course, widely different. The following are the most important and most popular among them: The "Summa confessorum" of the Dominican Johannes of Freiburg (d. 1314) which was published a few years previous to the "Summa Astensis"; its high reputation and wide circulation was due to its revision by another member of the Dominican Order, Bartholomæus of Pisa (d. 1347) who arranged it alphabetically and supplemented its canonical parts; it is commonly known as the "Summa Pisana". This work served as the foundation for the "Summa. angelica", a clear and concise treatise, composed about 1476 by the Franciscan Angelus Cerletus, called "Angelus a Clavasio" after his native city, Chiavasso. Its great popularity is attested by the fact that it went through at least thirty-one editions from 1476 to 1520. A like popularity was enjoyed by the "Summa casuum" of the Franciscan, J. B. Trovamala, which appeared a few years later (1484) and, after being revised by the author himself, in 1495, bore the title of "Summa rosella". One of the last and most renowned of these summoe was probably the "Summa Silvestrina" of the Dominican Silvester Prierias (d. 1523), after which moral theology began to be treated in a different manner. The summoe here mentioned, being exclusively written for the practical use of confessors, did not spurn the more elementary form; but they represented the results of a thorough, scientific study, which produced not only writings of this kind, but also other systematic works of a profound scholarship.

The twelfth century witnessed a busy activity in speculative theology, which centered about the cathedral and monastic schools. These produced men like Hugh and Richard of St. Victor, and especially Hugh's pupil, Peter the Lombard, called the Master of the Sentences, who flourished in the cathedral school of Paris towards the middle of the century, and whose "Libri sententiarum" served for several centuries as the standard text-book in theological lecture-halls. In those days, however, when dangerous heresies against the fundamental dogmas and mysteries of the Christian faith began to appear, the moral part of the Christian doctrine received scant treatment; Peter the Lombard incidentally discusses a few moral questions, as e.g., about sin, while speaking of creation and the original state of man, or more in particular, while treating of original sin. Other questions, e.g., about the freedom of our actions and the nature of human actions in general, are answered in the doctrine on Christ, where he discusses the knowledge and the will of Christ. Even the renowned commentator of the "Sentences", Alexander of Hales, O. Min., does not yet seriously enter into Christian morals. The work of constructing moral theology as a speculative science was at last undertaken and completed by that great luminary of theology, St. Thomas of Aquin, to whose "Summa theologica" we referred above. Aside from this masterpiece, of which the second part and portions of the third pertain to morals, there are several minor works extant which bear a moral and ascetical character; the last-named branch was cultivated with extraordinary skill by St. Bonaventure of the Franciscan Order, though he did not equal the systematic genius of St. Thomas.

This and the subsequent centuries produced a number of prominent theologians, some of whom contested various doctrines of Aquinas, as Duns Scotus and his adherents, while others followed in his footsteps and wrote commentaries on his works, as Ægidius Romanus and Capreolus. Nevertheless, purely moral-theological questions were rarely made the subject of controversy during this time; a new epoch in the method of moral theology did not dawn until after the Council of Trent. However, there are two extremely fertile writers of the fifteenth century who not only exerted a powerful influence on the advancement of theology but raised the standard of practical life. They are Dionysius the Carthusian and St. Antoninus, Bishop of Florence. The former is well known for his ascetical works, while the latter devoted himself to the practice of the confessional and the ordinary work of the pastor. His "Summa theologica" belongs specially to our subject. It went through several editions, and A. Ballerini's revision of it, which appeared in 1740 at Florence, contains four folios. The third volume treats chiefly of ecclesiastical law; it discusses at great length the legal position of the Church and its penal code. A few chapters of the first volume are devoted to the psychological side of man and his actions. The remainder of the whole work is a commentary, from the purely moral standpoint, on the second part of St. Thomas's "Summa theologica", to which it constantly refers. It is not a mere theoretical explanation, but is so replete with juridical and casuistical details that it may be called an inexhaustible fountain for manuals of casuistry. How highly the practical wisdom of Antoninus was esteemed even during his lifetime is attested by the surname "Antoninus consiliorum", Antoninus of good counsel, given to him in the Roman Breviary.

A new life was breathed into the Catholic Church by the Council of Trent. Reformation of morals gave a fresh impetus to theological science. These had gradually fallen from the high level to which they had risen at the time of St. Thomas; the desire of solid advancement had frequently given place to seeking after clever argumentations on unimportant questions. The sixteenth century witnessed a complete change. Even before the council convened, there were eminent scholars of a serious turn of mind as Thomas of Vio (usually called Cajetanus), Victoria, and the two Sotos, all men whose solid knowledge of theology proved of immense benefit to the Council itself. Their example was followed by a long series of excellent scholars, especially Dominicans and members of the newly-founded Society of Jesus. It was above all the systematic side of moral theology which was now taken up with renewed zeal. In former centuries, Peter the Lombard's "Sentences" had been the universal text-book, and more prominent theological works of subsequent ages professed to be nothing else than commentaries upon them; henceforth, however, the "Summa theologica" of St. Thomas was followed as guide in theology and a large number of the best theological works, written after the Council of Trent, were entitled "Commentarii in Summam Sti. Thomæ". The natural result was a more extensive treatment of moral questions, since these constituted by far the largest portion of St. Thomas's "Summa". Among the earliest classical works of this kind is the "Commentariorum theologicorum tomi quattuor" of Gregory of Valentia. It is well thought out and shows great accuracy; vols. III and IV contain the explanation of the "Prima Secundæ" and the "Secunda Secundæ" of St. Thomas. This work was succeeded, at the end of the sixteenth and the beginning of the seventeenth century, by a number of similar commentaries; among them stand out most prominently those of Gabriel Vásquez", Lessius, Francisco Suárez, Becanus, and the works of Thomas Sanchez "In decalogum" as well as "Consilia moralia", which are more casuistical in their method; the commentaries of Dominic Bánez, which had appeared some time before; and those of Medina.

Prominent among all those mentioned is Francis Francisco Suárez, S.J., in whose voluminous works the principle questions of the "Secunda" of St. Thomas are developed with great accuracy and a wealth of positive knowledge. Almost every question is searchingly examined, and brought nearer its final solution; the most varied opinions of former theologians are extensively discussed, subjected to a close scrutiny, and the final decision is given with great circumspection, moderation, and modesty. A large folio treats the fundamental questions of moral theology in general:

* (1) De fine et beatitudine;
* (2) De voluntario et involuntario, et de actibus humanis;
* (3) De bonitate et malitia humanorum actuum;
* (4) De passionibus et vitiis.

Another volume treats of "Laws": several folio volumes are devoted to treatises which do indeed belong to morals, but which are inseparably connected with other strictly dogmatic questions about God and His attributes, viz., "De gratia divina"; they are today assigned everywhere to dogma proper; a third series gives the entire doctrine of the sacraments (with the exception of matrimony) from their dogmatic and moral side. Not all of the various virtues were examined by Francisco Suárez; besides the treatise on the theological virtues, we possess only that on the virtue of religion. But if any of Francisco Suárez's works may be called classical it is the last-named, which discusses in four volumes the whole subject "De religione" Within the whole range of "religio", including its notion and relative position, its various acts and practices, as prayers, vows, oaths, etc., the sins against it, there can hardly be found a dogmatic or casuistic question that has not been either solved or whose solution has not at least been attempted. Of the last two volumes one treats of religious orders in general, the other of the "Institute" of the Society of Jesus.

In the course of the seventeenth and eighteenth century, there appeared a number of similar, though conciser, works which treat moral-theological questions as a part of universal theology with the genuine spirit of Scholastic science. There are those of Tanner, Coninck, Platel, Gotti, Billuart, and many others, the mere enumeration of whom would lead us too far afield. We must, however, mention one to whom nobody can deny the honour of having advanced both speculative and practical theology, and especially practical morals, John de Lugo. Endowed with uncommon, speculative genius and clear, practical judgment, he in many instances pointed out entirely new paths towards the solution of moral questions. Speaking of his moral theology, St. Alphonsus styles him "by all odds leader after St. Thomas". The works that have come down to us are: "De fide", "De Incarnatione", "De justitia et jure", "De sacramentis", viz., "De sacramentis in genere", "De baptismo et eucharistia", and "De poenitentia". It is above all the volume "De poenitentia" which, through its sixteenth disputation, has become the classical handbook for casuistical moral theology and particularly for the specific distinction of sins; to the same subject belong the posthumous "Responsa moralia", a collection of answers given by de Lugo in complicated cases of conscience. This is not the place to point out his eminence as a dogmatist; suffice it to say that many far-reaching questions receive original solutions, which, though not universally accepted, have yet shed considerable light on these subjects.

The method which Lugo applies to moral theological questions, may well be called mixed, that is, it is both speculative and casuistical. Such works of a mixed character now grow common, they treat the whole subject-matter of moral theology, in as far as it is serviceable for the confessor and the pastor, in this mixed manner, though they insist more on casuistry than did Lugo. A type of this kind is the "Theologia moralis" of Paul Laymann (d. 1635); in this category may also be numbered the "Theologia decalogalis" and "Theologia sacramentalis" of Sporer (d. 1683), the "Conferentiæ" of Elbel (d. 1756), and the "Theologia moralis" of Reuter* (d. 1762). Almost numberless are the manuals for confessors, written in a simple casuistical form, though even these justify their conclusions by internal reasons after legitimatizing them by an appeal to external authority. They are not unfrequently the fruit of thorough, speculative knowledge and extensive reading. One of the most solid is probably the "Manuale confessariorum et poenitentium" of Azpilcueta (1494-1586), the great canonist, commonly known as "Doctor Navarrus"; furthermore, the "Instructio sacerdotum" or "Summa casuum conscientiæ" of Cardinal Tolet (d. 1596), which was highly recommended by St. Francis of Sales. One other work must also be mentioned, viz., the so-called "Medulla theologiæ moralis" of Hermann Busenbaum (d. 1688), which has become famous on account of its very extensive use (forty editions in less than twenty years during the lifetime of the author) and the number of its commentators. Among these are included Claude Lacroix, whose moral theology is considered as one of the most valuable of the eighteenth century, and St. Alphonsus Liguori, with whom, however, an entirely new epoch of moral theology commences.

Before entering upon this new phase, let us glance at the development of the so-called systems of morals and the controversies which sprang up among Catholic scholars, as well as at the casuistical method of treating moral theology in general. For it is precisely the casuistry of moral theology around which these controversies centre, and which has experienced severe attacks in our own day. These attacks were for the most part confined to Germany. The champions of the adversaries are J. B. Hirscher (d. 1865), Döllinger, Reusch, and a group of Catholic scholars who, in the years 1901 and 1902, demanded a "reform of Catholic moral theology", though all were not moved by the same spirit. In Hirscher it was the zeal for a supposedly good cause, though he was implicated in theological errors; Döllinger and Reusch attempted to cover their defection from the Church and their refusal to acknowledge the papal infallibility by holding up to the ridicule of the world ecclesiastical conditions and affairs which they thought militated against that infallibility; the latest phase of this opposition is mainly the result of misunderstandings. In order to elucidate the accusations brought against casuistry, we use the wholly unjustifiable criticism which Hirscher launched against Scholastic theology in general in his work of 1832, "On the Relation between the Gospel and Theological Scholasticism"; it is quoted approvingly by Döllinger and Reusch (Moralstreitigkeiten, 13 sqq.):

(1) "Instead of penetrating into the spirit which makes virtue what it is and underlies everything that is good in this world, in other words, instead of beginning with the one indivisible nature of all goodness, they begin with the material of the various moral precepts and prohibitions without adverting to where these originate, on what foundation they rest, and what is their life-giving principle." This means that Scholastics and casuists know only individual things, see nothing universal and uniform in the virtues and duties.

(2) "Instead of deriving these precepts and prohibitions from the one, individual essence of all goodness and thereby creating certainty in the moral judgments of their audience, they, rejecting principles, string 'shalt' to 'shalt', provide them with innumerable statutes and clauses, confuse and oppress the hearer by the overflowing measure of duties, half-duties, non-duties." In other words, the Scholastics oppress and confuse by an unnecessary multiplication of duties and non-duties.

(3) "It is more in accordance with the spirit of Mosaism than with that of Christianity when Christian morality is treated less as a doctrine of virtues than of laws and duties, and when by adding commandment to

commandment, prohibition to prohibition, it gives us a full and shaken measure of moral rules instead of building up on the Christian spirit, deriving everything from it and pointing out all particular virtues in its light." Or briefly, casuistry promotes exterior sanctimoniousness without the interior spirit.

(4) "Those who treat morals from the standpoint of casuistry, assign an important part to the distinction between grave and light laws grave and light duties, serious and slight transgressions, mortal and venial sins. . . . Now, the distinction between grievous and venial sins is not without a solid foundation, and if it is chiefly based on the different qualities of the will, and if, besides, the various degrees of goodness and malice are measured by the presence, e.g., of a purely good and strong will, of one less pure and less strong, of a weak, inert, impure, malicious, perverted will, then nobody will raise his voice against it. But it is wholly different when the distinction between mortal and venial sins is taken objectively, and based on the gravity and lightness of the commandments. . . . Such a distinction between mortal and venial sins, founded on the material differences of the commandments and the prohibitions, is a source of torment and anxiety for many. . . . True morality cannot be advanced through such an anxiety. . . . The mass of the people will derive only this one profit from such a method: many will refrain from what is forbidden under pain of mortal sin and will do what is commanded under the same penalty, but they will care little

for what is commanded or forbidden under pain of venial sin only; on the contrary they will seek a compensation in the latter for what they sacrificed to the grave commandments. But can we call the lives of such men Christian?" In other words, casuistry falsifies the consciences by distinguishing objectively between mortal and venial sins, leads to a contempt of the latter, and renders a genuinely Christian life impossible.

It is not difficult to refute all these accusations. One glance at the "Summa theologica" of St. Thomas will prove how incorrect is the first charge that Scholasticism and casuistry know only individual good acts and individual virtues, without inquiring into the foundation common to all virtues. Before treating the individual virtues and the individual duties, St. Thomas gives us a whole volume of discussions of a general nature, of which we may note the profound speculations on the last end, the goodness and malice of human actions, the eternal law.

The second accusation, that the Scholastic casuistry confuses the mind by its mass of duties and non-duties, can only mean that the Scholastic casuistry sets these up arbitrarily and contrary to truth. The complaint can only refer to those works and lectures which aim at the instruction of the clergy, pastors, and confessors. The reader or hearer who is confused or oppressed by this "mass of duties etc." shows by this very fact that he has not the talent necessary for the office of confessor or spiritual guide, that he should therefore choose another vocation.

The third charge, directed against Judaical hypocrisy which neglects the fostering of the interior life, is refuted by every work on casuistry, however meagre, for every one of them states most emphatically that, without the state of grace and a good intention, all external works, no matter how difficult and heroic, are valueless in the sight of God. Can the necessity of the internal spirit be brought out more clearly? And even if, in some cases, the external fulfilment of a certain work is laid down as the minimum demanded by God or the Church, without which the Christian would incur eternal damnation, yet this is not banishing the internal spirit, but designating the external fulfilment as the low-water mark of morality.

Lastly, the fourth charge springs from a very grave theological error. There can be no doubt that, in judging the heinousness of sin and in distinguishing between mortal and venial sins, the subjective element must be taken into consideration, However, every compendium of moral theology, no matter how casuistical, meets this requirement. Every manual distinguishes sins which arise from ignorance, weakness, malice, without, however, labelling all sins of weakness as venial sins, or all sins of malice as mortal sins; for there are surely minor acts of malice which cannot be said to cause the death of the soul. Every manual also takes cognizance of sins which are committed without sufficient deliberation, knowledge, or freedom: all these, even though the matter be grave, are counted as venial sins. On the other hand, every manual recognizes venial and grievous sins which are such by the gravity of the matter alone. Or who would, abstracting from everything else, put a jocose lie on a par with the denial of faith? But even in these sins, mortal or venial according to their object, the casuists lay stress on the personal dispositions in which the sin was actually committed. Hence, their universal principle: the result of a subjectively erroneous conscience may be that an action which is in itself only venial, becomes a mortal sin, and vice versa, that an action which is in itself mortally sinful, that is, constitutes a grave violation of the moral law, may be only a venial sin. Nevertheless, all theologians, also casuists, consider a correct conscience a great boon and hence endeavour, by their casuistic discussions, to contribute towards the formation of correct consciences, so that the subjective estimate of the morality of certain actions may coincide, as far as possible, with the objective norm of morality.

When, lastly, various opponents of the casuistical method object that the moralist occupies himself exclusively with sins and their analysis, with the "dark side" of human life, let them remember that it is physically impossible to say everything in one breath, that, just as in many other arts and sciences, a division of labour may also be advantageous for the science of moral theology, that the particular purpose of manuals and lectures may be limited to the education of skilled confessors and that this purpose may very well be fulfilled by centering attention on the dark side of human life. Nevertheless, it must be granted that this cannot be the only purpose of moral theology: a thorough discussion of all Christian virtues and the means of acquiring them is Indispensable. If at any time this part of moral theology should be pushed to the background, moral theology would become one-sided and would need a revision, not by cutting down casuistry, but by devoting more time and energy to the doctrine of virtues in their scientific, parenetical, and ascetical aspect.

In all these branches of moral theology, a great advance was noticeable at the time of the Council of Trent. That more stress was laid on casuistry in particular, finds its explanation in the growing frequency of sacramental confession. This is freely conceded by our adversaries. Döllinger and Reusch say (op. cit., 19 sqq.): "The fact that casuistry underwent a further development after the sixteenth century, is connected with further changes in the penitential discipline. From that time on the custom prevailed of approaching the confessional more frequently, regularly before Communion, of confessing not only grievous, but also venial sins, and of asking the confessor's advice for all troubles of the spiritual life, so that the confessor became more and more a spiritual father and guide." The confessor needed this schooling and scientific training, which alone could enable him to give correct decisions in complex cases of human life, to form a correct estimate of moral goodness or defect, duty or violation of duty, virtue or vice. Now, it was inevitable that the confessor should meet cases where the existence or exact measure of the obligation remained obscure even after careful examination, where the moralist was therefore confronted by the question what the final decision in these cases should be: whether one was obliged to consider oneself bound when the duty was obscure and doubtful, or how one could remove this doubt and arrive at the definite conclusion that there was no strict obligation. That the former could not be the case, but that an obligation, to exist, must first be proved, had always been known and had been variously expressed in practical rules: "In dubiis benigniora sequenda", "odiosa sunt restringenda", etc. The basic principle, however, for solving such dubious cases and attaining the certitude necessary for the morality of an action was not always kept clearly in view. To establish this universal principle, was equivalent to establishing a moral system; and the various systems were distinguished by the principle to which each adhered.

    The history of Probabilism is given under this title, suffice it to say here that from the middle of the seventeenth century when the violent discussion of this question begins, the development of moral theology coincides with that of Probabilism and of other Probabilistic systems; although these systems touch only a small portion of morals and of moral truths and nothing is farther from the truth than the opinion, so wide-spread among the adversaries of Catholic morals, that Probabilism gave a new shape and a new spirit to the whole of moral theology. Probabilism and the other systems of morals are concerned only about cases which are objectively doubtful; hence they abstract entirely from the wide sphere of certain, established truths. Now, the latter class is by far the larger in moral theology also; were it not so, human reason would be in a sorry plight, and Divine providence would have bestowed little care on the noblest of its visible creatures and on their highest goods, even in the supernatural order, in which a full measure of gifts and graces was showered upon those ransomed in Christ. The certain and undoubted portion includes all the fundamental questions of Christian morals; it comprises those principles of the moral order by which the relations of man to himself, to God, to his neighbour, and to the various communities are regulated; it embraces the doctrine of the last end of man and of the supernatural means of attaining this end. There is only a comparatively small number of objectively obscure and doubtful laws or duties that appeal to Probabilism or Antiprobabilism for a decision. However, as has been said, since the middle of the seventeenth century, the interest of moral theologians centered in the question about Probabilism or Antiprobabilism.

      Just as far from the truth is the second opinion of the adversaries of Probabilism, viz., that this system induces people to evade the laws and hardens them into callousness. On the contrary, to moot the question of Probabilism at all, was the sign of a severely conscientious soul. He who proposes the question at all knows and confesses by that very fact: first, that it is not lawful to act with a doubtful conscience, that he who performs an action without being firmly convinced of its being allowed, commits sin in the sight of God; secondly, that a law, above all the Divine law, obliges us to take cognizance of it and that, therefore, whenever doubts arise about the probable existence of an obligation we must apply sufficient care in order to arrive at certainty, so that a frivolous disregard of reasonable doubts is in itself a sin against the submission due to God. In spite of all this, it may happen that all our pains and inquiries do not lead us to certainty, that solid reasons are found both for and against the existence of an obligation: under these circumstances, a conscientious man will naturally ask whether he must consider himself bound by the law or whether he can, by further reflections — reflex principles, as they are called — come to the plain conclusion that there is no obligation either to do or to omit the act in question. Were we obliged to consider ourselves bound in every doubt, the result, obviously, would be an intolerable severity. But since before performing an action the final verdict of our conscience must be free from doubt, the necessity of removing in one way or another such doubts as may have arisen, is self-evident.

At first there was a lack of clearness with regard to Probabilism and the questions connected with it. Conflicting definitions of opinion, probability, and certitude, could not but cause confusion. When works on moral theology and practical manuals began to multiply, it was inevitable that some individuals should take the word "probable" in too wide or in too lax a sense, although there can be no doubt that in itself it means "something acceptable to reason", in other words, since reason can accept nothing unless it has the appearance of truth, "something based on reasons which generally lead to the truth". Hence it is that opinions were actually advanced and spread as practicable which were little in accord with the demands of the Christian Faith, and which brought down upon them the censure of the Holy See. We refer particularly to the theses condemned by Alexander VII on 24 Sept., 1665, and on 18 March, 1666, and by Innocent XI on 2 March, 1679. It is not Probabilism that must be made responsible for them, but the vagaries of a few Probabilists.

As a result of these condemnations, some theologians thought themselves obliged to oppose the system itself and to side with Probabiliorism. Previous to this turn of affairs, the Jansenists had been the most pronounced adversaries of Probabilism. But they, too, had received a setback when Innocent X condemned (31 May, 1653) in the "Augustinus" of Jansenius, then recently deceased, the proposition: "Just men, with the strength now at their disposal, cannot keep certain commandments of God even if they wish and endeavour to do so; besides, they are without the help of grace which might make it possible for them", was taken from the work and rejected as heretical and blasphemous. Now Probabilism was least reconcilable with this Jansenistic thesis, which could be maintained the easier, the stricter the moral obligations laid upon man's conscience were and the severer the system proclaimed as solely justified was. Consequently, the adherents of the Jansenistic doctrine endeavoured to attack Probabilism, to throw suspicion on it as an innovation, to represent it even as leading to sin. The exaggerations of a few Probabilists who went too far in their laxity, gave an opportunity to the Jansenists to attack the system, and soon a number of scholars, notably among the Dominicans abandoned Probabilism, which they had defended till then, attacked it and stood up for Probabiliorism; some Jesuits also opposed Probabilism. But by far, the majority of the Jesuit writers as well as a vast number of other orders and of the secular clergy, adhered to Probabilism. An entire century was taken up with this controversy, which probably has not its equal in the history of Catholic theology.

Fortunately, the works on either side of this controversy were not popular writings. Nevertheless, exaggerated theories caused a glaring inequality and much confusion in the administration of the Sacrament of Penance and in the guidance of souls. This seems to have been the case particularly in France and Italy; Germany probably suffered less from Rigorism. Hence it was a blessing of Divine Providence that there arose a man in the middle of the eighteenth century, who again insisted on a gentler and milder practice, and who, owing to the eminent sanctity which he combined with solid learning, and which raised him soon after his death to the honour of the altar, received the ecclesiastical approbation of his doctrine, thereby definitively establishing the milder practice in moral theology.

This man is Alphonsus Maria Liguori, who died in 1787 at the age of 91, was beatified in 1816, canonized in 1839, and declared Doctor Ecclesiæ in 1871. In his youth Liguori had been imbued with the stricter principles of moral theology; but, as he himself confesses, the experience which a missionary life extending over fifteen years gave him, and careful study, brought him to a realization of their falseness and evil consequences. Chiefly for the younger members of the religious congregation which owed its existence to his fervent zeal, he worked out a manual of moral theology, basing it on the widely used "Medulla" of the Jesuit Hermann Busenbaum, whose theses he subjected to a thorough examination, confirmed by internal reasons and external authority, illustrated by adverse opinions, and here and there modified. The work, entirely Probabilistic in its principles, was first published in 1748. Received with universal applause and lauded even by popes, it went through its second edition in 1753; edition after edition then followed, nearly every one showing the revising hand of the author; the last, ninth, edition, published during the lifetime of the saint, appeared in 1785. After his beatification and canonization his "Theologia moralis" found an even wider circulation. Not only were various editions arranged, but it almost seemed as though the further growth of moral theology would be restricted to a reiteration and to compendious revisions of the works of St. Alphonsus. An excellent critical edition of the "Theologia moralis Sti. Alphonsi" is that of Léonard Gaudé, C.SS.R. (Rome, 1905), who has verified all the quotations in the work and illustrated it with scholarly annotations.

No future work on practical moral theology can pass without ample references to the writings of St. Alphonsus. Hence it would be impossible to gain a clear insight into the present state of moral theology and its development without being more or less conversant with the system of the saint, as narrated in the article PROBABILISM. The controversy, which is still being waged about Probabilism and Æquiprobabilism, has no significance unless the latter oversteps the limits set to it by St. Alphonsus and merges into Probabiliorism. However, though the controversy has not yet been abandoned theoretically, still in everyday practice it is doubtful if there is any one who follows other rules in deciding doubtful cases than those of Probabilism. This ascendancy of the milder school in moral theology over the more rigorous gained new impetus when Alphonsus was canonized and when the Church pointed out in particular that Divine Providence had raised him up as a bulwark against the errors of Jansenism, and that by his numerous writings he had blazed a more reliable path which the guides of souls might safely follow amid the conflicting opinions either too lax or too strict. During his lifetime the saint was forced to enter several literary disputes on account of his works on moral theology; his chief adversaries were Concina and

Patuzzi, both of the Dominican Order, and champions of Probabiliorism.

The last decades of the eighteenth century may well be called a period of general decadence as far as the sacred sciences, moral theology included, are concerned. The frivolous spirit of the French Encyclopedists had infected, as it were, the whole of Europe. The Revolution, which was its offspring, choked all scientific life. A few words about the state of moral theology during this period may suffice. Italy was torn asunder by the dispute about Rigorism and a milder practice; in France, Rigorism had received the full rights of citizenship through the Jansenistic movement and held its own till late in the nineteenth century; Germany was swayed by a spirit of shallowness which threatened to dislodge Christian morals by rationalistic and natural principles. The "general seminaries" which Joseph II established in the Austrian states, engaged professors who did not blush to advance heretical doctrines and to exclude Christian self-restraint from the catalogue of moral obligations. Other German institutions, too, offered their chairs of theology to professors who had imbibed the ideas of "enlightenment", neglected to insist on Catholic doctrines of faith and putting aside the supernatural life, sought the end and aim of education in a merely natural morality. But in the second decade of the nineteenth century the French Revolution had spent itself, quiet had again followed the turmoil, the political restoration of Europe had been begun. A restoration also of the ecclesiastical spirit and learning was also inaugurated and the gradual rise of moral theology became noticeable. Apart from the purely ascetical side there are three divisions in which this new life was plainly visible: catechism, popular instruction, pastoral work.

Though it is the purpose of catechetical teaching to instruct the faithful in the entire range of Christian religion, in the doctrines of faith no less than in those of morals, yet the former may also be conceived and discussed with respect to the duties and the way by which man is destined to obtain his last end. Hence, the catechetical treatment of religious questions may be regarded as a portion of moral theology. During the period of "enlightenment", this branch had been degraded to a shallow moralizing along natural lines. But that it rose again in the course of the past century to a lucid explanation of the sum-total of the Christian doctrine, is attested by numerous excellent works, both catechisms and extensive discussions. To these may be added the more thorough manuals of Christian doctrine intended for higher schools, in which the apologetical and moral portions of religious instruction are treated scientifically and adapted to the needs of the time. There is nothing, however, which prevents us from placing these writings in the second of the above-mentioned classes, since their aim is the instruction of the Christian people, though principally the educated laymen. It is true these works belong exclusively, even less than the catechetical, to moral theology, since their subject-matter embraces the whole of the Christian doctrine, yet the morally destructive tendencies of Atheism and the new moral questions brought forward by the conditions of our times, impressed upon writers the importance of moral instruction in manuals of Catholic faith. The last decades in particular prove that this side of theology has been well taken care of. Various questions bearing on Christian morals were extensively treated in monographs, as e.g., the social question, the significance of money, the Church's doctrine on usury, the woman question, etc. To quote single works or to enter on the different subjects in detail would exceed the limits of this article.

    The third line along which we noted an advance was called the pastoral, that is, instruction which has as its special aim the education and aid of pastors and confessors. That this instruction is necessarily, though not exclusively, casuistic, was mentioned above. The scarcity of priests, which was keenly felt in many places, occasioned a lack of time necessary for an all-round scientific education of the candidates for the priesthood. This circumstance explains why scientific manuals of moral theology, for decades, were merely casuistic compendia, containing indeed the gist of scientific investigations, but lacking in scientific argumentation. The correctness of ecclesiastical doctrine had been insured and facilitated by the approbation with which the Church distinguished the works of St. Alphonsus. Hence, many of these compendia are nothing else than recapitulations of St. Alphonsus's "Theologia moralis", or, if following a plan of their own, betray on every page that their authors had it always ready at hand. Two works may here find mention which enjoyed a wider circulation than any other book on moral theology and which are frequently used even today: the Scavini's "Theologia moralis universa", and the shorter "Compendium theologiæ moralis" by Jean-Pierre Gury, together with the numerous revisions which appeared in France, Germany, Italy, Spain, and North America.

    We must not, however, deceive ourselves by concluding that, owing to the ecclesiastical approbation of St. Alphonsus and his moral writings, moral theology is now settled forever and, so to speak, crystallized. Nor does this approbation assure us that all individual questions have been solved correctly, and therefore the discussion of certain moral questions remains still open. The Apostolic See itself, or rather the Sacred Penitentiary, when asked, "Whether a professor of moral theology may quietly follow and teach the opinions which St. Alphonsus Liguori teaches in his Moral Theology", gave indeed an affirmative answer on 5 July, 1831; it added, however, "but those must not be reprehended who defend other opinions supported by the authority of reliable doctors". He who would conclude the guarantee of absolute correctness from the ecclesiastical approbation of the saint's works, would make the Church contradict herself. St. Thomas of Aquin was at least as solemnly approved for the whole field of theology as St. Alphonsus for moral theology. Yet, e. g, on the subject of the efficacy of grace, which enters deeply into morals, St. Thomas and St. Alphonsus defend wholly contradictory opinions; both cannot be right, and so may be freely discussed. The same may be said of other questions. In our own days, Antonio Ballerini above all made a simple use of this freedom of discussion, first in his annotations to Gury's "Compendium", then in his "Opus theologicum morale", which was recast and edited after his death by Dominic Palmieri. It rendered an eminent service to casuistry; for though we cannot approve of everything, yet the authority of various opinions has been carefully sifted and fully discussed.

Lately, attempts have been made to develop moral theology along other lines. The reformers assert that the casuistical method has choked every other and that it must give place to a more scientific, systematic treatment. It is evident that a merely casuistical treatment does not come up to the demands of moral theology, and as a matter of fact, during the last decades, the speculative element was more and more insisted on even in works chiefly casuistic. Whether the one or the other element should prevail, must be determined according to the proximate aim which the work intends to satisfy. If there is question of a purely scientific explanation of moral theology which does not intend to exceed the limits of speculation, then the casuistical element is without doubt speculative, systematic discussion of the questions belonging to moral theology; casuistry then serves only to illustrate the theoretical explanations. But if there is question of a manual which is intended for the practical needs of a pastor and confessor and for their education, then the solid, scientific portion of general moral-theological questions must be supplemented by an extensive casuistry. Nay, when time and leisure are wanting to add ample theoretical explanations to an extensive casuistical drill, we should not criticize him who would under these circumstances insist on the latter at the expense of the former; it is the more necessary in actual practice.

XV.
Political Economy

Political economy (Greek, oikonomia — the management of a household or family, politike — pertaining to the state) or economics (ta oikonomika — the art of household management) is the social science which treats of man's activities in providing the material means to satisfy his wants.

Economy originally meant the management and regulation of the resources of the household; that is, of the immediate family with its slaves and dependents. Political economy originally meant the management of the household of the State. It was so used as late as Adam Smith (Wealth of Nations, 1776), who defined it thus:

Political economy considered as a branch of the science of a statesman or legislator proposes two distinct objects, first, to supply a plentiful revenue or subsistence for the people, or more properly to enable them to provide such a revenue or subsistence for themselves; and secondly, to supply the state or commonwealth with a revenue sufficient for the public service. It proposes to enrich both the people and the sovereign.

The sum of the efforts and activities of the members of the household in acquiring the means to satisfy their wants may be designated as the economy of the household. Where a household is not economically self-sufficing, that is, where households are economically interdependent, we have a broader economy. Where this interdependence is state- or nation-wide, there exists a national economy or political economy.

The term political economy is used in yet a third sense. It is the name of the science which treats of this nation-wide complexus of economic activities.

Method
Deductive

English economists in the early part of the nineteenth century, beginning with Malthus and Ricardo, hoped to establish a science of political economy independent of the art of the statesman, which would vie with the natural sciences in the exactness of its conclusions. They narrowed the field as conceived by Adam Smith by variously defining political economy as the science of wealth, the science of value, or the science of exchanges. But along with this narrowing of the field and the attainment of scientific precision in the use of terms went a divorce of their science from the economic realities of life. Their method was strictly deductive. Beginning with three or four principles for which they claimed universal validity, they proceeded to deduce a complete system without further appeal to the facts of life. These English writers, known as the Classical or Orthodox School, held that political economy must not concern itself with ethical or practical considerations. To do so, in their opinion, would degrade it to an art, for the science of political economy was concerned merely with the explanation of the causal relations existing among economic phenomena. It was their business as economists simply to explain the existing economic system not to defend or condemn it, nor to show how it might be replaced by a better one. To them good and bad were concepts which concerned moralists and not economists.

Inductive

In opposition to this narrow and non-ethical view of the Classical School, there arose in Germany in the middle of the nineteenth century, the Historical School, holding that political economy is an inductive and an ethical science. They derided the abstractions of the Orthodox School, some extremists even going so far as to contend that the time was not yet ripe for a science of political economy. The business of their generation, they held, was to gather from observation and history and to classify the economic facts upon which future economists might construct a science.

Deductive and Inductive

After a bitter struggle of half a century the opposition between the schools has almost disappeared, and it is now generally recognized that the economist must use both the deductive and the inductive methods, using now one predominantly and now the other, according to the nature of the problem upon which he happens to be engaged. The best usage of the present time is to make political economy an ethical science, that is, to make it include a discussion of what ought to be in the economic world as well as what is. This has all along been the practice of Catholic writers. Some of them even go so far as to make political economy a branch of ethics and not an independent science. (See Devas, "Principles of Political Economy".) For a further discussion of the relationship between the two sciences.

Scope

For purposes of exposition the field of political economy is often divided into four parts: production, consumption, distribution, and exchange. Some authors omit one or another of these divisions, treating its problems under the remaining heads.

Production

The department of production is concerned with the creation of wealth through the united efforts of land, labor, and capital. The creation of wealth involves the bringing into existence of utilities, that is, of capacities to satisfy wants. Utilities are created by changes in form of goods, or in their location, or by keeping them from a time of less demand to a time of greater demand.

Consumption

Consumption is concerned with the destruction of utilities in goods. It is the utilization of wealth, the carrying out of the purpose for which wealth is produced.

Distribution

The department of distribution considers the manner in which the wealth which has been produced is divided among the agents which have produced it. The shares in distribution are: rent, which is paid to the landlord for the use of the land; wages, which is the return to the labourer; interest, which goes to the capitalist for the use of his capital; and profit, which is the reward of the entrepreneur or undertaker of the business.

Exchange

Finally, exchange has to do with the transfer of ownership of wealth. Under this head are discussed money and credit and international exchanges.

Other Subjects

Outside of these four divisions separate chapters are usually devoted to a consideration of taxation, monopolies, transportation, economic progress, and other problems. Adam Smith and his immediate followers were more closely concerned with the problems of production. Owing to the world's remarkable progress in that direction in the last century, the inequalities of distribution have come more and more into prominence, and this is now the favourite field of the economist.

History
Ancient

In ancient Greece and Rome there was little likelihood of the emergence of a science of political economy. Their industrial system was founded on slavery, the great estates were for the most part self-sufficient economic units, leaving comparatively little room for commerce, and labour was held in contempt by the thinking element. However, fragmentary discussions on economic subjects, mingled with ethical and political considerations, are to be found. Xenophon has a rather extensive treatment of household economy. Plato, in the "Republic", advocates an ideal communistic State. Aristotle presents a defense of private property, and writes against the taking of interest on the ground that money is barren. He defends warmly the institution of slavery. Among the Romans there was not much originality. We find frequent discussions of the relative merits of large and small farms. Cicero, Pliny the Elder, and other writers deplored the introduction of gold as a medium of exchange and preferred the age of barter. Seneca wrote upon the ethics of political economy and pleaded for the simple life.

Patristic Writers

Under Christian influence labour, which had been held in contempt by the Pagans, came to be respected and honoured. The rigors of slavery were mitigated and the milder form of serfdom grew up, which later gave way to free labour. The Roman law had insisted on the rights of property; the early Fathers on the other hand, insisted on the rights of man. Some even went to the extent of advocating a system of communism as the ideal state, merely tolerating private property. "The soil," says St. Ambrose, "was given to rich and poor in common." St. Gregory the Great, St. Augustine, St. Basil the Great, St. John Chrysostom, and St. Jerome write in similar vein. The taking of usury was universally condemned.

Middle Ages

By the end of the Middle Ages there was developed a complete and systematic economic doctrine. This doctrine differed from modern political economy in two important aspects. In the first place it was made to fit the economic institutions of that day, and would be inadequate if applied to ours; and secondly, the emphasis was placed upon the ethically desirable rather than upon the actually existent, However, this latter distinction is now very much less marked than it was in the first half of the nineteenth century. Such questions as property, wealth, consumption, value, price, money, loans, monopoly, and taxation were treated in detail. To the medieval theologian, the "just price" of an article included enough to pay fair wages to the worker, that is, enough to enable him to maintain the standard of living of his class. In a like manner, a reasonable profit was defended as the wages of the merchant. With certain limitations, the taking of interest for money loans was forbidden. On the other hand, there were certain classes of productive investments, such as the buying of rent-charges, where interest was allowed. Among the writers of the period on economic subjects, St. Thomas Aquinas takes first place. Other writers of importance were Henry of Ghent, Ægidius Colonna, Petrarch, Nicholas Oresme, Bishop of Lisieux who wrote a work on money for his pupil Charles V, and finally St. Antoninus, Archbishop of Florence, and St. Bernardine of Siena.

Mercantile System

In the sixteenth and seventeenth centuries a revolution in industrial activities was taking place which had a profound influence upon the economic literature. The great geographical discoveries, the invention of gunpowder and printing, the decay of feudalism and the rise of modern states, the increase in the supply of the precious metals, and the growing use of credit — all these united to furnish problems for endless discussion. Statesmen, feeling the need of money to support war, adopted various restrictive measures to obtain it. The economic writers who defended these restrictions are usually classed together as the Mercantile School. Sometimes the attempt was made to keep money in the country by prohibiting its exportation or by debasing the coinage. Another way was to encourage the exportation of finished commodities and the importation of raw material in order to secure a balance of trade. Mercantilism reached its highest perfection under Colbert, the Minister of Finance under Louis XIV, and is sometimes referred to as Colbertism. Later imitators of Colbert were less successful, and Mercantilism often degenerated into a system of special privileges and exemptions, without any adequate advantage to the nation. Prominent among the Mercantilist writers were Jean Bodin (d. 1596), Giovanni Botero (d. 1617), Juan Mariana (d. 1623), Antonio Serra (published in 1613), Antoine* de Montchrétien (Traité d'économie politique, 1615), who was the originator of the term political economy, and Thomas Mun (d. 1641), author of "England's Treasure by Foreign Trade".

System of Natural Liberty

During the Mercantile period statesmen had interested themselves in industry principally for the purpose of carrying on war; in the following period wars were carried on in the interest of industry and commerce. Under Mercantile influence, the attitude of governments had been decidedly paternalistic. In the eighteenth century those who speak for commerce and industry demand that these be allowed to develop freely, unhampered by the guiding strings of government. In France there grew up a school of economic writers later known as the Physiocrats, who protested against the balance of trade doctrine of the Mercantile School and summed up the duties of the government towards industry and commerce in the famous phrase "laissez faire et laissez passer". They believed in a beneficent "order of nature" which should be allowed free play. To them, agriculture alone was productive. The Physiocrats had been strongly influenced by such English writers as Locke, Petty, and Hume, and they in turn were destined to further influence English political economy.

Adam Smith (1723-90), "the father of political economy" was a result of the combination of both the English and the French currents. His work, "An Inquiry into the Nature and Causes of the Wealth of Nations" (1776), gained immediate popularity and exercised profound political influence in the next generation. Smith held that while the individual selfishly seeks his private gain, he is led by an invisible hand to promote the public good, and that since the individual and social interests are identical, the sphere of state action should be narrowed. He thus followed up the attack on the Mercantile system begun by the Physiocrats. He differed from the Physiocrats in making labour as well as land productive. Among the followers of Smith are to be noted Malthus ("Essay on Population", 1798), author of the startling statement that population tends to increase in a geometrical ratio while subsistence tends to increase in an arithmetical ratio, and Ricardo ("Principles of Political Economy and Taxation", 1817), whose name is associated with the differential rent theory, the subsistence theory of wages, and the labour theory of value. Other writers of the English Classical School, who followed closely in the footsteps of Malthus and Ricardo, were James Mill, MacCulloch Senior, and John Stuart Mill. The last named in his later life renounced the individualism of the Orthodox School in favour of socialistic views.

Historical School

About the middle of the nineteenth century there began in Germany under the leadership of Wilhelm Roscher, Karl Knies, and Bruno Hildebrand, a reaction against the Orthodox-English School. These writers insisted on the relativity of economic theory, that is, they did not believe that economic principles, good for all times and places, and all degrees of economic development, could be established. Moreover, they insisted strongly on the need of the study of economic history and upon the ethical and practical character of political economy. They were soon in complete control of the economic teaching of Germany. They differ radically from the Physiocrats and Adam Smith in their repudiation of the doctrine of natural liberty. In fact many of them have gone so far in the opposite direction as to be designated Kathedersozialisten (Professorial Socialists), because of their reliance on state help in accomplishing social reforms.

Austrian School

Since 1871 there has grown up in Austria a group of writers who make of political economy a deductive and psychological science of value. They oppose to the cost-of-production explanation of value of the Classical School, a theory of value based upon marginal utility. It is a well known psychological fact that the utilities of additional units of a commodity to a consumer diminish as the supply increases. Now it is the utility of the last or marginal unit consumed, says the Austrian School, which determines value. Menger, Wieser, Boehm-Bawerk, in Austria, the late W. Stanley Jevons, in England, and J. B. Clark, in America, are the leading representatives of this school.

Socialism

Socialism represents the extreme of reaction against laissez faire or the system of natural liberty of the Physiocrats and Adam Smith. Laissez faire professes to believe in the identity of the interests of the different industrial classes and hence decries the need of restrictive legislation, while socialism emphatically denies that this solidarity exists under our present system and seeks to develop a "class consciousness" among the workers that will overthrow the influence of the dominant class. Economic socialism borrowed the labour theory of value from Ricardo and gave it an ethical interpretation, holding that since labour is the sole producer of wealth, the labourer should receive the entire product. Accordingly, the socialists deny the right of the capitalist to interest and of the landlord to rent, and would make capital and land common property. According to Karl Marx ("Das Kapital", 1867), the founder of so-called scientific socialism, the labourer under the present system does not receive more than a bare subsistence. The "surplus value" which he produces above this amount is appropriated by landlords and capitalists. Another contribution of Marx to socialism is the materialistic conception of history, according to which such factors in history as religion, ethics, and the family, undergo changes corresponding to the changes in the underlying economic organization of which they are a product.

Christian Democracy

The movement which has been gaining ground for the last half century among Christian churches, both Catholic and non-Catholic, to emphasize the importance of religious and moral elements in a healthy economic life, and which protests more or less strongly against laissez faire, is usually designated as Christian Socialism. This name is, however, not well chosen, since none of the so-called Christian socialists hold to the fundamental principle of socialism, namely the abolishment of private ownership in the means of production.

The Protestant writers in this field have naturally lacked an authority which would hold them together. In England their adoption of co-operative associations as a substitute for competition has given them a unity which they have not attained elsewhere.

The Catholic School agrees with the socialists in much of their criticism of the competitive system, but parts company with them by insisting on the place of religion, the family, property, and the employer system in the social scheme. In the matter of state intervention, there are among Catholic writers two general tendencies. The more "liberal" wing, led by such economists as Le Play, Périn, and Victor

Brants, would reduce state action to a minimum, while others, looking to Bishop Ketteler, Cardinal Manning, and Count de Mun, would invoke a considerable measure of so-called State socialism. A strong impulse towards unity of effort among Catholics was given by the publication of the encyclicals of Pope Leo XIII, "Rerum Novarum", of 15 May, 1891, and "Graves de Communi", of 18 January, 1901.

XVI.
Logic

Logic is the science and art which so directs the mind in the process of reasoning and subsidiary processes as to enable it to attain clearness, consistency, and validity in those processes. The aim of logic is to secure clearness in the definition and arrangement of our ideas and other mental images, consistency in our judgments, and validity in our processes of inference.

The name

The Greek word logos, meaning "reason", is the origin of the term logic--logike (techen, pragmateia, or episteme, understood), as the name of a science or art, first occurs in the writings of the Stoics. Aristotle, the founder of the science, designates it as "analytic", and the Epicureans use the term canonic. From the time of Cicero, however, the word logic is used almost without exception to designate this science. The names dialectic and analytic are also used.

The Definition

It is a curious fact that, although logic is the science which treats of definition, logicians are not agreed as to how logic itself should be defined. There are, in all, about two hundred different definitions of logic. It would, of course, be impossible to enumerate even the principal definitions here. It will be sufficient to mention and discuss a few typical ones.

Port Royal logic

The Port Royal logic ("L'Art de penser", published 1662) defines logic as "the art of using reason well in the acquisition of the knowledge of things, both for one's own instruction and that of others." More briefly "Logic is the art of reasoning." The latter is Arnauld's definition. Definitions of this type are considered too narrow, both because they define logic in terms of art, not leaving room for its claim to be considered a science, and because, by the use of the term reasoning, they restrict the scope of logic to one class of mental processes.

Hegel

Hegel goes to the other extreme when he defines logic as "the science of the pure idea." By idea he understands all reality, so that for him logic includes the science of subjective reality (logic of mental concepts) and the science of objective reality (logic of being, metaphysics). In like manner the definitions which fail to distinguish between logic and psychology, defining logic as "the science of mental processes", or "the science of the operations of the mind", are too wide. Definitions which characterize logic as "the science of sciences", "the art of arts", are also too wide: they set up too large a claim for logic.

St. Thomas Aquinas

In his commentary on Aristotle's logical treatises ("

In Post. Anal.", lect. i, Leonine ed., I, 138), he says: "Ars quædam necessaria est, quae sit directiva ipsius actus rationis, per quam scilicet homo in ipso actu rationis ordinate faciliter et sine errore procedat. Et haec ars est logica, id est rationalis scientia." Combining those two sentences, we may render St. Thomas's definition as follows: "Logic is the science and art which directs the act of the reason, by which a man in the exercise of his reason is enabled to proceed without error, confusion, or unnecessary difficulty." Taking reason in its broadest sense, so as to include all the operations of the mind which are strictly cognitive, namely, the formation of mental images, judgment, and ratiocination, we may expand St. Thomas' definition and define logic as "the science and art which so directs the mind in the process of reasoning and subsidiary processes as to enable it to attain clearness (or order), consistency, and validity in those processes". Logic is essentially directive. Therein it differs from psychology, which is essentially speculative or theoretical, and which concerns itself only in an Incidental and secondary manner with the direction of mental processes. Logic deals with processes of the mind. Therein it differs from metaphysics, which has for its field of inquiry and speculation the whole universe of being. Logic deals with mental processes in relation to truth or, more particularly, in relation to the attainment and exposition of truth by processes which aim at being valid, clear, orderly, and consistent. Therein it differs from ethics, which treats of human actions, external deeds as well as thoughts, in relation to man's final destiny. Validity, clearness, consistency, and order are logical qualities of thought, goodness and evil are ethical qualities. Finally, logic is not to be confounded with rhetoric. Rhetoric, in the old meaning of the word, was the art of persuasion; it used all the devices, such as emotional appeal, verbal arrangement, etc., in order to bring about a state of mind which had reference to action primarily, and to conviction only in a secondary sense. Logic is the science and art of conviction; it uses only arguments, discarding emotional appeal and employing merely words as the symbols of thoughts.

The question whether logic is a science or an art is now generally decided by asserting that it is both. It is a science, in so far as it not merely formulates rules for right thinking, but deduces those rules from general principles which are based on the nature of mind and of truth. It is an art, in so far as it is directly and immediately related to performance, namely, to the acts of the mind. As the fine arts direct the painter or the sculptor in the actions by which he aims at producing a beautiful picture or a beautiful statue, so logic directs the thinker in the actions by which he aims at attaining truth, or expounding truth which he has attained.

Division of Logic

The traditional mode of dividing logic, into "formal" and "material", is maintained in many modern treatises on the subject. In formal logic the processes of thought are studied independently of, or without consideration of, their content. In material logic the chief question is the truth of the content of mental processes. An example from arithmetic will serve to illustrate the function of formal logic. When we add two and two, and pronounce the result to be four, we are dealing with a process of addition in its formal aspect, without paying attention to the content. The process is valid whatever the content may be, whether the "two and two "refer to books, horses, trees, or circles. This is precisely how we study judgments and arguments in logic. From the judgment "All A is B" we infer "Therefore some B is A"; and the process is valid whether the original proposition be "All circles are round" or "All lions are carnivorous". In material logic, on the contrary, we inquire into the content of the judgments or premises and endeavour to determine whether they are true or false. Material logic was styled by the old writers "major logic", "critical logic", or simply" criticism". In recent times the word epistemology (science of knowledge), meaning an inquiry into the value of knowledge, has come into general use, and designates that portion of philosophy which inquires into the objective value of our concepts, the import and value of judgments and reasoning, the criteria of truth, the nature of evidence, certitude, etc. Whenever this new term is adopted there is a tendency to restrict the term logic to mean merely formal logic. Formal logic studies concepts, and other mental images, for the purpose of securing clearness and order among those contents of the mind. It studies judgments for the purpose of showing when and how they are consistent or inconsistent, that is, when one may be inferred from another (conversion), and when they are opposed (opposition) . It studies the two kinds of reasoning, deductive and inductive, so as to direct the mind to use these processes validly. Finally, it studies sophisms (or fallacies) and method for the purpose of showing what errors are to be avoided, and what arrangement is to be followed in a complex series of reasoning processes. But, while it is true in general that in all these tasks formal logic preserves its purely formal character, and does not inquire into the content of thought, nevertheless, in dealing with inductive reasoning and in laying down the rules for definition and division, formal logic does take account of the matter of thought. For this reason, it seems desirable to abandon the old distinction between formal and material, to designate as logic what was formerly called formal logic, and to reserve the term epistemology for that portion of philosophy which, while inquiring into the value of human knowledge in general, covers the ground which was the domain of material logic.

There remain certain kinds of logic which are not included under the heads formal and material. Transcendental logic (Kant) is the inquiry into human knowledge for the purpose of determining what elements or factors in human thought are a priori, that is, independent of experience. Symbolic logic (Lambert, Boole) is an application of mathematical methods to the processes of thought. It uses certain conventional symbols to represent terms, propositions, and the relations among them, and then, without any further reference to the laws of thought, applies the rules and methods of the mathematical calculus (Venn, "Symbolic Logic", London, 1881). Applied logic, in the narrower sense, is synonymous with material logic in the wider sense, it means logic applied to the study of the natural sciences, logic applied to education, logic applied to the study of law, etc. Natural logic is that native power of the mind by which most persons are competent to judge correctly and reason validly about the affairs and interests of everyday life; it is contrasted with scientific logic, which is logic as a science and cultivated art.

History of Logic

The history of logic possesses a more than ordinary interest, because, on the one hand, every change in the point of view of the metaphysician and the psychologist tended to produce a corresponding change in logical theory and practice, while, on the other hand, changes in logical method and procedure tended to affect the conclusions as well as the method of the philosopher. Notwithstanding these tendencies towards variation, the science of logic has undergone very few radical changes from the beginning of its history.

The Nyaya

A system of philosophy which was studied in India in the fifth century B.C., though it is perhaps, of much older date, takes its name from the word nyaya, meaning logical argument, or syllogism. This philosophy, like all the Indian systems, busied itself with the Problem of the deliverance of the soul from bondage, and its solution was that the soul is to be freed from the trammels of matter by means of systematic reasoning. This view of the question led naturally to an analysis of the methods of thinking, and to the construction of a type of reasoning which bears a remote resemblance to the syllogism. The nyaya, or Indian syllogism, as it is sometimes called, consists of five propositions. If, for instance, one wishes to prove that the hill is on fire, one begins with the assertion: "The hill is on fire." Next, the reason is given: "For it smokes." Then comes an instance, "Like the kitchen fire"; which is followed by the application, "So also the hill smokes." Finally comes the conclusion, "Therefore it is on fire." Between this and the clear-cut Aristotelean syllogism, with its major and minor premises and conclusion, there is all the difference that exists between the Oriental and the Greek mode of thinking. It is hardly necessary to say that there is no historical evidence that Aristotle was in any way influenced in his logic by Gotama, the reputed author of the nyaya.

Pre-Aristotelean Logic in Greece

  The first philosophers of Greece devoted attention

exclusively to the problem of the origin of the universe. The Eleatics, especially Zeno of Elea, the Sophists, and the Megarians developed the art of argumentation to a high degree of perfection. Zeno was especially remarkable in this respect, and is sometimes styled the Founder of Dialectic. None of these, however, formulated laws or rules of reasoning. The same is true of Socrates and Plato, although the former laid great stress on definition and induction, and the latter exalted dialectic, or discussion, into an important instrument of philosophical knowledge.

Aristotle, the founder of logic

In the six treatises which he devoted to the subject, Aristotle examined and analysed the thinking processes for the purpose of formulating the laws of thought. These treatises are

* "The Categories",
* "Interpretation",
* "Prior Analytics",
* "Posterior Analytics",
* "Topics", and
* "Sophisms". These were afterwards given the title of "Organon", or "Instrument of Knowledge"; this designation, however, did not come into common use until the fifteenth century.

The first four treatises contain, with occasional excursions into the domain of grammar and metaphysics, the science of formal logic essentially the same as it is taught at the present day. The "Topics" and the "Sophisms" contain the applications of logic to argumentation and the refutation of fallacies. In conformity with the fundamental principle of his theory of knowledge, namely, that all our knowledge comes from experience, Aristotle recognizes the importance of inductive reasoning, that is to say, reasoning from particular instances to general principles. If he and his followers did not develop more fully this portion of logic, it was not because they did not recognize its importance in principle. His claim to the title of Founder of Logic has never been seriously disputed; the most that his opponents in the modern era could do was to set up rival systems in which induction was to supplant syllogistic reasoning. One of the devices of the opponents of scholasticism is to identify the Schoolmen and Aristotle with the advocacy of an exclusively deductive logic.

Post-Aristotelean Logicians Among the Greeks

Among the immediate disciples of Aristotle, Theophrastus and Eudemus devoted special attention to logic. To the former is sometimes attributed the invention of the hypothetical syllogism, although the same claim is sometimes made for the Stoics. The latter, to whom, probably, we owe the name logic, recognized this science as one of the constitutive parts of philosophy. They included in it dialectic and rhetoric, or the science of argumentation and the science of persuasion. They busied themselves also with the question of the criterion of truth, which is still an important problem in major logic, or, as it is now called, epistemology. Undoubtedly, they improved on Aristotle's logic in many points of detail; but to what extent, and in what respect, is a matter of conjecture, owing to the loss of the voluminous Stoic treatises on logic. Their rivals, the Epicureans professed a contempt for logic — or "canonic", as they styled it. They maintained that it is an adjunct of physics, and that a knowledge of physical phenomena acquired through the senses is the only knowledge that is of value in the pursuit of happiness. After the Stoics and the Epicureans came the commentators. These may, for convenience, be divided into the Greeks and the Latins. The Greeks from Alexander of Aphrodisias, in the second, to St. John of Damascus in the eighth century of our era, flourished at Athens, at Alexandria, and in Asia Minor. With Photius, in the ninth century, the scene is shifted to Constantinople. To the first period belong Alexander of Aphrodisias, known as "the Commentator" Themistius, David the Armenian, Philoponus, Simplicius and Porphyry, author of the Isagoge (Eisagoge), or "Introduction" to the logic of Aristotle. In this work the author, by his explicit enumeration of the five predicables and his comment thereon, flung a challenge to the medieval logicians, which they took up in the famous controversy concerning universals. To the second period belong Photius, Michael Psellus the younger (eleventh century), Nicephorus Blemmydes, George Pachymeres, and Leo Magentinus (thirteenth century). All these did little more than abridge, explain, and defend the text of the

Aristotelean works on logic. An exception should, perhaps, be made in favour of the physician Galen (second century), who is said to have introduced the fourth syllogistic figure, and who wrote a special work, "On Fallacies of Diction".

Latin Commentators

Among the Latin commentators on Aristotle we find almost in every case more originality and more inclination to add to the science of logic than we do in the case of the Greeks. After the taking of Athens by Sulla (84 B.C.) the works of Aristotle were carried to Rome, where they were arranged and edited by Andronicus of Rhodes. The first logical treatise in Latin is Cicero's abridgment of the "Topics". Then came a long period of inactivity. About A.D.160, Apuleius wrote a short account of the "Interpretation". In the middle of the fourth century Marius Victorinus translated Porphyry's "Isagoge". To the time of St. Augustine belong the treatises "Categoriae Decem" and "Principia Dialectica". Both were attributed to St. Augustine, though the first is certainly spurious, and the second of doubtful authenticity. They were very often transcribed in the early Middle Ages, and the logical treatises of the ninth and tenth centuries make very free use of their contents. The most popular however, of all the Latin works on logic was the curious medley of prose and verse "De Nuptiis Mercurii et Philologiae" by Marcianus Capella (about A.D. 475). In it dialectic is treated as one of the seven liberal arts, and that portion of the work was the text in all the early medieval schools of logic. Another writer on logic who exerted a widespread influence during the first period of Scholasticism was Boethius (470 524), who wrote two commentaries on the "Isagoge" of Porphyry, two on Aristotle's "Interpretation", and one on the "Categories". Besides, he wrote the original treatises,"On Categorical Syllogisms", "On Division", and "On Topical Differences", and translated several portions of Aristotle's logical works. In fact, it was principally through his translations that the early Scholastic writers, who as a rule, were entirely ignorant of Greek, had access to Aristotle's writings. Cassiodorus a contemporary of Boethius, wrote a treatise, "On the Seven Liberal Arts", in which, in the portion devoted to dialectic, he gave a summary and analysis of the Aristotelean and Porphyrian writings on logic. Isidore of Seville (died 636), Venerable Bede (673-735) and Alcuin (736-804), the forerunners of the Scholastics, were content with abridging in their logical works the writings of Boethius and Cassiodorus.

The Scholastics

The first masters of the schools in the age of Charlemagne and the century immediately following were not acquainted at first hand with Aristotle's works. They used the works and translations of Boethius, the pseudo-Augustinian treatises mentioned above, and the work by Marcianus Capella. Little by little their interest became centred on the metaphysical and psychological problems suggested in those treatises especially on the problem of universals and the conflict between Realism and Nominalism. As a consequence of this shifting of the centre of interest, very little was done towards perfecting the technic of logic, and there is a very noticeable dearth of original work during the ninth and tenth centuries. John Scotus Eriugena, Eric and Remi of Auxerre, and the teachers at St. Gall in Switzerland confined their activity to glossing and commenting on the traditional texts, especially Pseudo-Augustine and Marcianus Capella. In the case of the St. Gall teachers we have however, by way of exception, a work on logic, which bears evident traces of the influence of Eriugena, and a collection of mnemonic verses containing the nineteen valid syllogisms.

Roscelin (about 1050-1100), by his outspoken profession of Nominalism concentrated the attention of his contemporaries and immediate successors on the problem of universals. In the discussion of that problem the art of dialectical disputation was developed, and a taste for argumentation was fostered, but none of the dialecticians of the twelfth century, with the exception of Abelard, contributed to the advancement of the science of logic. This Abelard did in several ways. In his work to which Cousin gave the title "Dialectica", and in his commentaries, he strove to widen the scope and enhance the utility of logic as a science. Not only is it the science of disputation, but also the science of discovery, by means of which the arguments supplied by a study of nature are examined. The principal

application of logic, however, is in the discussion of religious truth. Here Abelard, citing the authority of St. Augustine, contends that the methods of dialectic are applicable to the discussion of all truth, revealed as well as rational; they are applicable even to the mysteries of faith. In principle he was right, although in practice he went further than the example of St. Augustine would warrant him in going. His subsequent condemnation had for its ground, not the use of dialectic in theology, but the excessive use of dialectic to the point of rationalism. Abelard, it should be noted, was acquainted only with those treatises of Aristotle which had been translated by Boethius, and which constituted the logica vetus. His contemporary, Gilbert de la Porrée, added to the old logic a work entitled "Liber Sex Principiorum", a treatise on the last six of the Aristotelean Categories. Towards the middle of the twelfth century the remainder of the Aristotelean "Organon" became known, so that the logic of the schools, thenceforth known as logica nova, now contained:
* Aristotle's "Categories" and "Interpretation" and Porphyry's "Isagoge" (contents of the logica vetus);
* Aristotle's "Analytics", "Topics", and "Sophisms";
* Gilbert's "Liber Sex Principiorum".

This was the text in the schools when St. Thomas began to teach, and it continued to be used until superseded by the logica moderna, which embodied the contributions of Petrus Hispanus. The first writer of importance who reveals an acquaintance with the Aristotelean "Organon" in its entirety is John of Salisbury (died 1182), a disciple of Abelard, who explains and defends the legitimate use of dialectic in his work "Metalogicus".

The definite triumph of Aristotelean logic in the schools of the thirteenth century was influenced by the introduction into Christian Europe of the complete works of Aristotle in Greek. The occasion of this was the taking of Constantinople by the crusaders in 1204. The Crusades had also the effect of bringing Christian Europe into closer contact with the Arabian scholars who, ever since the ninth century, had cultivated Aristotelean logic as well as the neo-Platonic interpretation of Aristotle's metaphysics. It was the Arabians who distinguished logica docens and logica utens. The former is logic as a theoretical science; the latter is logic as an applied art, practical logic. To them also is attributed the distinction between first intentions and second intentions. The Arabians, however, did not exert a determining influence on the development of Scholastic logic; they contributed to that development only in an external manner, by helping to make Aristotelean literature accessible to Christian thinkers. St. Thomas Aquinas and his teacher, Blessed Albertus Magnus (Albert the Great) did signal service to Scholastic logic, not so much by adding to its technical rules as by defining its scope and determining the limits of its legitimate applications to theology. They both composed commentaries on Aristotle's logical works and, besides, wrote independent logical treatises. The work, however, which bears the name "Summa Totius Logicae", and is found among the "Opuscula" of St. Thomas, is now judged to be from the pen of a disciple of his, Herve of Nedellac (Hervaeus Natalis). John Duns Scotus was also a commentator on Aristotle's logic. His most important original treatises on logic are "De Universalibus", in which he goes over the ground covered by Porphyry in the "Isagoge", and "Grammatica Speculativa". The latter is an interesting contribution to critical logic.

The technic of logic received special attention from Petrus Hispanus (Pope John XXI, died 1277), author of the "Summulae Logicales". This is the first medieval work to cover the whole ground of Aristotelean logic in an original way. All its predecessors were merely summaries or abridgments of Aristotle's works. In it occur the mnemonic lines, "Barbara, Celarent", etc., and nearly all the devices of a similar kind which are now used in the study of logic. They are the first of the kind in the history of logic, the lines in the ninth-century manuscript mentioned above being verses to aid the memory, without the use of arbitrary signs, such as the designation of types of propositions by means of vowels. And the credit of having introduced them is now almost unanimously given to Petrus himself. The theory that he borrowed them from a Greek work by Psellus (see above) is discredited by an examination of the manuscripts, which shows that the Greek verses are of later date than those in the "Summulae". In fact, it was the Byzantine writer who copied the Parisian teacher, and not, as Prantl contended, the Latin who borrowed from the

Greek. William of Occam (1280-1349) improved on the arrangement and method of the "Summulae" in his "Summa Totius Logicae". He also made important contributions to the doctrine of supposition of terms. He did not, however, agree with St. Thomas and St. Albert the Great in their definition of the scope and application of logic. His own conception of the purpose of logic was sufficiently serious and dignified. It was his followers, the Occamists of the fourteenth and fifteenth centuries, who, by their abuse of dialectical methods brought Scholastic logic into disrepute. One of the most original of all the Scholastic logicians was Raymond Lully (1234-1315). In his "Dialectica" he expounds clearly and concisely the logic of Aristotle, together with the additions made to that science by Petrus Hispanus. In his "Ars Magna", however, he discards all the rules and prescriptions of the formal science, and undertakes by means of his "logical machine" to demonstrate in a perfectly mechanical way all truth, supernatural as well as natural.

Scholastic logic, as may be seen from this sketch, did not modify the logic of Aristotle in any essential manner. Nevertheless, the logic of the Schools is an improvement on Aristotelean logic. The Schoolmen made clear many points which were obscure in Aristotle's works: for example, they determined more accurately than he did the nature of logic and its place in the plan of sciences. This was brought about naturally by the exigencies of theological controversy. Moreover, the Schoolmen did much to fix the technical meanings of terms in the modern languages, and, though the scientific spirit of the ages that followed spurned the methods of the Scholastic logicians, its own work was very much facilitated by the efforts of the Scholastics to distinguish the significations of words, and trace the relationship of language to thought. Finally, to the Schoolmen logic owes the various memory-aiding contrivances by the aid of which the task of teaching or learning the technicalities of the science is greatly facilitated.

Modern Logic

The fifteenth century witnessed the first serious attempts to revolt against the Aristotelean logic of the Schools. Humanists like Ludovicus Vico and Laurentius Valla made the methods of the Scholastic logicians the object of their merciless attack on medievalism. Of more importance in the history of logic is the attempt of Ramus (Pierre de La Ramee, 1515-72) to supplant the traditional logic by a new method which he expounded in his works "Aristotelicae Animadversiones" and "Scholae Dialecticae". Ramus was imitated in Ireland by George Downame (or Downham), Bishop of Derry, in the seventeenth century, and in the same century he had a most distinguished follower in England in the person of John Milton, who, in 1672, published "Artis Logicae Plenior Institutio ad Petri Rami Methodum Concinnata". Ramus's innovations, however, were far from receiving universal approval, even among Protestants. Melanchthon's "Erotemata Dialectica", which was substantially Aristotelean, was extensively used in the Protestant schools, and exerted a wider influence than Ramus's "Animadversiones". Francis Bacon (1561-1626) inaugurated a still more formidable onslaught. Profiting by the hints thrown out by his countryman and namesake, Roger Bacon (1214-1294), he attacked the Aristotelean method, contending that it was utterly barren of results in science, that it was, in fact, essentially unscientific, and needed not so much to be reformed as to be entirely supplanted by a new method. This he attempted to do in his "Novum Organum", which was to introduce a new logic, an inductive logic, to take the place of the deductive logic of Aristotle and the Schoolmen. It is now recognized even by the partisans of Bacon that he erred in two respects. He erred in describing Aristotle's logic as exclusively deductive, and he erred in claiming for the inductive method the ability to direct the mind in scientific discovery and practical invention. Bacon did not succeed in overthrowing the authority of Aristotle. Neither did Descartes (1596-1649), who was as desirous to make logic serve the purposes of the mathematician as Bacon was to make it serve the cause of scientific discovery. The Port Royal Logic ("L'Art de penser" 1662), written by Descartes's disciples, is essentially Aristotelean. So, though in a less degree are the logical treatises of Hobbes (1588-1679) and Gassendi (1592-1655), both of whom underwent the influence of Bacon's ideas. In the seventeenth and eighteenth centuries, Father Buffier, Le Clerc (Clericus), Wolff, and Lambert strove to modify the Aristotelean logic in the direction of empiricism, sensism, or Leibnizian innatism. In the treatises which they wrote on logic there is nothing that one might consider of primary importance.

Kant and the other German Transcendentalists of the nineteenth century took a more equitable view of Aristotle's services to the science of logic. As a rule, they recognized the value of what he had accomplished and, instead of trying to undo his work, they attempted to supplement it. It is a question, however, whether they did not do as much harm to logic in one way as Bacon and Descartes did in another. By withdrawing from the domain of logic what is empirical, and confining the science to an examination of "the necessary laws of thought", the Transcendentalists gave occasion to Mill and other Associationists to accuse logic of being unreal, and out of touch with the needs of an age which was, above all things, an age of empirical science. Most of the recent German literature on logic is characterized by the amount of attention which it pays either to historical inquiries, or to inquiries into the value of knowledge, or to investigation of the philosophical foundations of the laws of logic. It has added very little to the technical portion of the science. In England, the most important event in the history of logic in the nineteenth century was the publication, in 1843, of John Stuart Mill's "System of Logic". Mill renewed all the claims put forward by Bacon, and with some measure of success. At least, he brought about a change in the method of teaching logic at the great English seats of learning. Carrying Locke's empiricism to its ultimate conclusion, and adopting the association theory of the human mind, he rejected all necessary truth, discarded the syllogism as not only useless but fallacious, and maintained that all reasoning is from particulars to particulars. He did not make many converts to these views, but he succeeded in giving inductive logic a place in every textbook on logic published since his time. Not so successful was the attempt of Sir William Hamilton to establish a new logic (the "new analytic"), on the principle that the predicate as well as the subject of a proposition should be quantified. Nor, indeed, was he quite original in this: the idea had been put forward in the seventeenth century by the Catholic philosopher Caramuel (1606-82). Recent logical literature in English has striven above all things to attain clearness, intelligibility, and practical utility in its exposition of the laws of thought. Whenever it indulges in speculation as to the nature of mental processes, it is, of course, coloured by the various philosophies of the time.

Indeed, the history of logic is interesting and profitable chiefly because it shows how the philosophical theories influence the method and the doctrine of the logician. The empiricism and sensism of the English school, descending from Hobbes through Locke, Hume, and the Associationists, could lead in logic to no other conclusion than that to which it does lead in Mill's rejection of the syllogism and of all necessary truth. On the other hand, Descartes's exaltation of deduction and Leibniz's adoption of the mathematical method have their origin in that doctrine of innatism which is the opposite of empiricism. Again, the domination of industrialism, and the insistence for recognition on the part of the social economist, have had in our own day the effect of pushing logic more and more towards the position of a purveyor of rules for scientific discovery and practical invention. The materialism of the last half of the nineteenth century demanded that logic prove its utility in a practical way. Hence the prominence given to induction. But, of all the crises through which logic has passed, the most interesting is that which is known as the "Storm and Stress of Scholasticism", in which mysticism on the one side rejected dialectic as "the devil's art", and maintained that "God did not choose logic as a means of saving his people", while rationalism on the other side set no bounds to the use of logic, going so far as to place it on a plane with Divine faith. Out of this conflict issued the Scholasticism of the thirteenth century, which gave due credit to the mystic contention in so far as that contention was sound, and at the same time acknowledged freely the claims of rationalism within the limits of orthodoxy and of reason. St. Thomas and his contemporaries looked upon logic as an instrument for the discovery and exposition of natural truth. They considered, moreover, that it is the instrument by which the theologian is enabled to expound, systematize, and defend revealed truth. This view of the theological use of logic is the basis for the charge of intellectualism which Modernist philosophers imbued with Kantism have made against the Scholastics. Modernism asserts that the logical nexus is "the weakest link" between the mind and spiritual truth. So that the contest waged in the twelfth century is renewed in slightly different terms in our own day, the application of logic to theology being now, as then, the principal point in dispute.

In every system of logic there is an underlying philosophical theory, though this is not always formulated in explicit terms. It is impossible to explain and demonstrate the laws of thought without falling back on some theory of the nature of mind. For this reason Catholic philosophers and educators, as well as those who by their position in the Church are responsible for the purity of doctrine in Catholic institutions, have recognized that there is in logic the Catholic and the non-Catholic point of view. Our objection to a good deal of recent logical literature is not based on an unfavourable estimate of its scientific quality: what we object to is the sensism, subjectivism, agnosticism or other philosophical doctrine, which underlies the logical theories of the author. Works on logic written by Catholics generally adhere very closely to the traditional Aristotelean logic of the schools. Yet that is not the reason why they are approved. They are approved because they are free from false philosophical assumptions.

In many non-Catholic works on logic the underlying philosophy is not only erroneous, but subversive of the whole body of natural spiritual truth which the Catholic Church guards as carefully as she does the deposit of faith.

XVII.
Knowledge

Knowledge, being a primitive fact of consciousness, cannot, strictly speaking, be defined; but the direct and spontaneous consciousness of knowing may be made clearer by pointing out its essential and distinctive characteristics. It will be useful first to consider briefly the current uses of the verb "to know". To say that I know a certain man may mean simply that I have met him, and recognize him when I meet him again. This implies the permanence of a mental image enabling me to discern this man from all others. Sometimes, also, more than the mere familiarity with external features is implied. To know a man may mean to know his character, his inner and deeper qualities, and hence to expect him to act in a certain way under certain circumstances. The man who asserts that he knows an occurrence to be a fact means that he is so certain of it as to have no doubt concerning its reality. A pupil knows his lesson when he has mastered it and is able to recite it, and this, as the case may be, requires either mere retention in memory, or also, in addition to this retention, the intellectual work of understanding. A science is known when its principles, methods, and conclusions are understood, and the various facts and laws referring to it co-ordinated and explained. These various meanings may be reduced to two classes, one referring chiefly to sense-knowledge and to the recognition of particular experiences, the other referring chiefly to the understanding of general laws and principles. This distinction is expressed in many languages by the use of two different verbs—by gnônai and eidénai, in Greek; by cognoscere and scire, in Latin, and by their derivatives in the Romance languages; in German by kennen and wissen.

Essentials of Knowledge

(1) Knowledge is essentially the consciousness of an object, i.e. of any thing, fact, or principle belonging to the physical, mental, or metaphysical order, that may in any manner be reached by cognitive faculties. An event, a material substance, a man, a geometrical theorem, a mental process, the immortality of the soul, the existence and nature of God, may be so many objects of knowledge. Thus knowledge implies the antithesis of a knowing subject and a known object. It always possesses an objective character and any process that may be conceived as merely subjective is not a cognitive process. Any attempt to reduce the object to a purely subjective experience could result only in destroying the fact itself of knowledge, which implies the object, or not-self, as clearly as it does the subject, or self.

(2) Knowledge supposes a judgment, explicit or implicit. Apprehension, that is, the mental conception of a simple present object, is generally numbered among the cognitive processes, yet, of itself, it is not in the strict sense knowledge, but only its starting-point. Properly speaking, we know only when we compare, identify, discriminate, connect; and these processes, equivalent to judgments, are found implicitly even in ordinary sense-perception. A few judgments are reached immediately, but by far the greater

number require patient investigation. The mind is not merely passive in knowing, not a mirror or sensitized plate, in which objects picture themselves; it is also active in looking for conditions and causes, and in building up science out of the materials which it receives from experience. Thus observation and thought are two essential factors in knowledge.

(3) Truth and certitude are conditions of knowledge. A man may mistake error for truth and give his unreserved assent to a false statement. He may then be under the irresistible illusion that he knows, and subjectively the process is the same as that of knowledge; but an essential condition is lacking, namely, conformity of thought with reality, so that there we have only the appearance of knowledge. On the other hand, as long as any serious doubt remains in his mind, a man cannot say that he knows. "I think so" is far from meaning "I know it is so"; knowledge is not mere opinion or probable assent. The distinction between knowledge and belief is more difficult to draw, owing chiefly to the vague meaning of the latter term. Sometimes belief refers to assent without certitude, and denotes the attitude of the mind especially in regard to matters that are not governed by strict and uniform laws like those of the physical world, but depend on many complex factors and circumstances, as happens in human affairs. I know that water will freeze when it reaches a certain temperature; I believe that a man is fit for a certain office, or that the reforms endorsed by one political party

will be more beneficial than those advocated by another. Sometimes, also, both belief and knowledge imply certitude, and denote states of mental assurance of the truth. But in belief the evidence is more obscure and indistinct than in knowledge, either because the grounds on which the assent rests are not so clear, or because the evidence is not personal, but based on the testimony of witnesses, or again because, in addition to the objective evidence which draws the assent, there are subjective conditions that predispose to it. Belief seems to depend on a great many influences, emotions, interests, surroundings, etc., besides the convincing reasons for which assent is given to truth. Faith is based on the testimony of someone else--God or man according as we speak of Divine or of human faith. If the authority on which it rests has all the required guarantees, faith gives the certitude of the fact, the knowledge that it is true; but, of itself, it does not give the intrinsic evidence why it is so.

Kinds of Knowledge

(1) It is impossible that all the knowledge a man has acquired should be at once present in consciousness. The greater part, in fact all of it with the exception of the few thoughts actually present in the mind, is stored up in the form of latent dispositions which enable the mind to recall it when wanted. Hence we may distinguish actual from habitual knowledge. The latter extends to whatever is preserved in memory and is capable of being recalled at

will. This capacity of being recalled may require several experiences; a science is not always known after it has been mastered once, for even then it may be forgotten. By habitual knowledge is meant knowledge in readiness to come back to consciousness, and it is clear that it may have different degrees of perfection.

(2) The distinction between knowledge as recognition and knowledge as understanding has already been noted. In the same connection may be mentioned the distinction between particular knowledge, or knowledge of facts and individuals, and general knowledge, or knowledge of laws and classes. The former deals with the concrete, the latter with the abstract.

(3) According to the process by which it is acquired, knowledge is intuitive and immediate or discursive and mediate. The former comes from the direct sense perception, or the direct mental intuition of the truth of a proposition, based as it were on its own merits. The latter consists in the recognition of the truth of a proposition by seeing its connection with another already known to be true. The self-evident proposition is of such a nature as to be immediately clear to the mind. No one who understands the terms can fail to know that two and two are four, or that the whole is greater than any one of its parts. But most human knowledge is acquired progressively. Inductive knowledge starts from self-evident facts, and rises to laws and causes. Deductive knowledge proceeds from general self-evident propositions in order to discover their

particular application. In both cases the process may be long, difficult, and complex. One may have to be satisfied with negative conception and analogical evidence, and, as a result, knowledge will be less clear, less certain, and more liable to error.

The Problem of Knowledge

    The question of knowledge belongs to various sciences, each of which takes a different point of view. Psychology considers knowledge as a mental fact whose elements, conditions, laws and growth are to be determined. It endeavours to discover the behaviour of the mind in knowing, and the development of the cognitive process out of its elements. It supplies the other sciences with the data on which they must work. Among these data are found certain laws of thought which the mind must observe in order to avoid contradiction and to reach consistent knowledge. Formal logic also takes the subjective point of view; it deals with these laws of thought, and neglecting the objective side of knowledge (that is, its materials), studies only the formal elements necessary to consistency and valid proof. At the other extreme, science, physical or metaphysical, postulating the validity of knowledge, or at least leaving this problem out of consideration, studies only the different objects of knowledge, their nature and properties. As to the crucial questions, the validity of knowledge, its limitations, and the relations between the knowing subject and the known object, these belong to the province of epistemology.

Knowledge is essentially objective. Such names as the "given" or the "content" of knowledge may be substituted for that of "object", but the plain fact remains that we know something external, which is not formed by, but offered to, the mind. This must not, however, cause us to overlook another fact equally evident. Different minds will frequently take different views of the same object. Moreover, even in the same mind, knowledge undergoes great changes in the course of time; judgments are constantly modified, enlarged or narrowed down, in accordance with newly discovered facts and ascertained truths. Sense-perception is influenced by past processes, associations, contrasts, etc. In rational knowledge a great diversity of assents is produced by personal dispositions, innate or acquired. In a word, knowledge clearly depends on the mind. Hence the assertion that it is made by the mind alone, that it is conditioned exclusively by the nature of the thinking subject, and that the object of knowledge is in no way outside of the knowing mind. To use Berkeley's words, to be is to be known (esse est percipi). The fact of the dependence of knowledge upon subjective conditions however, is far from sufficient to justify this conclusion. Men agree on many propositions, both of the empirical and of the rational order; they differ not so much on objects of knowledge as on objects of opinion, not so much on what they really know as on what they think they know. For two men with normal eyes, the vision of an object, as far as we can ascertain, is sensibly the same. For two men with normal minds, the proposition that the sum of the angles in a triangle equals two right angles has the same meaning, and, both for several minds and for the same mind at different times, the knowledge of that proposition is identical. Owing to associations and differences in mental attitudes, the fringe of consciousness will vary and somewhat modify the total mental state, but the focus of consciousness, knowledge itself, will be essentially the same. St. Thomas will not be accused of idealism, and yet he makes the nature of the mind an essential factor in the act of knowledge:

> Cognition is brought about by the presence of the known object in the knowing mind. But the object is in the knower after the fashion of the knower. Hence, for any knower, knowledge is after the fashion of his own nature (Summa theol., I, Q. xii, a. 4).

What is this presence of the object in the subject? Not a physical presence; not even in the form of a picture, a duplicate, or a copy. It cannot be defined by any comparison with the physical world; it is sui generis, a cognitive likeness, a species intentionalis.

When knowledge, either of concrete realities or of abstract propositions, is said to consist in the presence of an object in the mind, we cannot mean by this object something external in its absolute existence and isolated from the mind, for we cannot think outside of our own thought, and the mind cannot know what is not somehow present in the mind. But this is no sufficient ground for accepting extreme idealism and looking upon knowledge as purely subjective. If the object of an assent or experience cannot be absolute reality, it does not follow that to an assent or experience there is no corresponding reality; and the fact that an object is reached through the conception of it does not justify the conclusion that the mental conception is the whole of the object's reality. To say that knowledge is a conscious process is true, but it is only a part of the truth. And from this to infer, with Locke, that, since we can be conscious only of what takes place within ourselves, knowledge is only "conversant with ideas", is to take an exclusively psychological view of the fact which asserts itself primarily as establishing a relation between a mind and an external reality. Knowledge becomes conversant with ideas by a subsequent process, namely by the reflection of the mind upon its own activity. The subjectivist has his eyes wide open to the difficulty of explaining the transition from external reality to the mind, a difficulty which, after all, is but the mystery of consciousness itself. He keeps them obstinately closed to the utter impossibility of explaining the building up by the mind of an external reality out of mere conscious processes. Notwithstanding all theorizing to the contrary, the facts impose themselves that in knowing the mind is not merely active, but also passive; that it must conform, not simply to its own laws but to external reality as well; that it does not create facts and laws but discovers them; and that the right of truth to recognition persists even when it is actually ignored or violated. The mind, it is true, contributes its share to the knowing process, but, to use the metaphor of St. Augustine, the generation of knowledge requires another cause: "Whatever object we know is a co-factor in the generation of the knowledge of it. For knowledge is begotten both by the knowing subject and the known object" (De Trinitate, IX, xii). Hence it may be maintained that there are realities distinct from ideas without falling into the absurdity of maintaining that they are known in their absolute existence, that is apart from their relations to the knowing mind. Knowledge is essentially the vital union of both.

It has been said above that knowledge requires experience and thought. The attempt to explain knowledge by experience alone proved a failure, and the favour which Associationism found at first was short-lived. Recent criticism of the sciences has accentuated the fact, which already occupied a central place in scholastic philosophy, that knowledge, even of the physical and mental worlds, implies factors transcending experience. Empiricism fails completely in its endeavour to explain and justify universal knowledge, the knowledge of uniform laws under which facts are brought to unity. Without rational additions, the perception of what is or has been can never give the knowledge of what will certainly and necessarily be. True as this is of the natural sciences, it is still more evident in abstract and rational sciences like mathematics. Hence we are led back to the old Aristotelian and Scholastic view, that all knowledge begins with concrete experience, but requires other factors, not given in experience, in order to reach its perfection. It needs reason interpreting the data of observation, abstracting the contents of experience from the conditions which individualize them in space and time, removing, as it were, the outer envelope of the concrete, and going to the core of reality. Thus knowledge is not, as in Kantian criticism, a synthesis of two elements, one external, the other depending only on the nature of the mind; not the filling up of empty shells—a priori mental forms or categories—with the unknown and unknowable reality. Even abstract knowledge reveals reality, although its object cannot exist outside of the mind without conditions of which the mind in the act of knowing divests it.

Knowledge is necessarily proportioned or relative to the capacity of the mind and the manifestations of the object. Not all men have the same keenness of vision or hearing, or the same intellectual aptitudes. Nor is the same reality equally bright from all angles from which it may be viewed. Moreover, better eyes than human might perceive rays beyond the red and the violet of the spectrum; higher intellects might unravel many mysteries of nature, know more and better, with greater facility, certainty, and clearness. The fact that we do not know everything, and that all our knowledge is inadequate, does not invalidate the knowledge which we possess, any more than the horizon which bounds our view prevents us from perceiving more or less distinctly the various objects within its limits. Reality manifests itself to the mind in different ways and with varying degrees of clearness. Some objects are bright in themselves and are perceived immediately. Others are known indirectly by throwing on them light borrowed elsewhere, by showing by way of causality, similarity, analogy their connection with what we already know. This is essentially the condition of scientific progress, to find connections between various objects, to proceed from the known to the unknown. As we recede from the self-evident, the path may become more difficult, and the progress slower. But, with the Agnostic, to assign clearly defined boundaries to our cognitive powers is unjustifiable, for we pass gradually from one object to another without break, and there is no sharp limit between science and metaphysics. The same instruments, principles, and methods that are recognized in the various sciences will carry us higher and higher, even to the Absolute, the First Cause, the Source of all reality. Induction will lead us from the effect to the cause, from the imperfect to the perfect, from the contingent to the necessary, from the dependent to the self-existent, from the finite to the infinite.

And this same process by which we know God's existence cannot fail to manifest something—however little—of His nature and perfections. That we know Him imperfectly, by way chiefly of negation and analogy, does not deprive this knowledge of all value. We can know God only so far as He manifests Himself through His works which dimly mirror His perfections, and so far as our finite mind will allow. Such knowledge will necessarily remain infinitely far from being comprehension, but it is only by a misleading confusion of terms that Spencer identifies the unknowable with the incomprehensible, and denies the possibility of any knowledge of the Absolute because we can have no absolute-knowledge. Seeing "through a glass" and "in a dark manner" is far from the vision "face to face" of which our limited mind is incapable without a special light from God Himself. Yet it is knowledge of Him who is the source both of the world's intelligibility and truth, and of the mind's intelligence.

… XVIII.
Truth

Truth (Anglo-Saxon tréow, tryw, truth, preservation of a compact, from a Teutonic base Trau, to believe) is a relation which holds (1) between the knower and the known — Logical Truth; (2) between the knower and the outward expression which he gives to his knowledge — Moral Truth; and (3) between the thing itself, as it exists, and the idea of it, as conceived by God — Ontological Truth. In each case this relation is, according to the Scholastic theory, one of correspondence, conformity, or agreement (adoequatio) (St. Thomas, Summa I:21:2).

Ontological Truth

Every existing thing is true, in that it is the expression of an idea which exists in the mind of God, and is, as it were, the exemplar according to which the thing has been created or fashioned. Just as human creations — a cathedral, a painting, or an epic — conform to and embody the ideas of architect, artist, or poet, so, only in a more perfect way, God's creatures conform to and embody the ideas of Him who gives them being. (Q. D., De verit., a. 4; Summa 1:16:1.) Things that exist, moreover, are active as well as passive. They tend not only to develop, and so to realize more and more perfectly the idea which they are created to express, but they tend also to reproduce themselves. Reproduction obtains wherever there is interaction between different things, for an effect, in so far as it proceeds from a given cause, must resemble that cause. Now the cause of knowledge in man is — ultimately, at any rate — the thing that is known. By its activities it causes in man an idea that is like to the idea embodied in the thing itself. Hence, things may also be said to be ontologically true in that they are at once the object and the cause of human knowledge. (Cf. IDEALISM; and Summa, I:16:7 and 1:16:8; m 1. periherm., 1. III; Q.D., I, De veritate, a. 4.)

Logical Truth
The Scholastic Theory

To judge that things are what they are is to judge truly. Every judgment comprises certain ideas which are referred to, or denied of, reality. But it is not these ideas that are the objects of our judgment. They are merely the instruments by means of which we judge. The object about which we judge is reality itself — either concrete existing things, their attributes, and their relations, or else entities the existence of which is merely conceptual or imaginary, as in drama, poetry, or fiction, but in any case entities which are real in the sense that their being is other than our present thought about them. Reality, therefore, is one thing, and the ideas and judgments by means of which we think about reality, another; the one objective, and the other subjective. Yet, diverse as they are, reality is somehow present to, if not present in consciousness when we think, and somehow by means of thought the nature of reality is revealed. This being the case, the only term adequate to describe the relation that exists between thought and reality, when our judgments about the latter are true judgments, would seem to be conformity or correspondence. "Veritas logica est adaequatio intellectus et rei" (Summa, I:21:2). Whenever truth is predicable of a judgment, that judgment corresponds to, or resembles, the reality, the nature or attributes of which it reveals. Every judgment is, however, as we have said, made up of ideas, and may be logically analyzed into a subject and a predicate, which are either united by the copula is, or disjoined by the expression is not. If the judgment be true, therefore, these ideas must also be true, i.e. must correspond with the realities which they signify. As, however, this objective reference or significance of ideas is not recognized or asserted except in the judgment, ideas as such are said to be only "materially" true. It is the judgment alone that is formally true, since in the judgment alone is a reference to reality formally made, and truth as such recognized or claimed.

The negative judgment seems at first sight to form an exception to the general law that truth is correspondence; but this is not really the case. In the affirmative judgment both subject and predicate and the union between them, of whatever kind it may be, are referred to reality; but in the negative judgment subject and predicate are disjoined, not conjoined. In other words, in the negative judgment we deny that the predicate has reality in the particular case to which the subject refers. On the other hand, all such predicates presumably have reality somewhere, otherwise we should not talk about them. Either they are real qualities or real things, or at any rate somebody has conceived them as real. Consequently the negative judgment, if true, may also be said to correspond with reality, since both subject and predicate will be real somewhere, either as existents or as conceptions. What we deny, in fact, in the negative judgment is not the reality of the predicate, but the reality of the conjunction by which subject and predicate are united in the assertion which we implicitly challenge and negate. Subject and predicate may both be real, but if our judgment be true, they will be disjoined, not united in reality.

But what precisely is this reality with which true judgments and true ideas are said to correspond? It is easy enough to understand how ideas can correspond with realities that are themselves conceptual or ideal, but most of the realities that we know are not of this kind. How, then, can ideas and their conjunctions or disjunctions, which are psychical in character, correspond with realities which for the most part are not psychical but material? To solve this problem we must go back to ontological truth which, as we saw, implies the creation of the universe by One Who, in creating it, has expressed therein His own ideas very much as an architect or an author expresses his ideas in the things that he creates except that creation in the latter case supposes already existent material. Our theory of truth supposes that the universe is built according to definite and rational plan, and that everything within the universe expresses or embodies an essential and integral part of that plan. Whence it follows that just as in a building or in a piece of sculpture we see the plan or design that is realized therein, so, in our experience of concrete things, by means of the same intellectual power, we apprehend the ideas which they embody or express. The correspondence therefore, in which truth consists is not a correspondence between ideas and anything material as such, but between ideas as they exist in our mind and function in our acts of cognition, and the idea that reality expresses and embodies — ideas which have their origin and prototype in the mind of God.

With regard to judgments of a more abstract or general type, the working of this view is quite simple. The realities to which abstract concepts refer have no material existence as such. There is no such thing, for instance, as action or reaction in general; nor are there any twos or fours. What we mean when we say that "action and reaction are equal and opposite", or that "two and two make four", is that these laws which in their own proper nature are ideal, are realized or actualized in the material universe in which we live; or, in other words, that the material things we see about us behave in accordance with these laws and through their activities manifest them to our minds.

Perceptual judgments, i.e. the judgments which usually accompany and give expression to acts of perception, differ from the above in that they refer to objects which are immediately present to our senses. The realities in this case, therefore, are concrete existing things. It is, however, rather with the appearance of such things that our judgment is now concerned than with their essential nature or inner constitution. Thus, when we predicate colours, sounds, odours, flavours, hardness or softness, heat or cold of this or that object, we make no statement about the nature of such qualities, still less about the nature of the thing that possesses them. What we assert is

* that such and such a thing exists, and
* that it has a certain objective quality, which we call green, or loud, or sweet, or hard, or hot, to distinguish it from other qualities — red, or soft, or bitter, or cold — with which it is not identical; while
* our statement further implies that the same quality will similarly appear to any normally constituted man, i.e. will affect his senses in the same way that it affects our own.

Accordingly, if in the real world such a condition of things obtains — if, that is to say, the thing in question does exist and has in fact some peculiar and distinctive property whereby it affects my senses in a certain peculiar and distinctive way — my judgment is true.

The truth of perceptual judgments by no means implies an exact correspondence between what is perceived and the images, or sensation — complexes, whereby we perceive; nor does the Scholastic theory necessitate any such view. It is not the image, or sensation-complex, but the idea, that in judgment is referred to reality, and that gives us knowledge of reality. Colour and other qualities of objective things are doubtless perceived by means of sensation of peculiar and distinctive quality or tone, but no one imagines that this presupposes similar sensation in the object perceived. It is by means of the idea of colour and its specific differences that colours are predicated of objects, not by means of sensations Such an idea could not arise, indeed, were it not for the sensations which in perception accompany and condition it; but the idea itself is not a sensation, nor is it of a sensation. Ideas have their origin in sensible experience and are indefinable, so far as immediate experience goes, except by reference to such experience and by differentiation from experiences in which other and different properties of objects are presented Granted, therefore, that differences in what is technically known as the "quality" of sensation correspond to differences in the objective properties of things, the truth of perceptual judgments is assured. No further correspondence is required; for the correspondence which truth postulates is between idea and thing, not between sensation and thing. Sensation conditions knowledge, but as such it is not knowledge. It is, as it were, a connecting link between the idea and the thing. Differences of sensation are determined by the causal activity of things; and from the sensation-complex, or image the idea is derived by an instinctive and quasi-intuitive act of the mind which we call abstraction. Thus the idea which the thing unconsciously expresses finds conscious expression in the act of the knower, and the vast scheme of relations and laws which are de facto embodied in the material universe reproduce themselves in the consciousness of man.

Correspondence between thought and reality, idea and thing, or knower and known, therefore, turns out in all cases to be of the very essence of the truth relation. Whence, say the opponents of our theory, in order to know whether our judgments are true or not, we must compare them with the realities that are known — a comparison that is obviously impossible, since reality can only be known through the instrumentality of the judgment. This objection, which is to be found in almost every non-Scholastic book dealing with the subject, rests upon a grave misapprehension of the real meaning of the Scholastic doctrine. Neither St. Thomas nor any other of the great Scholastics ever asserted that correspondence is the scholastic criterion of truth. To inquire what truth is, is one question; to ask how we know that we have judged truly, quite another. Indeed, the possibility of answering the second is supposed by the mere fact that the first is put. To be able to define truth, we must first possess it and know that we possess it, i.e. must be able to distinguish it from error. We cannot define that which we cannot distinguish and to some extent isolate. The Scholastic theory supposes, therefore, that truth has already been distinguished from error, and proceeds to examine truth with a view to discovering in what precisely it consists. This standpoint is epistemological, not criteriological. When he says that truth is correspondence, he is stating what truth is, not by what sign or mark it can be distinguished from error. By the old

Scholastics the question of the criteria of truth was scarcely touched. They discussed the criteria of valid reasoning in their treatises on logic, but for the rest they left the discussion of particular criteria to the methodology of particular sciences. And rightly so, for there is really no criterion of universal application. The distinction of truth and error is at bottom intuitional. We cannot go on making criteria ad infinitum. Somewhere we must come to what is ultimate, either first principles or facts.

This is precisely what the Scholastic theory of truth affirms. In deference to the modern demand for an infallible and universal criterion of truth, not a few Scholastic writers of late have suggested objective evidence. Objective evidence, however, is nothing more than the manifestation of the object itself, directly or indirectly, to the mind, and hence is not strictly a criterion of truth, but its foundation. As Père Geny puts it in his pamphlet discussing "Une nouvelle théorie de la connaissance", to state that evidence is the ultimate criterion of truth is equivalent to stating that knowledge properly so called has no need of a criterion, since it is absurd to suppose a knowledge which does not know what it knows. Once grant, as all must grant who wish to avoid absolute scepticism, that knowledge is possible, and it follows that, properly used, our faculties must be capable of giving us truth. Doubtless, coherence and harmony with facts are pro tanto signs of truth's presence in our minds; but what we need for the most part are not signs of truth, but signs or criteria of error — not tests whereby to discover when our faculties have gone right, but tests whereby to discover when they have gone wrong. Our judgments will be true, i.e. thought will correspond with its object, provided that object itself, and not any other cause, subjective or objective, determines the content of our thought. What we have to do, therefore, is to take care that our assent is determined by the evidence with which we are confronted, and by this alone. With regard to the senses this means that we must look to it that they are in good condition and that the circumstances under which we are exercising them are normal; with regard to the intellect that we must not allow irrelevant considerations to weigh with us, that we must avoid haste, and, as far as possible, get rid of bias, prejudice, and an over-anxious will to believe. If this be done, granted there is sufficient evidence, true judgments will naturally and necessarily result. The purpose of argument and discussion, as of all other processes that lead to knowledge, is precisely that the object under discussion may manifest itself in its various relations, either directly or indirectly, to the mind. And the object as thus manifesting itself is what the Scholastic calls evidence. It is the object, therefore, which in his view is the determining cause of truth. All kinds of processes, both mental and physical, may be necessary to prepare the way for an act of cognition, but in the last resort such an act must be determined as to its content by the causal activity of the object, which makes itself evident by producing in the mind an idea that is like to the idea of which its own existence is the realization.

The Hegelian Theory

In the Idealism of Hegel and the Absolutism of the Oxford School (of which Mr. Bradley and Mr. Joachim are the leading representatives) both reality and truth are essentially one, essentially an organic whole. Truth, in fact, is but reality qua thought. It is an intelligent act in which the universe is thought as a whole of infinite parts or differences, all organically inter-related and somehow brought to unity. And because truth is thus organic, each element within it, each partial truth, is so modified by the others through and through that apart from them, and again apart from the whole, it is but a distorted fragment, a mutilated abstraction which in reality is not truth at all. Consequently, since human truth is always partial and fragmentary, there is in strictness no such thing as human truth. For us the truth is ideal, and from it our truths are so far removed that, to convert them into the truth, they would have to undergo a change of which we know neither the measure nor the extent.

The flagrantly sceptical character of this theory is sufficiently obvious, nor is there any attempt on the part of its exponents to deny it. Starting with the assumption that to conceive is "to hold many elements together in a connexion necessitated by their several contents", and that to be conceivable is to be "a significant whole", i.e. a whole, "such that all its constituent elements reciprocally determine one another's being as contributory features in a single concrete meaning", Dr. Joachim boldly identifies the true with the conceivable (Nature of Truth, 66). And since no human intellect can conceive in this full and magnificent sense, he frankly admits that no human truth can be more than approximate, and that to the margin of error which this approximation involves no limits can be assigned. Human truth draws from absolute or ideal truth "whatever being and conservability" it possesses (Green, "Prolegom.", article 77); but it is not, and never can be, identical with absolute truth, nor yet with any part of it, for these parts essentially and intrinsically modify one another. For his definition of human truth, therefore, the Absolutist is forced back upon the Scholastic doctrine of correspondence. Human truth represents or corresponds with absolute truth in proportion as it presents us with this truth as affected by more or less derangement, or in proportion as it would take more or less to convert the one into the other (Bradley, "Appearance and Reality", 363). While, therefore, both theories assign correspondence as the essential characteristic of human truth, there is this fundamental difference between them: For the Scholastic this correspondence, so far as it goes, must be exact; but for the Absolutist it is necessarily imperfect, so imperfect, indeed, that "the ultimate truth" of any given proposition "may quite transform its original meaning" (Appearance and Reality, 364).

To admit that human truth is essentially

representative is really to admit that conception is something more than the mere "holding together of many elements in a connexion necessitated by their several contents". But the fallacy of the "coherence theory" does not lie so much in this, nor yet in the identification of the true and the conceivable, as in its assumption that reality, and therefore truth, is organically one. The universe is undoubtedly one, in that its parts are inter-related and inter-dependent; and from this it follows that we cannot know any part completely unless we know the whole; but it does not follow that we cannot know any part at all unless we know the whole. If each part has some sort of being of its own, then it can be known for what it is, whether we know its relations to other parts or not; and similarly some of its relations to other parts can be known without our knowing them all. Nor is the individuality of the parts of the universe destroyed by their inter-dependence; rather it is thereby sustained.

The sole ground which the Hegelian and the Absolutist have for denying these facts is that they will not square with their theory that the universe is organically one. Since, therefore, it is confessedly impossible to explain the nature of this unity or to show how in it the multitudinous differences of the universe are "reconciled", and since, further, this theory is acknowledged to be hopelessly sceptical, it is surely irrational any longer to maintain it.

The Pragmatic Theory

Life for the Pragmatist is essentially practical. All human activity is purposive, and its purpose is the control of human experience with a view to its improvement, both in the individual and in the race. Truth is but a means to this end. Ideas, hypotheses, and theories are but instruments which man has "made" in order to better both himself and his environment; and, though specific in type, like all other forms of human activity they exist solely for this end, and are "true" in so far as they fulfil it. Truth is thus a form of value: it is something that works satisfactorily; something that "ministers to human interests, purposes and objects of desire" (Studies in Humanism, 362). There are no axioms or self-evident truths. Until an idea or a judgment has proved itself of value in the manipulation of concrete experience, it is but a postulate or claim to truth. Nor are there any absolute or irreversible truths. A proposition is true so long as it proves itself useful, and no longer. In regard to the essential features of this theory of truth W. James, John Dewey, and A.W. Moore in America, F.C.S. Schiller in England, G. Simmel in Germany, Papini in Italy, and Henri Bergson, Le Roy, and Abel Rey in France are all substantially in agreement. It is, they say, the only theory which takes account of the psychological processes by which truth is made, and the only theory which affords a satisfactory answer to the arguments of the sceptic.

In regard to the first of these claims there can be no doubt that Pragmatism is based upon a study of truth "in the making". But the question at issue is not whether interest, purpose, emotion, and volition do as a matter of fact play a part in the process of cognition. That is not disputed. The question is whether, in judging of the validity of a claim to truth, such considerations ought to have weight. If the aim of all cognitive acts is to know reality as it is, then clearly judgments are true only in so far as they satisfy this demand. But this does not help us in deciding what judgments are true and what are not, for the truth of a judgment must already be known before this demand can be satisfied. Similarly with regard to particular interests and purposes; for though such interests and purposes may prompt us to seek for knowledge, they will not be satisfied until we know truly, or at any rate think we know truly. The satisfaction of our needs, in other words, is posterior to, and already supposes, the possession of true knowledge about whatever we wish to use as a means to the satisfaction of those needs. To act efficiently, we must know what it is we are acting upon and what will be the effects of the action contemplated. The truth of our judgments is verified by their consequences only in those cases where we know that such consequences should ensue if our judgment be true, and then act in order to discover whether in reality they will ensue.

Theoretically, and upon Scholastic principles, since whatever is true is also good, true judgments ought to result in good consequences. But, apart from the fact that the truth of our judgment must in many cases be known before we can act upon them with success, the Pragmatic criterion is too vague and too variable to be of any practical use. "Good consequences", "successful operations on reality", "beneficial interaction with sensible particulars" denote experiences which it is not easy to recognize or to distinguish from other experiences less good, less successful, and less beneficial. If we take personal valuations as our test, these are proverbially unstable; while, if social valuations alone are admissible, where are they to be found, and upon what grounds accepted by the individual? Moreover, when a valuation has been made, how are we to know that it is accurate? For this, it would seem, further valuations will be required, and so on ad infinitum. Distinctively pragmatic criteria of truth are both impractical and unreliable, especially the criterion of felt satisfaction, which seems to be the favourite, for in determining this not only the personal factor, but the mood of the moment and even physical conditions play a considerable part. Consequently upon the second head the claim of the Pragmatist can by no means be allowed. The Pragmatist theory is not a whit less sceptical than the theory of the Absolutist, which it seeks to displace. If truth is relative to purposes and interests, and if these purposes and interests are, as they are admitted to be, one and all tinged by personal idiosyncrasy, then what is true for one man will not be true for another, and what is true now will not be true when a change takes place either in the interest that has engendered it or in the circumstances by which it has been verified.

All this the Pragmatist grants, but replies that such truth is all that man needs and all that he can get. True judgments do not correspond with reality, nor in true judgments do we know reality as it is. The function of cognition, in short, is not to know reality, but to control it. For this reason truth is identified with its consequences — theoretical, if the truth be merely virtual, but in the end practical, particular, concrete. "Truth means successful operations on reality" (Studies in Hum., 118). The truth-relation "consists of intervening parts of the universe which can in every particular case be assigned and catalogued" (Meaning of Truth, 234). "The chain of workings which an opinion sets up is the opinion's truth" (Ibid., 235). Thus, in order to refute the Sceptic, the Pragmatist changes the nature of truth, redefining it as the definitely experienceable success which attends the working of certain ideas and judgments; and in so doing he grants precisely what the Sceptic seeks to prove, namely, that our cognitive faculties are incapable of knowing reality as it is.

The "New" Realist's Theory

As it is a first principle with both Absolutist and Pragmatist that reality is changed by the very act in which we know it, so the negation of this thesis is the root principle of "New" Realism. In this the "New" Realist is at one with the Scholastic. Reality does not depend upon experience, nor is it modified by experience as such. The "New" Realist, however, has not as yet adopted the correspondence theory of truth. He regards both knowledge and truth as unique relations which hold immediately between knower and known, and which are as to their nature indefinable. "The difference between subject and object of consciousness is not a difference of quality or substance, but a difference of office or place in a configuration" (Journal of Phil. Psychol. and Scientific Meth., VII, 396). Reality is made up of terms and their relations, and truth is just one of these relations, sui generis, and therefore recognizable only by intuition. This account of truth is undoubtedly simple, but there is at any rate one point which it seems altogether to ignore, viz., the existence of judgments and ideas of which, and not of the mind as such, the truth-relation is predicable. We have not on the one hand objects and on the other bare mind; but on the one hand objects and on the other a mind that by means of the judgment refers its own ideas to objects — ideas which as such, both in regard to their existence and their content, belong to the mind which judges. What then is the relation that holds between these ideas and their objects when our judgments are true, and again when they are false? Surely both logic and criteriology imply that we know something more about such judgments than merely that they are different.

Bertrand Russell, who has given in his adhesion to "The Program and First Platform of Six Realists", drawn up and signed by six American professors in July, 1910, modifies somewhat the naïveté of their theory of truth.

"Every judgment", he says (Philos. Essays, 181), "is a relation of a mind to several objects, one of which is a relation. Thus, the judgment, 'Charles I died on the scaffold', denotes several objects or 'objectives' which are related in a certain definite way, and the relation is as real in this case as are the other objectives. The judgment 'Charles I died in his bed', on the other hand, denotes the objects, Charles I, death, and bed, and a certain relation between them, which in this case does not relate the objects as it is supposed to relate them. A judgment therefore, is true, when the relation which is one of the objects relates the other objects, otherwise it is false" (loc. cit.). In this statement of the nature of truth: correspondence between the mind judging and the objects about which we judge is distinctly implied, and it is precisely this correspondence which is set down as the distinguishing mark of true judgments. Russell however, unfortunately seems to be at variance with other members of the New Realist school on this point. G.E. Moore expressly rejects the correspondence theory of truth ("Mind", N. S., VIII, 179 sq.), and Prichard, another English Realist, explicitly states that in knowledge there is nothing between the object and ourselves (Kant's Theory of Knowledge, 21). Nevertheless, it is matter for rejoicing that in regard to the main points at issue — the non-alteration of reality by acts of cognition, the possibility of knowing it in some respects without its being known in all, the growth of knowledge by "accretion", the non-spiritual character of some of the objects of experience, and the necessity of ascertaining empirically and not by a priori methods, the degree of unity which obtains between the various parts of the universe—the "New" Realist and the Scholastic Realist are substantially in agreement.

Moral Truth, or Veracity

Veracity is the correspondence of the outward expression given to thought with the thought itself. It must not be confused with verbal truth (veritas locutionis), which is the correspondence of the outward or verbal expression with the thing that it is intended to express. The latter supposes on the part of the speaker not only the intention of speaking truly, but also the power so to do, i.e. it supposes (1) true knowledge and (2) a right use of words. Moral truth, on the other hand, exists whenever the speaker expresses what is in his mind even if de facto he be mistaken, provided only that he says what he thinks to be true. This latter condition however, is necessary. Hence a better definition of moral truth would be "the correspondence of the outward expression of thought with the thing as conceived by the speaker". Moral truth, therefore, does not imply true knowledge. But, though a deviation from moral truth would be only materially a lie, and hence not blameworthy, unless the use of words or signs were intentionally incorrect, moral truth does imply a correct use of words or other signs. A lie therefore, is an intentional deviation from moral truth, and is defined as a locutio contra mentem; i.e. it is the outward expression of a thought which is intentionally diverse from the thing as conceived by the speaker. It is important to observe, however, that the expression of the thought, whether by word or by sign, must in all cases be taken in its context; for both in regard to words and to signs, custom and circumstances make a considerable difference with respect to their interpretation. Veracity, or the habit of speaking the truth, is a virtue; and the obligation of practising it arises from a twofold source. First, "since man is a social animal, naturally one man owes to another that without which human society could not go on. But men could not live together if they did not believe one another to be speaking the truth. Hence the virtue of veracity comes to some extent under the head of justice [rationem debiti]" (St. Thomas, Summa Theologiæ II-II.109.3). The second source of the obligation to veracity arises from the fact that speech is clearly of its very nature intended for the communication of knowledge by one to another. It should be used, therefore, for the purpose for which it is naturally intended, and lies should be avoided. For lies are not merely a misuse, but an abuse, of the gift of speech, since, by destroying man's instinctive belief in the veracity of his neighbour, they tend to destroy the efficacy of that gift.

XIX.
Epistemology

Epistemology, in a most general way, is that branch of philosophy which is concerned with the value of human knowledge.

The name epistemology, is of recent origin, but especially since the publication of Ferrier's "Institutes of Metaphysics: the Theory of Knowing and Being" (1854), it has come to be used currently instead of other terms, still sometimes met with, like applied logic, material or critical logic, critical or initial philosophy, etc. To the same part of philosophy the name criteriology is given by the authors of some Latin textbooks and by the Louvain School.

The exact province of epistemology is as yet but imperfectly determined, the two main views corresponding to the two meanings of the Greek word epistéme. According as this is understood in its more general sense of knowledge, or in its more special sense of scientific knowledge, epistemology is "the theory of the origin, nature and limits of knowledge" (Baldwin, "Dict. of Philos. and Psychol.", New York, 1901, s.v. "Epistemology", I, 333; cf. "Gnosiology",I,414); or "the philosophy of the sciences", and more exactly, "the critical study of the principles, hypotheses and results of the various sciences, designed to determine their logical (not psychological) origin, their value and objective import" ("Bulletin de la Société fran‚aise de Philos.", June, 1905, fasc. no. 7 of the Vocabulaire philosophique, s.v. "Epistémologie", 221; cf. Aug., 1906, fasc. 9 of the Vocabul., s.v. "Gnoséologie", 332). The Italian usage agrees with the French. According to Ranzoli ("Dizionario di seienze filosofiche", Milan, 1905, s.v. "Epistemologia", 226; cf. "Gnosiologia", 286), epistemology "determines the objects of every science by ascertaining their differentiating characteristics, fixes their relations and common principles, the laws of their development and their special methods".

Here we shall consider epistemology in its first and broader meaning, which is the usual one in English, as applying to the theory of knowledge, the German Erkenntnistheorie, i.e. "that part of Philosophy which, in the first place, describes, analyses, examines genetically the facts of knowledge as such (psychology of knowledge), and then tests chiefly the value of knowledge and of its various kinds, its conditions of validity, range and limits (critique of knowledge)" (Eisler, Wörterbuch der philos. Begriffe, 2d ed., Berlin, 1904, I, 298). In that sense epistemology does not merely deal with certain assumptions of science, but undertakes to test the cognitive faculty itself in all its functions.

Historical Outline

The first efforts of Greek thinkers centre around the study of nature. This early philosophy is almost exclusively objective, and supposes, without examining it, the validity of knowledge. Doubt arose later chiefly from the disagreement of philosophers in determining the primordial elements of matter and in discussing the nature and attributes of reality. Parmenides holds that it is unchangeable; Heraclitus, that it is constantly changing; Democritus endows it with an eternal inherent motion, while Anaxagoras requires an independent and intelligent motor. This led the Sophists to question the possibility of certitude, and prepared the way for their sceptical tendencies. With Socrates, Plato, and Aristotle, who oppose the Sophists, the power of the mind to know truth and reach certitude is vindicated, and the conditions for the validity of knowledge are examined. But epistemological questions are not yet treated on their own merits, nor kept sufficiently distinct from purely logical and metaphysical inquiries. The philosophy of the Stoics is primarily practical, knowledge being looked upon as a means of right living and as a condition of happiness. As man must act according to guiding principles and rational convictions, human action supposes the possibility of knowledge. Subordinating science to ethics, the Epicureans admit the necessity of knowledge for conduct. And since Epicurean ethics rests essentially on the experience of pleasure and pain, these sensations are ultimately the practical criterion of truth. The conflict of opinions, the impossibility of demonstrating everything, the relativity of perception, became again the main arguments of scepticism. Pyrrho claims that the nature of things is unknowable, and consequently we must abstain from judging; herein consist human virtue and happiness. The representatives of the Middle Academy also are sceptical, although in a less radical manner. Thus Arcesilaus, while denying the possibility of certitude and claiming that the duty of a wise man is to refuse his assent to any proposition, admits nevertheless that a degree of probability sufficient for the conduct of life is attainable. Carneades develops the same doctrine and emphasizes its sceptical aspect. Later sceptics, Ænesidemus, Agrippa, and Sextus Empiricus, make no essential addition.

The Fathers of the Church are occupied chiefly in defending Christian dogmas, and thus indirectly in showing the harmony of revealed truth with reason St. Augustine goes farther than any other in the analysis of knowledge and in the inquiry concerning its validity. He wrote a special treatise against the sceptics of the Academy who admitted no certain, but only probable, knowledge. What is probability, he asks in an argument ad hominem, but a likeness of or an approach to truth and certitude? And then how can one speak of probability who does not first admit certitude? On one point at least, the existence of the thinking subject, doubt is impossible. Should a man doubt everything or be in error, the very fact of doubting or being deceived implies existence. First logical principles also are certain. Although the senses are not untrustworthy, perfect knowledge is intellectual knowledge based on the data of the senses and rising beyond them to general causes. In medieval philosophy the main epistemological issue is the objective value of universal ideas. After Plato and Aristotle the Scholastics hold that there is no science of the individual as such. As science deals with general principles and laws to know how far science is legitimate it is necessary to know first the value of general notions and the relations of the universal to the individual. Does the universal exist in nature, or is it a purely mental product? Such was the question raised by Porphyry in his introduction to Aristotle's "Categories". Up to the end of the twelfth century the answers are limited to two, corresponding to the two, possibilities mentioned by Porphyry. Hence if one may speak of Realism at that period, it does not seem altogether correct to speak of Conceptualism or Nominalism in the well-defined sense which these terms have since acquired (see De Wulf, Hist. de la phil. médiévale, 2d ed., Louvain 1905). Later, a distinction is introduced which St. Thomas formulates clearly and which avoids both extremes. The universal as such does not exist in nature, but only in the mind. Yet it is not a mere product of mental activity; it has a basis in really existing things; that is, by their individual and by their common features, existing things offer to the mind a basis for the exercise of its functions of abstraction and generalization. This moderate Realism, as it is called in opposition to Conceptualism on the one side, and on the other, to exaggerated, or absolute Realism, is also essentially the doctrine of Duns Scotus; and it prevailed in the School till the period of decadence when Nominalism or Terminism was introduced by Occam and his followers.

In modern times Descartes may be mentioned for his methodical doubt and his solution of it in the Cogito, ergo sum, i.e. I think, therefore, I exist. But Locke, in his "Essay concerning Human Understanding", is the first to give a clear statement of epistemological problems. To begin with ontological discussions is to begin "at the wrong end" and to take "a wrong coursed." Hence "it came to my thoughts that . . . before we set ourselves upon inquiries of that nature, it was necessary to examine our own abilities, and to see what objects our understandings were, or were not fitted to deal with" (Epistle to the Reader). Locke's purpose is to discover "the certainty, evidence and extent" of human knowledge (I, i, 3), to find "the horizon which sets the bounds between the enlightened and dark parts of things, between what is, and what is not comprehensible by us (I, i, 7), and "to search out the bounds between opinion and knowledge" (I, i, 3). One who reflects on the contradictions among men, and the assurance with which every man maintains his own opinion "may perhaps have reason to suspect that either there is no such thing as truth at all, or that mankind hath no sufficient means to attain a certain knowledge of it" (I, i, 2). This investigation will prevent us from undertaking the study of things that are "beyond the reach of our capacities" (I, i, 4), and will be "a cure of skepticism and idleness" (I, i, 6). Such is the problem; among the main points in its solution may be mentioned the following: "we have the knowledge of our own existence by intuition; of the existence of God by demonstration; and of other things by sensation" (IV, ix, 2). The nature of the soul cannot be known, nor does the trustworthiness of the senses extend to "secondary qualities"; a fortiori, substance and essences are unknowable. These and other conclusions, however, are not reached by a truly epistemological method, i.e. by the criticism of the processes and postulates of knowledge, but almost exclusively by the psychological method of mental analysis. Following in Locke's footsteps and proceeding farther, Berkeley denied the objectivity even of primary qualities of matter, and Hume held a universal and radical phenomenalism. Aroused from his "dogmatic slumber" by the skepticism of Hume, Kant took up again the same problem of the extent, validity, and limits of human knowledge. This is the task of criticism, not the criticism of books and systems, but of reason itself in the whole range of its powers, and in regard to its ability to attain knowledge transcending experience. Briefly stated, the solution reached by Kant is that we know things-as-they-appear, or phenomena, but not the noumena, or things-in-themselves. These latter, precisely because they are outside the mind, are also outside the possibility of knowledge. Kant's successors, identifying the theory of being with the theory of knowing, elaborated his "Critique" into a system of metaphysics in which the very existence of things-in-themselves was denied. After Kant we reach the present period in the evolution of epistemological problems.

Problems

Today epistemology stands in the foreground of philosophical sciences. The preceding outline, however, shows that it was the last to be constituted as a distinct investigation and to receive a special systematic treatment. In older philosophers are found partial discussions, not yet coordinated and regarding only special aspects of the problem. The problem itself is not formulated before Locke, and no true epistemological solution attempted before Kant. In the beginning of philosophical investigation, as well as in the beginning of cognitive life in the individual, knowledge and certitude are accepted as self-evident facts needing no discussion. Full of confidence in its own powers, reason at once rises to the highest metaphysical considerations regarding the nature, essential elements, and origin of matter and of the human soul. But contradiction and conflict of opinions oblige the mind to turn back upon itself, to reflect in order to compare, test, and perhaps revise its conclusions; for contradictions cause doubt; and doubt leads to reflection on the value of knowledge. Throughout history, also, interest in epistemological questions is aroused chiefly after periods characterized by ontological investigations implying the assumption of the validity of knowledge. As the psychology of knowledge develops problems of epistemology grow more numerous, and their solutions more varied. Originally the choice is almost exclusively between affirming the value of knowledge and denying it. For one who looks upon knowledge as a simple fact, these are the only two possible alternatives. After psychology has shown the complexity of the knowing-process, pointed out its various elements, examined its genesis, and followed its development, knowledge is no longer deemed either valid or invalid in its totality. Certain forms of it may be rejected and others retained; or knowledge may be held as valid up to, but not beyond, a certain point. In fact, at present, one would look in vain for absolute and unlimited dogmatism as well as for pure and complete skepticism. Opinions vary between these two extremes; and hence comes, partly at least, the confusion of terms by which various views are designated--a labyrinth in which even the most experienced can hardly find their way. Here a few systems only will be mentioned, and their names used in their most general and obvious sense.

The main problems of epistemology may be conveniently reduced to the following.

1. Starting from the fact of spontaneous certitude, the first question is: Does reflection also justify certitude? Is certain knowledge within man's power? In a general way Dogmatism gives an affirmative, Scepticism a negative answer. Modern Agnosticism attempts to indicate the limits of human knowledge and concludes that the ultimate reality is unknowable.

2. This leads to a second problem: How does knowledge arise, and what modes of knowledge are valid? Empiricism admits no other trustworthy information than the data of experience, while Rationalism claims that reason as a special faculty is more important.

3. A third question presents itself: What is

knowledge? Cognition is a process within the mind with the special feature of referring to something without the mind, of representing some extramental reality. What is the value of this representative aspect? Is it merely the result of the mind's inner activity, as Idealism claims? Or is the mind also passive in the act of knowing, and does it in fact reflect some other reality, as Realism asserts? And if there exist such realities, can we know anything about them in addition to the fact of their existence? What is the relation between the idea in the mind and the thing outside the mind? Finally, even if knowledge is valid, the fact of error is undeniable; what then will be the criterion by which truth may be distinguished from error? What signs decide whether certitude in any ease is justified? Such systems as Intellectualism, Mysticism, Pragmatism, Traditionalism, etc., have attempted to answer these questions in various ways.

Like all other sciences, epistemology should start from self-evident facts, namely the facts of knowledge and certitude. To begin, as Descartes did, with a universal doubt is to do away with the facts instead of interpreting them; nor is it possible consistently to emerge out of such a doubt. Locke's principle that "knowledge is conversant only with our ideas" is contrary to experience, since in fact it is for the psychologist alone that ideas become objects of knowledge. First to isolate the mind absolutely from external reality, and then to ask how it can nevertheless come into contact with this reality, is to propose an insoluble problem. As to the Kantian attitude, it has been criticized repeatedly for examining the validity of knowledge with the knowing faculty, for making reason its own critic and judge while its lights to criticize and judge are still held in doubt. Epistemology, the science of knowing, is closely related to metaphysics, the science of being, as its necessary introduction, and as gradually leading into it. The main epistemological issue cannot be met without stepping almost immediately on metaphysical ground, since the faculty of knowledge cannot be examined apart from its exercise and therefore from the contents of knowledge. Logic in its strict sense is the science of the laws of thought; it is concerned with the form, not the matter of knowledge, and in this it differs from epistemology. Psychology deals with knowledge as a mental fact, apart from its truth or falsity; it endeavours to determine the conditions, not only of cognitive, but of all mental processes and to discover their relations and the laws of their sequence. Thus logic and epistemology complement the work of psychology in two different directions, and epistemology forms a transition from psychology and logic to metaphysics. The importance of epistemology can hardly be overestimated, since it deals with the ground-work of knowledge itself, and therefore of all scientific, philosophical, moral, and religious principles. At the present time especially it is an indispensable requisite for apologetics, for the very foundations of religion are precisely the doctrines most frequently looked upon as beyond the reach of human intelligence. In fact much recent discussion concerning the value of knowledge has taken place on the ground of apologetics, and for the distinct purpose of testing the value of religious beliefs. If, contrary to the definitions of the Council of the Vatican, the existence of God and some at least of His attributes cannot be demonstrated, it is evident that there is no possibility of revelation and supernatural faith. As Pius X expresses it (Encycl. "Pascendi", 8 Sept., 1907), to confine reason within the field of phenomena and give it no right and no power to go beyond these limits as to make it "incapable of lifting itself up to God and of recognizing His existence by means of visible things. . . . And then all will readily perceive what becomes of natural theology, of the motives of credibility and of external revelation".

XX.
Faith

The meaning of the word

(Pistis, fides). In the Old Testament, the Hebrew means essentially steadfastness, cf. Exodus 17:12, where it is used to describe the strengthening of Moses' hands; hence it comes to mean faithfulness, whether of God towards man (Deuteronomy 32:4) or of man towards God (Psalm 118:30). As signifying man's attitude towards God it means trustfulness or fiducia. It would, however, be illogical to conclude that the word cannot, and does not, mean belief or faith in the Old Testament for it is clear that we cannot put trust in a person's promises without previously assenting to or believing in that person's claim to such confidence. Hence even if it could be proved that the Hebrew does not in itself contain the notion of belief, it must necessarily presuppose it. But that the word does itself contain the notion of belief is clear from the use of the radical, which in the causative conjugation, or Hiph'il, means "to believe", e.g. Genesis 15:6, and Deuteronomy 1:32, in which latter passage the two meanings — viz. of believing and of trusting — are combined. That the noun itself often means faith or belief, is clear from Habakkuk 2:4, where the context demands it. The witness of the Septuagint is decisive; they render the verb by pisteuo, and the noun by pistis; and here again the two factors, faith and trust, are connoted by the same term. But that even in classical Greek pisteuo was used to signify believe, is clear from Euripides (Helene, 710), logois d'emoisi pisteuson tade, and that pistis could mean "belief" is shown by the same dramatist's theon d'ouketi pistis arage (Medea, 414; cf. Hipp., 1007). In the New Testament the meanings "to believe" and "belief", for pisteon and pistis, come to the fore; in Christ's speech, pistis frequently means "trust", but also "belief" (cf. Matthew 8:10). In Acts it is used objectively of the tenets of the Christians, but is often to be rendered "belief" (cf. 17:31; 20:21; 26:8). In Romans 14:23, it has the meaning of "conscience" — "all that is not of faith is sin" — but the Apostle repeatedly uses it in the sense of "belief" (cf. Romans 4 and Galatians 3). How necessary it is to point this out will be evident to all who are familiar with modern theological literature; thus, when a writer in the "Hibbert Journal", Oct., 1907, says, "From one end of the Scripture to the other, faith is trust and only trust", it is hard to see how he would explain 1 Corinthians 13:13, and Hebrews 11:1. The truth is that many theological writers of the present day are given to very loose thinking, and in nothing is this so evident as in their treatment of faith. In the article just referred to we read: "Trust in God is faith, faith is belief, belief may mean creed, but creed is not equivalent to trust in God." A similar vagueness was especially noticeable in the "Do we believe?" controversy—one correspondent says—"We unbelievers, if we have lost faith, cling more closely to hope and — the greatest of these — charity" ("Do we believe?", p. 180, ed. W. L. Courtney, 1905). Non-Catholic writers have repudiated all idea of faith as an intellectual assent, and consequently they fail to realize that faith must necessarily result in a body of dogmatic beliefs. "How and by what influence", asks Harnack, "was the living faith transformed into the creed to be believed, the surrender to Christ into a philosophical Christology?" (quoted in Hibbert Journal, loc. cit.).

Faith may be Considered both Objectively and Subjectively

Objectively, it stands for the sum of truths revealed by God in Scripture and tradition and which the Church (see RULE OF FAITH) presents to us in a brief form in her creeds, subjectively, faith stands for the habit or virtue by which we assent to those truths. It is with this subjective aspect of faith that we are here primarily concerned. Before we proceed to analyze the term faith, certain preliminary notions must be made clear.

(a) The twofold order of knowledge. — "The Catholic Church", says the Vatican Council, III, iv, "has always held that there is a twofold order of knowledge, and that these two orders are distinguished from one another not only in their principle but in their object; in one we know by natural reason, in the other by Divine faith; the object of the one is truth attainable by natural reason, the object of the other is mysteries hidden in God, but which we have to believe and which can only be known to us by Divine revelation."

(b) Now intellectual knowledge may be defined in a general way as the union between the intellect and an intelligible object. But a truth is intelligible to us only in so far as it is evident to us, and evidence is of different kinds; hence, according to the varying character of the evidence, we shall have varying kinds of knowledge. Thus a truth may be self-evident — e.g. the whole is greater than its part — in which case we are said to have intuitive knowledge of it; or the truth may not be self-evident, but deducible from premises in which it is contained — such knowledge is termed reasoned knowledge; or again a truth may be neither self-evident nor deducible from premises in which it is contained, yet the intellect may be obliged to assent to it because It would else have to reject some other universally accepted truth; lastly, the intellect may be induced to assent to a truth for none of the foregoing reasons, but solely because, though not evident in itself, this truth rests on grave authority — for example, we accept the statement that the sun is 90,000,000 miles distant from the earth because competent, veracious authorities vouch for the fact. This last kind of knowledge is termed faith, and is clearly necessary in daily life. If the authority upon which we base our assent is human and therefore fallible, we have human and fallible faith; if the authority is Divine, we have Divine and infallible faith. If to this be added the medium by which the Divine authority for certain statements is put before us, viz. the Catholic Church, we have Divine-Catholic Faith.

(c) Again, evidence, whatever its source, may be of various degrees and so cause greater or less firmness of adhesion on the part of the mind which assents to a truth. Thus arguments or authorities for and against a truth may be either wanting or evenly balanced, in this case the intellect does not give in its adherence to the truth, but remains in a state of doubt or absolute suspension of judgment; or the arguments on one side may predominate; though not to the exclusion of those on the other side; in this case we have not complete adhesion of the intellect to the truth in question but only opinion. Lastly, the arguments or authorities brought forward may be so convincing that the mind gives its unqualified assent to the statement proposed and has no fear whatever lest it should not be true; this state of mind is termed certitude, and is the perfection of knowledge. Divine faith, then, is that form of knowledge which is derived from Divine authority, and which consequently begets absolute certitude in the mind of the recipient.

(d) That such Divine faith is necessary, follows from the fact of Divine revelation. For revelation means that the Supreme Truth has spoken to man and revealed to him truths which are not in themselves evident to the human mind. We must, then, either reject revelation altogether, or accept it by faith; that is, we must submit our intellect to truths which we cannot understand, but which come to us on Divine authority.

(e) We shall arrive at a better understanding of the habit or virtue of faith if we have previously analysed an act of faith; and this analysis will be facilitated by examining an act of ocular vision and an act of reasoned knowledge. In ocular vision we distinguish three things: the eye, or visual faculty the coloured object, and the light which serves as the medium between the eye and the object. It is usual to term colour the formal object (objectum formale quod) of vision, since it is that which precisely and alone makes a thing the object of vision, the individual object seen may be termed the material object, e.g. this apple, that man, etc. Similarly, the light which serves as the medium between the eye and the object is termed the formal reason (objectum formale quo) of our actual vision. In the same way, when we analyze an act of intellectual assent to any given truth, we must distinguish the intellectual faculty which elicits the act the intelligible object towards which the intellect is directed, and the evidence whether intrinsic to that object or extrinsic to it, which moves us to assent to it. None of these factors can be omitted, each cooperates in bringing about the act, whether of ocular vision or of intellectual assent.

(f) Hence, for an act of faith we shall need a faculty capable of eliciting the act, an object commensurate with that faculty, and evidence — not intrinsic but extrinsic to that object — which shall serve as the link between faculty and object. We will commence our analysis with the object:-

Analysis of the Object or Term in an Act of Divine Faith

(a) For a truth to be the object of an act of Divine faith, it must be itself Divine, and this not merely as coming from God, but as being itself concerned with God. Just as in ocular vision the formal object must necessarily be something coloured, so in Divine faith the formal object must be something Divine — in theological language, the objectum formale quod of Divine faith is the First Truth in Being, Prima Veritas in essendo — we could not make an act of Divine faith in the existence of India.

(b) Again, the evidence upon which we assent to this Divine truth must also be itself Divine, and there must be as close a relation between that truth and the evidence upon which it comes to us as there is between the coloured object and the light; the former is a necessary condition for the exercise of our visual faculty, the latter is the cause of our actual vision. But no one but God can reveal God; in other words, God is His own evidence. Hence, just as the formal object of Divine faith is the First Truth Itself, so the evidence of that First Truth is the First Truth declaring Itself. To use scholastic language once more, the objectum formale quod, or the motive, or the evidence, of Divine faith is the Prima Veritas in dicendo.

(c) There is a controversy whether the same truth can be an object both of faith and of knowledge. In other words, can we believe a thing both because we are told it on good authority and because we ourselves perceive it to be true? St. Thomas, Scotus, and others hold that once a thing is seen to be true, the adhesion of the mind is in no wise strengthened by the authority of one who states that it is so, but the majority of theologians maintain, with De Lugo, that there may be a knowledge which does not entirely satisfy the mind, and that authority may then find a place, to complete its satisfaction. — We may note here the absurd expression Credo quia impossibile, which has provoked many sneers. It is not an axiom of the Scholastics, as was stated in the "Revue de Metaphysique et de Morale" (March, 1896, p. 169), and as was suggested more than once in the "Do we believe?" correspondence. The expression is due to Tertullian, whose exact words are: "Natus est Dei Filius; non pudet, quia pudendum est: et mortuus est Dei Filius; prorsus credibile est, quia ineptum est; et sepultus, resurrexit; certum est, quia impossibile" (De Carne Christi, cap. v). This treatise dates from Tertullian's Montanist days, when he was carried away by his love of paradox. At the same time it is clear that the writer only aims at bringing out the wisdom of God manifested in the humiliation of the Cross; he is perhaps paraphrasing St. Paul's words in 1 Corinthians 1:25.

(d) Let us now take some concrete act of faith, e.g. "I believe in the Most Holy Trinity." This mystery is the material or individual object upon which we are now exercising our faith, the formal object is its character as being a Divine truth, and this truth is clearly inevident as far as we are concerned; it in no way appeals to our intellect, on the contrary it rather repels it. And yet we assent to it by faith, consequently upon evidence which is extrinsic and not intrinsic to the truth we are accepting. But there can be no evidence commensurate with such a mystery save the Divine testimony itself, and this constitutes the motive for our assent to the mystery, and is, in scholastic language, the *objectum formale quo* of our assent. If then, we are asked why we believe with Divine faith any Divine truth, the only adequate answer must be because God has revealed it.

(e) We may point out in this connexion the falsity of the prevalent notion that faith is blind. "We believe", says the Vatican Council (III, iii), "that revelation is true, not indeed because the intrinsic truth of the mysteries is clearly seen by the natural light of reason, but because of the authority of God Who reveals them, for He can neither deceive nor be deceived." Thus, to return to the act of faith which we make in the Holy Trinity, we may formulate it in syllogistic fashion thus: Whatever God reveals is true but God has revealed the mystery of the Holy Trinity therefore this mystery is true. The major premise is indubitable and intrinsically evident to reason; the minor premise is also true because it is declared to us by the infallible Church (cf. RULE OF FAITH), and also because, as the Vatican Council says, "in addition to the internal assistance of His Holy Spirit, it has pleased God to give us certain external proofs of His revelation, viz. certain Divine facts, especially miracles and prophecies, for since these latter clearly manifest God's omnipotence and infinite knowledge, they afford most certain proofs of His revelation and are suited to the capacity of all." Hence St. Thomas says: "A man would not believe unless he saw the things he had to believe, either by the evidence of miracles or of something similar" (II-II:1:4, ad 1). The saint is here speaking of the motives of credibility.

Motives of Credibility

(a) When we say that a certain statement is incredible we often mean merely that it is extraordinary, but it should be borne in mind that this is a misuse of language, for the credibility or incredibility of a statement has nothing to do with its intrinsic probability or improbability; it depends solely upon the credentials of the authority who makes the statement. Thus the credibility of the statement that a secret alliance has been entered into between England and America depends solely upon the authoritative position and the veracity of our informant. If he be a clerk in a government office it is possible that he may have picked up some genuine information, but if our informant be the Prime Minister of England, his statement has the highest degree of credibility because his credentials are of the highest. When we speak of the motives of credibility of revealed truth we mean the evidence that the things asserted are revealed truths. In other words, the credibility of the statements made is correlative with and proportionate to the credentials of the authority who makes them. Now the credentials of God are indubitable, for the very idea of God involves that of omniscience and of the Supreme Truth. Hence, what God says is supremely credible, though not necessarily supremely intelligible for us. Here, however, the real question is not as to the credentials of God or the credibility of what He says, but as to the credibility of the statement that God has spoken. In other words who or what is the authority for this statement, and what credentials does this authority show? What are the motives of credibility of the statement that God has revealed this or that?

(b) These motives of credibility may be briefly stated as follows: in the Old Testament considered not as an inspired book, but merely as a book having historical value, we find detailed the marvellous dealings of God with a particular nation to whom He repeatedly reveals Himself; we read of miracles wrought in their favour and as proofs of the truth of the revelation He makes; we find the most sublime teaching and the repeated announcement of God's desire to save the world from sin and its consequences. And more than all we find throughout the pages of this book a series of hints, now obscure, now clear, of some wondrous person who is to come as the world's saviour; we find it asserted at one time that he is man, at others that he is God Himself. When we turn to the New Testament we find that it records the birth, life, and death of One Who, while clearly man, also claimed to be God, and Who proved the truth of His claim by His whole life, miracles, teachings, and death, and finally by His triumphant resurrection. We find, moreover, that He founded a Church which should, so He said, continue to the end of time, which should serve as the repository of His teaching, and should be the means of applying to all men the fruits of the redemption He had wrought. When we come to the subsequent history of this

Church we find it speedily spreading everywhere, and this in spite of its humble origin, its unworldly teaching, and the cruel persecution which it meets at the hands of the rulers of this world. And as the centuries pass we find this Church battling against heresies schisms, and the sins of her own people—nay, of her own rulers—and yet continuing ever the same, promulgating ever the same doctrine, and putting before men the same mysteries of the life, death and resurrection of the world's Saviour, Who had, so she taught, gone before to prepare a home for those who while on earth should have believed in Him and fought the good fight. But if the history of the Church since New-Testament times thus wonderfully confirms the New Testament itself, and if the New Testament so marvellously completes the Old Testament, these books must really contain what they claim to contain, viz. Divine revelation. And more than all, that Person Whose life and death were so minutely foretold in the Old Testament, and Whose story, as told in the New Testament, so perfectly corresponds with its prophetic delineation in the Old Testament, must be what He claimed to be, viz. the Son of God. His work, therefore, must be Divine. The Church which He founded must also be Divine and the repository and guardian of His teaching. Indeed, we can truly say that for every truth of Christianity which we believe Christ Himself is our testimony, and we believe in Him because the Divinity He claimed rests upon the concurrent testimony of His miracles, His prophecies His personal character, the nature of His doctrine, the marvellous propagation of His teaching in spite of its running counter to flesh and blood, the united testimony of thousands of martyrs, the stories of countless saints who for His sake have led heroic lives, the history of the Church herself since the Crucifixion, and, perhaps more remarkable than any, the history of the papacy from St. Peter to Pius X.

(c) These testimonies are unanimous; they all point in one direction, they are of every age, they are clear and simple, and are within the grasp of the humblest intelligence. And, as the Vatican Council has said, "the Church herself, is, by her marvellous propagation, her wondrous sanctity, her inexhaustible fruitfulness in good works, her Catholic unity, and her enduring stability, a great and perpetual motive of credibility and an irrefragable witness to her Divine commission" (Const. Dei Filius) . "The Apostles", says St. Augustine, "saw the Head and believed in the Body; we see the Body let us believe in the Head" [Sermo ccxliii, 8 (al. cxliii), de temp., P.L., V 1143]. Every believer will echo the words of Richard of St. Victor, "Lord, if we are in error, by Thine own self we have been deceived—for these things have been confirmed by such signs and wonders in our midst as could only have been done by Thee!" (de Trinitate, 1, cap. ii).

(d) But much misunderstanding exists regarding the meaning and office of the motives of credibility. In the first place, they afford us definite and certain knowledge of Divine revelation; but this knowledge precedes faith; it is not the final motive for our assent to the truths of faith—as

St. Thomas says, "Faith has the character of a virtue, not because of the things it believes, for faith is of things that appear not, but because it adheres to the testimony of one in whom truth is infallibly found" (De Veritate, xiv, 8); this knowledge of revealed truth which precedes faith can only beget human faith it is not even the cause of Divine faith (cf. Francisco Suárez, be Fide disp. iii, 12), but is rather to be considered a remote disposition to it. We must insist upon this because in the minds of many faith is regarded as a more or less necessary consequence of a careful study of the motives of credibility, a view which the Vatican Council condemns expressly: "If anyone says that the assent of Christian faith is not free, but that it necessarily follows from the arguments which human reason can furnish in its favour; or if anyone says that God's grace is only necessary for that living faith which worketh through charity, let him be anathema" (Sess. IV). Nor can the motives of credibility make the mysteries of faith clear in themselves, for, as St. Thomas says, "the arguments which induce us to believe, e.g. miracles, do not prove the faith itself, but only the truthfulness of him who declares it to us, and consequently they do not beget knowledge of faith's mysteries, but only faith" (in Sent., III, xxiv, Q. i, art. 2, sol. 2, ad 4). On the other hand, we must not minimize the real probative force of the motives of credibility within their true sphere—"Reason declares that from the very outset the Gospel teaching was rendered conspicuous by signs and wonders which gave, as it were, definite proof of a definite truth" (Leo XIII, Æterni Patris).

(e) The Church has twice condemned the view that faith ultimately rests on an accumulation of probabilities. Thus the proposition, "The assent of supernatural faith . . is consistent with merely probable knowledge of revelation" was condemned by Innocent XI in 1679 (cf. Denzinger, Enchiridion, 10th ed., no. 1171); and the Syllabus Lamentabili sane (July, 1907) condemns the proposition (XXV) that "the assent of faith rests ultimately on an accumulation of probabilities." But since the great name of Newman has been dragged into the controversy regarding this last proposition, we may point out that, in the Grammar of Assent (chap. x, sect. 2), Newman refers solely to the proof of faith afforded by the motives of credibility, and he rightly concludes that, since these are not demonstrative, this line of proof may be termed "an accumulation of probabilities". But it would be absurd to say that Newman therefore based the final assent of faith on this accumulation—as a matter of fact he is not here making an analysis of an act of faith, but only of the grounds for faith; the question of authority does not come into his argument (cf. McNabb, Oxford Conferences on Faith, pp. 121-122).

Analysis of the Act of Faith from the Subjective Standpoint

(a) The light of faith. — An angel understands truths which are beyond man's comprehension; if then a man were called upon to assent to a truth beyond the ken of the human intellect, but within the grasp of the angelic intellect, he would require for the time being something more than his natural light of reason, he would require what we may call "the angelic light". If, now, the same man were called upon to assent to a truth beyond the grasp of both men and angels, he would clearly need a still higher light, and this light we term "the light of faith" — a light, because it enables him to assent to those supernatural truths, and the light of faith because it does not so illumine those truths as to make them no longer obscure, for faith must ever be "the substance of things to be hoped for, the evidence of things that appear not" (Hebrews 11:1). Hence St. Thomas (De Veritate, xiv, 9, ad 2) says: "Although the Divinely infused light of faith is more powerful than the natural light of reason, nevertheless in our present state we only imperfectly participate in it; and hence it comes to pass that it does not beget in us real vision of those things which it is meant to teach us; such vision belongs to our eternal home, where we shall perfectly participate in that light, where, in fine, in God's light we shall see light' (Ps. xxxv, 10)."

(b) The necessity of such light is evident from what has been said, for faith is essentially an act of assent, and just as assent to a series of deductive or inductive reasonings, or to intuition of first principles, would be impossible without the light of reason, so, too assent to a supernatural truth would be inconceivable without a supernatural strengthening of the natural light "Quid est enim fides nisi credere quod non vides?" (i.e. what is faith but belief in that which thou seest not?) asks St. Augustine;

but he also says: "Faith has its eyes by which it in some sort sees that to be true which it does not yet see—and by which, too, it most surely sees that it does not see what it believes" [Ep. ad Consent., ep. cxx 8 (al. ccxxii), P.L., II, 456].

(c) Again, it is evident that this "light of faith" is a supernatural gift and is not the necessary outcome of assent to the motives of credibility. No amount of study will win it, no intellectual conviction as to the credibility of revealed religion nor even of the claims of the Church to be our infallible guide in matters of faith, will produce this light in a man's mind. It is the free gift of God. Hence the Vatican Council (III, iii;) teaches that "faith is a supernatural virtue by which we with the inspiration and assistance of God's grace, believe those things to be true which He has revealed". The same decree goes on to say that "although the assent of faith is in no sense blind, yet no one can assent to the Gospel teaching in the way necessary for salvation without the illumination of the Holy Spirit, Who bestows on all a sweetness in believing and consenting to the truth". Thus, neither as regards the truth believed nor as regards the motives for believing, nor as regards the subjective principle by which we believe — viz. the infused light — can faith be considered blind.

(d) The place of the will in an act of faith. — So far we have seen that faith is an act of the intellect assenting to a truth which is beyond its grasp, e.g. the mystery of the Holy Trinity. But to many it will seem almost as futile to ask the intellect to assent to a proposition which is not intrinsically evident as it would be to ask the eye to see a sound. It is clear, however, that the intellect can be moved by the will either to study or not to study a certain truth, though if the truth be a self-evident one — e.g., that the whole is greater than its part — the will cannot affect the intellect's adhesion to it, it can, however, move it to think of something else, and thus distract it from the contemplation of that particular truth. If, now, the will moves the intellect to consider some debatable point—e.g. the Copernican and Ptolemaic theories of the relationship between the sun and the earth — it is clear that the intellect can only assent to one of these views in proportion as it is convinced that the particular view is true. But neither view has, as far as we can know, more than probable truth, hence of itself the intellect can only give in its partial adherence to one of these views, it must always be precluded from absolute assent by the possibility that the other view may be right. The fact that men hold much more tenaciously to one of these than the arguments warrant can only be due to some extrinsic consideration, e.g. that it is absurd not to hold what the vast majority of men hold. And here it should be noted that, as St. Thomas says repeatedly, the intellect only assents to a statement for one of two reasons: either because that statement is immediately or mediately evident in itself — e.g. a first principle or a conclusion from premises — or because the will moves it to do so. Extrinsic evidence of course comes into play when intrinsic evidence is wanting, but though it would be absurd, without weighty evidence in its support, to assent to a truth which we do not grasp, yet no amount of such evidence can make us assent, it could only show that the statement in question was credible, our ultimate actual assent could only be due to the intrinsic evidence which the statement itself offered, or, failing that, due to the will. Hence it is that St. Thomas repeatedly defines the act of faith as the assent of the intellect determined by the will (De Veritate, xiv, 1; II-II, Q. ii, a. 1, ad 3; 2, c.; ibid., iv, 1, c., and ad 2). The reason, then, why men cling to certain beliefs more tenaciously than the arguments in their favour would warrant, is to be sought in the will rather than in the intellect. Authorities are to be found on both sides, the intrinsic evidence is not convincing, but something is to be gained by assenting to one view rather than the other, and this appeals to the will, which therefore determines the intellect to assent to the view which promises the most. Similarly, in Divine faith the credentials of the authority which tells us that God has made certain revelations are strong, but they are always extrinsic to the proposition, "God has revealed this or that", and consequently they cannot compel our assent; they merely show us that this statement is credible. When, then, we ask whether we are to give in our free assent to any particular statement or not, we feel that in the first place we cannot do so unless there be strong extrinsic evidence in its favour, for to believe a thing merely because we wished to do so would be absurd. Secondly, the proposition itself does not compel our assent, since it is not intrinsically evident, but there remains the fact that only on condition of our assent to it shall we have what the human soul naturally yearns for, viz., the possession of God, Who is, as both reason and authority declare, our ultimate end; "He that believeth and is baptized, shall be saved", and "Without faith it is impossible to please God." St. Thomas expresses this by saying: "The disposition of a believer is that of one who accepts another's word for some statement, because it seems fitting or useful to do so. In the same way we believe Divine revelation because the reward of eternal life is promised us for so doing. It is the will which is moved by the prospect of this reward to assent to what is said, even though the intellect is not moved by something which it understands. Hence St. Augustine says (Tract. xxvi in Joannem, 2): Cetera potest homo nolens, credere nonnisi volens' [i.e. other things a man can do against his will but to believe he must will]" (De Ver., xiv, 1).

(e) But just as the intellect needed a new and special light in order to assent to the supernatural truths of faith, so also the will needs a special grace from God in order that it may tend to that supernatural good which is eternal life. The light of faith, then, illumines the understanding, though the truth still remains obscure, since it is beyond the intellect's grasp; but supernatural grace moves the will, which, having now a supernatural good put before it, moves the intellect to assent to what it does not understand. Hence it is that faith is described as "bringing into captivity every understanding unto the obedience of Christ" (2 Corinthians 10:5).

Definition of Faith

The foregoing analyses will enable us to define an act of Divine supernatural faith as "the act of the intellect assenting to a Divine truth owing to the movement of the will, which is itself moved by the grace of God" (St. Thomas, II-II, Q. iv, a. 2). And just as the light of faith is a gift supernaturally bestowed upon the understanding, so also this Divine grace moving the will is, as its name implies, an equally supernatural and an absolutely gratuitous gift. Neither gift is due to previous study neither of them can be acquired by human efforts, but "Ask and ye shall receive."

From all that has been said two most important corollaries follow:

* That temptations against faith are natural and inevitable and are in no sense contrary to faith, "since", says St. Thomas, "the assent of the intellect in faith is due to the will, and since the object to which the intellect thus assents is not its own proper object — for that is actual vision of an intelligible object — it follows that the intellect's attitude towards that object is not one of tranquillity, on the contrary it thinks and inquires about those things it believes, all the while that it assents to them unhesitatingly; for as far as it itself is concerned the intellect is not satisfied" (De Ver., xiv, 1).

* (b) It also follows from the above that an act of supernatural faith is meritorious, since it proceeds from the will moved by Divine grace or charity, and thus has all the essential constituents of a meritorious act (cf. II-II, Q. ii, a. 9). This enables us to understand St. James's words when he says, "The devils also believe and tremble" (ii, 19) . "It is not willingly that they assent", says St. Thomas, "but they are compelled thereto by the evidence of those signs which prove that what believers assent to is true, though even those proofs do not make the truths of faith so evident as to afford what is termed vision of them" (De Ver., xiv 9, ad 4); nor is their faith Divine, but merely philosophical and natural. Some may fancy the foregoing analyses superfluous, and may think that they savour too much of Scholasticism. But if anyone will be at the pains to compare the teaching of the Fathers, of the Scholastics, and of the divines of the Anglican Church in the seventeenth and eighteenth centuries, with that of the non-Catholic theologians of today, he will find that the Scholastics merely put into shape what the Fathers taught, and that the great English divines owe their solidity and genuine worth to their vast patristic knowledge and their strictly logical training.

Let anyone who doubts this statement compare Bishop Butler's Analogy of Religion, chaps. v, vi, with the paper on "Faith" contributed to Lux Mundi. The writer of this latter paper tells us that "faith is an elemental energy of the soul", "a tentative probation", that "its primary note will be trust", and finally that "in response to the demand for definition, it can only reiterate: "Faith is faith. Believing is just believing"'. Nowhere is there any analysis of terms, nowhere any distinction between the relative parts played by the intellect and the will; and we feel that those who read the paper must have risen from its perusal with the feeling that they had been wandering through — we use the writer's own expression — "a juggling maze of words."

The Habit of Faith and the Life of Faith

(a) We have defined the act of faith as the assent of the intellect to a truth which is beyond its comprehension, but which it accepts under the influence of the will moved by grace and from the analysis we are now in a position to define the virtue of faith as a supernatural habit by which we firmly believe those things to be true which God has revealed. Now every virtue is the perfection of some faculty, but faith results from the combined action of two faculties, viz., the intellect which elicits the act, and the will which moves the intellect to do so; consequently, the perfection of faith will depend upon the perfection with which each of these faculties performs its allotted task; the intellect must assent unhesitatingly, the will must promptly and readily move it to do so.

(b) The unhesitating assent of the intellect cannot be due to intellectual conviction of the reasonableness of faith, whether we regard the grounds on which it rests or the actual truths we believe, for "faith is the evidence of things that appear not"; it must, then, be referred to the fact that these truths come to us on Divine infallible testimony. And though faith is so essentially of "the unseen" it may be that the peculiar function of the light of faith, which we have seen to be so necessary, is in some sort to afford us, not indeed vision, but an instinctive appreciation of the truths which are declared to be revealed. St. Thomas seems to hint at this when he says: "As by other virtuous habits a man sees what accords with those habits, so by the habit of faith a man's mind is inclined to assent to those things which belong to the true faith and not to other things" (II-II:4:4, ad 3). In every act of faith this unhesitating assent of the intellect is due to the motion of the will as its efficient cause, and the same must be said of the theological virtue of faith when we consider it as a habit or as a moral virtue, for, as St. Thomas insists (I-II, Q. lvi,), there is no virtue, properly so called, in the intellect except in so far as it is subject to the will. Thus the habitual promptitude of the will in moving the intellect to assent to the truths of faith is not only the efficient cause of the intellect's assent, but is precisely what gives to this assent its virtuous, and consequently meritorious, character. Lastly, this promptitude of the will can only come from its unswerving tendency to the Supreme Good. And at the risk of repetition we must again draw attention to the distinction between faith as a purely intellectual habit, which as such is dry and barren, and faith resident, indeed, in the intellect, but motived by charity or love of God, Who is our beginning, our ultimate end, and our supernatural reward. "Every true motion of the will", says St. Augustine, "proceeds from true love" (de Civ. Dei, XIV, ix), and, as he elsewhere beautifully expresses it, "Quid est ergo credere in Eum? Credendo amare, credendo diligere, credendo in Eum ire, et Ejus membris incorporari. Ipsa est ergo fides quam de nobis Deus exigit—et non invenit quod exigat, nisi donaverit quod invenerit." (Tract. xxix in Joannem, 6. — "What, then, is to believe in God? — It is to love Him by believing, to go to Him by believing, and to be incorporated in His members. This, then, is the faith which God demands of us; and He finds not what He may demand except where He has given what He may find.") This then is what is meant by "living" faith, or as theologians term it, fides formata, viz., "informed" by charity, or love of God. If we regard faith precisely as an assent elicited by the intellect, then this bare faith is the same habit numerically as when the informing principle of charity is added to it, but it has not the true character of a moral virtue and is not a source of merit. If, then, charity be dead — if, in other words, a man be in mortal sin and so without the habitual sanctifying grace of God which alone gives to his will that due tendency to God as his supernatural end which is requisite for supernatural and meritorious acts — it is evident that there is no longer in the will that power by which it can, from supernatural motives, move the intellect to assent to supernatural truths. The intellectual and Divinely infused habit of faith remains, however, and when charity returns this habit acquires anew the character of "living" and meritorious faith.

(c) Again, faith being a virtue, it follows that a man's promptitude in believing will make him love the truths he believes, and he will therefore study them, not indeed in the spirit of doubting inquiry, but in order the better to grasp them as far as human reason will allow. Such inquiry will be meritorious and will render his faith more robust, because, at the same time that he is brought face to face with the intellectual difficulties which are involved, he will necessarily exercise his faith and repeatedly "bring his intellect into submission". Thus St. Augustine says, "What can be the reward of faith, what can its very name mean if you wish to see now what you believe? You ought not to see in order to believe, you ought to believe in order to see; you ought to believe so long as you do not see, lest when you do see you may be put to the blush" (Sermo, xxxviii, 2, P.L., V, 236). And it is in this sense we must understand his oft-repeated words: "Crede ut intelligas" (Believe that you may understand). Thus, commenting on the Septuagint version of Isaiah 7:9 which reads: "nisi credideritis non intelligetis", he says: "Proficit ergo noster intellectus ad intelligenda quae credat, et fides proficit ad credenda quae intelligat; et eadem ipsa ut magis magisque intelligantur, in ipso intellectu proficit mens. Sed hoc non fit propriis tanquam naturalibus viribus sed Deo donante atque adjuvante" (Enarration on Psalm 118, Sermo xviii, 3, "Our intellect therefore is of use to understand whatever things it believes, and faith is of use to believe whatever it understands; and in order that these same things may be more and more understood, the thinking faculty [mens] is of use in the intellect. But this is not brought about as by our own natural powers but by the gift and the aid of God." Cf. Sermo xliii, 3, in Is., vii, 9; P.L., V, 255).

(d) Further, the habit of faith may be stronger in one person than in another, "whether because of the greater certitude and firmness in the faith which one has more than another, or because of his greater promptitude in assenting, or because of his greater devotion to the truths of faith, or because of his greater confidence" (II-II:5:4).

(e) We are sometimes asked whether we are really certain of the things we believe, and we rightly answer in the affirmative; but strictly speaking, certitude can be looked at from two standpoints: if we look at its cause, we have in faith the highest form of certitude, for its cause is the Essential Truth; but if we look at the certitude which arises from the extent to which the intellect grasps a truth, then in faith we have not such perfect certitude as we have of demonstrable truths, since the truths believed are beyond the intellect's comprehension (II-II, Q. iv, 8; de Ver., xiv, and i, ad 7).

The Genesis of Faith in the Individual Soul

(a) Many receive their faith in their infancy, to others it comes later in life, and its genesis is often misunderstood. Without encroaching upon the article

REVELATION, we may describe the genesis of faith in the adult mind somewhat as follows: Man being endowed with reason, reasonable investigation must precede faith; now we can prove by reason the existence of God, the immortality of the soul, and the origin and destiny of man; but from these facts there follows the necessity of religion, and true religion must be the true worship of the true God not according to our ideas, but according to what He Himself has revealed. But can God reveal Himself to us? And, granting that He can, where is this revelation to be found? The Bible is said to contain it; does investigation confirm the Bible's claim? We will take but one point: the Old Testament looks forward, as we have already seen, to One Who is to come and Who is God; the New Testament shows us One Who claimed to be the fulfilment of the prophecies and to be God; this claim He confirmed by His life, death, and resurrection by His teaching, miracles, and prophecies. He further claimed to have founded a Church which should enshrine His revelation and should be the infallible guide for all who wished to carry out His will and save their souls. Which of the numerous existing Churches is His? It must have certain definite characteristics or notes. It must be One Holy, Catholic, and Apostolic, it must claim infallible teaching power. None but the Holy, Roman, Catholic, and Apostolic Church can claim these characteristics, and her history is an irrefragable proof of her Divine mission. If, then, she be the true Church, her teaching must be infallible and must be accepted.

(b) Now what is the state of the inquirer who has come thus far? He has proceeded by pure reason, and, if on the grounds stated he makes his submission to the authority of the Catholic Church and believes her doctrines, he has only human, reasonable, fallible, faith. Later on he may see reason to question the various steps in his line of argument, he may hesitate at some truth taught by the Church, and he may withdraw the assent he has given to her teaching authority. In other words, he has not Divine faith at all. For Divine faith is supernatural both in the principle which elicits the acts and in the objects or truths upon which it falls. The principle which elicits assent to a truth which is beyond the grasp of the human mind must be that same mind illumined by a light superior to the light of reason, viz. the light of faith, and since, even with this light of faith, the intellect remains human, and the truth to be believed remains still obscure, the final assent of the intellect must come from the will assisted by Divine grace, as seen above. But both this Divine light and this Divine grace are pure gifts of God, and are consequently only bestowed at His good pleasure. It is here that the heroism of faith comes in; our reason will lead us to the door of faith but there it leaves us; and God asks of us that earnest wish to believe for the sake of the reward — "I am thy reward exceeding great" — which will allow us to repress the misgivings of the intellect and say, "I believe, Lord, help Thou my unbelief." As St. Augustine expresses it, "Ubi defecit ratio, ibi est fidei aedificatio" (Sermo ccxlvii, P.L., V, 1157 —

"Where reason fails there faith builds up").

(c) When this act of submission has been made, the light of faith floods the soul and is even reflected back upon those very motives which had to be so laboriously studied in our search after the truth; and even those preliminary truths which precede all investigation e.g. the very existence of God, become now the object of our faith.

Faith in Relation to Works

(a) Faith and no works may be described as the Lutheran view. "Esto peccator, pecca fortiter sed fortius fide" was the heresiarch's axiom, and the Diet of Worms, in 1527, condemned the doctrine that good works are not necessary for salvation.

(b) Works and no faith may be described as the modern view, for the modern world strives to make the worship of humanity take the place of the worship of the Deity (Do we believe? as issued by the Rationalist Press, 1904, ch. x: "Creed and Conduct" and ch. xv: "Rationalism and Morality". Cf. also Christianity and Rationalism on Trial, published by the same press, 1904).

(c) Faith shown by works has ever been the doctrine of the Catholic Church and is explicitly taught by St. James, ii, 17: "Faith, if it have not works, is dead." The Council of Trent (Sess. VI, canons xix, xx, xxiv, and xxvi) condemned the various aspects of the Lutheran doctrine, and from what has been said above on the necessity of charity for "living" faith, it will be evident that faith does not exclude, but demands, good works, for charity or love of God is not real unless it induces us to keep the Commandments; "He that keepeth his word, in him in very deed the charity of God is perfected" (1 John 2:5). St. Augustine sums up the whole question by saying "Laudo fructum boni operis, sed in fide agnosco radicem" — i.e. "I praise the fruit of good works, but their root I discern in faith" (Enarration on Psalm 31).

Loss of Faith

From what has been said touching the absolutely supernatural character of the gift of faith, it is easy to understand what is meant by the loss of faith. God's gift is simply withdrawn. And this withdrawal must needs be punitive, "Non enim deseret opus suum, si ab opere suo non deseratur" (St. Augustine, Enarration on Psalm 145 — "He will not desert His own work, if He be not deserted by His own work"). And when the light of faith is withdrawn, there inevitably follows a darkening of the mind regarding even the very motives of credibility which before seemed so convincing. This may perhaps explain why those who have had the misfortune to apostatize from the faith are often the most virulent in their attacks upon the grounds of faith; "Vae homini illi", says St. Augustine, "nisi et ipsius fidem Dominus protegat", i.e. "Woe be to a man unless the Lord safeguard his faith" (Enarration on Psalm 120).

Faith is reasonable

(a) If we are to believe present-day Rationalists and

Agnostics, faith, as we define it, is unreasonable. An Agnostic declines to accept it because he considers that the things proposed for his acceptance are preposterous, and because he regards the motives assigned for our belief as wholly inadequate. "Present me with a reasonable faith based on reliable evidence, and I will joyfully embrace it. Until that time I have no choice but to remain an Agnostic" (Medicus in the Do we Believe? Controversy, p. 214). Similarly, Francis Newman says: "Paul was satisfied with a kind of evidence for the resurrection of Jesus which fell exceedingly short of the demands of modern logic, it is absurd in us to believe, barely because they believed" (Phases of Faith, p. 186). Yet the supernatural truths of faith, however they may transcend our reason, cannot be opposed to it, for truth cannot be opposed to truth, and the same Deity Who bestowed on us the light of reason by which we assent to first principles is Himself the cause of those principles, which are but a reflection of His own Divine truth. When He chooses to manifest to us further truths concerning Himself, the fact that these latter are beyond the grasp of the natural light which He has bestowed upon us will not prove them to be contrary to our reason. Even so pronounced a rationalist as Sir Oliver Lodge says: "I maintain that it is hopelessly unscientific to imagine it possible that man is the highest intelligent existence" (Hibbert Journal, July, 1906, p. 727).

Agnostics, again, take refuge in the unknowableness of truths beyond reason, but their argument is fallacious, for surely knowledge has its degrees. I may not fully comprehend a truth in all its bearings, but I can know a great deal about it; I may not have demonstrative knowledge of it, but that is no reason why I should reject that knowledge which comes from faith. To listen to many Agnostics one would imagine that appeal to authority as a criterion was unscientific, though perhaps nowhere is authority appealed to so unscientifically as by modern scientists and modern critics. But, as St. Augustine says, "If God's providence govern human affairs we must not despair or doubt but that He hath ordained some certain authority, upon which staying ourselves as upon a certain ground or step, we may be lifted up to God" (De utilitate credendi); and it is in the same spirit that he says: "Ego vero Evangelio non crederem, nisi me Catholicae Ecclesiae commoveret auctoritas" (Contra Ep. Fund., V, 6 — "I would not believe the Gospel if the authority of the Catholic Church did not oblige me to believe").

(b) Naturalism, which is only another name for Materialism, rejects faith because there is no place for it in the naturalistic scheme; yet the condemnation of this false philosophy by St. Paul and by the author of the Book of Wisdom is emphatic (cf. Romans 1:18-23; Wisdom 13:1-19). Materialists fail to see in nature what the greatest minds have always discovered in it, viz., "ratio cujusdam artis; scilicet divinae, indita rebus, qua ipsae res moventur ad finem determinatum" — "the manifestation of a Divine plan whereby all things are directed towards their appointed end" (St. Thomas, Lect. xiv, in II Phys.). Similarly, the vagaries of Humanism blind men to the fact of man's essentially finite character and hence preclude all idea of faith in the infinite and the supernatural (cf. "Naturalism and Humanism" in Hibbert Journal, Oct., 1907).

Faith is Necessary

"He that believeth and is baptized", said Christ, "shall be saved, but he that believeth not shall be condemned" (Mark 16:16); and St. Paul sums up this solemn declaration by saying: "Without faith it is impossible to please God" (Hebrews 11:6). The absolute necessity of faith is evident from the following considerations: God is our beginning and our end and has supreme dominion over us, we owe Him, consequently, due service which we express by the term religion. Now true religion is the true Now true religion is the true worship of the true God. But it is not for man to fashion a worship according to his own ideals; none but God can declare to us in what true worship consists, and this declaration constitutes the body of revealed truths, whether natural or supernatural. To these, if we would attain the end for which we came into the world, we are bound to give the assent of faith. It is clear, moreover, that no one can profess indifference in a matter of such vital importance. During the Reformation period no such indifference was professed by those who quitted the fold; for them it was not a question of faith or unfaith, so much as of the medium by which the true faith was to be known and put into practice. The attitude of many outside the Church is now one of absolute indifference, faith is regarded as an emotion, as a peculiarly subjective disposition which is regulated by no known psychological laws. Thus Taine speaks of faith as "une source vive qui s'est formee au plus profond de l'ame, sous la poussee et la chaleur des instincts immanents" — "a living fountain which has come into existence in the lowest depths of the soul under the impulse and the warmth of the immanent instincts". Indifferentism in all its phases was condemned by Pius IX in the Syllabus Quanta cura: in Prop. XV, "Any man is free to embrace and profess whatever form of religion his reason approves of"; XVI, "Men can find the way of salvation and can attain to eternal salvation in any form of religious worship"; XVII "We can at least have good hopes of the eternal salvation of all those who have never been in the true Church of Christ"; XVIII, "Protestantism is only another form of the same true Christian religion, and men can be as pleasing to God in it as in the Catholic Church."

The Objective Unity and Immutability of Faith

      Christ's prayer for the unity of His Church the highest form of unity conceivable, "that they all may be one as thou, Father, in me, and I in Thee" (John 17:21), has been brought into effect by the unifying force of a bond of a faith such as that which we have analysed. All Christians have been taught to be "careful to keep the unity of the spirit in the bond of peace, one body and one spirit, as you are called in one hope of your calling; one Lord, one faith, one baptism, one God and Father of all" (Ephesians 4:3-6). The objective unity of the Catholic Church becomes readily intelligible when we reflect upon the nature of the bond of union which faith offers us. For our faith comes to us from the one unchanging Church, "the pillar and ground of truth", and our assent to it comes as a light in our minds and a motive power in our wills from the one unchanging God Who can neither deceive nor be deceived. Hence, for all who possess it, this faith constitutes an absolute and unchanging bond of union. The teachings of this faith develop, of course, with the needs of the ages, but the faith itself remains unchanged. Modern views are entirely destructive of such unity of belief because their root principle is the supremacy of the individual judgment. Certain writers do indeed endeavour to overcome the resulting conflict of views by upholding the supremacy of universal human reason as a criterion of truth; thus Mr. Campbell writes: "One cannot really begin to appreciate the value of united Christian testimony until one is able to stand apart from it, so to speak, and ask whether it rings true to the reason and moral sense" (The New Theology, p. 178; cf. Cardinal Newman, "Palmer on Faith and Unity" in Essays Critical and Historical, vol. 1, also, Thomas Harper, S.J., Peace Through the Truth, London, 1866, 1st Series.)

XXI.
Scepticism

Scepticism (Gr. sképsis, speculation, doubt; sképtesthai, to scrutinize or examine carefully) may mean (1) doubt based on rational grounds, or (2) disbelief based on rational grounds (cf. Balfour, "Defence of Phil. Doubt", p. 296), or (3) a denial of the possibility of attaining truth; and in any of these senses it may extend to all spheres of human knowledge (Universal Scepticism), or to some particular spheres of the same (Mitigated Scepticism). The third is the strictly philosophical sense of the term Scepticism, which is taken, unless otherwise specified, to be universal. Scepticism is then a systematic denial of the capacity of the human intellect to know anything whatsoever with certainty. It differs from Agnosticism because the latter denies only the possibility of metaphysics and natural theology; from Positivism in that Positivism denies that we do de facto know anything beyond the laws by which phenomena are related to one another; from Atheism in that the atheist denies only the fact of God's existence, not our capacity for knowing whether He exists.

History of Scepticism

The great religions of the East are for the most part essentially sceptical. They treat life as one vast illusion, destined some time or other to give place to a state of nescience, or to be absorbed in the life of the Absolute. But their Scepticism is a tone of mind rather than a reasoned philosophical doctrine based upon a critical examination of the human mind or upon a study of the history of human speculation. If we wish for the latter we must seek it among the philosophies of ancient Greece. Among the Greeks the earliest form of philosophical speculation was directed towards an explanation of natural phenomena, and the contradictory theories which were soon evolved by the prolific genius of the Greek mind, inevitably led to Scepticism. Heraclitus, Parmenides, Democritus, Empedocles, Anaxagoras, though differing on other points, one and all came to the conclusion that the senses, whence they had derived the data upon which their theories were built, could not be trusted. Accordingly Protagoras and the Sophists distinguish "appearances" from "reality"; but, finding that no two philosophers could agree as to the nature of the latter, they pronounced reality unknowable. The thorough-going Scepticism which resulted is apparent in the three famous propositions of Gorgias: "Nothing exists"; "If anything did exist it could not be known"; "If it was known, the knowledge of it would be incommunicable."

The first step towards the refutation of this Scepticism was the Socratic doctrine of the concept. There can be no science of the particular, said Socrates. Hence, before any science at all is possible, we must clear up our general notions of things and come to some agreement in regard to definitions. Plato, adopting this attitude, but still holding to the view that the senses can give only dóxa (opinion) and not epistéme (true knowledge), worked out an intellectual theory of the universe. Aristotle, who followed, rejected Plato's theory, and proposed a very different one in its place, with the result that another epidemic of Scepticism succeeded. But Aristotle did more than this. He propounded the doctrine of intuition or self-evident truth. All things cannot be proved, he said; yet an infinite regress is impossible. Hence there must be somewhere self-evident principles which are no mere assumptions, but which underlie the structure of human knowledge and are presupposed by the very nature of things (Metaph., 1005 b, 1006 a). This doctrine, later on, was to prove one of the chief forces that checked the destructive onslaught of the Sceptics; for, even if Aristotle's dictum cannot be proved, it none the less states a fact which to many is itself self-evident. It was the Stoics who first took "evidence" as the ultimate criterion of truth. Perceptions, they taught, are valid when they are characterized by enárgeia, i.e. when their objects are manifest, clear, or obvious. Similarly conceptions and judgments are valid when we are conscious that in them there is katálepsis an apprehension of reality. Contemporaneously, however, with Zeno, the founder of Stoicism, lived Pyrrho the Sceptic (d. about 270 B.C.), who, though he admitted that we can know "appearance," denied that we can know anything of the reality that underlies it. Oudèn mâllon — nothing is more one thing than another. Contradictory statements, therefore, may both be true. A scepticism so radical as this, the Stoics argued, is useless for practical life; and this argument bore fruit.

Arcesilaus, founder of the Middle Academy (third century B.C.), though rejecting the Stoic criterion and affirming that nothing could be known for certain, nevertheless admitted that some criterion is needed whereby to direct our actions in practice, and with this in view suggested that we should assent to what is reasonable (tò eúlogon). For "the reasonable" Carneades, who founded the Third Academy (second century B.C.), substituted "the probable": propositions which after careful examination manifest no contradiction, external or internal, are pithané (probable) kaà aperístatos (secure) kaì perideuméne (thoroughly tested) (Sextus Empiricus "Adv. Math.", VII, 166). A subsequent attempt to reconcile conflicting doctrines having proved futile, however, the Academy lapsed into Pyrrhonism. Ænesidemus sums up the traditional arguments of the Sceptics under ten heads, which later on (second century A.D.) were reduced by Sextus Empiricus to five:

1. human judgments and human theories are contradictory;
2. all proof involves an infinite regress;
3. perceptual data are relative both to the percipient and to one another;
4. axioms, or self-evident truths, are really assumptions;
5. all syllogistic reasoning involves diállelos (a vicious circle), for the major premise can be proved only by complete induction, and the possibility of complete induction supposes the truth of the conclusion (Sextus Emp., "Hyp. Pyrrh.", I, 164; II, 134; Diogenes Laertius, IX,

88).

From Scepticism the neo-Platonists sought refuge in the immediacy of a mystic experience; Augustine and Anselm in faith which in supernatural matters must precede both experience and knowledge (cf. Augustine, "De vera relig.", xxiv, xxv; "De util. cred.", ix; Anselm, "De fid. Trin.", ii); St. Thomas and the Scholastics in a rational, coherent, and systematic theory of the ultimate nature of things, based on self-evident truths but consistent also with the facts of experience, and consistent too with the truth of revelation, which thus serves to confirm what we have already discovered by the light of natural reason. But with the Renaissance, characterized as it was by an indiscriminate enthusiasm for all forms of Greek thought, it was only natural that the Scepticism of the Greeks should be revived. In this movement Montaigne (d. 1592), Charron (d. 1603), Sanchez (d. 1632), Pascal (d. 1662), Sorbière (d. 1670), Le Vayer (d. 1672), Hirnhaym (d. 1679), Foucher (d. 1696), Bayle (d. 1706), Huet (d. 1721), all took part. Its aim was to discredit reason on the old grounds of contradiction and of the impossibility of proving anything. Huet, Bishop of Avranches, and others sought to argue from the bankruptcy of reason to the necessity and sufficiency of faith. But for the most part, faith, understood in the Catholic sense of belief in a system of revealed doctrines capable of intelligent expression and rational interpretation, so far from being exempt from the attacks of the Sceptics, was rather (as it still is) the chief object against which their efforts were directed. Faith, as they understood it, was blind and unreasoning. The diversity of doctrine introduced by Protestantism had rendered all other faith, in their view no less contradictory than philosophy and natural belief.

In Hume Scepticism finds a new argument derived from the psychology of Locke. A critical examination of human cognition, it was said, reveals the fact that the data of knowledge consist merely of impressions — distinct, successive, discreet. These the mind connects in various ways, and these ways of connecting things become habitual. Thus the principle of causality, the propositions of arithmetic, geometry, and algebra, physical laws etc., in short all forms of synthesis and relations are subjective in origin. They have no objective validity, and their alleged "necessity" is but a psychological feeling arising from the force of habit. We undoubtedly believe in real things and real causes; but this is merely because we have grown accustomed so to group and connect our mental impressions. The arguments of Pyrrho and other Sceptics are unanswerable, their Scepticism reasonable and well-founded; but in practical life it is too much trouble to think otherwise than we do think, and we could not get on if we did. Kant's answer to Hume was embodied in a philosophy as eminently subjective as that of Hume himself. Consequently it failed, and resulted only in further Scepticism, implicit, if not actually professed. And nowadays physical science, which in Kant's time alone held its own against the inroads of Scepticism, is as thoroughly permeated with it as the rest of our beliefs. One instance must suffice — that of Mr. A. J. Balfour, who in his "Defense of Philosophic Doubt" seeks to uphold religious belief on the equivocal ground that it is no less certain than scientific theory and method. There is, he says,

* no satisfactory means of inferring the general from the particular (c. ii),
* no empirical proof of the law of causality (c. iii),
* no adequate guarantee of the uniformity of nature and the persistence of physical law (cc. iv, v).

Again, of the popular philosophic arguments which are "put forward as final and conclusive grounds of belief" p. 138), the argument from general consent is not ultimate; that from success in practice, though it gives us grounds for confidence in the future, cannot be conclusive, since it is empirical in character; whilst the argument from common sense which affirms that the intellect, when working normally, is trustworthy, involves a vicious circle, since normal workings can be distinguished from abnormal only on the ground that they lead to truth (c. vii). Similarly the original "deliverances of consciousness", to which Scottish Intuitionists appeal, are of no avail because it is impossible to determine what deliverances of consciousness are original and what are not. Returning to the question of science, Mr. Balfour finds that it contradicts common sense in that (e.g.) it declares bodies, which appear coloured to our senses, to be made up in reality of uncoloured particles, and, while thus discrediting the trustworthiness of observation, provides no criterion whereby to distinguish observations which are trustworthy from those which are not. Its method, too, is inconclusive, for there may always be other hypotheses which would explain the facts equally well (c. xii). Lastly the evolution of belief tends wholly to discredit its validity, for our beliefs are largely determined by non-rational causes, and, even when evidence is their motive, what we regard as evidence is settled by circumstances altogether beyond our control (c. xiii).

Critical Examination of Scepticism

A reply to the copious arguments of the Sceptic enumerated above, might take the following line:
* The Sceptic fails to distinguish between practical moral certainty which excludes all reasonable grounds for doubt, and absolute certainty which excludes all possible grounds for doubt. The latter can be had only when evidence is complete, proof wholly adequate, obvious, and conclusive, and when all difficulties and objections can be completely solved. In mathematics this is sometimes possible, though not always; but in other matters "practical certainty" as a rule is all we can get. And this is sufficient, since "practical certainty" is certainty for reasonable beings.
* Axiomatic, or self-evident, truth must be insisted on. The truth of an axiom can never be proved, yet may become manifest, even to those who for the time being doubt it, when its meaning and its application are clearly understood.

* Perceptual judgments refer qualities (not sensations) to things, but they do not declare what is the nature of these qualities, and hence do not contradict scientific theory.

* Perception is trustworthy in that it reveals to us the general character and behaviour of things — both of ourselves and of external objects. We do not often mistake a spade for a table-knife or a turkey for a hippopotamus. The senses do not pretend to be accurate in detail (unless assisted by instruments) or in abnormal circumstances.

* The "normal" working of our faculties can be determined independently of any question as to the truth of their deliverances. The work of our faculties is "normal", (1) when they are free from the influence of subjective factors, other than those which belong to their proper nature (i.e. free from disease, impediment, the influence of prejudice, expectancy desire, etc.), and (2) when they are exercised upon their own proper objects. In the case of the senses this means upon objects we meet with day by day under ordinary circumstances. If the circumstances are extraordinary, our senses are still trustworthy, however, provided the circumstances be taken into account.

* Alleged contradictions inherent in philosophical terms are due to ambiguity, misunderstanding, the lack of precise definition, or the influence of a false philosophy. For instance, the contradictions which Mr. Bradley points out (Appearance and Reality, bk. I) in terms such as time, space, substance and accident, causality, self, are not to be found in these terms as defined by the Scholastics.

* Contradictions between different philosophical theories may be (a) accounted for, and (b) eliminated. (a) They arise from ambiguity, variety of definition, misconception, misinterpretation, careless inference, groundless assumption, unverified hypothesis, and the neglect of relevant facts. Yet (b) all error contains an element of truth, and contradictions suppose a common principle already granted anterior to their divergence; and these underlying principles and elements of truth contained in all theories can be distinguished from the errors in which they are wrapped up.

* Beliefs arising from non-rational or from unknown grounds should either be re-established on rational grounds or discarded. All beliefs should be evident either (1) immediately, as in the case (e.g.) of our belief in external reality, or (2) mediately by inference from known truth, or (3) on the ground of adequate testimony.

* The Sceptic assumes the capacity of the intellect to criticize the faculty of knowledge, and thus, in so far as he denies its capacity to know anything, implicitly contradicts himself.

XXII.
St. Thomas Aquinas

St. Thomas Aquinas was a philosopher, theologian, and doctor of the Church (Angelicus Doctor). He is the patron of Catholic universities, colleges, and schools. He was born at Rocca Secca in the Kingdom of Naples, 1225 or 1227; and died at Fossa Nuova, 7 March, 1274.

Life

The great outlines and all the important events of his life are known, but biographers differ as to some details and dates. Death prevented Henry Denifle from executing his project of writing a critical life of the saint. Denifle's friend and pupil, Dominic Prümmer, O.P., professor of theology in the University of Fribourg, Switzerland, took up the work and published the "Fontes Vitae S. Thomae Aquinatis, notis historicis et criticis illustrati"; and the first fascicle (Toulouse, 1911) has appeared, giving the life of St. Thomas by Peter Calo (1300) now published for the first time. From Tolomeo of Lucca . . . we learn that at the time of the saint's death there was a doubt about his exact age (Prümmer, op. cit., 45). The end of 1225 is usually assigned as the time of his birth. Father Prümmer, on the authority of Calo, thinks 1227 is the more probable date (op. cit., 28). All agree that he died in 1274.

Landulph, his father, was Count of Aquino; Theodora, his mother, Countess of Teano. His family was related to the Emperors Henry VI and Frederick II, and to the Kings of Aragon, Castile, and France. Calo relates that a holy hermit foretold his career, saying to Theodora before his birth: "He will enter the Order of Friars Preachers, and so great will be his learning and sanctity that in his day no one will be found to equal him" (Prümmer, op. cit., 18). At the age of five, according to the custom of the times, he was sent to receive his first training from the Benedictine monks of Monte Cassino. Diligent in study, he was thus early noted as being meditative and devoted to prayer, and his preceptor was surprised at hearing the child ask frequently: "What is God?"

About the year 1236 he was sent to the University of Naples. Calo says that the change was made at the instance of the Abbot of Monte Cassino, who wrote to Thomas's father that a boy of such talents should not be left in obscurity (Prümmcr, op. cit., 20). At Naples his preceptors were Pietro Martini and Petrus Hibernus. The chronicler says that he soon surpassed Martini at grammar, and he was then given over to Peter of Ireland, who trained him in logic and the natural sciences. The customs of the times divided the liberal arts into two courses: the Trivium, embracing grammar, logic, and rhetoric; the Quadrivium, comprising music, mathematics, geometry, and astronomy . . . . Thomas could repeat the lessons with more depth and lucidity than his masters displayed. The youth's heart had remained pure amidst the corruption with which he was surrounded, and he resolved to embrace the religious life.

Some time between 1240 and August, 1243, he received the habit of the Order of St. Dominic, being attracted and directed by John of St. Julian, a noted preacher of the convent of Naples. The city wondered that such a noble young man should don the garb of poor friar. His mother, with mingled feelings of joy and sorrow, hastened to Naples to see her son. The Dominicans, fearing she would take him away, sent him to Rome, his ultimate destination being Paris or Cologne. At the instance of Theodora, Thomas's brothers, who were soldiers under the Emperor Frederick, captured the novice near the town of Aquapendente and confined him in the fortress of San Giovanni at Rocca Secca. Here he was detained nearly two years, his parents, brothers, and sisters endeavouring by various means to destroy his vocation. The brothers even laid snares for his virtue, but the pure-minded novice drove the temptress from his room with a brand which he snatched from the fire. Towards the end of his life, St. Thomas confided to his faithful friend and companion, Reginald of Piperno, the secret of a remarkable favour received at this time. When the temptress had been driven from his chamber, he knelt and most earnestly implored God to grant him integrity of mind and body. He fell into a gentle sleep, and, as he slept, two angels appeared to assure him that his prayer had been heard. They then girded him about with a white girdle, saying: "We gird thee with the girdle of perpetual virginity." And from that day forward he never experienced the slightest motions of concupiscence.

    The time spent in captivity was not lost. His mother relented somewhat, after the first burst of anger and grief; the Dominicans were allowed to provide him with new habits, and through the kind offices of his sister he procured some books — the Holy Scriptures, Aristotle's Metaphysics, and the "Sentences" of Peter Lombard. After eighteen months or two years spent in prison, either because his mother saw that the hermit's prophecy would eventually be fulfilled or because his brothers feared the threats of Innocent IV and Frederick II, he was set at liberty, being lowered in a basket into the arms of the Dominicans, who were delighted to find that during his captivity "he had made as much progress as if he had been in a studium generale" (Calo, op. cit., 24).

Thomas immediately pronounced his vows, and his superiors sent him to Rome. Innocent IV examined closely into his motives in joining the Friars Preachers, dismissed him with a blessing, and forbade any further interference with his vocation. John the Teutonic, fourth master general of the order, took the young student to Paris and, according to the majority of the saint's biographers, to Cologne, where he arrived in 1244 or 1245, and was placed under Albertus Magnus, the most renowned professor of the order. In the schools Thomas's humility and taciturnity were misinterpreted as signs of dullness, but when Albert had heard his brilliant defence of a difficult thesis, he exclaimed: "We call this young man a dumb ox, but his bellowing in doctrine will one day resound throughout the world."

In 1245 Albert was sent to Paris, and Thomas accompanied him as a student. In 1248 both returned to

Cologne. Albert had been appointed regent of the new studium generale, erected that year by the general chapter of the order, and Thomas was to teach under him as Bachelor. During his stay in Cologne, probably in 1250, he was raised to the priesthood by Conrad of Hochstaden, archbishop of that city. Throughout his busy life, he frequently preached the Word of God, in Germany, France, and Italy. His sermons were forceful, redolent of piety, full of solid instruction, abounding in apt citations from the Scriptures.

In the year 1251 or 1252 the master general of the order, by the advice of Albertus Magnus and Hugo a S. Charo (Hugh of St. Cher), sent Thomas to fill the office of Bachelor (sub-regent) in the Dominican studium at Paris. This appointment may be regarded as the beginning of his public career, for his teaching soon attracted the attention both of the professors and of the students. His duties consisted principally in explaining the "Sentences" of Peter Lombard, and his commentaries on that text-book of theology furnished the materials and, in great part, the plan for his chief work, the "Summa theologica".

In due time he was ordered to prepare himself to obtain the degree of Doctor in Theology from the University of Paris, but the conferring of the degree was postponed, owing to a dispute between the university and the friars. The conflict, originally a dispute between the university and the civic authorities, arose from the slaying of one of the students and the wounding of three others by the city guard. The university, jealous of its autonomy, demanded satisfaction, which was refused. The doctors closed their schools, solemnly swore that they would not reopen them until their demands were granted, and decreed that in future no one should be admitted to the degree of Doctor unless he would take an oath to follow the same line of conduct under similar circumstances. The Dominicans and Franciscans, who had continued to teach in their schools, refused to take the prescribed oath, and from this there arose a bitter conflict which was at its height when St. Thomas and St. Bonaventure were ready to be presented for their degrees. William of St-Amour extended the dispute beyond the original question, violently attacked the friars, of whom he was evidently jealous, and denied their right to occupy chairs in the university. Against his book, "De periculis novissimorum temporum" (The Perils of the Last Times), St. Thomas wrote a treatise "Contra impugnantes religionem", an apology for the religious orders (Touron, op. cit., II, cc. vii sqq.). The book of William of St-Amour was condemned by Alexander IV at Anagni, 5 October, 1256, and the pope gave orders that the mendicant friars should be admitted to the doctorate.

About this time St. Thomas also combated a dangerous book, "The Eternal Gospel" (Touron, op. cit., II, cxii). The university authorities did not obey immediately; the influence of St. Louis IX and eleven papal Briefs were required before peace was firmly established, and St. Thomas was admitted to the degree of Doctor in Theology.

The date of his promotion, as given by many biographers, was 23 October, 1257. His theme was "The Majesty of Christ". His text, "Thou waterest the hills from thy upper rooms: the earth shall be filled with the fruit of thy works" (Psalm 103:13), said to have been suggested by a heavenly visitor, seems to have been prophetic of his career. A tradition says that St. Bonaventure and St. Thomas received the doctorate on the same day, and that there was a contest of humility between the two friends as to which should be promoted first.

From this time St. Thomas's life may be summed up in a few words: praying, preaching, teaching, writing, journeying. Men were more anxious to hear him than they had been to hear Albert, whom St. Thomas surpassed in accuracy, lucidity, brevity, and power of exposition, if not in universality of knowledge. Paris claimed him as her own; the popes wished to have him near them; the studia of the order were eager to enjoy the benefit of his teaching; hence we find him successively at Anagni, Rome, Bologna, Orvieto, Viterbo, Perugia, in Paris again, and finally in Naples, always teaching and writing, living on earth with one passion, an ardent zeal for the explanation and defence of Christian truth. So devoted was he to his sacred task that with tears he begged to be excused from accepting the Archbishopric of Naples, to which he was appointed by Clement IV in 1265. Had this appointment been accepted, most probably the "Summa theologica" would not have been written.

Yielding to the requests of his brethren, he on several occasions took part in the deliberations of the general chapters of the order. One of these chapters was held in London in 1263. In another held at Valenciennes (1259) he collaborated with Albertus Magnus and Peter of Tarentasia (afterwards Pope Innocent V) in formulating a system of studies which is substantially preserved to this day in the studia generalia of the Dominican Order (cf. Douais, op. cit.).

It is not surprising to read in the biographies of St. Thomas that he was frequently abstracted and in ecstasy. Towards the end of his life the ecstasies became more frequent. On one occasion, at Naples in 1273, after he had completed his treatise on the Eucharist, three of the brethren saw him lifted in ecstasy, and they heard a voice proceeding from the crucifix on the altar, saying "Thou hast written well of me, Thomas; what reward wilt thou have?" Thomas replied, "None other than Thyself, Lord" (Prümmer, op. cit., p. 38). Similar declarations are said to have been made at Orvieto and at Paris.

On 6 December, 1273, he laid aside his pen and would write no more. That day he experienced an unusually long ecstasy during Mass; what was revealed to him we can only surmise from his reply to Father Reginald, who urged him to continue his writings: "I can do no more. Such secrets have been revealed to me that all I have written now appears to be of little value" (modica, Prümmer, op. cit., p. 43). The "Summa theologica" had been completed only as far as the ninetieth question of the third part (De partibus poenitentiae).

Thomas began his immediate preparation for death. Gregory X, having convoked a general council, to open at Lyons on 1 May, 1274, invited St. Thomas and St. Bonaventure to take part in the deliberations, commanding the former to bring to the council his treatise "Contra errores Graecorum" (Against the Errors of the Greeks). He tried to obey, setting out on foot in January, 1274, but strength failed him; he fell to the ground near Terracina, whence he was conducted to the Castle of Maienza, the home of his niece the Countess Francesca Ceccano. The Cistercian monks of Fossa Nuova pressed him to accept their hospitality, and he was conveyed to their monastery, on entering which he whispered to his companion: "This is my rest for ever and ever: here will I dwell, for I have chosen it" (Psalm 131:14). When Father Reginald urged him to remain at the castle, the saint replied: "If the Lord wishes to take me away, it is better that I be found in a religious house than in the dwelling of a lay person." The Cistercians were so kind and attentive that Thomas's humility was alarmed. "Whence comes this honour", he exclaimed, "that servants of God should carry wood for my fire!" At the urgent request of the monks he dictated a brief commentary on the Canticle of Canticles.

The end was near; extreme unction was administered. When the Sacred Viaticum was brought into the room he pronounced the following act of faith:

If in this world there be any knowledge of this sacrament stronger than that of faith, I wish now to use it in affirming that I firmly believe and know as certain that Jesus Christ, True God and True Man, Son of God and Son of the Virgin Mary, is in this Sacrament . . . I receive Thee, the price of my redemption, for Whose love I have watched, studied, and laboured. Thee have I preached; Thee have I taught. Never have I said anything against Thee: if anything was not well said, that is to be attributed to my ignorance. Neither do I wish to be obstinate in my opinions, but if I have written anything erroneous concerning this sacrament or other matters, I submit all to the judgment and correction of the Holy Roman Church, in whose obedience I now pass from this life.

He died on 7 March, 1274. Numerous miracles attested his sanctity, and he was canonized by John XXII, 18 July, 1323. The monks of Fossa Nuova were anxious to keep his sacred remains, but by order of Urban V the body was given to his Dominican brethren, and was solemnly translated to the Dominican church at Toulouse, 28 January, 1369. A magnificent shrine erected in 1628 was destroyed during the French Revolution, and the body was removed to the Church of St. Sernin, where it now reposes in a sarcophagus of gold and silver, which was solemnly blessed by Cardinal Desprez on 24 July, 1878. The chief bone of his left arm is preserved in the cathedral of Naples. The right arm, bestowed on the University of Paris, and originally kept in the St. Thomas's Chapel of the

Dominican church, is now preserved in the Dominican Church of S. Maria Sopra Minerva in Rome, whither it was transferred during the French Revolution.

A description of the saint as he appeared in life is given by Calo (Prümmer, op. cit., p. 401), who says that his features corresponded with the greatness of his soul. He was of lofty stature and of heavy build, but straight and well proportioned. His complexion was "like the colour of new wheat": his head was large and well shaped, and he was slightly bald. All portraits represent him as noble, meditative, gentle yet strong. St. Pius V proclaimed St. Thomas a Doctor of the Universal Church in the year 1567. In the Encyclical "Aeterni Patris", of 4 August, 1879, on the restoration of Christian philosophy, Leo XIII declared him "the prince and master of all Scholastic doctors". The same illustrious pontiff, by a Brief dated 4 August, 1880, designated him patron of all Catholic universities, academies, colleges, and schools throughout the world.

Writings (General Remarks)

Although St. Thomas lived less than fifty years, he composed more than sixty works, some of them brief, some very lengthy. This does not necessarily mean that every word in the authentic works was written by his hand; he was assisted by secretaries, and biographers assure us that he could dictate to several scribes at the same time. Other works, some of which were composed by his disciples, have been falsely attributed to him.

In the "Scriptores Ordinis Praedicatorum" (Paris, 1719) Fr. Echard devotes eighty-six folio pages to St. Thomas's works, the different editions and translations (I, pp. 282-348). Touron (op. cit., pp. 69 sqq.) says that manuscript copies were found in nearly all the libraries of Europe, and that, after the invention of printing, copies were multiplied rapidly in Germany, Italy, and France, portions of the "Summa theologica" being one of the first important works printed. Peter Schöffer, a printer of Mainz, published the "Secunda Secundae" in 1467. This is the first known printed copy of any work of St. Thomas. The first complete edition of the "Summa" was printed at Basle, in 1485. Many other editions of this and of other works were published in the sixteenth and seventeenth centuries, especially at Venice and at Lyons. The principal editions of all the work (Opera Omnia) were published as follows: Rome, 1570; Venice, 1594, 1612, 1745; Antwerp, 1612; Paris, 1660, 1871-80 (Vives); Parma, 1852-73; Rome, 1882 (the Leonine). The Roman edition of 1570, called "the Piana", because edited by order of St. Pius V, was the standard for many years. Besides a carefully revised text it contained the commentaries of Cardinal Cajetan and the valuable "Tabula Aurea" of Peter of Bergamo. The Venetian edition of 1612 was highly prized because the text was accompanied by the Cajetan-Porrecta commentaries . . . . The Leonine edition, begun under the patronage of Leo XIII, now continued under the master general of the Dominicans, undoubtedly will be the most perfect of all. Critical dissertations on each work will be given, the text will be carefully revised, and all references will be verified. By direction of Leo XIII (Motu Proprio, 18 Jan., 1880) the "Summa contra gentiles" will be published with the commentaries of Sylvester Ferrariensis, whilst the commentaries of Cajetan go with the "Summa theologica".

The latter has been published, being volumes IV-XII of the edition (last in 1906). St. Thomas's works may be classified as philosophical, theological, scriptural, and apologetic, or controversial. The division, however, cannot always be rigidly maintained. The "Summa theologica", e.g., contains much that is philosophical, whilst the "Summa contra gentiles" is principally, but not exclusively, philosophical and apologetic. His philosophical works are chiefly commentaries on Aristotle, and his first important theological writings were commentaries on Peter Lombard's four books of "Sentences"; but he does not slavishly follow either the Philosopher or the Master of the Sentences (on opinions of the Lombard rejected by theologians, see Migne, 1841, edition of the "Summa" I, p. 451).

Writings (Principal Works)

Amongst the works wherein St. Thomas's own mind and method are shown, the following deserve special mention:

(1) "Quaestiones disputatae" (Disputed Questions) — These were more complete treatises on subjects that had

not been fully elucidated in the lecture halls, or concerning which the professor's opinion had been sought. They are very valuable, because in them the author, free from limitations as to time or space, freely expresses his mind and gives all arguments for or against the opinions adopted. These treatises, containing the questions "De potentia", "De malo", "De spirit. creaturis", "De anima", "De unione Verbi Incarnati", "De virt. in communi", "De caritate", "De corr. fraterna", "De spe", "De virt. cardinal.", "De veritate", were often reprinted, e.g. recently by the Association of St. Paul (2 vols., Paris and Fribourg, Switzerland, 1883).

(2) "Quodlibeta" (may be rendered "Various Subjects", or "Free Discussions") — They present questions or arguments proposed and answers given in or outside the lecture halls, chiefly in the more formal Scholastic exercises, termed circuli, conclusiones, or determinationes, which were held once or twice a year.

(3) "De unitate intellectus contra Averroistas" -- This opusculum refuted a very dangerous and widespread error, viz., that there was but one soul for all men, a theory which did away with individual liberty and responsibility.

(4) "Commentaria in Libros Sententiarum" (mentioned above) -- This with the following work are the immediate forerunners of the "Summa theologica".

(5) "Summa de veritate catholicae fidei contra gentiles" (Treatise on the Truth of the Catholic Faith, against Unbelievers) -- This work, written at Rome, 1261-64, was composed at the request of St. Raymond of

Pennafort, who desired to have a philosophical exposition and defence of the Christian Faith, to be used against the Jews and Moors in Spain. It is a perfect model of patient and sound apologetics, showing that no demonstrated truth (science) is opposed to revealed truth (faith). The best recent editions are those of Rome, 1878 (by Uccelli), of Paris and Fribourg, Switzerland, 1882, and of Rome, 1894. It has been translated into many languages. It is divided into four books: I. Of God as He is in Himself; II. Of God the Origin of Creatures; III. Of God the End of Creatures; IV. Of God in His Revelation. It is worthy of remark that the Fathers of the Vatican Council, treating the necessity of revelation (Constitution "Dei Filius", c. 2), employed almost the very words used by St. Thomas in treating that subject in this work (I, cc. iv, V), and in the "Summa theologica" (I:1:1).

(6) Three works written by order of Urban IV --

* The "Opusculum contra errores Graecorum" refuted the errors of the Greeks on doctrines in dispute between them and the Roman Church, viz., the procession of the Holy Ghost from the Father and the Son, the primacy of the Roman pontiff, the Holy Eucharist, and purgatory. It was used against the Greeks with telling effect in the Council of Lyons (1274) and in the Council of Florence (1493). In the range of human reasonings on deep subjects there can be found nothing to surpass the sublimity and depth of the argument adduced by St. Thomas to prove that the Holy Ghost proceeds from the Father and the Son (cf.

Summa I:36:2); but it must be borne in mind that our Faith is not based on that argument alone.

* "Officium de festo Corporis Christi". Mandonnet (Ecrits, p. 127) declares that it is now established beyond doubt that St. Thomas is the author of the beautiful Office of Corpus Christi, in which solid doctrine, tender piety, and enlightening Scriptural citations are combined, and expressed in language remarkably accurate, beautiful, chaste, and poetic. Here we find the well-known hymns, "Sacris Solemniis", "Pange Lingua" (concluding in the "Tantum Ergo"), "Verbum Supernum" (concluding with the "O Salutaris Hostia") and, in the Mass, the beautiful sequence "Lauda Sion". In the responses of the office, St. Thomas places side by side words of the New Testament affirming the real presence of Christ in the Blessed Sacrament and texts from the Old Testament referring to the types and figures of the Eucharist. Santeuil, a poet of the seventeenth century, said he would give all the verses he had written for the one stanza of the "Verbum Supernum": "Se nascens dedit socium, convescens in edulium: Se moriens in pretium, Se regnans dat in praemium" — "In birth, man's fellow-man was He, His meat, while sitting at the Board: He died his Ransomer to be, He reigns to be his Great Reward" (tr. by Marquis of Bute). Perhaps the gem of the whole office is the antiphon "O Sacrum Convivium" (cf. Conway, "St. Thomas Aquinas", London and New York, 1911, p. 61).

* The "Catena Aurea", though not as original as his

other writings, furnishes a striking proof of St. Thomas's prodigious memory and manifests an intimate acquaintance with the Fathers of the Church. The work contains a series of passages selected from the writings of the various Fathers, arranged in such order that the texts cited form a running commentary on the Gospels. The commentary on St. Matthew was dedicated to Urban IV. An English translation of the "Catena Aurea" was edited by John Henry Newman (4 vols., Oxford, 1841-1845; see Vaughan, op. cit., vol. II,) pp. 529 sqq..

(7) The "Summa theologica"-- This work immortalized St. Thomas. The author himself modestly considered it simply a manual of Christian doctrine for the use of students. In reality it is a complete scientifically arranged exposition of theology and at the same time a summary of Christian philosophy (see SUMMÆ). In the brief prologue St. Thomas first calls attention to the difficulties experienced by students of sacred doctrine in his day, the causes assigned being: the multiplication of useless questions, articles, and arguments; the lack of scientific order; frequent repetitions, "which beget disgust and confusion in the minds of learners". Then he adds: "Wishing to avoid these and similar drawbacks, we shall endeavour, confiding in the Divine assistance, to treat of these things that pertain to sacred doctrine with brevity and clearness, in so far as the subject to be treated will permit." In the introductory question, "On Sacred Doctrine", he proves that, besides the knowledge which reason affords,

Revelation also is necessary for salvation first, because without it men could not know the supenatural end to which they must tend by their voluntary acts; secondly, because, without Revelation, even the truths concerning God which could be proved by reason would be known "only by a few, after a long time, and with the admixture of many errors". When revealed truths have been accepted, the mind of man proceeds to explain them and to draw conclusions from them. Hence results theology, which is a science, because it proceeds from principles that are certain (Answer 2). The object, or subject, of this science is God; other things are treated in it only in so far as they relate to God (Answer 7). Reason is used in theology not to prove the truths of faith, which are accepted on the authority of God, but to defend, explain, and develop the doctrines revealed (Answer 8). He thus announces the division of the "Summa": "Since the chief aim of this sacred science is to give the knowledge of God, not only as He is in Himself, but also as He is the Beginning of all things, and the End of all, especially of rational creatures, we shall treat first of God; secondly, of the rational creature's advance towards God (de motu creaturae rationalis in Deum); thirdly, of Christ, Who, as Man, is the way by which we tend to God." God in Himself, and as He is the Creator; God as the End of all things, especially of man; God as the Redeemer — these are the leading ideas, the great headings, under which all that pertains to theology is contained.

(a) Sub-divisions

The First Part is divided into three tracts:

* On those things which pertain to the Essence of God;

* On the distinction of Persons in God (the mystery of the Trinity);

* On the production of creatures by God and on the creatures produced.

The Second Part, On God as He is in the End of man, is sometimes called the Moral Theology of St. Thomas, i.e., his treatise on the end of man and on human acts. It is subdivided into two parts, known as the First Section of the Second (I-II, or 1a 2ae) and the Second of the Second (II-II, or 2a 2ae).

The First of the Second. The first five questions are devoted to proving that man's last end, his beatitude, consists in the possession of God. Man attains to that end or deviates from it by human acts, i.e. by free, deliberate acts. Of human acts he treats, first, in general (in all but the first five questions of the I-II), secondly, in particular (in the whole of the II-II). The treatise on human acts in general is divided into two parts: the first, on human acts in themselves; the other, on the principles or causes, extrinsic or intrinsic, of those acts. In these tracts and in the Second of the Second, St. Thomas, following Aristotle, gives a perfect description and a wonderfully keen analysis of the movements of man's mind and heart.

The Second of the Second considers human acts, i.e., the virtues and vices, in particular. In it St. Thomas treats, first, of those things that pertain to all men, no matter what may be their station in life, and, secondly, of those things that pertain to some men only. Things that pertain to all men are reduced to seven headings: Faith, Hope, and Charity; Prudence, Justice, Fortitude, and Temperance. Under each title, in order to avoid repetitions, St. Thomas treats not only of the virtue itself, but also of the vices opposed to it, of the commandment to practise it, and of the gift of the Holy Ghost which corresponds to it. Things pertaining to some men only are reduced to three headings: the graces freely given (gratia gratis datae) to certain individuals for the good of the Church, such as the gifts of tongues, of prophecy, of miracles; the active and the contemplative life; the particular states of life, and duties of those who are in different states, especially bishops and religious.

The Third Part treats of Christ and of the benefits which He has conferred upon man, hence three tracts: On the Incarnation, and on what the Saviour did and suffered; On the Sacraments, which were instituted by Christ, and have their efficacy from His merits and sufferings; On Eternal Life, i.e., on the end of the world, the resurrection of bodies, judgment, the punishment of the wicked, the happiness of the just who, through Christ, attain to eternal life in heaven.

Eight years were given to the composition of this work, which was begun at Rome, where the First Part and the First of the Second were written (1265-69). The Second of the Second, begun in Rome, was completed in Paris (1271). In 1272 St. Thomas went to Naples, where the Third Part was written, down to the ninetieth question of the tract On Penance (see Leonine edition, I, p. xlii). The work has been completed by the addition of a supplement, drawn from other writings of St. Thomas, attributed by some to Peter of Auvergne, by others to Henry of Gorkum. These attributions are rejected by the editors of the Leonine edition (XI, pp. viii, xiv, xviii). Mandonnet (op. cit., 153) inclines to the very probable opinion that it was compiled by Father Reginald de Piperno, the saint's faithful companion and secretary.

The entire "Summa" contains 38 Treatises, 612 Questions, subdivided into 3120 articles, in which about 10,000 objections are proposed and answered. So admirably is the promised order preserved that, by reference to the beginning of the Tracts and Questions, one can see at a glance what place it occupies in the general plan, which embraces all that can be known through theology of God, of man, and of their mutual relations . . . "The whole Summa is arranged on a uniform plan. Every subject is introduced as a question, and divided into articles. . . . Each article has also a uniform disposition of parts. The topic is introduced as an inquiry for discussion, under the term Utrum, whether — e.g. Utrum Deus sit? The objections against the proposed thesis are then stated. These are generally three or four in number, but sometimes extend to seven or more. The conclusion adopted is then introduced by the words, Respondeo dicendum. At the end of the thesis expounded the objections are answered, under the forms, ad primum, ad secundum, etc." . . . . The "Summa" is Christian doctrine in scientific form; it is human reason rendering its highest service in defence and explanation of the truths of the Christian religion. It is the answer of the matured and saintly doctor to the question of his youth: What is God? Revelation, made known in the Scriptures and by tradition; reason and its best results; soundness and fulness of doctrine, order, conciseness and clearness of expression, effacement of self, the love of truth alone, hence a remarkable fairness towards adversaries and calmness in combating their errors; soberness and soundness of judgment, together with a charmingly tender and enlightened piety — these are all found in this "Summa" more than in his other writings, more than in the writings of his contemporaries, for "among the Scholastic doctors, the chief and master of all, towers Thomas Aquinas, who, as Cajetan observes (In 2am 2ae, Q. 148, a. 4) 'because he most venerated the ancient doctors of the Church in a certain way seems to have inherited the intellect of all'" (Encyclical, "Aeterni Patris", of Leo XIII).

(b) Editions and Translations

It is impossible to mention the various editions of the "Summa", which has been in constant use for more than seven hundred years. Very few books have been so often republished. The first complete edition, printed at Basle in 1485, was soon followed by others, e.g., at Venice in 1505,

1509, 1588, 1594; at Lyons in 1520, 1541, 1547, 1548, 1581, 1588, 1624,1655; at Antwerp in 1575. These are enumerated by Touron (op. cit., p. 692), who says that about the same time other editions were published at Rome, Antwerp, Rouen, Paris, Douai, Cologne, Amsterdam, Bologna, etc. The editors of the Leonine edition deem worthy of mention those published at Paris in 1617, 1638, and 1648, at Lyons in 1663, 1677, and 1686, and a Roman edition of 1773 (IV, pp. xi, xii). Of all old editions they consider the most accurate two published at Padua, one in 1698, the other in 1712, and the Venice edition of 1755. Of recent editions the best are the following: the Leonine; the Migne editions (Paris, 1841, 1877); the first volume of the 1841 edition containing the "Libri quatuor sententiarum" of Peter Lombard; the very practical Faucher edition (5 vols. small quarto, Paris, 1887), dedicated to Cardinal Pecci, enriched with valuable notes; a Roman edition of 1894. The "Summa" has been translated into many modern languages as well.

Writings (Method and Style)

It is not possible to characterize the method of St. Thomas by one word, unless it can be called eclectic. It is Aristotelean, Platonic, and Socratic; it is inductive and deductive; it is analytic and synthetic. He chose the best that could he find in those who preceded him, carefully sifting the chaff from the wheat, approving what was true, rejecting the false. His powers of synthesis were extraordinary. No writer surpassed him in the faculty of expressing in a few well-chosen words the truth gathered from a multitude of varying and conflicting opinions; and in almost every instance the student sees the truth and is perfectly satisfied with St. Thomas's summary and statement. Not that he would have students swear by the words of a master. In philosophy, he says, arguments from authority are of secondary importance; philosophy does not consist in knowing what men have said, but in knowing the truth (In I lib. de Coelo, lect. xxii; II Sent., D. xiv, a. 2, ad 1um). He assigns its proper place to reason used in theology (see below: Influence of St. Thomas), but he keeps it within its own sphere. Against the Traditionalists the Holy See has declared that the method used by St. Thomas and St. Bonaventure does not lead to Rationalism (Denzinger-Bannwart, n. 1652). Not so bold or original in investigating nature as were Albertus Magnus and Roger Bacon, he was, nevertheless, abreast of his time in science, and many of his opinions are of scientific value in the twentieth century. Take, for instance, the following: "In the same plant there is the two-fold virtue, active and passive, though sometimes the active is found in one and the passive in another, so that one plant is said to be masculine and the other feminine" (3 Sent., D. III, Q. ii, a 1).

The style of St. Thomas is a medium between the rough expressiveness of some Scholastics and the fastidious elegance of John of Salisbury; it is remarkable for accuracy, brevity, and completeness. Pope Innocent VI (quoted in the

Encyclical, "Aeterni Patris", of Leo XIII) declared that, with the exception of the canonical writings, the works of St. Thomas surpass all others in "accuracy of expression and truth of statement" (habet proprietatem verborum, modum dicendorum, veritatem sententiarum). Great orators, such as Bossuet, Lacordaire, Monsabré, have studied his style, and have been influenced by it, but they could not reproduce it. The same is true of theological writers. Cajetan knew St. Thomas's style better than any of his disciples, but Cajetan is beneath his great master in clearness and accuracy of expression, in soberness and solidity of judgment. St. Thomas did not attain to this perfection without an effort. He was a singularly blessed genius, but he was also an indefatigable worker, and by continued application he reached that stage of perfection in the art of writing where the art disappears. "The author's manuscript of the Summa Contra Gentiles is still in great part extant. It is now in the Vatican Library. The manuscript consists of strips of parchment, of various shades of colour, contained in an old parchment cover to which they were originally stitched. The writing is in double column, and difficult to decipher, abounding in abbreviations, often passing into a kind of shorthand. Throughout many passages a line is drawn in sign of erasure" (Rickaby, Op. cit., preface: see Ucelli ed., "Sum. cont. gent.", Rome, 1878).

Influences Exerted on St. Thomas

How was this great genius formed? The causes that exerted an influence on St. Thomas were of two kinds, natural and supernatural.

Natural causes

(1) As a foundation, he "was a witty child, and had received a good soul" (Wisdom 8:19). From the beginning he manifested precocious and extraordinary talent and thoughtfulness beyond his years.

(2) His education was such that great things might have been expected of him. His training at Monte Cassino, at Naples, Paris, and Cologne was the best that the thirteenth century could give, and that century was the golden age of education. That it afforded excellent opportunities for forming great philosophers and theologians is evident from the character of St. Thomas's contemporaries. Alexander of Hales, Albertus Magnus, St. Bonaventure, St. Raymond of Pennafort, Roger Bacon, Hugo a S. Charo, Vincent of Beauvais, not to mention scores of others, prove beyond all doubt that those were days of really great scholars. (See Walsh, "The Thirteenth, Greatest of Centuries", New York, 1907.) The men who trained St. Thomas were his teachers at Monte Cassino and Naples, but above all Albertus Magnus, under whom he studied at Paris and Cologne.

(3) The books that exercised the greatest influence on his mind were the Bible, the Decrees of the councils and of the popes, the works of the Fathers, Greek and Latin,

especially of St. Augustine, the "Sentences" of Peter Lombard, the writings of the philosophers, especially of Plato, Aristotle, and Boethius. If from these authors any were to be selected for special mention, undoubtedly they would be Aristotle, St. Augustine, and Peter Lombard. In another sense the writings of St. Thomas were influenced by Averroes, the chief opponent whom he had to combat in order to defend and make known the true Aristotle.

(4) It must be borne in mind that St. Thomas was blessed with a retentive memory and great powers of penetration. Father Daniel d'Agusta once pressed him to say what he considered the greatest grace he had ever received, sanctifying grace of course excepted. "I think that of having understood whatever I have read", was the reply. St. Antoninus declared that "he remembered everything be had read, so that his mind was like a huge library" (cf. Drane, op. cit., p. 427; Vaughan, op. cit., II, p. 567). The bare enumeration of the texts of Scripture cited in the "Summa theologica" fills eighty small-print columns in the Migne edition, and by many it is not unreasonably supposed that he learned the Sacred Books by heart while he was imprisoned in the Castle of San Giovanni. Like St. Dominic he had a special love for the Epistles of St. Paul, on which he wrote commentaries (recent edition in 2 vols., Turin, 1891).

(5) Deep reverence for the Faith, as made known by tradition, characterizes all his writings. The consuetudo ecclesiae — the practice of the Church — should prevail

over the authority of any doctor (Summa II-II:10:12). In the "Summa" he quotes from 19 councils, 41 popes, and 52 Fathers of the Church. A slight acquaintance with his writings will show that among the Fathers his favourite was St. Augustine (on the Greek Fathers see Vaughan, op. cit., II, cc. iii sqq.).

(6) With St. Augustine (On Christian Doctrine II.40), St. Thomas held that whatever there was of truth in the writings of pagan philosophers should be taken from them, as from "unjust possessors", and adapted to the teaching of the true religion (Summa I:84:5). In the "Summa" alone he quotes from the writings of 46 philosophers and poets, his favourite authors being Aristotle, Plato, and, among Christian writers, Boethius. From Aristotle he learned that love of order and accuracy of expression which are characteristic of his own works. From Boethius he learned that Aristotle's works could be used without detriment to Christianity. He did not follow Boethius in his vain attempt to reconcile Plato and Aristotle. In general the Stagirite was his master, but the elevation and grandeur of St. Thomas's conceptions and the majestic dignity of his methods of treatment speak strongly of the sublime Plato.

Supernatural Causes

Even if we do not accept as literally true the declaration of John XXII, that St. Thomas wrought as many miracles as there are articles in the "Summa", we must, nevertheless, go beyond causes merely natural in attempting to explain his extraordinary career and wonderful writings.

(1) Purity of mind and body contributes in no small degree to clearness of vision (see St. Thomas, "Commentaries on I Cor., c. vii", Lesson v). By the gift of purity, miraculously granted at the time of the mystic girdling, God made Thomas's life angelic; the perspicacity and depth of his intellect, Divine grace aiding, made him the "Angelic Doctor".

(2) The spirit of prayer, his great piety and devotion, drew down blessings on his studies. Explaining why he read, every day, portions of the "Conferences" of Cassian, he said: "In such reading I find devotion, whence I readily ascend to contemplation" (Prümmer, op. cit., p. 32). In the lessons of the Breviary read on his feast day it is explicitly stated that he never began to study without first invoking the assistance of God in prayer; and when he wrestled with obscure passages of the Scriptures, to prayer he added fasting.

(3) Facts narrated by persons who either knew St. Thomas in life or wrote at about the time of his canonization prove that he received assistance from heaven. To Father Reginald he declared that he had learned more in prayer and contemplation than he had acquired from men or books (Prümmer, op. cit., p. 36). These same authors tell of mysterious visitors who came to encourage and enlighten him. The Blessed Virgin appeared, to assure him that his

life and his writings were acceptable to God, and that he would persevere in his holy vocation. Sts. Peter and Paul came to aid him in interpreting an obscure passage in Isaias. When humility caused him to consider himself unworthy of the doctorate, a venerable religious of his order (supposed to be St. Dominic) appeared to encourage him and suggested the text for his opening discourse (Prümmer, op. cit., 29, 37; Tocco in "Acta SS.", VII Mar.; Vaughan, op. cit., II, 91). His ecstasies have been mentioned. His abstractions in presence of King Louis IX (St. Louis) and of distinguished visitors are related by all biographers. Hence, even if allowance be made for great enthusiasm on the part of his admirers, we must conclude that his extraordinary learning cannot be attributed to merely natural causes. Of him it may truly be said that he laboured as if all depended on his own efforts and prayed as if all depended on God.

Influence of St. Thomas (On Sanctity)

The great Scholastics were holy as well as learned men. Alexander of Hales, St. Albertus Magnus, St. Thomas, and St. Bonaventure prove that learning does not necessarily dry up devotion. The angelic Thomas and the seraphic Bonaventure represent the highest types of Christian scholarship, combining eminent learning with heroic sanctity. Cardinal Bessarion called St. Thomas "the most saintly of learned men and the most learned of saints". His works breathe the spirit of God, a tender and enlightened piety, built on a solid foundation, viz. the knowledge of God, of Christ, of man. The "Summa theologica" may be made a manual of piety as well as a text-book for the study of theology (Cf. Drane, op. cit., p. 446). St. Francis de Sales, St. Philip Neri, St. Charles Borromeo, St. Vincent Ferrer, St. Pius V, St. Antoninus constantly studied St. Thomas. Nothing could be more inspiring than his treatises on Christ, in His sacred Person, in His life and sufferings. His treatise on the sacraments, especially on penance and the Eucharist, would melt even hardened hearts. He takes pains to explain the various ceremonies of the Mass ("De ritu Eucharistiae" in Summa III:83), and no writer has explained more clearly than St. Thomas the effects produced in the souls of men by this heavenly Bread (Summa III:79). The principles recently urged, in regard to frequent Communion, by Pius X ("Sacra Trid. Synodus", 1905) are found in St. Thomas (Summa III:79:8, III:80:10), although he is not so explicit on this point as he is on the Communion of children. In the Decree "Quam Singulari" (1910) the pope cites St. Thomas, who teaches that, when children begin to have some use of reason, so that they can conceive some devotion to the Blessed Sacrament, they may be allowed to communicate (Summa III:80:9). The spiritual and devotional aspects of St. Thomas's theology have been pointed out by Father Contenson, O.P., in his "Theologia mentis et cordis". They are more fully explained by Father Vallgornera, O.P., in his "Theologia Mystica D. Thomae", wherein the author leads the soul to God through the purgative, illuminative, and unitive ways. The Encyclical Letter of Leo XIII on the

Holy Spirit is drawn largely from St. Thomas, and those who have studied the "Prima Secundae" and the "Secunda Secundae" know how admirably the saint explains the gifts and fruits of the Holy Ghost, as well as the Beatitudes, and their relations to the different virtues Nearly all good spiritual writers seek in St. Thomas definitions of the virtues which they recommend.

Influence of St. Thomas (On Intellectual Life)

Since the days of Aristotle, probably no one man has exercised such a powerful influence on the thinking world as did St. Thomas. His authority was very great during his lifetime. The popes, the universities, the studia of his order were anxious to profit by his learning and prudence. Several of his important works were written at the request of others, and his opinion was sought by all classes. On several occasions the doctors of Paris referred their disputes to him and gratefully abided by his decision (Vaughan, op. cit., II, 1 p. 544). His principles, made known by his writings, have continued to influence men even to this day. This subject cannot be considered in all its aspects, nor is that necessary. His influence on matters purely philosophical is fully explained in histories of philosophy. His paramount importance and influence may be explained by considering him as the Christian Aristotle, combining in his person the best that the world has known in philosophy and theology. It is in this light that he is proposed as a model by Leo XIII in the famous Encyclical

"Aeterni Patris". The work of his life may be summed up in two propositions: he established the true relations between faith and reason; he systematized theology.

(1) Faith and Reason

The principles of St. Thomas on the relations between faith and reason were solemnly proclaimed in the Vatican Council. The second, third, and fourth chapters of the Constitution "Dei Filius" read like pages taken from the works of the Angelic Doctor. First, reason alone is not sufficient to guide men: they need Revelation; we must carefully distinguish the truths known by reason from higher truths (mysteries) known by Revelation. Secondly, reason and Revelation, though distinct, are not opposed to each other. Thirdly, faith preserves reason from error; reason should do service in the cause of faith. Fourthly, this service is rendered in three ways:

* reason should prepare the minds of men to receive the Faith by proving the truths which faith presupposes (praeambula fidei);

* reason should explain and develop the truths of Faith and should propose them in scientific form;

* reason should defend the truths revealed by Almighty God.

This is a development of St. Augustine's famous saying (On the Holy Trinity XIV.1), that the right use of reason is "that by which the most wholesome faith is begotten . . . is nourished, defended, and made strong." These principles are proposed by St. Thomas in many places, especially in the following: "In Boethium, da Trin. Proem.", Q. ii, a. 1; "Sum. cont. gent.", I, cc. iii-ix; Summa I:1:1, I:1:5, I:1:8, I:32:1, I:84:5. St. Thomas's services to the Faith are thus summed up by Leo XIII in the Encyclical "Aeterni Patris": "He won this title of distinction for himself: that singlehanded he victoriously combated the errors of former times, and supplied invincible arms to put to rout those which might in after times spring up. Again, clearly distinguishing, as is fitting, reason and faith, he both preserved and had regard for the rights of each; so much so, indeed, that reason, borne on the wings of Thomas, can scarcely rise higher, while faith could scarcely expect more or stronger aids from reason than those which she has already obtained through Thomas."

St. Thomas did not combat imaginary foes; he attacked living adversaries. The works of Aristotle had been introduced into France in faulty translations and with the misleading commentaries of Jewish and Moorish philosophers. This gave rise to a flood of errors which so alarmed the authorities that the reading of Aristotle's Physics and Metaphysics was forbidden by Robert de Courçon in 1210, the decree being moderated by Gregory IX in 1231. There crept into the University of Paris an insidious spirit of irreverence and Rationalism, represented especially by Abelard and Raymond Lullus, which claimed that reason could know and prove all things, even the mysteries of Faith. Under the authority of Averroes dangerous doctrines were propagated, especially two very pernicious errors: first, that philosophy and religion being in different regions, what is true in religion might be false in philosophy; secondly, that all men have but one soul. Averroes was commonly styled "The Commentator", but St. Thomas says he was "not so much a Peripatetic as a corruptor of Peripatetic philosophy" (Opusc. de unit. intell.). Applying a principle of St. Augustine (see I:84:5), following in the footsteps of Alexander of Hales and Albertus Magnus, St. Thomas resolved to take what was true from the "unjust possessors", in order to press it into the service of revealed religion. Objections to Aristotle would cease if the true Aristotle were made known; hence his first care was to obtain a new translation of the works of the great philosopher. Aristotle was to be purified; false commentators were to be refuted; the most influential of these was Averroes, hence St. Thomas is continually rejecting his false interpretations.

(2) Theology Systematized

The next step was to press reason into the service of the Faith, by putting Christian doctrine into scientific form. Scholasticism does not consist, as some persons imagine, in useless discussions and subtleties, but in this, that it expresses sound doctrine in language which is accurate, clear, and concise. In the Encyclical "Aeterni Patris" Leo XIII, citing the words of Sixtus V (Bull "Triumphantis", 1588), declares that to the right use of philosophy we are indebted for "those noble endowments which make Scholastic theology so formidable to the enemies of truth", because "that ready coherence of cause and effect, that order and array of a disciplined army in battle, those clear definitions and distinctions, that strength of argument and those keen discussions by which light is distinguished from darkness, the true from the false, expose and lay bare, as it were, the falsehoods of heretics wrapped around by a cloud of subterfuges and fallacies". When the great Scholastics had written, there was light where there had been darkness, there was order where confusion had prevailed. The work of St. Anselm and of Peter Lombard was perfected by the Scholastic theologians. Since their days no substantial improvements have been made in the plan and system of theology, although the field of apologetics has been widened, and positive theology has become more important.

Influence of St. Thomas (His Doctrine Followed)

Within a short time after his death the writings of St. Thomas were universally esteemed. The Dominicans naturally took the lead in following St. Thomas. The general chapter held in Paris in 1279 pronounced severe penalties against all who dared to speak irreverently of him or of his writings. The chapters held in Paris in 1286, at Bordeaux in 1287, and at Lucca in 1288 expressly required the brethren to follow the doctrine of Thomas, who at that time had not been canonized (Const. Ord. Praed., n. 1130). The University of Paris, on the occasion of Thomas's death, sent an official letter of condolence to the general chapter of the Dominicans, declaring that, equally with his brethren, the university experienced sorrow at the loss of one who was their own by many titles (see text of letter in Vaughan, op. cit., II, p. 82). In the Encyclical "Aeterni Patris" Leo XIII mentions the Universities of Paris, Salamanca, Alcalá, Douai, Toulouse, Louvain, Padua, Bologna, Naples, Coimbra as "the homes of human wisdom where Thomas reigned supreme, and the minds of all, of teachers as well as of taught, rested in wonderful harmony under the shield and authority of the Angelic Doctor". To the list may be added Lima and Manila, Fribourg and Washington.

Seminaries and colleges followed the lead of the universities. The "Summa" gradually supplanted the "Sentences" as the textbook of theology. Minds were formed in accordance with the principles of St. Thomas; he became the great master, exercising a world-wide influence on the opinions of men and on their writings; for even those who did not adopt all of his conclusions were obliged to give due consideration to his opinions. It has been estimated that 6000 commentaries on St. Thomas's works have been written. Manuals of theology and of philosophy, composed with the intention of imparting his teaching, translations, and studies, or digests (études), of portions of his works have been published in profusion during the last six hundred years and today his name is in honour all over the world.

In every one of the general councils held since his

death St. Thomas has been singularly honoured. At the Council of Lyons his book "Contra errores Graecorum" was used with telling effect against the Greeks. In later disputes, before and during the Council of Florence, John of Montenegro, the champion of Latin orthodoxy, found St. Thomas's works a source of irrefragable arguments. The "Decretum pro Armenis" (Instruction for the Armenians), issued by the authority of that council, is taken almost verbatim from his treatise, "De fidei articulis et septem sacramentis" (see Denzinger-Bannwart, n. 695). "In the Councils of Lyons, Vienne, Florence, and the Vatican", writes Leo XIII (Encyclical "Aeterni Patris"), "one might almost say that Thomas took part in and presided over the deliberations and decrees of the Fathers contending against the errors of the Greeks, of heretics, and Rationalists, with invincible force and with the happiest results."

But the chief and special glory of Thomas, one which he has shared with none of the Catholic doctors, is that the Fathers of Trent made it part of the order of the conclave to lay upon the altar, together with the code of Sacred Scripture and the decrees of the Supreme Pontiffs, the Summa of Thomas Aquinas, whence to seek counsel, reason, and inspiration. Greater influence than this no man could have.

Before this section is closed mention should be made of two books widely known and highly esteemed, which were inspired by and drawn from the writings of St. Thomas. The Catechism of the Council of Trent, composed by disciples of the Angelic Doctor, is in reality a compendium of his theology, in convenient form for the use of parish priests. Dante's "Divina Commedia" has been called "the Summa of St. Thomas in verse", and commentators trace the great Florentine poet's divisions and descriptions of the virtues and vices to the "Secunda Secundae".

Influence of St. Thomas (Appreciation)
(1) In the Church

The esteem in which he was held during his life has not been diminished, but rather increased, in the course of the six centuries that have elapsed since his death. The position which he occupies in the Church is well explained by that great scholar Leo XIII, in the Encyclical "Aeterni Patris", recommending the study of Scholastic philosophy: "It is known that nearly all the founders and framers of laws of religious orders commanded their societies to study and religiously adhere to the teachings of St. Thomas. . . To say nothing of the family of St. Dominic, which rightly claims this great teacher for its own glory, the statutes of the Benedictines, the Carmelites, the Augustinians, the Society of Jesus, and many others, all testify that they are bound by this law." Amongst the "many others" the Servites, the Passionists, the Barnabites, and the Sulpicians have been devoted in an especial manner to the study of St. Thomas. The principal ancient universities where St. Thomas ruled as the great master have been enumerated above. The Paris doctors called him the morning star, the luminous sun, the light of the whole Church. Stephen, Bishop of Paris, repressing those who dared to attack the doctrine of "that most excellent Doctor, the blessed Thomas", calls him "the great luminary of the Catholic Church, the precious stone of the priesthood, the flower of doctors, and the bright mirror of the University of Paris" (Drane, op. cit., p. 431). In the old Louvain University the doctors were required to uncover and bow their heads when they pronounced the name of Thomas (Goudin, op. cit., p. 21).

"The ecumenical councils, where blossoms the flower of all earthly wisdom, have always been careful to hold Thomas Aquinas in singular honour" (Leo XIII in "Aeterni Patris"). This subject has been sufficiently treated above. The "Bullarium Ordinis Praedicatorum", published in 1729-39, gives thirty-eight Bulls in which eighteen sovereign pontiffs praised and recommended the doctrine of St. Thomas (see also Vaughan, op. cit., II, c. ii; Berthier, op. cit., pp. 7 sqq.). These approbations are recalled and renewed by Leo XIII, who lays special stress on "the crowning testimony of Innocent VI: 'His teaching above that of others, the canons alone excepted, enjoys such an elegance of phraseology, a method of statement, a truth of proposition, that those who hold it are never found swerving from the path of truth, and he who dare assail it will always be suspected of error (ibid.).'" Leo XIII surpassed his predecessors in admiration of St. Thomas, in whose works he declared a remedy can be found for many evils that afflict society (see Berthier, op. cit., introd.). The notable Encyclical Letters with which the name of that illustrious pontiff will always be associated show how he had studied the works of the Angelic Doctor. This is very noticeable in the letters on Christian marriage, the Christian constitution of states, the condition of the working classes, and the study of Holy Scripture. Pope Pius X, in several letters, e.g. in the "Pascendi Dominici Gregis" (September, 1907), has insisted on the observance of the recommendations of Leo XIII concerning the study of St. Thomas. An attempt to give names of Catholic writers who have expressed their appreciation of St. Thomas and of his influence would be an impossible undertaking; for the list would include nearly all who have written on philosophy or theology since the thirteenth century, as well as hundreds of writers on other subjects. Commendations and eulogies are found in the introductory chapters of all good commentaries. An incomplete list of authors who have collected these testimonies is given by Father Berthier (op. cit., p. 22). . . .

(2) Outside the Church

(a) Anti-Scholastics -- Some persons have been and are still opposed to everything that comes under the name of Scholasticism, which they hold to be synonymous with subtleties and useless discussions. From the prologue to the "Summa" it is clear that St. Thomas was opposed to all that was superfluous and confusing in Scholastic studies. When people understand what true Scholasticism means, their objections will cease.

(b) Heretics and Schismatics -- "A last triumph was reserved for this incomparable man — namely, to compel the homage, praise, and admiration of even the very enemies of the Catholic name" (Leo XIII, ibid.). St. Thomas's orthodoxy drew upon him the hatred of all Greeks who were opposed to union with Rome. The united Greeks, however, admire St. Thomas and study his works (see above Translations of the "Summa"). The leaders of the sixteenth-century revolt honoured St. Thomas by attacking him, Luther being particularly violent in his coarse invectives against the great doctor. Citing Bucer's wild boast, "Take away Thomas and I will destroy the Church", Leo XIII (ibid.) remarks, "The hope was vain, but the testimony has its value".

Calo, Tocco, and other biographers relate that St. Thomas, travelling from Rome to Naples, converted two celebrated Jewish rabbis, whom he met at the country house of Cardinal Richard (Prümmer, op. cit., p. 33; Vaughan, op. cit., I, p. 795). Rabbi Paul of Burgos, in the fifteenth century, was converted by reading the works of St. Thomas. Theobald Thamer, a disciple of Melancthon, abjured his heresy after he had read the "Summa", which he intended to refute. The Calvinist Duperron was converted in the same way, subsequently becoming Archbishop of Sens and a cardinal (see Conway, O.P., op. cit., p. 96).

After the bitterness of the first period of Protestantism had passed away, Protestants saw the necessity of retaining many parts of Catholic philosophy and theology, and those who came to know St. Thomas were compelled to admire him. Überweg says "He brought the Scholastic philosophy to its highest stage of development, by effecting the most perfect accommodation that was possible of the Aristotelian philosophy to ecclesiastical orthodoxy" (op. cit., p. 440). R. Seeberg in the "New Schaff-Herzog Religious Encyclopedia" (New York, 1911) devotes ten columns to St. Thomas, and says that "at all points he succeeded in upholding the church doctrine as credible and reasonable" (XI, p. 427).

For many years, especially since the days of Pusey and Newman, St. Thomas has been in high repute at Oxford. Recently the "Summa contra gentiles" was placed on the list of subjects which a candidate may offer in the final honour schools of Litterae Humaniores at that university (cf. Walsh, op. cit., c. xvii). For several years Father De Groot, O.P., has been the professor of Scholastic philosophy in the University of Amsterdam, and courses in Scholastic philosophy have been established in some of the leading non-Catholic universities of the United States. Anglicans have a deep admiration for St. Thomas. Alfred Mortimer, in the chapter "The Study of Theology" of his work entitled "Catholic Faith and Practice" (2 vols., New York, 1909), regretting that "the English priest has ordinarily no scientific acquaintance with the Queen of Sciences", and proposing a remedy, says, "The simplest and most perfect sketch of universal theology is to be found in the Summa of St. Thomas" (vol. II, pp. 454, 465).

St. Thomas and Modern Thought

In the Syllabus of 1864 Pius IX condemned a proposition in which it was stated that the method and principles of the ancient Scholastic doctors were not suited to the needs of our times and the progress of science (Denzinger-Bannwart, n. 1713).

In the Encyclical "Aeterni Patris" Leo XIII points out the benefits to be derived from "a practical reform of philosophy by restoring the renowned teaching of St. Thomas Aquinas". He exhorts the bishops to "restore the golden wisdom of Thomas and to spread it far and wide for the defence and beauty of the Catholic Faith, for the good of society, and for the advantage of all the sciences". In the pages of the Encyclical immediately preceding these words he explains why the teaching of St. Thomas would produce such most desirable results: St. Thomas is the great master to explain and defend the Faith, for his is "the solid doctrine of the Fathers and the Scholastics, who so clearly and forcibly demonstrate the firm foundations of the Faith, its Divine origin, its certain truth, the arguments that sustain it, the benefits it has conferred on the human race, and its perfect accord with reason, in a manner to satisfy completely minds open to persuasion, however unwilling and repugnant". The career of St. Thomas would in itself have justified Leo XIII in assuring men of the nineteenth century that the Catholic Church was not opposed to the right use of reason. The sociological aspects of St. Thomas are also pointed out: "The teachings of Thomas on the true meaning of liberty, which at this time is running into license, on the Divine origin of all authority, on laws and their force, on the paternal and just rule of princes, on obedience to the highest powers, on mutual charity one towards another — on all of these and kindred subjects, have very great and invincible force to overturn those principles of the new order which are well known to be dangerous to the peaceful order of things and to public safety" (ibid.).

The evils affecting modern society had been pointed out by the pope in the Letter "Inscrutabili" of 21 April, 1878, and in the one on Socialism, Communism, and Nihilism ("The Great Encyclicals of Leo XIII", pp. 9 sqq.; 22 sqq.). How the principles of the Angelic Doctor will furnish a remedy for these evils is explained here in a general way, more particularly in the Letters on the Christian constitution of states, human liberty, the chief duties of Christians as citizens, and on the conditions of the working classes (ibid., pp. 107, 135, 180, 208).

It is in relation to the sciences that some persons doubt the reliability of St. Thomas's writings; and the doubters are thinking of the physical and experimental sciences, for in metaphysics the Scholastics are admitted to be masters. Leo XIII calls attention to the following truths: (a) The Scholastics were not opposed to investigation. Holding as a principle in anthropology "that the human intelligence is only led to the knowledge of things without body and matter by things sensible, they well understood that nothing was of greater use to the philosopher than diligently to search into the mysteries of nature, and to be earnest and constant in the study of physical things" (ibid., p. 55). This principle was reduced to practice: St. Thomas, St. Albertus Magnus, Roger Bacon, and others "gave large attention to the knowledge of natural things" (ibid., p. 56). (b) Investigation alone is not sufficient for true science. "When facts have been established, it is necessary to rise and apply ourselves to the study of the nature of corporeal things, to inquire into the laws which govern them and the principles whence their order and varied unity and mutual attraction in diversity arise" (p. 55).

Will the scientists of today pretend to be better reasoners than St. Thomas, or more powerful in synthesis? It is the method and the principles of St. Thomas that Leo XIII recommends: "If anything is taken up with too great subtlety by the Scholastic doctors, or too carelessly stated; if there be anything that ill agrees with the discoveries of a later age or, in a word, is improbable in any way, it does not enter into our mind to propose that for imitation to our age" (p. 56). Just as St. Thomas, in his day, saw a movement towards Aristotle and philosophical studies which could not be checked, but could be guided in the right direction and made to serve the cause of truth, so also, Leo XIII, seeing in the world of his time a spirit of study and investigation which might be productive of evil or of good, had no desire to check it, but resolved to propose a moderator and master who could guide it in the paths of truth.

No better guide could have been chosen than the clear-minded, analytic, synthetic, and sympathetic Thomas Aquinas. His extraordinary patience and fairness in dealing with erring philosophers, his approbation of all that was true in their writings, his gentleness in condemning what was false, his clear-sightedness in pointing out the direction to true knowledge in all its branches, his aptness and accuracy in expressing the truth — these qualities mark him as a great master not only for the thirteenth century, but for all times. If any persons are inclined to consider him too subtle, it is because they do not know how clear, concise, and simple are his definitions and divisions. His two summae are masterpieces of pedagogy, and mark him as the greatest of human teachers. Moreover, he dealt with errors similar to many which go under the name of philosophy or science in our days. The Rationalism of Abelard and others called forth St. Thomas's luminous and everlasting principles on the true relations of faith and reason. Ontologism was solidly refuted by St. Thomas nearly six centuries before the days of Malebranche, Gioberti, and Ubaghs (see Summa I:84:5). The true doctrine on first principles and on universals, given by him and by the other great Scholastics, is the best refutation of Kant's criticism of metaphysical ideas (see, e.g., "Post. Analyt.", I, lect. xix; "De ente et essentia", c. iv; Summa I:17:3 corp. and ad 2um; I:79:3; I:84:5; I:84:6 corp and ad 1um; I:85:2 ad 2um;

I:85:3 ad 1um, ad 4um; Cf. index to "Summa": "Veritas", "Principium", "Universale"). Modern psychological Pantheism does not differ substantially from the theory of one soul for all men asserted by Averroes (see "De unit. intell." and Summa I:76:2; I:79:5). The Modernistic error, which distinguishes the Christ of faith from the Christ of history, had as its forerunner the Averroistic principle that a thing might be true in philosophy and false in religion.

In the Encyclical "Providentissimus Deus" (18 November, 1893) Leo XIII draws from St. Thomas's writings the principles and wise rules which should govern scientific criticism of the Sacred Books. From the same source recent writers have drawn principles which are most helpful in the solution of questions pertaining to Spiritism and Hypnotism. Are we to conclude, then, that St. Thomas's works, as he left them, furnish sufficient instruction for scientists, philosophers, and theologians of our times? By no means. Vetera novis augere et perficere — "To strengthen and complete the old by aid of the new" — is the motto of the restoration proposed by Leo XIII. Were St. Thomas living today he would gladly adopt and use all the facts made known by recent scientific and historical investigations, but he would carefully weigh all evidence offered in favour of the facts. Positive theology is more necessary in our days than it was in the thirteenth century. Leo XIII calls attention to its necessity in his Encyclical, and his admonition is renewed by Pius X in his Letter on Modernism. But both pontiffs declare that positive theology must not be extolled to the detriment of Scholastic theology. In the Encyclical "Pascendi", prescribing remedies against Modernism, Pius X, following in this his illustrious predecessor, gives the first place to "Scholastic philosophy, especially as it was taught by Thomas Aquinas"; St. Thomas is still "The Angel of the Schools".

XXIII.
Thomism

In a broad sense, Thomism is the name given to the system which follows the teaching of St. Thomas Aquinas in philosophical and theological questions. In a restricted sense the term is applied to a group of opinions held by a school called Thomistic, composed principally, but not exclusively, of members of the Order of St. Dominic, these same opinions being attacked by other philosophers or theologians, many of whom profess to be followers of St. Thomas.

* To Thomism in the first sense are opposed, e.g., the Scotists, who deny that satisfaction is a part of the proximate matter (materia proxima) of the Sacrament of Penance. Anti-Thomists, in this sense of the word, reject opinions admittedly taught by St. Thomas.

* To Thomism in the second sense are opposed, e.g. the Molinists, as well as all who defend the moral instrumental causality of the sacraments in producing grace against the system of physical instrumental causality, the latter being a doctrine of the Thomistic School.

Anti-Thomism in such cases does not necessarily imply opposition to St. Thomas: It means opposition to tenets of the Thomistic School. Cardinal Billot, for instance, would not admit that he opposed St. Thomas by rejecting the Thomistic theory on the causality of the sacraments. In the Thomistic School, also, we do not always find absolute unanimity. Bañez and Billuart do not always agree with Cajetan, though all belong to the Thomistic School. It does not come within the scope of this article to determine who have the best right to be considered the true exponents of St. Thomas.

The subject may be treated under the following headings:

I. Thomism in general, from the thirteenth century down to the nineteenth;

II. The Thomistic School;

III. Neo-Thomism and the revival of Scholasticism.

IV. Eminent Thomists

The doctrine in general

Early Opposition Overcome

Although St. Thomas (d. 1274) was highly esteemed by all classes, his opinions did not at once gain the ascendancy and influence which they acquired during the first half of the fourteenth century and which they have since maintained. Strange as it may appear, the first serious opposition came from Paris, of which he was such an ornament, and from some of his own monastic brethren. In the year 1277 Stephen Tempier, Bishop of Paris, censured certain philosophical propositions, embodying doctrines taught by St. Thomas, relating especially to the principle of individuation and to the possibility of creating several angels of the same species. In the same year Robert Kilwardby, a Dominican, Archbishop of Canterbury, in conjunction with some doctors of Oxford, condemned those same propositions and moreover attacked St. Thomas's doctrine of the unity of the substantial form in man.

Kilwardby and his associates pretended to see in the condemned propositions something of Averroistic Aristoteleanism, whilst the secular doctors of Paris had not fully forgiven one who had triumphed over them in the controversy as to the rights of the mendicant friars. The storm excited by these condemnations was of short duration. Blessed Albertus Magnus, in his old age, hastened to Paris to defend his beloved disciple. The Dominican Order, assembled in general chapter at Milan in 1278 and at Paris in 1279, adopted severe measures against the members who had spoken injuriously of the venerable Brother Thomas. When William de la Mare, O.S.F., wrote a "Correptorium fratris Thomæ", an English Dominican, Richard Clapwell (or Clapole), replied in a treatise "Contra corruptorium fratris Thomae". About the same time there appeared a work, which was afterwards printed at Venice (1516) under the title, "Correctorium corruptorii S. Thomae", attributed by some to Ægidius Romanus, by others to Clapwell, by others to Father John of Paris. St. Thomas was solemnly vindicated when the Council of Vienna (1311-12) defined, against Peter John Olivi, that the rational soul is the substantial form of the human body (on this definition see Zigliara, "De mente Conc. Vicnn.", Rome, 1878). The canonization of St. Thomas by John XXII, in 1323, was a death-blow to his detractors. In 1324 Stephen de Bourret, Bishop of Paris, revoked the censure pronounced by his predecessor, declaring that "that blessed confessor and excellent doctor, Thomas Aquinas, had never believed, taught, or written anything contrary to the Faith or good morals". It is doubtful whether Tempier and his associates acted in the name of the University of Paris, which had always been loyal to St. Thomas. When this university, in 1378, wrote a letter condemning the errors of John de Montesono, it was explicitly declared that the condemnation was not aimed at St. Thomas: "We have said a thousand times, and yet, it would seem, not often enough, that we by no means include the doctrine of St. Thomas in our condemnation." An account of these attacks and defences will be found in the following works: Echard, "Script. ord. prad.", I, 279 (Paris, 1719); De Rubeis, "Diss. crit.", Diss. xxv, xxvi, I, p. cclxviii; Leonine edit. Works of St. Thomas; Denifle, "Chart. univ. Paris" (Paris, 1890-91), I, 543, 558, 566; II, 6, 280; Duplessis d'Argentré, "Collectio judiciorum de novis erroribus" (3 vols., Paris, 1733-36), 1, 175 sqq.; Du Boulay, "Hist. univ. Par.", IV, 205, 436, 618, 622, 627; Jourdain, "La phil. de S. Thomas d'Aquin" (Paris, 1858), II, i; Douais, "Essai sur l'organization des études dans l'ordre des ff. prêcheurs" (Paris and Toulouse, 1884), 87 sqq.; Mortier, "Hist. des maîtres gén. de l'ordre des ff. prêch.", II, 115142, 571; "Acta cap. gen. ord. praed.", ed. Reichert (9 vols., Rome, 1893-1904, II; Turner, "Hist. of Phil." (Boston, 1903), xxxix.

Progress of Thomism

The general chapter of the Dominican Order, held at Carcassonne in 1342, declared that the doctrine of St.

Thomas had been received as sound and solid throughout the world (Douais, op. cit., 106). His works were consulted from the time they became known, and by the middle of the fourteenth century his "Summa Theologica" had supplanted the "Libri quatuor sententiarum", of Peter Lombard as the text-book of theology in the Dominican schools. With the growth of the order and the widening of its influence Thomism spread throughout the world; St. Thomas became the great master in the universities and in the studia of the religious orders (see Encyc. "Aeterni Patris" of Leo XIII). The fifteenth and sixteenth centuries saw Thomism in a triumphal march which led to the crowning of St. Thomas as the Prince of Theologians, when his "Summa was laid beside the Sacred Scriptures at the Council of Trent, and St. Pius V, in 1567, proclaimed him a Doctor of the Universal Church. The publication of the "Piana" edition of his works, in 1570, and the multiplication of editions of the "Opera omnia" and of the "Summa" during the seventeenth century and part of the eighteenth show that Thomism flourished during that period. In fact it was during that period that some of the great commentators (for example, Francisco Suárez, Sylvius, and Billuart) adapted his works to the needs of the times.

Decline of Scholasticism and of Thomism

Gradually, however, during the seventeenth and eighteenth centuries, there came a decline in the study of the works of the great Scholastics. Scholars believed that there was need of a new system of studies, and, instead of building upon and around Scholasticism, they drifted away from it. The chief causes which brought about the change were Protestantism, Humanism, the study of nature, and the French Revolution. Positive theology was considered more necessary in discussions with the Protestants than Scholastic definitions and divisions. Elegance of diction was sought by the Humanists in the Greek and Latin classics, rather than in the works of the Scholastics, many of whom were far from being masters of style. The discoveries of Copernicus (d. 1543), Kepler (d. 1631), Galileo (d. 1642), and Newton (d. 1727) were not favourably received by the Scholastics. The experimental sciences were in honour; the Scholastics including St. Thomas, were neglected (cf. Turner, op cit., 433). Finally, the French Revolution disorganized all ecclesiastical studies, dealing to Thomisn a blow from which it did not fully recover until the last quarter of the nineteenth century. At the time when Billuart (d. 1757) published his "Summa Sancti Thoma hodiernis academiarum moribus accomodata" Thomism still held an important place in all theological discussion. The tremendous upheaval which disturbed Europe from 1798 to 1815 affected the Church as well as the State. The University of Louvain, which had been largely Thomistic, was compelled to close its doors, and other important institutions of learning were either closed or seriously hampered in their work. The Dominican Order, which naturally had supplied the most ardent

Thomists, was crushed in France, Germany, Switzerland, and Belgium. The province of Holland was almost destroyed, whilst the provinces of Austria and Italy were left to struggle for their very existence. The University of Manila (1645) continued to teach the doctrines of St. Thomas and in due time gave to the world Cardinal Zephyrinus González, O.P., who contributed in no small degree to the revival of Thomism under Leo XIII.

Distinctive Doctrines of Thomism in General
    (1) In Philosophy
* The angels and human souls are without matter, but every material composite being (compositum) has two parts, prime matter and substantial form. In a composite being which has substantial unity and is not merely an aggregate of distinct units, there can be but one substantial form. The substantial form of man is his soul (anima rationalis) to the exclusion of any other soul and of any other substantial form. The principle of individuation, for material composites, is matter with its dimensions: without this there can be no merely numerical multiplication: distinction in the form makes specific distinction: hence there cannot be two angels of the same species.

* The essences of things do not depend on the free will of God, but on His intellect, and ultimately on His essence, which is immutable. The natural law, being derived from the eternal law, depends on the mind of God, ultimately on the essence of God; hence it is intrinsically immutable.

Some actions are forbidden by God because they are bad: they are not bad simply because He forbids them [see Zigliara, "Sum. phil." (3 vols., Paris, 1889), ccx, xi, II, M. 23, 24, 25].

* The will moves the intellect quoad exercitium, i.e. in its actual operation: the intellect moves the will quoad specificationem, i.e. by presenting objects to it: nil volitum nisi praecognitum. The beginning of all our acts is the apprehension and desire of good in general (bonum in communi). We desire happiness (bonum in communi) naturally and necessarily, not by a free deliberate act. Particular goods (bona particularia) we choose freely; and the will is a blind faculty, always following the last practical judgment of the intellect (Zigliara, 51).

* The senses and the intellect are passive, i.e. recipient, faculties; they do not create, but receive (i.e. perceive) their objects (St. Thomas, I, Q. lxxviii, a. 3; Q. lxxix, a. 2; Zigliara, 26, 27). If this principle is borne in mind there is no reason for Kant's "Critique of Pure Reason". On the other hand those faculties are not like wax, or the sensitive plate used by photographers, in the sense that they are inert and receive impressions unconsciously. The will controls the exercise of the faculties, and the process of acquiring knowledge is a vital process: the moving cause is always within the living agent.

* The Peripatetic axiom: "Nihil est in intellectu quod non prius in sensu" (Nothing is in the intellect that was not first in the senses), is admitted; but St. Thomas modifies it by saying: first, that, once the sense objects have been perceived, the intellect ascends to the knowledge of higher things, even of God; and, secondly, that the soul knows its own existence by itself (i.e. by its own act), although it knows its own nature only by reflection on its acts. Knowledge begins by sense perception, but the range of the intellect is far beyond that of the senses. In the soul as soon as it begins to act are found the first principles (prima principia) of all knowledge, not in the form of an objective illumination, but in the form of a subjective inclination to admit them on account of their evidence. As soon as they are proposed we see that they are true; there is no more reason for doubting them than there is for denying the existence of the sun when we see it shining (see Zigliara, op. cit., pp. 32-42).

* The direct and primary object of the intellect is the universal, which is prepared and presented to the passive intellect (intellectus possibilis) by the active intellect (intellectus agens) which illuminates the phantasmata, or mental images, received through the senses, and divests them of all individuating conditions. This is called abstracting the universal idea from the phantasmata, but the term must not be taken in a materialistic sense. Abstraction is not a transferring of something from one place to another; the illumination causes all material and individuating conditions to disappear, then the universal alone shines out and is perceived by the vital action of the intellect (Q. lxxxiv, a. 4; Q. lxxxv, a. 1, ad lum, 3um, 4um).

The process throughout is so vital, and so far elevated above material conditions and modes of action, that the nature of the acts and of the objects apprehended proves the soul to be immaterial and spiritual.

* The soul, by its very nature, is immortal. Not only is it true that God will not annihilate the soul, but from its very nature it will always continue to exist, there being in it no principle of disintegration (Zigliara, p. 9). Hence human reason can prove the incorruptibility (i.e. immortality) of the soul.

* The existence of God is not known by an innate idea, it cannot be proved by arguments a priori or a simultaneo; but it can be demonstrated by a posteriori arguments. Ontologism was never taught by St. Thomas or by Thomists (see Lepidi, "Exam. phil. theol. de ontologismo", Louvain, 1874, c. 19; Zigliara, Theses I, VIII).

* There are no human (i.e. deliberate) acts indifferent in individuo.

(2) In Theology

* Faith and science, i.e. knowledge by demonstration, cannot co-exist in the same subject with regard to the same object (Zigliara, O, 32, VII); and the same is true of knowledge and opinion.

* The metaphysical essence of God consists, according to some Thomists, in the intelligere actualissimum, i.e. fulness of pure intellection, according to others in the perfection of aseitas, i.e. in dependent existence (Zigliara, Th. VIII, IX).

* The happiness of heaven, formally and in the ultimate

analysis, consists in the vision, not in the fruition, of God.

* The Divine attributes are distinguished from the Divine nature and from each other by a virtual distinction, i.e. by a distinctio rationis cum fundamento a parte rei. The distinctio actualis formalis of Scotus is rejected.

* In attempting to explain the mystery of the Trinity — in as far as man can conceive it — the relations must be considered perfectiones simpliciter simplices, i.e. excluding all imperfection. The Holy Ghost would not be distinct from the Son if He did not proceed from the Son as well as from the Father.

* The angels, being pure spirits, are not, properly speaking, in any place; they are said to be in the place, or in the places, where they exercise their activity (Summa, I, Q. lii, a. 1). Strictly speaking, there is no such thing as an angel passing from place to place; but if an angel wishes to exercise its activity first in Japan and afterwards in America, it can do so in two instants (of angelic time), and need not pass through the intervening space (Q. liii). St. Thomas does not discuss the question "How many angels can dance on the point of a needle?" He reminds us that we must not think of angels as if they were corporeal, and that, for an angel, it makes no difference whether the sphere of his activity be the point of a needle or a continent (Q. lii, a. 2). Many angels cannot be said to be in the same place at the same time, for this would mean that whilst one angel is producing an effect others could be producing the same effect at the same time. There can be but one angel in the

same place at the same time (Q. lii, a. 3). The knowledge of the angels comes through ideas (species) infused by God (QQ. lv, a.2, lvii, a.2, lviii, a.7). They do not naturally know future contingents, the secrets of souls, or the mysteries of grace (Q. lvii, aa. 3, 45). The angels choose either good or evil instantly, and with full knowledge; hence their judgment is naturally final and irrevocable (Q. lxiv, a. 2).

* Man was created in the state of sanctifying grace. Grace was not due to his nature, but God granted it to him from the beginning (I, Q. xcv, a. 1). So great was the perfection of man in the state of original justice, and so perfect the subjection of his lower faculties to the higher, that his first sin could not have been a venial sin (I-II:89:3).

* It is more probable that the Incarnation would not have taken place had man not sinned (III, Q. i, a. 3). In Christ there were three kinds of knowledge: the scientia beata, i.e. the knowledge of things in the Divine Essence; the scientia infusa, i.e. the knowledge of things through infused ideas (species), and the scientia acquisita, i.e. acquired or experimental knowledge, which was nothing more than the actual experience of things which he already knew. On this last point St. Thomas, in the "Summa" (Q. ix, a. 4), explicitly retracts an opinion which he had once held (III Sent., d. 14, Q. iii, a. 3).

* All sacraments of the New Law, including confirmation and extreme unction, were instituted immediately by Christ. Circumcision was a sacrament of the Old Law and conferred grace which removed the stain of original sin.

The children of Jews or of other unbelievers may not be baptized without the consent of their parents (III, Q. lxviii, a. 10; II-II, Q. x, a. 12; Denzinger-Bannwart, n. 1481). Contrition, confession, and satisfaction are the proximate matter (materia proxima) of the Sacrament of Penance. Thomists hold, against the Scotists, that when Transubstantiation takes place in the Mass the Body of Christ is not made present per modum adduclionis, i.e. is not brought to the altar, but they do not agree in selecting the term which should be used to express this action (cf. Billuart, "De Euchar.", Diss. i, a. 7). Cardinal Billot holds ("De eccl. sacr.", Rome, 1900, Th. XI, "De euchar.", p. 379) that the best, and the only possible, explanation is the one given by St. Thomas himself: Christ becomes present by transubstantiation, i.e. by the conversion of the substance of bread into the substance of His body (III, Q. lxxv, a. 4; Sent., d. XI, Q. i, a. 1, q. 1). After the consecration the accidents (accidentia) of the bread and wine are preserved by Almighty God without a subject (Q. lxxxvii, a. 1). It was on this question that the doctors of Paris sought enlightenment from St. Thomas (see Vaughan, "Life and Labours of St. Thomas", London, 1872, II, p. 544). The earlier Thomists, following St. Thomas (Suppl., Q. xxxvii, a. 2), taught that the sub-diaconate and the four minor orders were partial sacraments. Some recent Thomists — e.g., Billot (op. cit., p. 282) and Tanquerey (De ordine, n. 16) — defend this opinion as more probable and more in conformity with the definitions of the councils.

The giving of the chalice with wine and of the paten with bread Thomists generally held to be an essential part of ordination to the priesthood. Some, however, taught that the imposition of hands was at least necessary. On the question of divorce under the Mosaic Law the disciples of St. Thomas, like the saint himself (Suppl., Q. lxvii, a. 3), wavered, some holding that a dispensation was granted, others teaching that divorce was merely tolerated in order to avoid greater evils.

The Thomistic School

The chief doctrines distinctive of this school, composed principally of Dominican writers, are the following:

In Philosophy

1. The unity of substantial form in composite beings, applied to man, requires that the soul be the substantial form of the man, so as to exclude even the forma corporeitatis, admitted by Henry of Ghent, Scotus, and others (cf. Zigliara, P. 13; Denzinger-Bannwart, in note to n. 1655).

2. In created beings there is a real distinction between the essentia (essence) and the existentia (existence); between the essentia and the subsistentia; between the real relation and its foundation; between the soul and its faculties; between the several faculties. There can be no medium between a distinctio realis and a

distinctio rationis, or conceptual distinction; hence the distinctio formalis a parte rei of Scotus cannot be admitted. For Thomistic doctrines on free will, God's knowledge, etc., see below.

In Theology

1. In the beatific vision God's essence takes the place not only of the species impressa, but also of the species expressa.

2. All moral virtues, the acquired as well as the infused, in their perfect state, are interconnected.

3. According to Billuart (De pecc., diss. vii, a. 6), it has been a matter of controversy between Thomists whether the malice of a mortal sin is absolutely infinite.

4. In choosing a medium between Rigorism and Laxism, the Thomistic school has been Antiprobabilistic and generally has adopted Probabiliorism. Some defended Equiprobabilism, or Probabilism cum compensatione. Medina and St. Antoninus are claimed by the Probabilists.

5. Thomistic theologians generally, whilst they defended the infallibility of the Roman pontiff, denied that the pope had the power to dissolve a matrimonium ratum or to dispense from a solemn vow made to God. When it was urged that some popes had granted such favours, they cited other pontiffs who declared that they could not grant them (cf. Billuart, "De matrim.", Diss. v, a. 2), and said, with Dominic Soto, "Factum pontificium non facit articulum fidei" (The action of a pope does not constitute an article of

faith, in 4 dist., 27, Q. i, a. 4). Thomists of today are of a different mind, owing to the practice of the Church.

6. The hypostatic union, without any additional grace, rendered Christ impeccable. The Word was hypostatically united to the blood of Christ and remained united to it, even during the interval between His death and resurrection (Denzinger-Bannwart, n. 718). During that same interval the Body of Christ had a transitory form, called forma cadaverica (Zigliara, P. 16, 17, IV).

7. The sacraments of the New Law cause grace not only as instrumental moral causes, but by a mode of causality which should be called instrumental and physical. In the attrition required in the Sacrament of Penance there should be at least a beginning of the love of God; sorrow for sin springing solely from the fear of hell will not suffice.

8. Many theologians of the Thomistic School, especially before the Council of Trent, opposed the doctrine of Mary's Immaculate Conception, claiming that in this they were following St. Thomas. This, however, has not been the opinion either of the entire school or of the Dominican Order as a body. Father Rouard de Card, in his book "L'ordre des freres precheurs et l'Immaculée Conception "(Brussels, 1864), called attention to the fact that ten thousand professors of the order defended Mary's great privilege. At the Council of Trent twenty-five Dominican bishops signed a petition for the definition of the dogma. Thousands of Dominicans, in taking degrees at

the University of Paris, solemnly pledged themselves to defend the Immaculate Conception.

9. The Thomistic School is distinguished from other schools of theology chiefly by its doctrines on the difficult questions relating to God's action on the free will of man, God's foreknowledge, grace, and predestination. In the articles on these subjects will be found an exposition of the different theories advanced by the different schools in their effort to explain these mysteries, for such they are in reality. As to the value of these theories the following points should be borne in mind:

* No theory has as yet been proposed which avoids all difficulties and solves all doubts;

* on the main and most difficult of these questions some who are at times listed as Molinists — notably Bellarmine, Francisco Suárez, Francis de Lugo, and, in our own days, Cardinal Billot ("De deo uno et trino", Rome, 1902, Th. XXXII) — agree with the Thomists in defending predestination ante praevisa merita. Bossuet, after a long study of the question of physical premotion, adapted the Thomistic opinion ("Du libre arbitre", c. viii).

* Thomists do not claim to be able to explain, except by a general reference to God's omnipotence, how man remains free under the action of God, which they consider necessary in order to preserve and explain the universality of God's causality and the independent certainty of His foreknowledge. No man can explain, except by a reference to God's infinite power, how the world was created out of

nothing, yet we do not on this account deny creation, for we know that it must be admitted. In like manner the main question put to Thomists in this controversy should be not "How will you explain man's liberty?" but "What are your reasons for claiming so much for God's action?" If the reasons assigned are insufficient, then one great difficulty is removed, but there remains to be solved the problem of God's foreknowledge of man's free acts. If they are valid, then we must accept them with their necessary consequences and humbly confess our inability fully to explain how wisdom "reacheth . . . from end to end mightily, and ordereth all things sweetly" (Wisdom 8:1).

* Most important of all, it must be clearly understood and remembered that the Thomistic system on predestination neither saves fewer nor sends to perdition more souls than any other system held by Catholic theologians. In regard to the number of the elect there is no unanimity on either side; this is not the question in dispute between the Molinists and the Thomists. The discussions, too often animated and needlessly sharp, turned on this point: How does it happen that, although God sincerely desires the salvation of all men, some are to be saved, and must thank God for whatever merits they may have amassed, whilst others will be lost, and will know that they themselves, and not God, are to be blamed? — The facts in the case are admitted by all Catholic theologians. The Thomists, appealing to the authority of St. Augustine and St. Thomas, defend a system which follows the admitted facts to their logical conclusions. The elect are saved by the grace of God, which operates on their wills efficaciously and infallibly without detriment to their liberty; and since God sincerely desires the salvation of all men, He is prepared to grant that same grace to others, if they do not, by a free act, render themselves unworthy of it. The faculty of placing obstacles to Divine grace is the unhappy faculty of sinning; and the existence of moral evil in the world is a problem to be solved by all, not by the Thomists alone. The fundamental difficulties in this mysterious question are the existence of evil and the non-salvation of some, be they few or be they many, under the rule of an omnipotent, all-wise, and all-merciful God, and they miss the point of the controversy who suppose that these difficulties exist only for the Thomists. The truth is known to lie somewhere between Calvinism and Jansenism on the one hand, and Semipelagianism on the other. The efforts made by theologians and the various explanations offered by Augustinians, Thomists, Molinists, and Congruists show how difficult of solution are the questions involved. Perhaps we shall never know, in this world, how a just and merciful God provides in some special manner for the elect and yet sincerely loves all men. The celebrated Congregatio de Auxiliis did not forever put an end to the controversies, and the question is not yet settled.

Neo-Thomism and the Revival of Scholasticism
    When the world in the first part of the nineteenth

century began to enjoy a period of peace and rest after the disturbances caused by the French Revolution and the Napoleonic Wars, closer attention was given to ecclesiastical studies and Scholasticism was revived. This movement eventually caused a revival of Thomism, because the great master and model proposed by Leo XIII in the encyclical "Aeterni Patris" (4 Aug., 1879) was St. Thomas Aquinas. . . . The Thomistic doctrine had received strong support from the older universities. Among these the Encyclical "Aeterni Patris" mentions Paris, Salamanca, Alcalá Douai, Toulouse, Louvain, Padua, Bologna, Naples, and Coimbra as "the homes of human wisdom where Thomas reigned supreme, and the minds of all, teachers as well as taught, rested in wonderful harmony under the shield and authority of the Angelic Doctor". In the universities established by the Dominicans at Lima (1551) and Manila (1645) St. Thomas always held sway. The same is true of the Minerva school at Rome (1255), which ranked as a university from the year 1580, and is now the international Collegio Angelico. Coming down to our own times and the results of the Encyclical, which gave a new impetus to the study of St. Thomas's works, the most important centres of activity are Rome, Louvain, Fribourg (Switzerland), and Washington. At Louvain the chair of Thomistic philosophy, established in 1880, became, in 1889-90, the "Institut supérieur de philosophie" or "Ecole St. Thomas d'Aquin," where Professor Mercier, now Cardinal Archbishop of Mechlin, ably and wisely directed the new Thomistic movement (see De Wulf, "Scholasticism Old and New", tr. Coffey, New York, 1907, append., p. 261; "Irish Ecel. Record", Jan. 1906). The theological department of the University of Fribourg, Switzerland, established in 1889, has been entrusted to the Dominicans. By the publication of the "Revue thomiste" the professors of that university have contributed greatly to a new knowledge and appreciation of St. Thomas. The Constitution of the Catholic University of America at Washington enjoins special veneration for St. Thomas; the School of Sacred Sciences must follow his leadership ("Const. Cath. Univ. Amer.", Rome, 1889, pp. 38, 43). The University of Ottawa and Laval University are the centres of Thomism in Canada. The appreciation of St. Thomas in our days, in Europe and in America, is well set forth in Perrier's excellent "Revival of Scholastic Philosophy in the Nineteenth Century" (New York, 1909).

Eminent Thomists

After the middle of the fourteenth century the vast majority of philosophical and theological writers either wrote commentaries on the works of St. Thomas or based their teachings on his writings. It is impossible, therefore, to give here a complete list of the Thomists: only the more important names can be given. Unless otherwise noted, the authors belonged to the Order of St. Dominic. Those marked (*) were devoted to Thomism in general, but were not of the Thomistic School. A more complete list will be found in the works cited at the end of this article.

Thirteenth Century

Thomas de Cantimpré (1270); Hugh of St. Cher (1263); Vincent of Bauvais (1264); St. Raymond de Pennafort (1275); Peter of Tarentaise (Pope Innocent V — 1276); Giles de Lassines (1278); Reginald de Piperno (1279); William de Moerbeka (1286); Raymond Marti (1286); Bernard de Trilia (1292); Bernard of Hotun, Bishop of Dublin (1298); Theodoric of Apoldia (1299); Thomas Sutton (1300).

Fourteenth Century

Peter of Auvergne (1301); Nicholas Boccasini, Benedict XI (1304); Godfrey of Fontaines (1304); Walter of Winterburn (1305); Ægidius Colonna (Aigidius Romanus), O.S.A (1243-1316); William of Paris (1314); Gerard of Bologna, Carmelite (1317); four biographers, viz Peter Calo (1310); William de Tocco (1324); Bartolommeo of Lucca (1327); Bernard Guidonis* (1331); Dante (1321); Natalis Hervieus (1323); Petrus de Palude (Paludanusi — 1342); Thomas Bradwardin, Archbishop of Canterbury (1349); Robert Holkott (1349); John Tauler (1361); Bl. Henry Suso (1365); Thomas of Strasburg, O.S.A. (1357); Jacobus Passavante (1357); Nicholas Roselli (1362); Durandus of Aurillac (1382), sometimes called Durandulus, because he wrote against Durandus a S. Portiano*, who was first a Thomist, afterwards an independent writer, attacking many of St. Thomas's doctrines; John Bromyard (1390); Nicholas Eymeric (1399).

Fifteenth Century

Manuel Calecas (1410); St. Vincent Ferrer (1415); Bl. John Dominici (1419); John Gerson*, chancellor of the University of Paris (1429); Luis of Valladolid (1436); Raymond Sabunde (1437); John Nieder (1437); Capreolus (1444), called the "Prince of Thomists"; John de Montenegro (1445); Fra Angelico (1455); St. Antoninus (1459); Nicholas of Cusa*, of the Brothers of the Common Life (1464); John of Torquemada (de Turrecremata¡, 1468); Bessarion, Basilian (1472); Alanus de Rupe (1475); John Faber (1477); Petrus Niger (1471); Peter of Bergamo (1482); Jerome Savonarola (1498).

Sixteenth Century

Felix Faber (1502); Vincent Bandelli (1506); John Tetzel (1519); Diego de Deza (1523); Sylvester Mazzolini (1523); Francesco Silvestro di Ferrara (1528); Thomas de Vio Cajetan (1534) (commentaries by these two are published in the Leonine edition of the works of St. Thomas); Conrad Koellin (1536); Chrysostom Javelli (1538); Santes Pagnino (1541); Francisco de Vitoria (1546); Franc. Romseus (1552); Ambrosius Catherinus* (Lancelot Politi, 1553); St. Ignatius of Loyola (1556) enjoined devotion to St. Thomas; Matthew Ory (1557); Dominic Soto (1560); Melchior Cano (1560); Ambrose

Pelargus (1561); Peter Soto (1563); Sixtus of Siena (1569); John Faber (1570); St. Pius V (1572); Bartholomew Medina (1581); Vincent Justiniani (1582); Maldonatus* (Juan Maldonado, 1583); St. Charles Borromeo* (1584); Salmerón* (1585); Ven. Louis of Granada (1588); Bartholomew of Braga (1590); Toletus* (1596); Bl. Peter Canisius* (1597); Thomas Stapleton*, Doctor of Louvain (1598); Fonseca (1599); Molina* (1600).

Seventeenth Century

Valentia* (1603); Domingo Bañez (1604); Vásquez* (1604); Bart. Ledesma (1604); Sánchez* (1610); Baronius * (1607); Capponi a Porrecta (1614); Aur. Menochio * (1615); Petr. Ledesma (1616); Francisco Suárez* (1617); Du Perron, a converted Calvinist, cardinal (1618); Bellarmine* (1621); St. Francis de Sales* (1622); Hieronymus Medices (1622); Lessius* (1623); Becanus* (1624); Malvenda (1628); Thomas de Lemos (1629); Alvarez; Laymann* (1635); Joann. Wiggers*, doctor of Louvain (1639); Gravina (1643); John of St. Thomas (1644); Serra (1647); Ripalda*, S.J.* (1648); Sylvius (Du Bois), doctor of Douai (1649); Petavius* (1652); Goar (1625); Steph. Menochio, S.J.* (1655); Franc. Pignatelli* (1656); De Lugo* (1660); Bollandus* (1665); Jammy (1665); Vallgornera (1665); Labbe* (1667); Pallavicini* (1667); Busenbaum* (1668); Nicolni* (1673); Contenson (1674); Jac. Pignatelli* (1675); Passerini* (1677); Gonet (1681); Bancel (1685); Thomassin* (1695); Goudin (1695);

Sfrondati* (1696); Quetif (1698); Rocaberti (1699); Casanate (1700). To this period belong the Carmelite Salmanticenses, authors of the "Cursus theologicus" (1631-72).

Eighteenth Century

Guerinois (1703); Bossuet, Bishop of Meaux; Norisins, O.S.A. (1704); Diana (1705); Thyrsus González* (1705); Massoulié (1706); Du hamel* (1706); Wigandt (1708); Piny (1709); Lacroix* (1714); Carrières* (1717); Natalis Alexander (1724); Echard (1724); Tourney*, doctor of the Sorbonne (1729); Livarius de Meyer* (1730); Benedict XIII* (1730); Graveson (1733); Th. du Jardin (1733); Hyacintha Serry (1738); Duplessis d'Argentré* (1740); Gotti (1742); Drouin* (1742); Antoine* (1743); Lallemant* (1748); Milante* (1749); Preingue (1752); Concina (1759); Billuart (1757); Benedict XIV* (1758); Cuiliati (1759); Orsi (1761); Charlevoix* (1761); Reuter* (1762); Baumgartner* (1764); Berti* (1766); Patuzzi (1769); De Rubeis (1775); Touron (1775); Thomas de Burgo (1776); Gener* (1781); Roselli (1783); St. Alphonsus Liguori (1787); Mamachi (1792); Richard (1794).

Nineteenth Century

In this century there are few names to be recorded outside of those who were connected with the Thomistic revival either as the forerunners, the promoters, or the writers of the Neo-Scholastic period.

XXIV.
Scholasticism

Scholasticism is a term used to designate both a method and a system. It is applied to theology as well as to philosophy. Scholastic theology is distinguished from Patristic theology on the one hand, and from positive theology on the other. The schoolmen themselves distinguished between theologia speculativa sive scholastica and theologia positiva. Applied to philosophy, the word "Scholastic" is often used also, to designate a chronological division intervening between the end of the Patristic era in the fifth century and the beginning of the modern era, about 1450. It will, therefore, make for clearness and order if we consider:

I. The origin of the word "Scholastic";

II. The history of the period called Scholastic in the history of philosophy;

III. The Scholastic method in philosophy, with incidental reference to the Scholastic method in theology; and

IV. The contents of the Scholastic system.

The revival of Scholasticism in recent times has been already treated under the head NEO-SCHOLASTICISM.

Origin of the Name "Scholastic"

There are in Greek literature a few instances of the use of the word scholastikos to designate a professional philosopher. Historically, however, the word, as now used, is to be traced, not to Greek usage, but to early Christian institutions. In the Christian schools, especially after the beginning of the sixth century, it was customary to call the head of the school magister scholae, capiscola, or scholasticus. As time went on, the last of these appellations was used exclusively. The curriculum of those schools included dialectic among the seven liberal arts, which was at that time the only branch of philosophy studied systematically. The head of the school generally taught dialectic, and out of his teaching grew both the manner of philosophizing and the system of philosophy that prevailed during all the Middle Ages. Consequently, the name "Scholastic" was used and is still used to designate the method and system that grew out of the academic curriculum of the schools or, more definitely, out of the dialectical teaching of the masters of the schools (scholastici). It does not matter that, historically, the Golden Age of Scholastic philosophy, namely, the thirteenth century, falls within a period when the schools, the curriculum of which was the seven liberal arts, including dialectic had given way to another organization of studies, the studia generalia, or universities. The name, once given, continued, as it almost always does, to designate the method and system which had by this time passed into a new phase of development. Academically, the philosophers of the thirteenth century are known as magistri, or masters; historically, however, they are Scholastics, and continue to be so designated until the end of the medieval period. And, even after the close of the Middle Ages, a philosopher or theologian who adopts the method or the system of the medieval Scholastics is said to be a Scholastic.

The Scholastic Period

The period extending from the beginning of Christian speculation to the time of St. Augustine, inclusive, is known as the Patristic era in philosophy and theology. In general, that era inclined to Platonism and underestimated the importance of Aristotle. The Fathers strove to construct on Platonic principles a system of Christian philosophy. They brought reason to the aid of Revelation. They leaned, however, towards the doctrine of the mystics, and, in ultimate resort, relied more on spiritual intuition than on dialectical proof for the establishment and explanation of the highest truths of philosophy. Between the end of the Patristic era in the fifth century and the beginning of the Scholastic era in the ninth there intervene a number of intercalary thinkers, as they may be called, like Claudianus Mamertus, Boethius, Cassiodorus, St. Isidore of Seville, Venerable Bede etc., who helped to hand down to the new generation the traditions of the Patristic age and to continue into the Scholastic era the current of Platonism. With the Carolingian revival of learning in the ninth century began a period of educational activity which resulted in a new phase of Christian thought known as Scholasticism. The first masters of the schools in the ninth century Alcuin, Rabanus, etc., were not indeed, more original than Boethius or Cassiodorus; the first original thinker in the Scholastic era was John the Scot.

Nevertheless they inaugurated the Scholastic movement because they endeavoured to bring the Patristic (principally the Augustinian) tradition into touch with the new life of European Christianity. They did not abandon Platonism. They knew little of Aristotle except as a logician. But by the emphasis they laid on dialectical reasoning, they gave a new direction to Christian tradition in philosophy. In the curriculum of the schools in which they taught, philosophy was represented by dialectic. On the textbooks of dialectic which they used they wrote commentaries and glosses, into which. Little by little, they admitted problems of psychology, metaphysics, cosmology, and ethics. So that the Scholastic movement as a whole may be said to have sprung from the discussions of the dialecticians.

Method, contents, and conclusions were influenced by this origin. There resulted a species of Christian Rationalism which more than any other trait characterizes Scholastic philosophy in every successive stage of its development and marks it off very definitely from the Patristic philosophy, which, as has been said, was ultimately intuitional and mystic. With Roscelin, who appeared about the middle of the eleventh century, the note of Rationalism is very distinctly sounded, and the first rumbling is heard of the inevitable reaction, the voice of Christian mysticism uttering its note of warning, and condemning the excess into which Rationalism had fallen. In the eleventh and twelfth centuries, therefore, Scholasticism passed through its period of storm and stress.

On the one side were the advocates of reason, Roscelin, Abelard, Peter Lombard; on the other were the champions of mysticism, St. Anselm, St. Peter Damian, St. Bernard, and the Victorines. Like all ardent advocates, the Rationalists went too far at first, and only gradually brought their method within the lines of orthodoxy and harmonized it with Christian reverence for the mysteries of Faith. Like all conservative reactionists, the mystics at first condemned the use as well as the abuse of reason; they did not reach an intelligent compromise with the dialecticians until the end of the twelfth century. In the final outcome of the struggle, it was Rationalism that, having modified its unreasonable claims, triumphed in the Christian schools, without, however driving the mystics from the field.

Meantime, Eclectics, like John of Salisbury, and Platonists, like the members of the School of Chartres, gave to the Scholastic movement a broader spirit of toleration, imparted, so to speak, a sort of Humanism to philosophy, so that, when we come to the eve of the thirteenth century, Scholasticism has made two very decided steps in advance. First, the use of reason in the discussion of spiritual truth and the application of dialectic to theology are accepted with. out protest, so long as they are kept within the bounds of moderation. Second, there is a willingness on the part of the Schoolmen to go outside the lines of strict ecclesiastical tradition and learn, not only from Aristotle, who was now beginning to be known as a metaphysician and a psychologist, but also from the Arabians and the Jews, whose works had begun to penetrate in Latin translations into the schools of Christian Europe. The taking of Constantinople in 1204, the introduction of Arabian, Jewish, and Greek works into the Christian schools, the rise of the universities, and the foundation of the mendicant orders — these are the events which led to the extraordinary intellectual activity of the thirteenth century, which centered in the University of Paris. At first there was considerable confusion, and it seemed as if the battles won in the twelfth century by the dialecticians should be fought over again. The translations of Aristotle made from the Arabian and accompanied by Arabian commentaries were tinged with Pantheism, Fatalism, and other Neoplatonic errors. Even in the Christian schools there were declared Pantheists, like David of Dinant, and outspoken Averroists, like Siger of Brabant, who bade fair to prejudice the cause of Aristoteleanism.

These developments were suppressed by the most stringent disciplinary measures during the first few decades of the thirteenth century. While they were still a source of danger, men like William of Auvergne and Alexander of Hales hesitated between the traditional Augustinianism of the Christian schools and the new Aristoteleanism, which came from a suspected source. Besides, Augustinianism and Platonism accorded with piety, while Aristoteleanism was found to lack the element of mysticism. In time, however, the translations made from the Greek revealed an Aristotle free from the errors attributed to him by the

Arabians, and, above all, the commanding genius of St. Albertus Magnus and his still more illustrious disciple, St. Thomas Aquinas, who appeared at the critical moment, calmly surveyed the difficulties of the situation, and met them fearlessly, won the victory for the new philosophy and continued successfully the traditions established in the preceding century. Their contemporary, St. Bonaventure, showed that the new learning was not incompatible with mysticism drawn from Christian sources, and Roger Bacon demonstrated by his unsuccessful attempts to develop the natural sciences the possibilities of another kind which were latent in Aristoteleanism.

With Duns Scotus, a genius of the first order, but not of the constructive type, begins the critical phase, of Scholasticism. Even before his time, the Franciscan and the Dominican currents had set out in divergent directions. It was his keen and unrelenting search for the weak points in Thomistic philosophy that irritated and wounded susceptibilities among the followers of St. Thomas, and brought about the spirit of partisanship which did so much to dissipate the energy of Scholasticism in the fourteenth century. The recrudescence of Averroism in the schools, the excessive cultivation of formalism and subtlety, the growth of artificial and even barbarous terminology, and the neglect of the study of nature and of history contributed to the same result. Ockham's Nominalism and Durandus's attempt to "simplify" Scholastic philosophy did not have the effect which their authors intended. "The glory and power of scholasticism faded into the warmth and brightness of mysticism," and Gerson, Thomas à Kempis, and Eckhart are more representative of what the Christian Church was actually thinking in the fourteenth and fifteenth centuries than are the Thomists, Scotists, and Ockhamists of that period, who frittered away much valuable time in the discussion of highly technical questions which arose within the schools and possess little interest except for adepts in Scholastic subtlety. After the rise of Humanism, when the Renaissance, which ushered in the modern era, was in full progress, the great Italian, Spanish, and Portuguese commentators inaugurated an age of more healthy Scholasticism, and the great Jesuit teachers, Toletus, Vasquez, and Francisco Suárez, seemed to recall the best days of thirteenth century speculation. The triumph of scientific discovery, with which, as a rule, the representatives of Scholasticism in the seats of academic authority had, unfortunately, too little sympathy, led to new ways of philosophizing, and when, finally, Descartes in practice, if not in theory, effected a complete separation of philosophy from theology, the modern era had begun and the age known as that of Scholasticism had come to an end.

The Scholastic Method

No method in philosophy has been more unjustly condemned than that of the Scholastics. No philosophy has been more grossly misrepresented. And this is true not only of the details, but also of the most essential elements of

Scholasticism. Two charges, especially, are made against the Schoolmen: First, that they confounded philosophy with theology; and second, that they made reason subservient to authority. As a matter of fact, the very essence of Scholasticism is, first, its clear delimitation of the respective domains of philosophy and theology, and, second, its advocacy of the use of reason.

Theology and Philosophy

Christian thinkers, from the beginning, were confronted with the question: How are we to reconcile reason with revelation, science with faith, philosophy with theology? The first apologists possessed no philosophy of their own. They had to deal with a pagan world proud of its literature and its philosophy, ready at any moment to flaunt its inheritance of wisdom in the face of ignorant Christians. The apologists met the situation by a theory that was as audacious as it must have been disconcerting to the pagans. They advanced the explanation that all the wisdom of Plato and the other Greeks was due to the inspiration of the Logos; that it was God's truth, and, therefore, could not be in contradiction with the supernatural revelation contained in the Gospels. It was a hypothesis calculated not only to silence a pagan opponent, but also to work constructively. We find it in St. Basil, in Origen, and even in St. Augustine. The belief that the two orders of truth, the natural and the supernatural, must harmonize, is the inspiration of intellectual activity in the Patristic era. But that era did little to define the limits of the two realms of truth. St. Augustine believes that faith aids reason (credo ut intelligam) and that reason aids faith (intelligo ut credam); he is, however, inclined to emphasize the first principle and not the second. He does not develop a definite methodology in dealing with them. The Scholastics, almost from the first, attempted to do so.

John Scotus Eriugena, in the ninth century, by his doctrine that all truth is a theophany, or showing forth of God, tried to elevate philosophy to the rank of theology, and identify the two in a species of theosophy. Abelard, in the twelfth century, tried to bring theology down to the level of philosophy, and identify both in a Rationalistic system. The greatest of the Scholastics in the thirteenth century, especially St. Thomas Aquinas, solved the problem for all time, so far as Christian speculation is concerned, by showing that the two are distinct sciences, and yet that they agree. They are distinct, he teaches, because, while philosophy relies on reason alone, theology uses the truths derived from revelation, and also because there are some truths, the mysteries of Faith, which lie completely outside the domain of philosophy and belong to theology. They agree, and must agree, because God is the author of all truth, and it is impossible to think that He would teach in the natural order anything that contradicts what He teaches in the supernatural order. The recognition of these principles is one of the crowning achievements of Scholasticism. It is one of the characteristics that mark it off from the Patristic era, in which the same principles were, so to speak, in solution, and not crystallized in definite expression. It is the trait which differentiates Scholasticism from Averroism. It is the inspiration of all Scholastic effort. As long as it lasted Scholasticism lasted, and as soon as the opposite conviction became established, the conviction, namely, that what is true in theology may be false in philosophy, Scholasticism ceased to exist. It is, therefore, a matter of constant surprise to those who know Scholasticism to find it misrepresented on this vital point.

Scholastic Rationalism

Scholasticism sprang from the study of dialectic in the schools. The most decisive battle of Scholasticism was that which it waged in the twelfth century against the mystics who condemned the use of dialectic. The distinguishing mark of Scholasticism in the age of its highest development is its use of the dialectical method. It is, therefore, a matter, once more, for surprise, to find Scholasticism accused of undue subservience to authority and of the neglect of reason. Rationalism is a word which has various meanings. It is sometimes used to designate a system which, refusing to acknowledge the authority of revelation, tests all truth by the standard of reason. In this sense, the Scholastics were not Rationalists. The Rationalism of Scholasticism consists in the conviction that reason is to be used in the elucidation of spiritual truth and in defence of the dogmas of Faith. It is opposed to mysticism, which distrusted reason and placed emphasis on intuition and contemplation. In this milder meaning of the term, all the Scholastics were convinced Rationalists, the only difference being that some, like Abelard and Roscelin, were too ardent in their advocacy of the use of reason, and went so far as to maintain that reason can prove even the supernatural mysteries of Faith, while others, like St. Thomas, moderated the claims of reason, set limits to its power of proving spiritual truth, and maintained that the mysteries of faith could not be discovered and cannot be proved by unaided reason.

The whole Scholastic movement, therefore, is a Rationalistic movement in the second sense of the term Rationalism. The Scholastics used their reason; they applied dialectic to the study of nature, of human nature and of supernatural truth. Far from depreciating reason, they went as far as man can go — some modern critics think they went too far — in the application of reason to the discussion of the dogmas of Faith. They acknowledged the authority of revelation, as all Christian philosophers are obliged to do. They admitted the force of human authority when the conditions of its valid application were verified. But in theology, the authority of revelation did not coerce their reason and in philosophy and in natural science they taught very emphatically that the argument from authority is the weakest of all arguments. They did not subordinate reason to authority in any unworthy sense of that phrase. It was an opponent of the Scholastic movement who styled philosophy "the handmaid of theology", a designation which, however, some of the Schoolmen accepted to mean that to philosophy belongs the honourable task of carrying the light which is to guide the footsteps of theology. One need not go so far as to say, with Barthélemy Saint Hilaire, that "Scholasticism, in its general result, is the first revolt of the modern spirit against authority." Nevertheless, one is compelled by the facts of history to admit that there is more truth in that description than in the superficial judgment of the historians who describe Scholasticism as the subordination of reason to authority.

Details of Scholastic Method

The Scholastic manner of treating the problems of philosophy and theology is apparent from a glance at the body of literature which the Schoolmen produced. The immense amount of commentary on Aristotle, on Peter Lombard, on Boethius, on Pseudo-Dionysius, and on the Scriptures indicates the form of academic activity which characterizes the Scholastic period. The use of texts dates from the very beginning of the Scholastic era in philosophy and theology, and was continued down into modern times. The mature teacher, however, very often embodied the results of his own speculation in a Summa, which, in time became a text in the hands of his successors. The Questiones disputatae were special treatises on the more difficult or the more important topics, and as the name implied, followed the method of debate prevalent in the schools, generally called disputation or determination. The Quodlibeta were miscellanies generally in the form of answers to questions which as soon as a teacher had attained a widespread renown, began to come to him, not only from the academic world in which he lived, but from all classes of persons and from every part of Christendom. The division of topics in theology was determined by the arrangement followed in Peter Lombard's "Books of Sentences", and in philosophy it adhered closely to the order of treatises in Aristotle's works. There is a good deal of divergence among the principal Scholastics in the details of arrangement, as well as in the relative values of the sub-titles, "part", "question", "disputation", "article", etc. All, however, adopt the manner of treatment by which thesis, objections, and solutions of objections stand out distinctly in the discussion of each problem. We find traces of this in Gerbert's little treatise "De rational) et ratione uti" in the tenth century, and it is still more definitely adopted in Abelard's "Sic et non". It had its root in Aristotelean method, but was determined more immediately by the dialectical activity of the early schools, from which, as was said, Scholasticism sprang.

Much has been said both in praise and in blame of Scholastic terminology in philosophy and theology. It is rather generally acknowledged that whatever precision there is in the modern languages of Western Europe is due largely to the dialectic disquisitions of the Scholastics. On the other hand, ridicule has been poured on the stiffness, the awkwardness, and the barbarity of the Scholastic style. In an impartial study of the question, it should be remembered that the Scholastics of the thirteenth century—and it was not they but their successors who were guilty of the grossest sins of style—were confronted with a terminological problem unique in the history of thought. They came suddenly into possession of an entirely new literature, the works of Aristotle. They spoke a language, Latin, on which the terminology of Aristotle in metaphysics psychology etc., had made no impression. Consequently, they were obliged to create all at once Latin words and phrases to express the terminology of Aristotle, a terminology remarkable for its extent, its variety, and its technical complexity. They did it honestly and humbly, by translating Aristotle's phrases literally; so that many a strange-sounding Latin phrase in the writings of the Schoolmen would be very good Aristotelean Greek, if rendered word for word into that language. The Latin of the best of the Scholastics may be lacking in elegance and distinction; but no one will deny the merits of its rigorous severity of phrase and its logical soundness of construction. Though wanting the graces of what is called the fine style, graces which have the power of pleasing but do not facilitate the task of the learner in philosophy, the style of the thirteenth-century masters possesses the fundamental qualities, clearness, conciseness, and richness of technical phrase.

The Contents of the Scholastic System

In logic the Scholastics adopted all the details of the Aristotelean system, which was known to the Latin world from the time of Boethius. Their individual contributions consisted of some minor improvements in the matter of teaching and in the technic of the science. Their underlying theory of knowledge is also Aristotelean. It may be described by saying that it is a system of Moderate Realism and Moderate Intellectualism. The Realism consists in teaching that outside the mind there exist things fundamentally universal which correspond to our universal ideas. The Moderate Intellectualism is summed up in the two principles:

* all our knowledge is derived from sense-knowledge; and
* intellectual knowledge differs from sense-knowledge, not only in degree but also in kind.

In this way, Scholasticism avoids Innatism, according to which all our ideas, or some of our ideas, are born with the soul and have no origin in the world outside us. At the same time, it avoids Sensism, according to which our so-called intellectual knowledge is only sense-knowledge of a higher or finer sort. The Scholastics, moreover, took a firm stand against the doctrine of Subjectivism. In their discussion of the value of knowledge they held that there is an external world which is real and independent of our thoughts. In that world are the forms which make things to be what they are. The same forms received into the mind in the process of knowing cause us not to be the object but to know the object. This presence of things in the mind by means of forms is true representation, or rather presentation. For it is the objective thing that we are first aware of, not its representation in us.

The Scholastic outlook on the world of nature is Aristotelean. The Schoolmen adopt the doctrine of matter and form, which they apply not only to living things but also to inorganic nature. Since the form, or entelechy is always striving for its own realization or actualization, the view of nature which this doctrine leads to is teleological. Instead, however, of ascribing purpose in a vague, unsatisfactory manner to nature itself, the Scholastics attributed design to the intelligent, provident author of nature. The principle of finality thus acquired a more precise meaning, and at the same time the danger of a Pantheistic interpretation was avoided. On the question of the universality of matter the Schoolmen were divided among themselves, some, like the Franciscan teachers, maintaining that all created beings are material, others, like St. Thomas, holding the existence of "separate forms", such as the angels, in whom there is potency but no matter. Again, on the question of the oneness of substantial forms, there was a lack of agreement. St. Thomas held that in each individual material substance, organic or inorganic, there is but one substantial form, which confers being, substantiality and, in the case of man, life, sensation, and reason. Others, on the contrary, believed that in one substance, man, for instance, there are simultaneously several forms, one of which confers existence, another substantiality, another life, and another, reason. Finally, there was a divergence of views as to what is the principle of individuation, by which several individuals of the same species are differentiated from one another. St. Thomas taught that the principle of individuation is matter with its determined dimensions, materia signata.

In regard to the nature of man, the first Scholastics were Augustinians. Their definition of the soul is what may be called the spiritual, as opposed to the biological, definition. They held that the soul is the principle of thought-activity, and that the exercise of the senses is a process from the soul through the body not a process of the whole organism, that is, of the body animated by the soul. The Scholastics of the thirteenth century frankly adopted the Aristotelean definition of the soul as the principle of life, not of thought merely. Therefore, they maintained, man is a compound of body and soul, each of which is an incomplete substantial principle the union being, consequently, immediate, vital, and substantial. For them there is no need of an intermediary "body of light" such as St. Augustine imagined to exist. All the vital activities of the individual human being are ascribed ultimately to the soul, as to their active principle, although they may have more immediate principles namely the faculties, such as intellect, the senses, the vegetative and muscular powers. But while the soul is in this way concerned with all the vital functions, being, in fact, the source of them, and the body enters as a passive principle into all the activities of the soul, exception must be made in the case of immaterial thought-activities. They are, like all the other activities, activities of the individual. The soul is the active principle of them. But the body contributes to them, not in the same intrinsic manner in which it contributes to seeing, hearing, digesting etc., but only in an extrinsic manner, by supplying the materials out of which the intellect manufactures ideas. This extrinsic dependence explains the phenomena of fatigue, etc. At the same time it leaves the soul so independent intrinsically that the latter is truly said to be immaterial.

From the immateriality of the soul follows its immortality. Setting aside the possibility of annihilation, a possibility to which all creatures, even the angels are subject, the human soul is naturally immortal, and its immortality, St. Thomas believes, can be proved from its immateriality. Duns Scotus, however, whose notion of the strict requirements of a demonstration was influenced by his training in mathematics, denies the conclusive force of the argument from immateriality, and calls attention to Aristotle's hesitation or obscurity on this point. Aristotle, as interpreted by the Arabians, was, undoubtedly, opposed to immortality. It was, however, one of St. Thomas's greatest achievements in philosophy that, especially in his opusculum "De unitate intellectus", he refuted the Arabian interpretation of Aristotle, showed that the active intellect is part of the individual soul, and thus removed the uncertainty which, for the Aristoteleans, hung around the notions of immateriality and immortality. From the immateriality of the soul follows not only that it is immortal, but also that it originated by an act of creation. It was created at the moment in which it was united with the body: creando infunditur, et infundendo creatur is the Scholastic phrase.

Scholastic metaphysics added to the Aristotelean system a full discussion of the nature of personality, restated in more definite terms the traditional arguments for the existence of God, and developed the doctrine of the providential government of the universe. The exigencies of theological discussion occasioned also a minute analysis of the nature of accident in general and of quantity in particular. The application of the resulting principles to the explanation of the mystery of the Eucharist, as contained in St. Thomas's works on the subject, is one of the most successful of all the Scholastic attempts to render faith reasonable by means of dialectical discussion. Indeed, it may be said, in general, that the peculiar excellence of the Scholastics as systematic thinkers consisted in their ability to take hold of the profoundest metaphysical distinctions, such as matter and form, potency and actuality, substance and accident, and apply them to every department of thought. They were no mere apriorists, they recognized in principle and in practice that scientific method begins with the observation of facts. Nevertheless, they excelled most of all in the talent which is peculiarly metaphysical, the power to grasp abstract general principles and apply them consistently and systematically.

So far as the ethics of Scholasticism is not distinctly Christian, seeking to expound and justify Divine law and the Christian standard of morals, it is Aristotelean. This is clear from the adoption and application of the Aristotelean definition of virtue as the golden mean between two extremes. Fundamentally, the definition is eudemonistic. It rests on the conviction that the supreme good of man is happiness, that happiness is the realization, or complete actualization, of one's nature, and that virtue is an essential means to that end. But what is vague and unsatisfactory in Aristotelean Eudemonism is made definite and safe in the Scholastic system, which determines the meaning of happiness and realization according to the Divine purpose in creation and the dignity to which man is destined as a child of God.

In their discussion of the problems of political philosophy the philosophers of the thirteenth century while not discarding the theological views of St. Augustine contained in "The City of God", laid a new foundation for the study of political organizations by introducing Aristotle's scientific definition of the origin and purpose of civil society. Man, says St. Thomas, is naturally a social and political animal. By giving to human beings a nature which requires the co-operation of other human beings for its welfare, God ordained man for society, and thus it is His will that princes should govern with a view to the public welfare. The end for which the state exists is, then, not merely vivere but bene vivere. All that goes to make life better and happier is included the Divine charter from which kings and rulers derive their authority. The Scholastic treatises on this subject and the commentaries on the "Polities" of Aristotle prepared the way for the medieval and modern discussions of political problems. In this department of thought, as in many others, the Schoolmen did at least one service which posterity should appreciate: they strive to express in clear systematic form what was present in the consciousness of Christendom in their day.

Printed in Great Britain
by Amazon

27015745R00377